Energy Poverty and Vulnerability

T0372548

Human health and wellbeing are closely intertwined with the ability to access affordable and modern domestic energy services, including heating, cooling, lighting, cooking, and information technology. Energy poverty is said to occur when such amenities cannot be secured up to a socially- and physically-necessitated level. Millions of people across the world suffer from energy poverty due to a combination of financial, social and technical circumstances.

Energy Poverty and Vulnerability provides novel and critical perspectives on the drivers and consequences of energy-related injustices in the home. Drawing together original research conducted by leading experts, the book offers fresh insights into the ways in which hitherto unexplored factors such as cultural norms, environmental conditions and household needs combine to shape vulnerability to energy poverty. Case studies from a wide range of countries are presented, thus providing the first globally-integrated account of a policy and research domain that has previously been divided between the Global South and North. An examination of the diverse manifestations of energy poverty is supplemented by an identification of this condition's shared and context-specific causes.

Conveying policy-relevant insights that can inform decision-making, this book can be of interest to students and scholars of energy demand, social justice, and sustainability transitions, as well as decision-makers and practitioners who wish to find out more about this complex issue.

Neil Simcock is a Research Associate at the University of Manchester, UK.

Harriet Thomson is a Research Associate at the University of Manchester, UK.

Saska Petrova is a Lecturer in the School of Environment, Education and Development at the University of Manchester, UK.

Stefan Bouzarovski is a Professor at the Department of Geography and Director of the Collaboratory for Urban Resilience and Energy at the University of Manchester, UK.

Routledge Explorations in Energy Studies

Energy Poverty and Vulnerability
A Global Perspective
Edited by Neil Simcock, Harriet Thomson, Saska Petrova and
Stefan Bouzarovski

Energy Poverty and Vulnerability

A Global Perspective

Edited by Neil Simcock,
Harriet Thomson, Saska Petrova
and Stefan Bouzarovski

Routledge
Taylor & Francis Group
LONDON AND NEW YORK

earthscan
from Routledge

First published 2018 by Routledge

2 Park Square, Milton Park, Abingdon, Oxfordshire OX14 4RN
52 Vanderbilt Avenue, New York, NY 10017

Routledge is an imprint of the Taylor & Francis Group, an informa business

First issued in paperback 2019

British Library Cataloguing-in-Publication Data
A catalogue record for this book is available from the British Library

Library of Congress Cataloging-in-Publication Data
A catalog record for this book has been requested

ISBN: 978-1-138-29445-5 (hbk)
ISBN: 978-0-367-24944-1 (pbk)

Typeset in Goudy
by Apex CoVantage, LLC

Contents

Illustrations

Figures

Tables

Boxes

Notes on contributors

Dorice Agol is a consultant in environment and international development and is a Research Fellow at the School of International Development, University of East Anglia (UEA), UK. Her interest lies at the interface between research, policy and practice, and she has published various subjects such as water-energy-food nexus, natural resources management, sustainability, corporate social responsibility, education and health. She recently co-edited a book, *Sustainability Indicators in Practice*, published by De Guyter Open Ltd. She has extensive research experience in Sub-Saharan Africa and the United Kingdom.

Branko Ančić is a Research Associate at the Institute for Social Research in Zagreb, Croatia, where he is a Head of the Centre for Research in Social Inequalities and Sustainability. His scientific and research interests include sociology of religion, sociology of health and sociology of sustainable development. His publications include an analysis of atheism and non-religiosity in Europe (*Oxford Handbook of Atheism*, Oxford University Press, 2014); an exploration of connection between religion and health (*Sociology and Space*, 2011); research of pro-environmental attitudes and behaviour in Europe (*Sustainability Perspectives from the European Semi-Periphery*, Institute for Social Research in Zagreb and Heinrich Böll Stiftung Croatia, 2014); public perception of climate change (*Croatian Meteorological Journal*, 2016) and interpretation of degrowth attitudes in Europe (*Green European – Environmental Behaviour and Attitudes in Europe in a Historical and Cross-Cultural Comparative Perspective*, Routledge, 2017).

Stefan Bouzarovski is a Professor of Geography at the University of Manchester and Director of the Collaboratory for Urban Resilience and Energy within the Manchester Urban Institute, UK. He is also External Professor at the Department of Economic Geography, University of Gdansk, Poland, and a Visiting Professor at the Department of Geography, University of Bergen, Norway. He is an internationally leading expert in energy and urban policy, with a particular focus on energy poverty in Europe – reflected in his role as Chair of the European Energy Poverty Observatory. He has undertaken research, consultancy, advocacy and policy-orientated work on this subject for more than 15 years. His work been funded by a wide range of governmental bodies, charities and private sector organizations (in more than 60 different projects or consultancy engagements) and has been published in more than 80 scientific and policy papers, including the books *Energy Poverty in Eastern Europe* (Ashgate, 2007) and *Retrofitting the City* (IB Tauris, 2016). Its outcomes have informed the work of the European Union, United Nations, World Bank and the International Energy Agency. He was one of the founding members of the UK Royal Geographical Society's Energy Geographies Research Group.

Beth Brockett is an Interdisciplinary Environmental Scientist. She has worked in academia and the third sector and is currently working as a land management and conservation adviser within the public sector. She has a background in ecology, soil science and critical social science and now specialises in working with different knowledge communities to promote sustainable land management. Her doctoral research at Lancaster University developed ways of incorporating qualitative data and alternative representations of landscape within Geographical Information Systems and critiqued the way maps and other spatial representations have been used within agri-environment schemes. She has published in a range of peer-reviewed journals, a Parliamentary Office of Science and Technology briefing paper and specialist blogs and magazines. She enjoys working with people to address environmental problems.

Alison Browne is a Lecturer in Human Geography and a Research Fellow at the Sustainable Consumption Institute (SCI), University of Manchester, UK. She has published extensively on the social, performative and material dynamics of everyday life and sustainability, including an emerging expertise in the everyday life practices underpinning water, energy, food and air pollution transitions and sustainability in Chinese cities. She has led and collaborated on several high-profile interdisciplinary research projects on water, energy and food in recent years funded by the EPSRC, ESRC, Interreg IVB, the Chinese Academy of Social Sciences/Sustainable Consumption Institute, British Academy etc. She works in collaboration with a range of commercial businesses, NGOs and governmental departments to bring about substantial non-academic impact from her research.

Evangelia Chatzikonstantinou is an architect (AUTH) with an MSc in Urban and Regional Planning and a PhD in Urban History (NTUA). Her dissertation discusses the socio-spatial dynamics that made roads one of the most important symbols of the Greek modernization. Her research focuses on urban history, critical geography and environmental planning. She has participated in several research projects at Urban Environment Laboratory NTUA; has worked at the Organization for the Regulatory Plan of Athens and has taught urban history, planning and sustainability at NTUA, National and Kapodistrian University of Athens and College Year in Athens, Greece.

Irena L.C. Connon is a Social Anthropologist and Postdoctoral Research Fellow in Human Geography at the University of Dundee, Scotland, UK. Her areas of research expertise are: 1) examining the human responses to environmental hazard events and improving policy and practices of disaster preparedness and recovery; 2) understanding the contested meanings and socio-cultural dimensions of vulnerability, resilience and adaptation to environmental hazards, including oil spills and extreme weather events; and 3) analysing the role of culture in energy hardship and the links between energy poverty and risk during weather-related power outages. She has conducted research in various sites within the UK, in Alaska and, more recently, in Australia. To date, she has published a number of peer-reviewed articles and book chapters and is now working on a collaborative project with the University of Technology Sydney, Australia, which focuses on the remediation of contaminated lands in residential sites.

Anna Cronin de Chavez is a Senior Research Fellow working for the Born in Bradford project, Bradford Teaching Hospitals NHS Foundation Trust, on infant and maternal health and green spaces. She is a medical anthropologist who has been involved in applied health and wellbeing research projects with vulnerable communities in Central America and the UK. These projects include the impact of fuel poverty on children and adults with sickle cell disease (Northern England and Midlands), child health and fuel poverty (South Yorkshire), thermal care of infants (Bradford and Guatemala), infant and maternal health and green spaces (Bradford), and she has conducted several months of ethnographic fieldwork in a remote part of Panama.

Jiska R. de Groot is a Development and Energy Geographer at the University of Cape Town's Energy Research Centre, South Africa. Her work focuses on the social processes surrounding changes in energy use, access to clean and reliable energy technologies and considerations of fairness and justice in energy systems. As a researcher, she is committed to conducting research that is policy- and practice-relevant with a focus on achieving local development benefits. She is currently involved in research projects funded by the EPSRC, the ESRC/NRF's Newton Fund, and DfID. She has published her work in several journals including *Energy Research & Social Science*, *Ocean and Coastal Management*, and *Development Southern Africa* and has contributed to several edited books in the field of energy and development.

Katrin Großmann is a Professor of Urban and Spatial Sociology at the Erfurt University of Applied Sciences, Germany. She was previously a Research Associate at the Department of Environmental and Urban Sociology, Helmholtz-Centre for Environmental Research, from 2007 to 2014. Her research specialises in issues of residential segregation, social diversity and inequalities in the context of urban spaces. Recently she has begun applying these ideas to energy poverty, studying the dynamics of energy vulnerability in relation to housing markets and residential mobility. She has published on these issues in a range of journals including *Geografiska Annaler Series B* and *European Urban & Regional Studies*. In 2016, she was lead editor on the volume *Energy and Social Inequality* (published by Springer in German).

Philippa Howden-Chapman, Professor of Public Health at the University of Otago, Wellington, New Zealand, is a director of *He Kainga Oranga*/Housing and Health Research Programme and the NZ Centre for Sustainable Cities. Her team's randomised community trials, in partnership with local communities, provide evidence to inform housing, health and energy policy. Their work focuses on reducing inequalities in the determinants of health, and they have received a number of awards including the Prime Minister's Science Prize. She is currently the chair of the WHO Housing and Health International Guideline Development Group.

Antje Kahlheber is part of the Department of Energy and Buildings at the Consumer Centre ('Verbraucherzentrale') in Rhineland-Palatinate, Germany, where she has established and manages a project on 'Systemic Consultancy on Energy and Costs for Energy-Poor Households'. She has a background in systemic consulting as well as energy consultation. As a Research Associate in Biology, her research focused on changes of aquatic ecosystems after human impacts. Her research interests are interactions between and regeneration of complex systems. She has published on a range of different topics like overfishing, sustainable land use and systemic approaches in consumer consulting. Besides her scientific career, she worked as a journalist for newspapers and science magazines.

Abigail J. Knox is a PhD candidate in the Department of Sociology at the University of Cape Town, South Africa. Her research focuses on electricity consumption behaviours and energy strategies of people living in informal settlements and backyard shacks. With the Energy Research Centre at the same university, she is also part of a Research Consortium led by the University of Twente in the Netherlands, focusing on productive uses of energy in the informal food sector. She is also co-founder of the social enterprise start-up TaxiMap – a website sharing information about minibus taxi routes in Durban, Cape Town and Johannesburg. Her consulting research experience includes sustainable energy markets, sustainable economic development, informal public transport and urban studies in South Africa.

Rob Lawson is a Professor in Marketing Department at University of Otago, New Zealand. He has applied consumer behaviour theory to research sustainability and consumer ethics and has been involved in consumer rights and justice in the marketplace. He has also researched tourist behaviour and analysed the values and lifestyles of NZ consumers. He was the Principal Investigator on a large Energy Cultures multidisciplinary project aimed at understanding why the adoption of energy-efficient technologies and behaviours has been slow in New Zealand households.

Sarah Lindley is a Reader in GIS in the Department of Geography, School of Environment, Education and Development, at the University of Manchester, UK. Most of her work is focused on understanding human-environment interactions through collaborative, multidisciplinary research with a strong geographical information science dimension. One strand of her research has developed improved spatial assessments of hazards, vulnerabilities and risks, including for heat-related hazard and urban air quality. Her work has been funded by a range of UK Research Councils and charities as well as government and international sources and has involved collaborations with engineering, atmospheric science, social science, ecology and the health sciences. She also works closely with users of research and has held local, national and international advisory roles. Current projects include climatejust.org.uk and the NERC/AHRC/ESRC-funded Green Infrastructure and the Health and Wellbeing Influences on an Ageing Population (GHIA) project (NE/N013530/1).

Maciej Lis holds a PhD degree in economics from the Warsaw School of Economics, Poland. He is a Research Fellow at the Institute for Structural Research (IBS) in Poland, where he developed a micro-simulation model of energy poverty. His research focuses on micro-simulation, health economics, labour economics and social policy.

Fatima McKague is a PhD candidate at the Centre for Sustainability at the University of Otago, New Zealand. Her PhD explores the energy-housing-poverty nexus in New Zealand. She is researching the consumption patterns of low-income energy users, particularly focusing on energy hardship and quality of life of these households. She hopes to provide evidence-based policy recommendations to alleviate fuel poverty in New Zealand. In addition to her PhD, she has worked for the Dunedin City Council as a Policy Advisor on energy and has provided consultancy to community organisations on housing and energy. She has also coordinated the Otago Energy Research Centre and the Otago Climate Change Network.

Agata Miazga graduated in Economics (MA) from the University of Warsaw, Poland. She was an analyst at the Institute for Structural Research (IBS) in Warsaw. Her research interests focused on defining and measuring energy poverty in Poland, as well as on education and the labour market. She is an author of several working papers describing the problem of energy poverty in Poland. Since 2017, she has changed her career path in IBS and now uses her scientific experience to promote her colleagues' research.

Nthabiseng Mohlakoana is employed by the Department of Governance and Technology for Sustainability (CSTM) at the University of Twente, the Netherlands, as a Post-Doctorial Researcher. She is currently coordinating a multi-partner project on Productive Uses of Energy in South Africa, Senegal and Rwanda under the DFID-funded ENERGIA Gender and Energy Research Programme. She also supervises Bachelor's and Master's student projects as well as some lecturing. She has more than 15 years of research experience in the area of energy poverty and development as well as in gender and energy research. Throughout her career, her work has mainly focused on research that influences policy to provide low-income households and communities in developing countries with better energy access while taking gender issues into consideration.

Kimberley C. O'Sullivan is a Research Fellow with *He Kainga Oranga*/Housing and Health Research Programme at the University of Otago, Wellington, New Zealand. She has been conducting energy poverty research since 2008; her work has included qualitative interviews with older people, mixed methods investigation into prepayment metering and energy poverty, and mixed methods participatory action research to explore youth experiences of energy poverty in NZ. She is interested finding solutions for achieving energy transition without entrenching energy injustice.

Saska Petrova is a Lecturer in Human Geography at the School of Environment, Education and Development and Director of the MSc in Environmental Governance at the University of Manchester, UK. Her work focuses on how local people are rendered vulnerable and governable via different regimes of environmental governance and low-carbon urban transformation processes. She has published extensively on these issues, including a monograph on *Communities in Transition* (Routledge, 2014) as well as a number of articles in leading scientific journals. She has an extensive professional background as a public advocate and consultant for a range of government institutions and think tanks.

Yachika Reddy is a Project Manager for Sustainable Energy Africa, a not-for-profit sustainable urban energy development organization in South Africa. She has an MSc in Energy Studies from the University of Cape Town. She has worked in the energy and development arena for over 10 years focusing on energy poverty, assisting cities with energy and climate change policy and strategy development and implementation and training. She has extensive experience in local government policy, planning and sustainable energy implementation. She was one of the co-authors of *The State of Energy in South African Cities 2015* and has written numerous reports and conference papers on energy poverty and sustainable urban energy development in South Africa.

Slavica Robić is a Program Director at the Society for Sustainable Development Design (DOOR), Croatia, and a PhD candidate at the University of Zagreb's Faculty of Electrical Engineering and Computing, pursuing research in the field of energy poverty. She has worked on many national and international energy-related projects both on an expert and advocacy level. She has authored and co-authored numerous reports, strategic and policy documents and has published the results of her work on energy efficiency in *Energy Policy*. Her expertise is primarily in the South-East European context, focusing on evidence-based advocacy work for promoting changes in social and energy policy.

Caitlin Robinson is a Doctoral Researcher at the University of Manchester, UK, currently completing her PhD in Human Geography within the School of Environment, Education and Development. Her research forms part of the multi-disciplinary EPSRC Centre for Doctoral Training in Power Networks. She is primarily interested in exploring inequalities and social vulnerabilities using spatial analysis. Her PhD research focuses upon mapping vulnerability to fuel poverty in England, considering the implications of the spatial distribution of these vulnerabilities for the governance of the sector.

Ivana Rogulj is the Program Coordinator at the Society for Sustainable Development Design (DOOR), Croatia, and an energy expert on the 'European Calculator, Trade-offs and Pathways towards Sustainable and Low-carbon European Societies' project, under the Research and Innovation EU Program. Her work focuses on energy efficiency and climate change mitigation, particularly energy and climate modelling and planning. She has previously worked for the Energy Service Company, dealing with large-scale energy efficiency projects. She has been involved in various interdisciplinary projects and participated in the development of the South East Europe Climate Calculator.

Katarzyna Sałach is an Analyst at the Institute for Structural Research (IBS) in Warsaw, Poland. Her research interests involve econometrics and environmental economics, poverty and inequalities. Her work at IBS is focused mainly on energy poverty, but currently, she is also involved in projects concerning the gender wage gap and labour market impacts of energy retrofits on buildings. Within the subject of energy poverty, she focuses on working out the most suitable indicator of energy poverty in Poland. She graduated in Mathematics (BSc) and Econometrics (MA), as well as in Musicology (BA), from the University of Warsaw.

Michelle Scott is currently working as a Postdoctoral Research Assistant at the University of Dundee, Scotland, UK. Her research is on participatory sensing and citizen science. Previously she worked as a postdoc at the Centre for Sustainability at the University of Otago on understanding people's energy-related choices and behaviours. She completed her PhD in Human Computer Interaction at the Madeira Interactive Technologies Institute at the University of Madeira, Portugal. Her research interests lie in encouraging awareness of the environment and understanding and changing sustainable behaviours. Recent research has produced both policy and design recommendations for encouraging more fuel-efficient driving practices and for the design of effective household energy efficiency interventions.

Neil Simcock is a Research Associate at the University of Manchester, UK, where he works on the Energy Vulnerability and Urban Transitions in Europe (EVALUATE) project. He has previously worked at Keele University and Lancaster University. His research expertise focuses on social and environmental justice, inequalities, poverty and vulnerability in the context of low-carbon energy transitions. He has published on these topics in several journals including *Local Environment*, *Energy Research & Social Science*, *Land Use Policy* and *Energy Policy*. He was also Co-Guest Editor of a Special Issue of *Energy Research & Social Science* on 'Energy demand for mobility and domestic life: new insights from energy justice' (Volume 18, 2016).

Harriet Thomson is a Research Associate at the University of Manchester, UK, working on the Energy Vulnerability and Urban Transitions in Europe (EVAL-UATE) project. She is also a Project Manager of the European Commission-funded European Energy Poverty Observatory (EPOV). Her background is in comparative social policy, and her doctoral research, which she undertook at the University of York, examined energy poverty in the European Union. Her research interests broadly concern institutional theory, the EU polity, climate change and domestic energy deprivation. She has published in a variety of academic journals and is Associate Editor of the international journal *Energy Research & Social Science*.

Fereniki Vatavali is an architect engineer and has received an MSc and a PhD on Urban and Regional Planning from National Technical University of Athens, Greece (NTUA). She has taught urban planning, regional planning and environmental planning at NTUA, Democritus University of Thrace, University of Thessaly, Hellenic Open University and Polis University of Tirana. She has participated in several research projects on issues related to the processes of urban development. Her research interests focus on the production of urban space, housing, landownership, urban policies, the environment and energy.

Helen Viggers is a Research Fellow at the University of Otago, Wellington, New Zealand, where she works in *He Kainga Oranga*/Housing and Health Research Programme. Her research focuses on New Zealand's cold housing – including the reasons for it, extent of it and interventions to improve it. She has also investigated the effect of housing on mobility and factors protecting against mortgagee sale.

Peta Wolpe is the Managing Director of Sustainable Energy Africa, a not-for-profit sustainable urban energy development organization in South Africa. She has a BA degree in Sociology from the University of Essex and a Master of Science in Social Administration and Social Work Studies from the London School of Economics and Political Science. She has worked in the development sector for many years. She is engaged in urban energy and climate change strategy development and implementation for local, provincial and national government in Sub-Saharan Africa. She has facilitated workshops and written papers on climate change, urban energy poverty and sustainable development.

Ben Wooliscroft is the Associate Dean Research in the Otago Business School, New Zealand. His research focuses on sustainability, ethical consumption, quality of life and active travel. An Associate Editor of the *Journal of Macromarketing*, he has published widely, including in *Marketing Theory*, the *Journal of the Academy of Marketing Science*, the *Journal of Macromarketing*, the *Journal of Sustainable Tourism*, *Transportation Research A* and *Energy Policy*.

Acknowledgements

The editors' work on this collection was inspired, developed and funded as part of the Energy Vulnerability and Urban Transitions in Europe (EVALUATE) project, which would have been impossible without the financial support of the European Research Council (FP7/2007–2013/ERC grant agreement number 313478). Our deep thanks to the many contributing authors for all their hard work and diligence in putting together such an exciting group of chapters. Many thanks to the staff at Routledge, particularly Margaret Farrelly and Annabelle Harris, for their guidance and patience throughout the duration of putting together this book. Special gratitude is also due to the Eaga Charitable Trust for providing financial support towards the organisation an early career researchers' symposium in Manchester during September 2016, as well as the Energy Geographies Working Group of the Royal Geographical Society with the Institute of British Geographers (RGS-IBG) for offering free guest passes that allowed some delegates to attend a session organised by the book editors at the RGS-IBG 2016 Annual International Conference. Presentations at the Manchester early career symposium and 2016 RGS-IBG conference session provided the basis for some of the chapters included here. The book has also benefited from the intellectual environment and resources provided by the Department of Geography within the School of Environment, Education and Development at the University of Manchester, as well as the Collaboratory for Resilience and Energy within the Manchester Urban Institute. We would single out previous members of the EVALUATE team – Sergio Tirado Herrero and Tomas Maltby – as well as colleagues at the Universities of Skopje and Gdańsk, Charles University, Central European University, and EkoSvest. Last but not least, we are grateful to the funding from the Global Development Institute's Conference Fund Award, which supports a session linked to this book at the Royal Geographical Society's 2017 Annual International Conference.

1 Introduction

Stefan Bouzarovski, Neil Simcock,
Harriet Thomson, and Saska Petrova

When Brenda Boardman published her seminal book *Fuel Poverty: From Cold Homes to Affordable Warmth* (Boardman 1991), there was little public acceptance of the idea that significant numbers of households may suffer from a form of deprivation that cannot be easily subsumed under the aegis of low incomes. Revisiting her work after two decades, a special section of the journal *Energy Policy* was subtitled 'Fuel poverty comes of age' (Liddell 2012, 2). It was underpinned by an acknowledgment that 'the concept has attained unprecedented prominence, mainly as a consequence of a new energy crisis far more complex and wide-ranging than any before' (Liddell 2012, 5). In recent years, this has aided the emergence of a global understanding of energy poverty, in which the condition (often recognized via the term 'fuel poverty' or 'domestic energy deprivation') can be conceptualized as a household's inability to secure a socially- and materially-necessitated level of energy services in the home (Bouzarovski and Petrova 2015).

Current public understandings, scientific research and policy action concerning insufficient energy provision in the home are a world away from the circumstances encountered by Boardman. Energy poverty is a now an official component of many European Union policies, with a new European Energy Poverty Observatory having been launched in December 2016. In the United Kingdom, cold homes are the subject of extensive public attention and political debate – even if a previously well-developed suite of state policies to address the issue has been subject to significant downgrading of late. France and Ireland have also mobilized significant governmental capacity towards the monitoring and amelioration of their own energy poverty-related challenges. At the same time, the predicament is gaining significant public attention in Spain, Germany, Poland, Slovakia, Greece, Bulgaria and Belgium. Beyond Europe, debates on the topic are emerging in Australia, New Zealand, Japan, South Africa and even in the United States. These efforts and deliberations have evolved parallel to the significant number of initiatives and analyses of energy poverty in the Global South – where issues of infrastructural access and development, rather than affordability, have traditionally taken precedence.

This book aims to provide a global perspective on energy poverty, with the aid of novel theoretical approaches that disturb entrenched scientific preconceptions and policy prescriptions. We are particularly interested in deepening existing conceptualizations of the systemic drivers of energy poverty, by drawing attention to the manner in which the condition is embedded in deeper forms and practices of social exclusion and injustice. Starting from the fact that energy poverty is an inherently spatial phenomenon – it is both experienced in and caused by the entanglement of the socio-technical infrastructures of the home, while varying significantly across cities, regions and nations – there is a strong focus on the geographic processes and contingencies that underpin the emergence of this predicament. We draw together the findings of original research conducted by leading experts from a wide range of countries in order to capture the rapidly expanding corpus of scientific and policy expertise on energy poverty. By furthering knowledge on the driving forces of the condition, the book also produces policy-relevant insights that can aid decision-making on how domestic energy deprivation can be ameliorated.

The book also speaks to recent advances in the state of the art in energy poverty research, largely developed in response to the limitations of early scholarship on the subject. Historically, the causes of energy poverty were considered through the 'triad' of high energy prices, poor housing efficiency and low incomes. More recent work has introduced a much wider set of factors into the debate, including, but not limited to cultural norms; the dynamic and evolving nature of household needs and circumstances; and underlying socio-technical, spatial and political issues that shape housing efficiency and energy prices. Considering that 'fuel poverty is rapidly becoming one of the most hazardous remaining elements of human housing' (Liddell 2012, 4), many recent contributions have involved a strong focus on the interconnections between energy poverty and health, as well as the mediating role that poor housing plays in this regard. Recent uses of relational geography (Buzar 2007), assemblage thinking (Harrison and Popke 2011), justice-based approaches (Walker and Day 2012) and vulnerability and resilience frameworks (Bouzarovski and Tirado Herrero 2017; Bouzarovski et al. 2016) to theorize energy poverty have been useful in highlighting more complex and nuanced issues that underpin and drive the condition. Whilst these indicate fruitful directions for further scholarship, more remains to be done in terms of both consolidating and advancing research agendas on the issue. We would make the case for a fuller incorporation of arguments that seek to understand the linkages between domestic energy deprivation, on the one hand, and the wider performativities of socio-technical service provision in residential buildings, on the other (Graham and Marvin 2002; Luque-Ayala and Silver 2016; Rutherford and Coutard 2014; Bouzarovski 2015).

Exposing and confronting infrastructural inequalities: new research directions

As noted above, recent years have seen the rise of a planetary sensibility with regard to energy poverty, moving beyond the dichotomy between 'Global North' vs. 'Global South' contexts in the study of the issue. A number of authors have aimed to address the lack of conversation or exchange of concepts, ideas and findings between these two realms of research (Li et al. 2014). In terms of policy, such a move also helps position domestic energy deprivation as a major human security issue that should receive urgent attention. It is predicated upon the premise that regardless of the drivers of domestic energy deprivation, its consequences remain the same – households are unable to meet their energy needs in the home. Moreover, empirical evidence challenges the notion that infrastructural access to modern energy is primarily an issue faced by citizens of the Global South, while households in the Global North are meant to struggle with high prices and incomes: affordability problems are common in many countries that are commonly classified as 'developing' – particularly in urban areas – while more technologically advanced networked forms of energy provision are often absent in large tracts of states that are conventionally labelled 'developed' (Bouzarovski and Petrova 2015).

Unpacking the North-South binary has been enabled by energy vulnerability thinking – an approach that highlights the distinction between energy poverty as a descriptor of a state at a given point in time, on the one hand, and vulnerability as a set of conditions that characterize the emergence and persistence of deprivation, on the other (Bouzarovski 2013; Hall et al. 2013; Middlemiss and Gillard 2015). The vulnerability approach hinges upon the notion that energy poverty itself is a fluid state, which a household may enter or exit after an externally- or internally-induced change in housing, social, political or economic circumstances; as a result, the energy vulnerability demographic will always be larger than that of people who are energy poor. In essence, energy vulnerability thinking operates with risks and probabilities, because they express the likelihood of becoming energy poor. When combined with approaches that focus on the entire 'energy chain' via which utility services get delivered to consumers, the vulnerability paradigm destabilizes the 'affordability-access binary to encompass the nature and structure of the built environment of the home, as well as the articulation of social practices and energy needs' (Bouzarovski and Petrova 2015, 35).

Energy vulnerability thinking is closely connected to approaches that focus on how the demand for energy services in the home is constructed via, and embedded in, a much wider set socio-technical relations (Walker et al. 2016). However, recognizing the need for energy as a socially necessitated phenomenon problematizes the idea that basic energy standards can be easily defined in any kind of social setting (Simcock and Petrova forthcoming). This also suggests that the reduction of energy poverty measurement and indicator frameworks to particular carriers cannot capture the entirety of household needs and situations across the world. Vulnerability thinking exposes the risks faced by groups that have received little policy recognition to date. This includes urban households living in transitory housing arrangements within the Global North – mainly young people, immigrants, tenants in private rental housing and residents of informal settlements – which are difficult to detect and target via conventional policy frameworks (Bouzarovski and Cauvain 2016; Jencks and Peterson 2001; Visagie 2008). In developing country contexts, the framework highlights the need to ensure that the technical and financial availability of energy carriers is matched with socially-necessitated household needs.

Recent years have also seen increasing understanding and acknowledgement of the serious health impacts of energy poverty across the globe. In places where domestic access to advanced heating and electricity infrastructure is limited, households face a range of health outcomes including physical injury during fuel-wood collection and inadequate storage of medicines due to a lack of refrigeration, to more serious issues relating to indoor air pollution (IAP) (Sovacool 2012). Globally, many households rely on polluting solid fuels – such as wood, dung and coal – for heating and cooking. When open or poorly ventilated stoves or open fires are used indoors, large quantities of harmful pollutants are released, which have been implicated as a causal agent of several diseases, including stroke, lung cancer and chronic obstructive pulmonary disease (Jin et al. 2006). As Sovacool notes, there is a hazardous spatial and temporal dimension to IAP, with it being spatially concentrated indoors within small rooms, and occurring at times when people (typically women) are preparing and eating food (Sovacool 2012, 275). Furthermore, lighting in energy poor households that lack electricity access is often provided by candles or diesel/kerosene lanterns, both of which pose health and safety risks to occupants, including poisoning from ingesting fuel, explosions and burns (Lam et al. 2012).

Meanwhile, a growing evidence base is forming on the diverse range of adverse health and well-being effects that manifest when households are unable to attain the energy services necessary to keep their homes sufficiently warm or cool (Tod and Thomson 2016). This body of work provides a nuanced picture of the impacts of extreme temperatures on those with pre-existing health conditions (Osman et al. 2008; Snell et al. 2015), as well as offering evidence on the ways in which energy poverty can lead to a deterioration of health and well-being (Harrington et al. 2005; Liddell and Morris 2010), creating a situation in which impaired health becomes both the outcome of and additional risk factor for experiencing energy poverty (Liddell and Guiney 2015). More recently, the spatial character-istics of health and well-being in relation to energy poverty has received atten-tion in a comparative study of 32 countries in Europe (Thomson et al. 2017). This work draws attention to a paradoxical situation whereby the disparity in poor health and well-being between those who are energy vulnerable and those that are not is greatest within some countries that experience higher levels of income equality and lower rates of energy poverty (compared to European aver-ages). The links between energy poverty and increased mortality during winter (termed excess winter mortality) has been known for some time (Braubach et al. 2011; Healy 2003). More recently, new advances have been made in how cli-matic variations are captured in the measurement of this phenomenon (Hajat and Gasparrini 2016; Liddell et al. 2016) with attention also shifting to how we calculate excess summer mortality.

A further conceptual direction has been the move toward theorizing energy poverty as a distinct form and manifestation of social, environmental and energy injustice (Christman and Russell 2016; Sovacool et al. 2016; Walker and Day

2012). Such work has made clear that the amelioration of energy poverty should be considered a fundamental moral and political obligation, rather than an optional act of charity or benevolence. It has also helped to enrich understandings of the leading causes of the condition, with the three tenets of distributional, recognition and procedural justice offering a useful lens through which to examine the underpinnings of domestic energy deprivation. The recent move toward a 'whole systems' perspective on energy justice (McCauley et al. 2013) has highlighted how the occurrence of energy poverty at the household level results from distributional inequities operating 'upstream' in the energy system – such as unfair or regressive pricing structures, subsidies for energy technologies, poorly designed or targeted energy efficiency policies or dated transmission infrastructure (Bouzarovski et al. 2017; Hiteva 2013). The concept of 'justice as recognition', meanwhile, focuses on how institutionalized patterns of cultural stereotyping, exclusion and stigmatization work to (re)produce energy poverty by devaluing and marginalizing some groups in policy design. Examples include a lack of consideration of the particular and highly varied needs of disabled people (Snell et al. 2015) and the negative stereotyping of tenants in multiple occupancy housing in the UK that results in such groups receiving little policy attention or support to improve the energy efficiency of their homes (Bouzarovski and Cauvain 2016). Where policy support is available, fear of stigmatization can also discourage households from revealing their situation in order to access support or advice (Reid et al. 2015). Finally, authors have also argued that procedural injustice also underpins energy deprivation, with inadequate opportunities for vulnerable groups to participate in policy-making leading to a lack of consideration for their situation (Walker and Day 2012).

Contents of this book

The chapters that constitute the remainder of the book expand some of these theoretical ideas while introducing a number of new frameworks to the debate. The studies are geographically diverse and encompass a wide range of economic, cultural and political contexts, cutting across the developed/developing country divide and exploring energy poverty in territories that have received little academic attention to date.

The initial three chapters in the book introduce a diversity of new conceptual insights and reflections on the underpinning drivers of energy deprivation. This begins with a discussion of the theory of intersectionality by Katrin Großmann and Antje Kahlheber. They powerfully argue that energy poverty is fundamentally the result of deep structures of mutually reinforcing inequalities – economic, racial, gender-based and others – that exist in societies. In this conceptualization, the classic 'triad' of energy poverty causes – low incomes, poor energy efficiency and high energy prices – is understood as a *symptom* of these deeper, more systemic forms of discrimination. Drawing on documentary analysis, energy poverty is often most severe and difficult to escape, Großmann and Kahlheber suggest, in households that are simultaneously disadvantaged along multiple axes inequality – such as race, income, gender or health. Focusing on the household scale, Fatima McKague, Rob Lawson, Michelle Scott and Ben Wooliscroft utilize the emerging 'energy cultures' framework to understand how energy poverty is constituted through an interaction between a household's material culture (such as the energy efficiency of the home), practices (routinized behaviours) and norms (expectations and values). The interaction between these dimensions, they argue, can produce a self-reinforcing situation, in which households are 'trapped' in vulnerable predicaments, whilst 'external' influences from beyond the home space, such as policy changes, can help to break this feedback loop. Their findings lend support to holistic approaches to policy-making that address each of the dimensions of energy culture. Following this, Irena L.C. Connon focuses on the role of socio-cultural values and norms – often overlooked in many traditional conceptualizations of energy poverty – in (re)producing domestic energy deprivation. Drawing on a rich set of qualitative interviews with households in Scotland and England, her findings reveal a cultural stigma toward being unable to heat one's home and a norm of distrust toward energy companies and national government. These work to encourage householders to conceal their vulnerability and discline them from seeking support or advice that may partly relieve their situation.

The next five chapters then move on to take a more explicitly geographical approach, focusing particularly on the multi-scalar spatial contingencies that underpin energy vulnerability and its manifestation in different localities, alongside an examination of the uneven spatial distribution of the condition. This commences with a persuasive exploration of energy poverty in post-apartheid urban South Africa, by Abigail J. Knox, Jiska R. de Groot and Nthabiseng Mohlakoana. Taking a highly contextualized historical and spatial approach, they explore the ways that apartheid legacies of spatial segregation, housing policy and energy service provision act as systemic drivers of urban energy vulnerability. Uniquely, their chapter moves beyond the traditional focus of energy poverty studies to incorporate *mobility* as an important energy service for households, and they thus analyze the lack of adequate transport options as a form of energy deprivation. Moving to very different context, Alison Browne, Saska Petrova and Beth Brockett discuss energy vulnerability in China. They do so through a unique 'nexus' approach that examines the connections between energy and water services. Their analysis illustrates how infrastructures of provision – connected, as in South Africa, to particular path-dependencies resulting from historical policy decisions – interconnect with everyday practices to produce a range of household vulnerabilities that vary between urban and rural areas, the north and south of the country and different socio-economic groups. Evangelia Chatzikonstantinou and Fereniki Vatavali then examine the spatialities of energy deprivation in Athens in the context of the Greek debt crisis. Combining data from city, neighbourhood and household levels, and using both quantitative and qualitative methods, they argue that energy deprivation has emerged as a crucial for the geography of the city, though the condition displays no clear spatial segregation. They also find that established perspectives on the relative vulnerability of high-/low-income households, and homeowners and tenants, are somewhat disrupted and redefined: for example, they found tenants to often be less vulnerable due to their ability to move apartment, whilst homeowners may be 'trapped' in their cold homes and overburdened by significant property taxes. Meanwhile, some low-income households can attain sufficient energy services if they live in an apartment building with supportive neighbours or an effective heating system – in these ways, apartment buildings are a crucial geographic site and scale in determining energy vulnerability.

Maciej Lis, Agata Miazga and Katarzyna Sałach then explore the regional distribution of energy poverty in Poland through the use of statistical methods. Although they find significant regional disparities, the geography is complex and changes depending on the precise indicator of energy poverty that is used – rural areas are more susceptible to issues with energy affordability (as defined by the 'low-income high-cost' indicator), whilst urban areas face issues with a lack of adequate thermal comfort (as defined by subjective perceptions of households). They argue that spatial variations in energy efficiency, prices of energy carriers, household incomes and average outdoor temperatures explain these regional inequalities. Subsequently, Caitlin Robinson, Stefan Bouzarovski and Sarah Lindley use a GIS approach to interrogate whether two dominant ways of modelling and measuring energy poverty – the '10%' and the low-income high-cost (LIHC) indicators, respectively – adequately capture the complex and uneven geographic distribution of energy in England. Their analysis shows that both measures have blind spots, with the 10% measure emphasizing pensioners and households lacking gas central heating and the LIHC emphasizing low-income families, and thus both fail to capture the full spatial complexity of energy vulnerability. A more explicitly geographic approach to the design of composite indicators, capturing the unique spatial distributions of vulnerability dimensions, is required if energy poverty measures are to reveal those most in need.

The role of divergent household needs in shaping energy vulnerability has begun to be acknowledged in recent years (e.g. Bouzarovski and Petrova 2015; Snell et al. 2015), and the chapter by Anna Cronin de Chavez helps to further this agenda through a rich qualitative analysis of households living with sickle cell disease. Her study powerfully demonstrates what she terms the 'triple-hit' effect of disability, encompassing a difficulty in gaining and sustaining income, increased needs for and costs relating to home heating and the potential for a vicious circle in which poor health is worsened by an inability to obtain or afford increased heating needs. Young people are another group that face heightened susceptibility to the impacts of colder temperature. The particular vulnerabilities of this group are analyzed in the chapter by Kimberley C. O'Sullivan, Helen Viggers and Philippa Howden-Chapman, who argue that, as well as being physiologically less able to cope with cold temperatures, young people also have reduced agency to make changes that improve their ability to attain adequate energy services and can also face exposure to cold temperatures outside the home – particularly at school. Drawing on their own experiences, they make a strong case for participatory methodologies that fully involve young people through the entire research process, arguing that this results in richer and more successful investigations.

The next three chapters adopt a stronger policy and solutions-based focus, critically analyzing current policy responses to energy deprivation and proposing how these might be improved. Slavica Robić, Ivana Rogulj and Branko Ančić begin, with a focus on the Western Balkans region of Europe. They argue that energy poverty policies in this region focus too strongly on providing households with financial relief, whilst doing little to improve the quality of dwellings. Partly, they suggest, this is symptomatic of a lack of full awareness and recognition of the condition – notably, none of the countries have official definitions of energy poverty. They argue for a more comprehensive energy efficiency strategy, the provision of advice to help households manage their energy use, and a general campaign to raise awareness of energy poverty as a distinct and pressing concern. The next chapter moves to an East African context, as Dorice Agol critically examines rural electrification programmes (REPs) in rural Kenya. Her findings show that, while REPs are designed to ameliorate energy poverty in rural areas, they encounter multiple challenges that shape their outcomes and impacts. These include technological issues (e.g. poor infrastructure and housing quality); institutional barriers (poor service provision, corruption); households' socio-cultural practices and preferences; the logistics of connecting geographically dispersed households; and the fact that electricity can be unaffordable to use once a household has been connected. Moreover, by targeting only specific demographics or narrowly defined spaces, REPs can produce new inequalities of access. She argues that, when assessing the relative 'success' of REPs, rather than considering only the crude figure of number of households connected to electricity infrastructure, greater attention is needed on the equitability of the outcomes and the quality of energy services households are able to achieve. The book's final chapter then returns to South Africa, as Peta Wolpe and Yachika Reddy build on the earlier chapter by Knox and colleagues to examine the difficulties of alleviating energy poverty in the country. They identify a series of challenges that policies have faced and provide suggestions for how they might be made more effective; of crucial importance, they argue, is the need for integrated, coordinated and holistic governance that goes beyond exclusively 'energy' departments to also incorporate issues of housing and neighbourhood planning, as well as greater incorporation of the voices of civil society and community groups.

The concluding chapter of the book, co-written by the editors, revisits the commonalities and differences observed in the preceding 14 chapters. It also identifies a set of policy implications at the global scale, as well as avenues for future research.

References

Boardman, B. (1991). *Fuel poverty: From cold homes to affordable warmth*. London: Bellhaven.

Bouzarovski, S. (2013). Energy poverty in the European Union: Landscapes of vulnerability. *Wiley Interdisciplinary Reviews: Energy and Environment.* Available at: http://online library.wiley.com/doi/10.1002/wene.89/abstract.

Bouzarovski, S. (2015). *Retrofitting the city: Residential flexibility, resilience and the built environment.* London: IB Tauris.

Bouzarovski, S. and Cauvain, J. (2016). Spaces of exception: Governing fuel poverty in England's multiple occupancy housing sector. *Space and Polity,* 20(3), 310–329.

Bouzarovski, S. and Petrova, S. (2015). A global perspective on domestic energy deprivation: Overcoming the energy poverty – fuel poverty binary. *Energy Research & Social Science,* 10, 31–40.

Bouzarovski, S. and Tirado Herrero, S. (2017). Geographies of injustice: The socio-spatial determinants of energy poverty in Poland, Czechia and Hungary. *Post-Communist Economies,* 29, 27–50.

Bouzarovski, S., Herrero, S. T., Petrova, S., Frankowski, J., Matoušek, R. and Maltby, T. (2017). Multiple transformations: Theorizing energy vulnerability as a socio-spatial phenomenon. *Geografiska Annaler: Series B, Human Geography,* 1–22.

Bouzarovski, S., Sýkora, L. and Matoušek, R. (2016). Locked-in post-socialism: Rolling path dependencies in liberec's district heating system. *Eurasian Geography and Economics.* Available at: http://dx.doi.org/10.1080/15387216.2016.1250224.

Braubach, M., Jacobs, D. E. and Ormandy, D. (2011). *Environmental burden of disease associated with inadequate housing.* Copenhagen: WHO Regional Office for Europe.

Buzar, S. (2007). *Energy poverty in Eastern Europe: Hidden geographies of deprivation.* Aldershot: Ashgate.

Christman, B. and H. Russell. (2016). Readjusting the political thermostat: Fuel poverty and human rights in the UK. *Journal of Human Rights in the Commonwealth,* 2(2). Available at: http://journals.sas.ac.uk/jhrc/article/view/2273.

Graham, S. and Marvin, S. (2002). *Splintering urbanism: Networked infrastructures, technological mobilities and the urban condition.* London and New York: Routledge.

Hajat, S. and Gasparrini, A. (2016). The excess winter deaths measure: Why its use is misleading for public health understanding of cold-related health impacts. *Epidemiology,* 27(4), 486–491.

Hall, S. M., Hards, S. and Bulkeley, H. (2013). New approaches to energy: Equity, justice and vulnerability: Introduction to the special issue. *Local Environment,* 18(4), 413–421.

Harrington, B. E., Heyman, B., Merleau-Ponty, N., Stockton, H., Ritchie, N. and Heyman, A. (2005). Keeping warm and staying well: Findings from the qualitative arm of the warm homes project. *Health & Social Care in the Community,* 13(3), 259–267.

Harrison, C. and Popke, J. (2011). "Because you got to have heat": The networked assemblage of energy poverty in Eastern North Carolina. *Annals of the Association of American Geographers,* 101(4), 949–961.

Healy, J. D. (2003). Excess winter mortality in Europe: A cross country analysis identifying key risk factors. *Journal of Epidemiology & Community Health,* 57(10), 784–789.

Hiteva, R. P. (2013). Fuel poverty and vulnerability in the EU low-carbon transition: The case of renewable electricity. *Local Environment,* 18(4), 487–505.

Jencks, C. and Peterson, P. E. (eds.) (2001). *The urban underclass.* Washington, DC: Brookings Institution Press.

Jin, Y., Ma, X., Chen, X., Cheng, Y., Baris, E. and Ezzati, M. (2006). Exposure to indoor air pollution from household energy use in rural China: The interactions of technology, behavior, and knowledge in health risk management. *Social Science & Medicine,* 62(12), 3161–3176.

Lam, N. L., Smith, K. R., Gauthier, A. and Bates, M. N. (2012). Kerosene: A review of household uses and their hazards in low- and middle-income countries. *Journal of Toxicology and Environmental Health, Part B*, 15(6), 396–432.

Li, K., Lloyd, B., Liang, X-J. and Wei, Y-M. (2014). Energy poor or fuel poor: What are the differences? *Energy Policy*, 68, 476–481.

Liddell, C. (2012). Fuel poverty comes of age: Commemorating 21 years of research and policy. *Energy Policy*, 49, 2–5.

Liddell, C. and Guiney, C. (2015). Living in a cold and damp home: Frameworks for understanding impacts on mental well-being. *Public Health*, 129(3), 191–199.

Liddell, C. and Morris, C. (2010). Fuel poverty and human health: A review of recent evidence. *Energy Policy*, 38(6), 2987–2997.

Liddell, C., Morris, C., Thomson, H. and Guiney, C. (2016). Excess winter deaths in 30 European countries 1980–2013: A critical review of methods. *Journal of Public Health*, 38(4), 806–814.

Luque-Ayala, A. and Silver, J. (2016). Introduction. In Luque-Ayala, A. and Silver, J. (eds.) *Energy, power and protest on the urban grid: Geographies of the electric city*. London and New York: Routledge.

McCauley, D. A., Heffron, R. J., Stephan, H. and Jenkins, K. (2013). Advancing energy justice: The triumvirate of tenets. *International Energy Law Review*, 32(3), 107–110.

Middlemiss, L. and Gillard, R. (2015). Fuel poverty from the bottom-up: Characterising household energy vulnerability through the lived experience of the fuel poor. *Energy Research & Social Science*, 6, 146–154.

Osman, L. M., Ayres, J. G., Garden, C., Reglitz, K., Lyon, J. and Douglas, J. G. (2008). Home warmth and health status of COPD patients. *European Journal of Public Health*, 18(4), 399–405.

Reid, L., McKee, K. and Crawford, J. (2015). Exploring the stigmatization of energy efficiency in the UK: An emerging research agenda. *Energy Research & Social Science*, 10, 141–149.

Rutherford, J. and Coutard, O. (2014). Urban energy transitions: Places, processes and politics of socio-technical change. *Urban Studies*, 51(7), 1353–1377.

Simcock, N. and S. Petrova. forthcoming. Energy poverty and vulnerability: A geographical perspective. In Solomon, B. and Calvert, K. (eds.) *Handbook on the geographies of energy*. Cheltenham: Edward Elgar Publishing.

Snell, C., Bevan, M. and Thomson, H. (2015). Justice, fuel poverty and disabled people in England. *Energy Research & Social Science*, 10, 123–132.

Sovacool, B. K. (2012). The political economy of energy poverty: A review of key challenges. *Energy for Sustainable Development*, 16(3), 272–282.

Sovacool, B. K., Heffron, R. J., McCauley, D. and Goldthau, A. (2016). Energy decisions reframed as justice and ethical concerns. *Nature Energy*, 1(5), 16024.

Thomson, H., Bouzarovski, S. and Snell, C. (2017). Rethinking the measurement of energy poverty in Europe: A critical analysis of indicators and data. *Indoor and Built Environment*. Available at: http://dx.doi.org/10.1177/1420326X17699260.

Tod, A. and Thomson, H. (2016). Health impacts of cold housing and energy poverty. In Csiba, K. (ed.) *Energy poverty handbook*. Brussels: The Greens/European Free Alliance in the European Parliament, pp. 39–56.

Visagie, E. (2008). The supply of clean energy services to the urban and peri-urban poor in South Africa. *Energy for Sustainable Development*, 12(4) (December), 14–21.

Walker, G. and Day, R. (2012). Fuel poverty as injustice: Integrating distribution, recognition and procedure in the struggle for affordable warmth. *Energy Policy*, 49, 69–75.

Walker, G., Simcock, N. and Day, R. (2016). Necessary energy uses and a minimum standard of living in the United Kingdom: Energy justice or escalating expectations? *Energy Research & Social Science*, 18. Available at: www.sciencedirect.com/science/article/pii/S2214629616300184.

2 Energy poverty in an intersectional perspective

On multiple deprivation, discriminatory systems, and the effects of policies

Katrin Großmann and Antje Kahlheber

Introduction

The debate on energy poverty is currently extending its geographical focus. Whereas the focus of debate, research, and policy development has long been in the UK – where the topic was initiated and where most of its terminology was coined in the 1980s – its focus now extends throughout Europe (Thomson and Snell 2013; Dubois and Meier 2016; Bouzarovski 2014). Meanwhile, concerns related to the causes and scope of energy deprivation bridge the Global North and South (Bouzarovski and Petrova 2015; Day et al. 2016; see also the Introduction to this volume). Together with such shifting geographical foci, new perspectives on the phenomenon have come to the fore. A focus on Southern European countries has raised the issue of electricity for cooling, studies from the Global South have elaborated the availability of different energy sources, and comparative work has evoked a new conceptual awareness, such as about the impact of political change and regimes (Bouzarovski and Petrova 2015; for a survey, see Day et al. 2016).

Taking the geographical context of Germany, we aim to contribute to such conceptual advances. In Germany, rising energy, electricity and gas disconnections are the most debated issue, whereas the housing stock is, in large parts and compared to other European countries, more energy efficient. The classic triad of causes found in the energy poverty literature – low incomes, poor energy efficiency, and high energy prices – can only partially explain which households are affected by energy poverty.

Drawing from documented counselling sessions for households struggling with energy costs, debts, and impending or executed energy cut-offs, we will address a conceptual gap in current energy poverty research: the underlying social structures involved in the creation of energy deprivation. Utilising the intersectionality approach as developed by Crenshaw (1991), we will analyse how various 'axes of inequality'[1] – such as income, gender, age, education, health status, and ethnicity – play a role in the constitution of households' energy-related struggles. The intersectionality approach, a strand of social stratification theory engaged with unravelling the mechanisms of multiple discriminations occurring along the intersections of axes of inequalities (Crenshaw 1991), will be used as a theoretical inspiration to interpret cases of energy deprivation. We intend to offer a deeper and more nuanced account of the causes of energy deprivation, moving beyond superficial theorisations to provide a richer understanding of the underpinning constellations in which energy deprivation emerges. The 'triad' theory of the causes of energy poverty first provided in the pioneering works of Boardman (1991) certainly served to help increase recognition of energy poverty and to measure the scope of the problem, in close connection with social movements and policy advice. However, we would argue that this theory fails to engage with the deeper systemic structures and inequalities that underpin domestic energy deprivation. The only axis of inequality, as defined by intersectionality theory,[2] that is included in this approach is income. In addition, the current debate on the appropriateness of the 10% indicator and alternative indicators, which triggered enormous attention, follows the same lines: income (as the only axis of inequality for social groups), energy prices, and housing conditions (Moore 2012). We would argue that the 'income-dimension' of the triad is an important axis of inequality that helps constitute the social position of a person (or household) in society and therefore deserves more analytical attention. However, in similar housing circumstances, some income poor households suffer energy deprivation whilst others do not. How can we explain this?

Other dimensions of inequality or social characteristics of individuals/households are sometimes present in the energy poverty debate, but they tend to be descriptive and not integrated into conceptual reasoning, particularly with regard to the recent shift towards identifying 'vulnerable consumers' in the EU policy debate (Pye and Dobbins 2015). Age and health have long been parameters of attention, especially because excess mortality studies have placed a focus on the enhanced vulnerability of elderly people (Rudge and Gilchrist 2005; Braubach und Fairburn 2010; Marmot Review Team 2011; Anderson et al. 2012; Chard and Walker 2016). Illness can be both a trigger of energy poverty by causing increased energy needs and consumption and a consequence of energy deprivation. It is a trigger because people who (need to) spend more time at home, or are awake at night and thus need longer hours of heating, therefore consume greater amounts of energy – leading to higher bills and thus an increased risk of energy poverty. Such changes in temporal patterns have also been highlighted for households with dependent children, especially if they are very young. For single parents, the prevalence of young children often coincides with low incomes (Anderson et al. 2012; Lawson et al. 2015).

As mentioned, however, these observations are not fully integrated with, or related to, deeper theoretical reasoning regarding the wider dynamics and structures of inequality in societies. Furthermore, other mechanisms such as housing market discrimination and subsequent residential segregation, which would cause low-income households to live in low-quality housing, remain largely invisible (see Großmann et al. 2014). In particular, information from major charities or consumer protection agencies, who are in close contact with households affected by energy deprivation, indicates that such households find themselves in 'multiple problems' (cf. Cremer 2013; e-fect/VZ RLP 2014; Verbraucherzentrale NRW 2015). In a study in Austria, Brunner et al. (2011) point out that for energy poor households energy bills are just one problem among several. This article intends to contribute to a conceptual shift: from energy poverty as a specific form of economic poverty, to energy as a field of inequality in which multiple factors merge to form a state of deprivation.

Debate and policies on energy poverty in Germany

There was a short period of public and political attention on the issue of households struggling to pay their energy bills when, after the Fukushima nuclear disaster, the German government executed an energy transition fostering both renewable energy production and energy efficiency measures – frequently termed the 'Energiewende' or 'energy transition'. For approximately 2 years, energy poverty became a surrogate battlefield between opposing opinions on energy policies, arguing for or against the energy transition (see Haas 2016). With this debate, both scholarly and institutional awareness of energy poverty increased, leading to programmes aimed at supporting households experiencing difficulties with energy bills and energy provision. Unlike the situation in the UK and in most other countries, electricity costs were at the centre of attention. Figures on the number of electricity cut-offs were made public, and they ranged from official figures of around 331,000 executed cut-offs annually (Bundesnetzagentur – German Network Agency 2017) and estimates from consumer protection agencies that ranged between 600,000 or even 800,000 cut-offs.[3]

Policy responses aimed at providing support for low-income households to better save energy and to negotiate with institutions to end or prevent electricity cut-offs (quite similar to Austria – see Brunner et al. 2016). Counselling programmes were established for households facing energy cut-offs or who were unable to pay their energy bills, most prominently the national-scale 'Stromsparcheck' ('check for energy savings') of the large charity Caritas, but also regional programmes with different foci led by consumer agencies in North-Rhine Westphalia (NRW) and Rhineland-Palatinate (RLP).

Within the academic debate, pioneering publications (e.g. Pietsch et al. 2010; Kopatz et al. 2010) used the triad of low incomes, high energy prices, and poor energy efficiency to develop a definition and an analytical base for the German context. Tews (2013), again leaning on Boardman's conceptualisation, argues that the appropriate policy response to energy poverty is retrofitting housing in order to improve energy efficiency. Some criticism of the emphasis on reducing of energy consumption of poor households has emerged recently, because studies show that low-income households often already save and even 'under-consume' energy (Brunner et al. 2016; Wolff et al. 2016). Besides income and energy costs, household composition is also highlighted. One-person households and households with either care-dependent elderly or toddlers are reported to require higher energy consumption (Cremer 2013; Verbraucherzentrale NRW 2015). On occasion, the influence of a migration background is highlighted because collecting information, understanding procedures, and checking expenditures are more difficult for migrants (e-fect/VZ RLP 2014; Verbraucherzentrale NRW 2015). In its policy recommendations, Caritas suggests that cases of energy hardship be more clearly defined, with the inclusion of social indicators such as age, health status, physical disabilities, pregnancy, or dependent children (Cremer 2013).

An important aspect of the debate addresses the appropriateness of welfare mechanisms. Households in the lowest income segment, i.e. purely welfare-dependent households living on what German law calls 'Grundsicherung' (basic financial security), are mostly covered for heating but struggle with rising electricity costs (see Aigeltinger et al. 2015). Households receiving financial support for housing ('Wohngeld') in addition to a low income, or those working on low wages, do not receive support for heating and, thus, are considered even more vulnerable (Kopatz 2013; Cischinsky et al. 2016). Low-income households lack the ability to exchange inefficient appliances for more efficient ones or to move to better insulated buildings (e.g. Kopatz 2013; Cremer 2013; Verbraucherzentrale NRW 2015).

Rising energy prices are in focus as a further cause of energy poverty. Prices for electricity rose for private consumers, although purchasing prices for providers declined considerably during the same period. Energy providers justify the high price level with reference to increasing costs for energy infrastructures and rising taxes on energy, some of which were imposed to finance the Energiewende. Transparency, here, is difficult to achieve. However, prices had been rising already since the early 2000s (Heindl et al. 2014; Tews 2013), before investments in Energiewende measures became crucial. The situation for heating fuels is different. Gas prices declined for consumers in recent years, following the decrease in purchasing prices for providers. Heavy competition in oil production and marketing led to unpredictable fluctuations, with a historic high in 2012 and a recent lower level comparable to 2006.

The German debate reveals the necessity to think beyond the classic 'triad' of energy poverty drivers to also include other social characteristics of households, the overlap of these characteristics with policies and institutional practices, and how this leads to a constellation of energy deprivation. In their evaluation of case studies of consumers facing energy debts, consumer organisations summarise: a central component of energy poverty is the sum of challenges households face in relation to their capabilities to cope with unfavourable situations. Even more, the complex requirements of energy delivery can be seen as a fundamental discrimination of households which have to deal with many burdens and are therefore restricted in their capacities to act and react (Kahlheber 2016). Interestingly, contributions to the field of energy justice and those from a perspective on needs (e.g. Day et al. 2016; Sovacool 2012; Walker and Day 2012) are starting to develop a way of thinking that conceptualises energy deprivation as a complex socio-technical phenomenon rather than just as a dimension of poverty. However, a full and coherent conceptualisation of these social inequalities, and how they work to reproduce energy poverty, is missing.

The intersectionality debate as an inspiration for conceptualising deprivation

Starting from feminist debates about how life chances for women differ, the triangle of race, class, and gender was discussed as influencing the relative position of individuals in social space. From here, the concept of intersectionality was developed, drawing attention to the overlapping effects of different axes of social difference. The seminal article by Crenshaw (1991) claims that overlapping disprivileging social characteristics, such as being a woman, being black, being old, and being disabled, lead to multiple deprivations. In these multiple deprivations, the disadvantages and discriminations arising from the various characteristics do not just add up, they intersect. At such intersections, disadvantages mutually reinforce each other.

> Intersectionality is a conceptualisation of the problem [of inequality] that attempts to capture both the structural and dynamic consequences of the interaction between two or more axes of subordination. It specifically addresses the manner in which racism, patriarchy, class oppression and other discriminatory systems create background inequalities that structure the relative position of women, races, ethnicities, classes and the like. Moreover, it addresses the way that specific acts and policies create burdens that flow along these axes constituting the dynamic or active aspects of disempowerment.
>
> (Crenshaw 2000, cited from Lutz 2014, 3)

This is a very new way of thinking about social inequalities. From an intersectional point of view, the relative position of an individual in society is not determined separately by selected social characteristics. Life chances thus would not be defined by resources as such, or by education, age, or skin colour, but by mutually reinforcing restrictions that a person faces in society. Seemingly small differences can thus lead to significantly different life chances. These restrictions turn characteristics that could be just random, horizontal, and unchangeable differences into drivers for discrimination. Crenshaw refers to 'discriminatory regimes' as the mechanisms that turn personal characteristics into disprivileging characteristics which mutually reinforce each other; 'racism and sexism readily intersect in the lives of real people' (Crenshaw 1991, 1242). As we shall illustrate, in the field of energy poverty, such discriminatory regimes can be found to operate in the systems of energy supply, in housing markets, in class distinction found in institutional practices, and so on. In this way, personal characteristics like health, communication skills or education can turn into disadvantages in the access to energy.

In the citation above, Crenshaw draws attention to the functioning of policies. Policies, she writes, flow along the intersecting axes of discrimination. Empowering policies for women thus do not automatically reach all women equally but best reach those women who do not face other discriminations by, for example, age, sexual orientation, legal status, or class. Crenshaw illustrates this by examining the outreach of policies to protect immigrant women from domestic violence within immigration policies in the US. In order to prevent women from accepting domestic violence merely to retain the right of residence, a 'waiver for hardship caused by domestic violence' was introduced. In order to make use of this waiver, official proof is needed, for example from the police or physicians. For those who cannot obtain such proof, such as Latinas living in illegality, immigrants without language skills, or otherwise without the ability to stand up for their own rights, this waiver is not accessible (Crenshaw 1991, 1246–1248). To put it differently, policies addressing a specific target group without anticipating the impact of intersections with other axes of inequalities do not equally reach everyone in the target group.

Drawing from our own experience, such intersections also play a role in how – and which – households can profit from energy counselling (described below). It takes a certain level of all knowledge, education, and motivation to make use of consumer counselling offers, which is generally a social practice of middle-class households. Low-income households, instead, access such offers through other institutions, so that a certain trust in institutions, as well as the ability to communicate with them, is a precondition for counselling. Language skills or psychological problems are burdens that can make it difficult for some vulnerable people to profit from these policies and programmes (see George et al. 2011 for a UK example). In this article, we attempt to interpret these observations more systematically.

There has been, however, intensive scholarly debate as to how an intersectionality approach can be operationalised in empirical research (survey in Lutz 2014). One challenge for empirical research focused on inequalities is that it is accustomed to working with statistical indicators such as income and education, gender, and age. The question about how intersectionality thinking can be integrated into empirical work that tries to depict deprivation or discrimination thus arises. Answers range from a denial of categories, in general, through working with intra-categorical (dividing categories into sub-categories), up to inter-categorical analyses (McCall 2005; Winker und Degele 2011). However, qualitative research has an important place in intersectional research because it allows for the detection of mechanisms of deprivation via in-depth studies.

Data and methods

This chapter is based on theoretical work combined with an exploratory secondary analysis of existing data on households in a state of energy-related deprivation. These data stem from the accompanying research of a consultancy project run by the Rhineland-Palatinate consumer protection agency for households with energy debts or cut-offs. In this project, households meet and discuss their issues with a trained consultant, who attempts to find a sustainable solution to the household's problems. The consultants consider factors such as the extent of debts, energy consumption, heating, housing and appliances, income, and other liabilities, as well as the individual's personal situation and abilities. Consulters offer, in up to 20 sessions, juridical and technical support and mediate with social services and energy providers.

The clients come on their own motivation, most often at the advice of other institutions such as charities, debt counselling, and social services. Each case and individual session is documented in separate report sheets defining specific variables. At the beginning of a contact, a questionnaire is filled out; the advisor completes the data sheet during the contact and reports on variables such as housing, energy use, socio-demographics, and so on and verbally describes the situation, the steps undertaken, and the (potential) success of the counselling.[4]

For this chapter, we analysed 149 such cases with descriptive statistical methods as well as with a qualitative analysis of the verbal aspects of the reports. Only cases that were closed at the time of analysis were included. The cases are by no means statistically representative of the population in the cities where offices are located, nor do they represent a group of energy poor households. Clients often accessed the counselling service when a problematic situation occurred; for example, an electricity cut-off of their home was announced or already executed, high energy debts had occurred, or people felt overburdened in their contact with institutions.

The qualitative analysis interpreted the data with an intersectional lens to see how characteristics of households, housing situations, and external factors intermixed. For this, we combined deductive and inductive steps. Cases were coded and interpreted in a contrasting fashion, seeking patterns leading to the state of energy deprivation.

Results will now be presented in two steps. First, we describe the group of clients in a quantitative overview. Second, we provide the results of the qualitative analysis.

Who is seeking advice?

Demographic structures

Demographically, the clients differ from the average population of the state Rhineland-Palatinate (RLP) with respect to gender, the share of single parents, and age, as shown in Figure 2.1. More women (62%) than men (38%) sought advice. The majority of cases are singles without a partner (72%) (RLP: 50.2%)[5] but only 42% are actually one-person households (state average: 37.1%). A high proportion, 26%, are single parents, mostly mothers (RLP: 22% in 2015). In half of the households, children under 18 are present, which is in line with the state's average of 49.6%. People seeking advice are younger than average. The mean age of clients is 42 years (RLP mean: 46), the majority is below 40 years. Nearly a fifth is younger than 30 years old (in RLP: 12.1% are between 20 and 30 years); the share of people above 60 years is surprisingly small (9%) (RLP: 21% older than 65 years).

Socio-economic structures

The sample represents relatively low social strata with a majority of 62% being unemployed (RLP: 5%), only a quarter of the clients are earning an income, and again only about 15% are in regular employment. Educational level is also relatively low, with only 3.3% of clients holding a university degree (RLP: 13.5%),

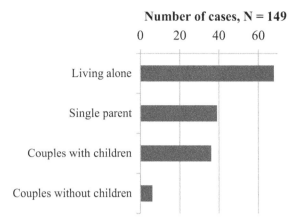

Figure 2.1 Demographic structures of the client sample

Source: Authors' own database, Verbraucherzentrale RLP 2016

but 30% of clients have no professional training at all (RLP: 17.2% among 25–65 year-old persons). 13% of clients receive a pension, although half of the pensioners are still below 65 years old, meaning that they receive a pension before the official German pension age has been reached. This is often due to severe illness and the physical inability to work. Thus, we see a specific group of vulnerable people here with rather low economic and educational status.

Ethnic structures

Among the clients, non-German households are over-represented compared to the RLP as a whole. 65% of clients have exclusively German citizenship (RLP: 90.5% have German or double citizenship); 75% speak German as their mother tongue. Out of the 25% non-natives, 11% have difficulties in speaking and understanding German.

Duration of residence

The cases divide largely into two groups: one group has been living in their flat or house for more than 3 years (51%); the other group moved in within the last 18 months (34%). A first interpretation is that energy-related problems often occur while moving house, with mistakes in billing or an underestimation of costs (moving can also be a way to try to escape debts), and/or that debts build up over time.

Burdening living conditions

Although comparable data are lacking here, illness is an important component in the sample: 32% of clients are physically or psychologically ill or are experiencing

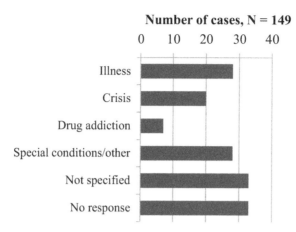

Figure 2.2 Clients with burdening living conditions

Source: Authors' own database, Verbraucherzentrale RLP 2016

a troubling period of their lives, such as the loss of a close person. Another 36% did not want to answer health-related questions or the situation was not clear. The information shown in Figure 2.2 depends on the openness of clients and thus cannot be considered completely reliable.

Energy costs, debts, and cut-offs in the sample

The majority of clients seek counselling because of problems related to their electricity costs. Every second client has difficulties covering the annual settlement bill, which can lead to unexpected supplementary payments of several hundred euros. This was often the case when the advance payments were underestimated by the energy provider, or bills have not been paid because of a sudden increase in expenditures, such as the birth of children, illness, or sudden unemployment. For 80% of clients, cut-off of electricity or heating were either announced (45%) or enforced (35%) (see Figure 2.3). In a third of the cases, an unfavourable contract led to high energy costs. Interestingly, 44% of clients had electric warm water devices, which are expensive to run (because of the high price of electricity per kWh and because electricity is an inefficient means of generating heat) and so contribute to high energy bills.

In sum, clients are, first and foremost, on a low income, often suffering from illness, and often living alone. Women are over-represented, partly because single mothers – but also couples – with small children are among the typically affected households. In addition, a migration background and difficulties in speaking and understanding the German language are over-represented, compared to the general population. Therefore, it seems that energy deprivation often coincides with other burdens and life crises.

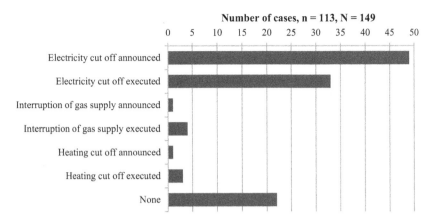

Figure 2.3 Electricity disconnections in the client sample

Notes: Electricity cut-offs can also affect heating because some households use electric heating devices or boilers for warm water provision The small n indicates the number of cases that have this information and the large N is the overall number of cases.

Source: Authors' own database, Verbraucherzentrale RLP 2016

Energy deprivation and how it relates to social structures

In the following, we investigate the verbal descriptions of the cases and identify patterns of how problematic situations have evolved. We distinguish between 'internal' disprivileging characteristics of the households, such as income, household composition, or age that interact with 'external conditions' such as energy efficiency of housing and the wider circumstances of the household. From an intersectional perspective, the household characteristics are 'axes of inequality', which open an entry point for discrimination and energy deprivation at their intersections. Together with external factors or conditions, these lead to the emergence of energy deprivation. Thus, prices and energy-inefficient housing and appliances are, here, building a context that unfolds an impact in interrelation with the (intersecting) characteristics of households.

Single characteristics leading to unexpected payment difficulties

In some cases, households experience problems when external conditions suddenly emerge that demand more coping capacities than currently existing ones. These often lie beyond the triad of low incomes, inefficiency, and rising costs. They include technical problems, lack of knowledge, lack of awareness, conflicts in one's private life, and conflicts with institutions or with the landlord; inefficient appliances are mentioned in only a few cases.[6] Clients show just one disprivileging characteristic, usually a low income, but a minority in this group might not even have low incomes. In all of these cases, the clients were of German nationality.

For example, a family of six with a decent monthly household income of 5,000 euro experienced the announcement of a heat disconnection. The consultation revealed that their landlord kept energy payments from the tenants instead of paying the bills to the energy provider. The consultant managed to set up a special agreement with the energy provider, allowing the family to pay directly for heating to the provider without being charged for the debts on the landlord's account. A further example is a family of four with two children and an average income of 3,000 euro, who received a disconnection announcement because the energy provider under-charged over several years and the family was then suddenly presented a 1,500 euro electricity bill to make up for the underpayments. These two issues, fraud with unfulfilled payments, either by the landlord or a partner, and mistakes or technical problems with the billing, occur repeatedly throughout the cases. In one case, a household had very low costs for 10 years, due to a defective energy meter, before a new meter was installed routinely, and suddenly, their high energy use caused enormous energy debts. Only support in negotiations can then lower such bills.

What we see here is that a problematic situation concerning access to energy services can arise suddenly and unexpectedly, with the conditions leading to this situation often located outside the household. Even though households with higher incomes are also affected, low-income households are more vulnerable. However, all of these cases are relatively non-severe, and solutions were found easily.

More severe problems occurring at simple intersections

We call a situation in which energy deprivation is caused by external conditions coinciding with at least two disprivileging social characteristics of the household (such as a low-income alongside an illness, disability, or a migration background) a simple intersection. For example, a 51-year-old woman, German, who was ill and on low income (her main income source was welfare) sought support because of a high energy payment of 140 euros she could not afford to pay all at once. Due to the combination of her illness (which creating additional expenses in her life) and her low income, she had only partly paid her electricity bills during the last year. The problem was solved by reducing the monthly rates based on a reconsideration of her actual energy consumption, alongside an agreement on paying off existing debts by instalment. In this case, illness and additional costs intersected with low incomes to cause an inability to pay the bills.

Simple intersections often become problematic when coupled with a change in circumstances, such as a divorce or moving house, and the respective difficulties in adapting to a new situation, setting up routines, and establishing the correct payment procedures with energy suppliers. In such dynamic moments, misunderstandings, mistakes, and technical errors in the billing occur – as described above in the section on 'single characteristics'. But for the households in this category, the overlap of two disprivileging characteristics, such as low incomes and illness or low income and small children in the household, limit and constrain their coping capacities in a more severe way. After a breakup in partnerships, women (and in our sample only women) came to seek help because they were left with unexpected cost burdens. Usually, the ex-partner caused high energy (and other) debts and then left the common flat, leaving the debts behind. For example, a German woman of 57, who was recently separated from her partner, received the energy cut-off announcement rather unexpectedly. It had been her male partner's responsibility within the household to manage the energy bills, she maintained, but after the separation, it emerged that he had often not paid these bills and had hidden the energy provider's reminders. Due to a small income, she was unable to pay these debts. In this situation, the male partner executed power and control, whilst the woman did not engage with or understand the matter of energy bills. Coupled with her low income, the situation became problematic.

Simple intersections tend to result in announced energy cut-offs, and solutions are often found by making the inability to pay clear and negotiating with the welfare institutions and energy providers. The described situations caused by simple intersections are usually not very severe; cuts are normally just announced rather than executed. Problems are short term rather than persistent.

Situations become more severe if a psychological deprivation or a lack of capacity to manage costs and contact with institutions is one of the intersecting disprivileging characteristics. For example, a woman in her 40s seemed to have (had) a partner with a shopping addiction, or she herself was addicted. Due to constant payment difficulties, she neglected her energy bills and ended up with increasing debts; a cut-off was announced, and penalties were executed. She was in a legal conflict with the Job Centre, but the energy provider agreed to payment by instalment.

Some such clients seemed to live for years in conflict with the rules of energy provision, did not comply with contracts, spent money beyond their resources, and, sooner or later, a gas or electricity cut-off was announced or executed. A young single mother with a 2-year-old child sought help because an electricity cut-off was executed. Warm water in her flat was provided through an electric boiler (typically inefficient and expensive to run), and she had high energy-consuming habits, such as taking a warm bath every day, without being aware of the related costs. The Job Centre and housing agency both refused to cover these costs. After intervention by the consumer protection agency, the energy provider rescinded the cut-off as a young child was involved. Such households lack the capacity to reduce consumption and expenditures, as well as to manage their relationships to institutions (unless one acknowledges the non-compliant behaviour as a coping strategy). The documentation of these cases does not allow for an interpretation of the causes of such circumstances; a much deeper investigation with, perhaps, biographical interviews would be needed to understand such cases.

In sum, households with two intersecting disprivileging characteristics face more severe problems with energy deprivation. Low incomes are usually one of these characteristics. The problems are most difficult to solve when a household exhibits a characteristic, such as a psychological illness, that negatively affects their coping capacities and ability to take informed action. In terms of gender, women who live in a household that follows more traditional role models in terms of handling financial issues, and so do not have control over the energy costs and spending, can be potentially vulnerable when a relationship ends.

Multiple intersections and the experience of severe energy deprivation

Many of the most severe cases occurred when households faced multiple disprivileging characteristics that intersected and combined with external conditions such as high energy prices or inefficient appliances. At these multiple intersections, the deepest and most severe energy deprivation occurs. A low income is usually a basic ingredient, but this overlaps with several other characteristics that deepen the state of deprivation, such as illness, the presence of small children in the household, a migration background, and language barriers.

Typical representatives of multiple intersections are single mothers. For them, several problems coincide. Low financial difficulties and/or welfare dependency can be long-term companions, and relationships with institutions are often burdened with other stress so that negotiations become difficult. When they contact the consumer protection agency, the clients often seek to reverse an announced cut-off or to reactivate energy provision. This is particularly important as a youth welfare office might remove children from a mother's care in the case of an energy cut-off, in order to protect them from physical harm. Clearly, gender is an important characteristic in such situations because gender norms imply that children stay with their mothers after a breakup in a partnership. There was no single father in our sample, and some women were severely overburdened by the whole situation. In one of the cases, the mother received medical support to combat depression – poor health thus intersected with other disprivileging characteristics such as gender, status as a single parent, and low income. Her energy debts amounted to 250 euro, a seemingly small sum, but one that already threatened her with not being able to continue living together with her children. Such households tend to avoid contact with institutions so as to not draw the attention of the youth welfare office.

In our sample, a migration background was also one of the intersecting characteristics that turned a difficult situation into a state of energy deprivation. Here, language barriers are a central problem that leads to conflicts and debts, as well as to announced or executed energy cut-offs. For example, in the case of a single mother from Somalia, gender intersected with household composition, low income, and her status as a migrant. Due to the presence of a small child plus a low energy efficiency of the home, energy costs were rather high. A relatively significant debt in electricity bills (2,220 euro) had evolved and could not, realistically, be paid from her low income. The energy provider had proposed a payment plan that she had agreed to, but language difficulties meant she had not understood the proposal. In the counselling, it became clear that the monthly rates in this plan were very unrealistic for her. Unfamiliar with the German welfare system, she did not even know that the Job Centre covers heating costs. Following support in contacting institutions, the debt was reduced to 800 euro, and a more realistic payment plan was developed. The client, apparently very grateful for the support, dropped by at the consumer protection agency's office occasionally just to 'say hello' even after the counselling had finished.

In some of the cases, material factors of the home and energy prices are also at work. Here, disprivileging characteristics intersect, and the deprivation is further caused by 'external triggers' such as low efficiency of housing and appliances and/ or rising prices. For example, a physically disabled woman, who was ill and living on a low income of 360 euro, also lived in difficult housing conditions. She had no central heating infrastructure and instead relied on portable electric heaters that she only switched on in winter for 1 hour a day. Her electricity was cut off; a reconnection would have cost 1,200 euro, according to the energy provider. After interventions, the Job Centre agreed to cover some of the debts but refused to cover heating costs above 0.99 euro per m², which is low for a situation when electricity is used for heating and warming water. Because the client sometimes worked on a temporary and short-term basis (for example, in ecological projects), the Job Centre disagreed with her over parts of her welfare payments. In addition, the client reported problems related to criminality in the neighbourhood, including suspected theft of mail and electricity.

In another case, a family with two children, one below 3 years of age, lived in a relatively spacious flat that was in a bad physical condition. They struggled with mould in both the parents' and the children's bedrooms. The heating was based on electricity, their energy consumption was already low, and the monthly income was approximately 2,000 euro. Moving to a different house or flat would have been a good solution, but unfortunately the family could not find a better place due to housing market restrictions. Here, the inability to move house, which is more closely related to the family's weak position on the housing market, appears as an obstacle to overcoming energy deprivation.

In sum, what these cases show is that a severe state of energy deprivation can occur at the intersection of disprivileging characteristics plus poor material conditions of the home. It can, however, occur even when the home can be heated efficiently, the flat is rather small, and the house has seen energy refurbishments. Intersections between a low income, having small children, and lacking knowledge of German and/or of the German welfare and energy system become relevant, here. Given that energy prices have, in general, been rising over several years for German households, the triad of causes made prominent in the literature (low incomes, high prices, and low efficiency) is basically present but does not, in itself, sufficiently explain the situation.

Limits of the data and open questions

The secondary analyses of data gathered in counselling projects are, of course, limited in what they reveal, so that many questions remain open. Much information is not given systematically and thus does not allow for an in-depth and systematic intersectionality-based interpretation. Not all clients talk equally openly about the problems they face; their estimation of their own situation differs.

What is more, five different counsellors with differing foci and professional experience performed the documentation. Especially for clients who came to the agency just once, the documents are incomplete, thus decreasing the quality of the data. There are many hints in the reports on conflicts, but they do not reveal the actual causes of these conflicts. Some characteristics of the households might have been important, but they were not documented. The same holds for current or former housing situations. Coping capacities are not reported systematically; it is often not known how households fell into income poverty, and details about the quality of housing, let alone housing type, are often not available. Conflicts with institutions are also reported, but few hints are given about their causes. The most severe information gap is the lack of details reported about the quality of contacts with institutions. However, despite these limitations, the data can still provide some powerful initial insights into the causes of energy poverty and illustrate the potential value of an intersectionality approach.

Energy deprivation reinterpreted

Energy deprivation rooted in interdependencies

The added value of the intersectionality approach for energy deprivation research lies in a more complex and nuanced, but nevertheless clear, understanding of how a situation of energy poverty emerged and why some households are more prone to a spiral of deep deprivation than others. What we can see in the data is how energy deprivation becomes more severe as an increasing number of disprivileging characteristics of households intersect. Some characteristics lead more clearly to deprivation than others. Low incomes act as a seedbed of energy deprivation. The stories of one-person households or households with single parents suggest that coping with energy poverty alone is more difficult than coping as a couple, partly because costs can be shared but also because other mutual support mechanisms are at play. To date, intersectionality theory has not engaged with inequalities and deprivations faced by households and has instead focused mostly on individuals. Within households, interactions of different member's characteristics seem even more complex than for individuals. Intersections here affect also coping capacities.

Problems become most severe, however, when illness enters the picture, whereby psychological illness seems to be even worse than physical illness; this supports the quantitative findings of Reibling and Jutz (2016). Another characteristic that deeply affects the state of deprivation is a migration background, often in combination with a lack of language skills. These two factors strictly limit coping capacities, so that an already difficult situation becomes a nearly unsolvable problem.

Energy deprivation and discriminatory systems

Characteristics of households are, however, not a problem per se; they become problematic as discriminatory systems turn them into problems, or, in Crenshaw's wording, into background inequalities. Such a view on discriminating structures and power relationships in society is still underdeveloped in energy poverty research. Vulnerable households are depicted as actors trapped in 'unfortunate' or 'unlucky' circumstances, rather than in discriminatory systems of society. The lack of adequate energy efficiency in homes is a relatively static factor, whilst the discriminatory mechanisms of the housing markets, which tend to segregate low-income households in low-quality housing, remain out of sight. Figure 2.4 thus adds more analytic layers to the formation of energy poverty and depicts housing as a field of discrimination creating inequalities.

Restrictions and discrimination in housing markets are, again, not just a matter of income. Migrant households or households with (many) children and households with existing, documented debts face discrimination on the free market. The rules of access to social housing in Germany hinder welfare-dependent households in gaining access to refurbished segments with high levels of energy efficiency because of price regulations (see Großmann et al. 2014). Thus, it is not the low energy-efficiency housing itself that is a cause of energy deprivation; rather, it becomes a problem through discriminatory housing markets.

Our data show that discrimination by institutions (energy providers, Job Centres, etc.) is likely to play a role in announcing or executing energy cut-offs, as

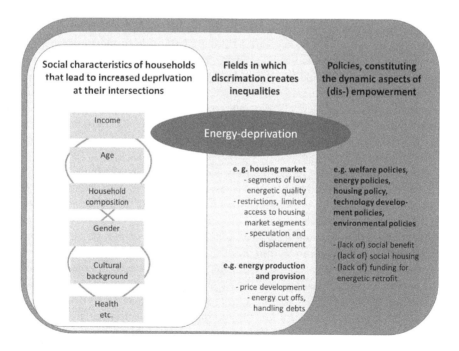

Figure 2.4 Energy deprivation in an intersectional perspective

Source: Authors' own model, reworked from Großmann 2017

do similar analyses by other consumer protection agencies (Verbraucherzentrale NRW 2015). Energy providers and the Job Centres refuse negotiations if they assume intentional misuse of welfare payments. Both Job Centres and energy providers have leeway for negotiations and support. Whether or not a payment by instalment can be negotiated, how high monthly rates are, and whether or not a cut-off is announced or enforced, is to some extent steered by legal rules – for example, protection in cases of hardship when young children are present in a household – but there is much room for interpretation. Furthermore, a migration background is an entry point for discrimination. We know from our own experience that staff in some Job Centres refuse to speak English even if they are able to, because the 'official' language is German, and this is said to be important for legal certainty.

Intersections of characteristics are also important for explaining coping capacities. In order to deal at all with the bureaucratic regimes of billing, to deal with institutions on a level playing field, or to defend oneself against discriminatory practices, cultural and social competencies are essential, alongside language skills. Social networks are crucial for coping with acute cut-offs. Good health is a basic precondition for dealing with difficulties or for generating income, irrespective of other factors.

Impacts of energy policies on multiple deprivations and discriminatory systems

The suggested reconceptualisation of energy deprivation also implies different views on policies, which then create a third analytic layer of energy deprivation (Figure 2.4). As Crenshaw has pointed out, the effects of policies flow along the intersecting axes of inequalities. Thus, energy (poverty) policies necessarily affect different households differently. If research and policy assessments focus solely on affordability and the effects of policies on incomes, their social impact is not evaluated in sufficient complexity. The questions are, instead: which measures reach which households, for whom are funding and support instruments accessible, and – finally but importantly – which unintended side-effects occur?

An example from the German context is the social impact of energy efficiency retrofitting. Funding and support schemes address owners, but the majority of low-income households are tenants. Tenants depend on the decisions of their landlords, who are often large private or municipal housing companies. This can mean that retrofit does not occur because owners do not see a rationale for such investments or efforts. Retrofitting of social housing often prioritises simplification of administrative processes, e.g. outsourcing of services around heating and the apartment-wide installation of electric flow heaters, both a rather expensive source for warmth and hot water. Tenants are then vulnerable to rising energy prices. In other cases, owners use the funding schemes for speculative investments followed by steep rent increases and evictions of low-income tenants, as blogs and media coverage have documented.[7] Intersecting axes of inequalities also affect the capacities of households to fight and resist such disinvestments, evictions, or energy cut-offs. A decent education and cultural capital is necessary to access information, to fight illegal measures of landlords, or to search for professional help and advice.

To sum up, legal regulations and policies do not reach households equally but along intersecting, disprivileging characteristics, acting as background inequalities and defining which households can profit from measures – and which cannot.

Conclusions

In this chapter, we have argued that the inability to pay for energy costs results from a complex state of deprivation, in which a variety of disprivileging characteristics of a household intersect and further interact with external conditions. Attempts to support these households need to address the multiplicity of their problematic situation. These German specifics can be an inspiration for finding new ways of understanding and addressing energy deprivation and for drawing from wider inequality debates and theories.

The intersectionality approach proves to be rich in inspiration. It helps to reason better about the multiplicity of problems households face and how they are related to their characteristics such as income, age, health, nationality and ethnicity, language skills, or education. It also draws attention to wider societal structures and the power relationships. The presented material points to at least two discriminatory systems: the housing market and bureaucratic procedures of energy providers and welfare institutions. Given the limits of secondary analyses of reports on energy counselling, more research would be needed to further explore the mechanisms of discrimination and also the coping capacities of households from an intersectional perspective. The assessment of policies would also provide new insights.

Notes

1 For axes of inequalities, various wording is used in intersectionality literature, such as 'dimensions of inequalities', or 'social characteristics' or 'categories' when talking about an individual. Together these characteristics form the identity of a person. Crenshaw (1991) speaks of social categories or/and of axes of subordination (race, class, and gender). The subordination occurs from discrimination such as in racism, patriarchy, and class oppression.
2 In intersectionality approaches, axes of inequality relate to those characteristics of persons that are important in constituting their identity in multiple facets of society – age, gender, income, and so on.
3 These estimates are based on representative surveys conducted by Verbraucherzentrale NRW and RLP (2012) among energy providers.
4 Limitations of this data are discussed at the end of the empirical section of this chapter.
5 Comprises single, widowed, and divorced residents.
6 This aspect is monitored as follows: energy consumption is monitored in all cases but only if values indicate an efficiency problem; if the client emphasises technical issues, a counsellor would engage with the technical side of consumption.
7 Examples are: for Stuttgart, www.s-oe-s.de/leitartikel/verkauf-der-lbbw-wohnungen-von-schwarz-rot-gruen-an-heuschrecken-verfuettert/ (Zugriff vom 02.10.2014); for

Berlin, www.berliner-zeitung.de/berlin/streit-um-sanierungskosten-auch-ohne-luxus-un bezahlbar,10809148,24165934.html, RBB Klartext vom 15.04.2015 (http://pankow ermieterprotest.jimdo.com/); RBB Abendschau vom 14.06.2014 (www.youtube.com/ watch?v=1hfY-gnR3lw); allgemein www.zeit.de/news/2014-03/22/wohnen-mieterbund vermieter-nutzen-sanierung-immer-oefter-als-waffe-22100406, and WDR vom 28.9. 2015 (www1.wdr.de/themen/verbraucher/themen/wohnen/mieterhoehung-nach-mod-ernisierung-104.html).

References

Aigeltinger, G., Heindl, P., Liessem, V., Römer, D., Schwengers, C. and Vogt, C. (2015). Zum Stromkonsum von Haushalten in Grundsicherung: Eine empirische Analyse für Deutschland. *ZEW Discussion Papers*, 15–75.

Anderson, W., White, V. and Finney, A. (2012). Coping with low incomes and cold homes. *Energy Policy*, 49, 40–52.

Boardman, B. (1991). *Fuel poverty: From cold homes to affordable warmth*. London and New York: Belhaven Press.

Bouzarovski, S. (2014). Energy poverty in the European Union: Landscapes of vulnerability. *Wiley Interdisciplinary Reviews: Energy and Environment*, 3(3), 276–289.

Bouzarovski, S. and Petrova, S. (2015). A global perspective on domestic energy deprivation: Overcoming the energy poverty – fuel poverty binary. *Energy Research & Social Science*, 10, 31–40.

Braubach, M. and Fairburn, J. (2010). Social inequities in environmental risks associated with housing and residential location – a review of evidence. *The European Journal of Public Health*, 20(1), 36–42.

Brunner, K-M., Christanell, A. and Mandl, S. (2016). Energiearmut in Österreich: Erfahrungen, Umgangsweisen und Folgen. In Großmann, K., Schaffrin, A. and Smigiel, C. (eds.) *Energie und soziale Ungleichheit: Zur gesellschaftlichen Dimension der Energiewende in Deutschland und Europa*. Wiesbaden: Springer VS S, pp. 131–155.

Brunner, K-M., Spitzer, M. and Christanell, A. (2011). *NELA. Nachhaltiger Energieverbrauch und Lebens-stile in armen und armutsgefährdeten Haushalten* (final report). Wien: Österreichisches Institut für Nachhaltige Entwicklung.

Bundesnetzagentur für Elektrizität, Gas, Telekommunikation, Post und Eisenbahnen. (2017). *Monitoringbericht 2016*. Bonn. Available at: www.bundesnetzagentur.de/SharedDocs/Downloads/DE/Sachgebiete/Energie/Unternehmen_Institutionen/DatenaustauschUndMonitoring/Monitoring/Monitoringbericht2016.pdf?__blob=publicationFile&v=2.

Chard, R. and Walker, G. (2016). Living with fuel poverty in older age: Coping strategies and their problematic implications. *Energy Research & Social Science*, 18, 62–70.

Cischinsky, H., Kirchner, J. and von Malottki, C. (2016). Das deutsche transfersystem in Zeiten von Klimaschutz und Energiewende. In Großmann, K., Schaffrin, A. and Smigiel, C. (eds.) *Energie und soziale Ungleichheit: Zur gesellschaftlichen Dimension der Energiewende in Deutschland und Europa*. Wiesbaden: Springer VS S, pp. 349–376.

Cremer, G. (2013). Energiearmut – Teilhabe ermöglichen: Eckpunkte und Position des DCV zur Bekämpfung von Energiearmut. *neue caritas spezial. Politik-Praxis-Forschung*, 2/2013, 2–5. Deutscher Caritasverband.

Crenshaw, K. (1991). Mapping the margins: Intersectionality, identity politics, and violence against women of color. *Stanford Law Review*, 43(6), 1241–1299.

Day, R., Walker, G. and Simcock, N. (2016). Conceptualising energy use and energy poverty using a capabilities framework. *Energy Policy*, 93, 255–264.

Dubois, U. and Meier, H. (2016). Energy affordability and energy inequality in Europe: Implications for policymaking. *Energy Research & Social Science*, 18, 21–35.

e-fect/ VZ RLP. (2014). *Zwischenbericht über die formative Evaluation des Pilotprojektes Energiearmut in Rheinland-Pfalz – systemische Energiekostenberatung*, Unpublished manuscript.

George, M., Graham, C. and Lennard, L. (2011). *Too many hurdles: Information and advice barriers in the energy market*. Leicester: Centre for Consumers and Essential Services.

Großmann, K. (2017). Energiearmut als multiple Deprivation vor dem Hintergrund diskriminierender Systeme. In Großmann, K., Schaffrin, A. and Smigiel, C. (eds.) *Energie und soziale Ungleichheit: Zur gesellschaftlichen Dimension der Energiewende in Deutschland und Europa*. Wiesbaden: Springer Fachmedien Wiesbaden, pp. 55–78.

Großmann, K., Buchholz, J., Buchmann, C., Hedke, C., Hoehnke, C. and Schwarz, N. (2014). Energy costs, residential mobility, and segregation in a shrinking city. *Open House International*, 39, 14–24.

Haas, T. (2016). Energiearmut als neues Konfliktfeld in der Stromwende. In Großmann K., Schaffrin, A. and Smigiel, C. (eds.) *Energie und soziale Ungleichheit: Zur gesellschaftlichen Dimension der Energiewende in Deutschland und Europa*. Wiesbaden: Springer VS S, pp. 377–402.

Heindl, P., Schüßler, R. and Löschel, A. (2014). Ist die Energiewende sozial gerecht? *Wirtschaftsdienst*, 94(7), 508–514.

Kahlheber, A. (2016). Spielräume am Limit: Energiearmut in der systemisch-lösungs orientierten Beratungspraxis der Verbraucherzentrale Rheinland-Pfalz – Ursachenkonstellationen und Beratungsansätze. In Großmann, K., Schaffrin, A. and Smigiel, C. (eds.) *Energie und soziale Ungleichheit: Zur gesellschaftlichen Dimension der Energiewende in Deutschland und Europa*. Wiesbaden: Springer VS S, pp. 209–238.

Kopatz, M. (2013). *Energiewende. Aber fair! Wie sich die Energiezukunft sozial tragfähig gestalten lässt*. München: Oekom-Verl.

Kopatz, M., Spitzer, M. and Christanell, A. (2010). *Energiearmut: Stand der Forschung, nationale Programme und regionale Modellprojekte in Deutschland, Österreich und Großbritannien, Wuppertal Wuppertal Inst. Umwelt, Energie: für Klima*.

Lawson, R., Williams, J. and Wooliscroft, B. (2015). Contrasting approaches to fuel poverty in New Zealand. *Energy Policy*, 81, 38–42.

Lutz, H. (2014). Intersectionality´s (brilliant) career – how to understand the attraction of the concept? Goethe-Universität Frankfurt, *Working Paper Series 'Gender, Diversity and Migration'*. Available at: www.fb03.uni-frankfurt.de/51634119/Lutz_WP.pdf.

Marmot Review Team. (2011). *The health impacts of cold homes and fuel poverty*. London: Department of Epidemiology & Public Health University College London.

McCall, L. (2005). The complexity of intersectionality. *Signs: Journal of Women in Culture & Society*, 30(3), 1771–1800.

Moore, R. (2012). Definitions of fuel poverty: Implications for policy. *Energy Policy*, 49, 19–26.

Pietsch, L., Benz, I. and Schweizer-Ries, P. (2010). Strategien zur Senkung von Energiekosten in einkommensschwachen Haushalten. *Informationen zur Raumentwicklung*, 12, 911–918.

Pye, S. and Dobbins, A. (2015). *Energy poverty and vulnerable consumers in the energy sector across the EU: Analysis of policies and measures*. Policy Report. Available at: https://ec.europa.eu/energy/sites/ener/files/documents/INSIGHT_E_Energy%20Poverty%20-%20Main%20Report_FINAL.pdf [Accessed 30 December 2015].

Reibling, N. and Jutz, R. (2016). Energiearmut und Gesundheit. In Großmann, K., Schaffrin, A. and Smigiel, C. (eds.) *Energie und soziale Ungleichheit: Zur gesellschaftlichen Dimension der Energiewende in Deutschland und Europa*. Wiesbaden: Springer VS S, pp. 157–184.

Rudge, J. and Gilchrist, R. (2005). Excess winter morbidity among older people at risk of cold homes: A population-based study in a London borough. *Journal of Public Health*, 27(4), 353–358.

Sovacool, B. K. (2012). The political economy of energy poverty: A review of key challenges. *Energy for Sustainable Development*, 16(3), 272–282.

Tews, K. (2013). *Energiearmut definieren, identifizieren und bekämpfen – Eine Herausforderung der sozialverträglichen Gestaltung der Energiewende: Vorschlag für eine Problemdefinition und Diskussion des Maßnahmenportfolios*, FFU-Report.

Thomson, H. and Snell, C. (2013). Quantifying the prevalence of fuel poverty across the European Union. *Special Section: Transition Pathways to a Low Carbon Economy*, 52, 563–572.

Verbraucherzentrale NRW. (2015). *Gemeinsame Wege aus der Energiearmut: Erfahrungen und Erfolge aus Nordrhein-Westfalen*. Available at: www.vz-nrw.de/mediabig/237456A.pdf.

Verbraucherzentralen NRW und RLP. (2012). *Hochrechnung der bundesweiten Versorgungsunterbrechungen auf Grundlage einer repräsentativen Befragung der Grundversorger*, Unpublished manuscript.

Walker, G. and Day, R. (2012). Fuel poverty as injustice: Integrating distribution, recognition and procedure in the struggle for affordable warmth. *Energy Policy*, 49, 69–75.

Winker, G. and Degele, N. (2011). Intersectionality as multi-level analysis: Dealing with social inequality. *European Journal of Women's Studies*, 18(1), 51–66.

Wolff, A., Schubert, J. and Gill, B. (2016). Risiko energetische Sanierung? Untersuchungen zur Differenz von Energiebedarf und – verbrauch sowie deren Auswirkungen auf einkommensschwache Haushalte. In Großmann, K., Schaffrin, A. and Smigiel, C. (eds.) *Energie und soziale Ungleichheit: Zur gesellschaftlichen Dimension der Energiewende in Deutschland und Europa*. Wiesbaden: Springer VS S, pp. 611–634.

3 Understanding energy poverty through the energy cultures framework

Fatima McKague, Rob Lawson, Michelle Scott, and Ben Wooliscroft

Introduction

Energy poverty occurs in many parts of the world (DECC 2015; AGECC 2010). Energy poverty, or the inability to access or afford energy, impacts on the capability of households to attain the level of energy services necessary to participate in society (Day et al. 2016; Bouzarovski and Petrova 2015; Sovacool et al. 2012; Sovacool 2014). One in five people lacks access to modern electricity, and 3 billion people rely on biomass and other 'traditional' fuels for cooking and heating (United Nations 2016). Over 10% of households in the United Kingdom, 14% in Europe and 25% in New Zealand cannot afford to keep their houses adequately warm in winter (DECC 2015; Howden-Chapman et al. 2012; Intelligent Energy Europe 2009).

Energy poverty can trigger a number of health and social effects. For example, exposure to indoor air pollution leads to respiratory infections, asthma and other diseases (WHO 2007; Bruce et al. 2000), whilst the inability to afford adequate warmth in winter has been associated with adverse effects on physical health and mental well-being and with excess winter mortality (Liddell 2010). Recent research has shown the wider effects of energy poverty, including social impacts and effects on households' quality of life (McKague et al. 2016).

Energy poverty is exacerbated by widening income and wealth inequality, making it harder for those with low incomes to have access to clean, affordable energy (Wilkinson et al. 2007). These households may pay a significant percentage of their income on energy, yet still live in cold, damp homes as a result of energy-inefficient appliances or lack of insulation (Goldthau and Sovacool 2012; Lloyd 2006; Geller 2003). Reports from New Zealand show that the average percentage of household income spent on energy in the home has increased across all income groups in New Zealand between 1988 and 2013; however, the biggest increase was for the lowest income group, with rates rising from 6% in 2007 to 13% in 2013. In contrast, the highest income group spent just 3% of household income on energy in the home in 2013, an increase from 1.6% in 2007 (New Zealand Government, 2013). While energy poverty is closely related to wider poverty and inequality, it is a distinct phenomenon that requires urgent attention (Hills 2012; Stephenson et al. 2015; Lawson et al. 2015).

Understanding the drivers and underlying causes of energy poverty is impor-tant for designing measures to eradicate it. Yet, many existing ways of conceptu-alising such causes do not capture their full complexity. (Walker 2014; Petrova et al. 2013; Lawson et al. 2015; Jansen and Seebregts 2010; Barton et al. 2013). The dominant literature on energy poverty has focused on the physical structure of dwellings and appliances, the economics of household expenses on energy and the epidemiological aspects of cold housing on health (Hills 2012; Clinch and Healy 2001; Harrington et al. 2005). While economic and technical approaches are useful, they do not adequately depict the wide-ranging variables implicated in the emergence of the condition in space and time (Harrington et al. 2005; Lid-dell,2012; Stern 2014; Pachauri and Spreng 2004). In particular, we would argue that the social, cultural and behavioural underpinnings of energy poverty, and how these interact with material and technical dimensions, could provide new insights into how energy vulnerability is formed and changes over time.

The aim of this chapter is to demonstrate the value of the energy cultures framework (Lawson et al. 2016; Hopkins and McCarthy 2016; Hoica 2012; Bell et al. 2013; Sweeney et al. 2013; Stephenson et al. 2010) in offering a nuanced and holistic framework through which to understand the drivers of energy pov-erty. The framework brings together multiple elements to conceptualise how the technical, behavioural and social components interact to structure energy consumption. The framework also captures the barriers and support systems in place that must be identified for effective policy targeting. Such a comprehensive understanding of energy poor households will provide insights that aid in design-ing targeted policy measures to alleviate energy poverty.

Understanding the drivers of energy poverty

One of the challenges of adequately addressing energy poverty is that it has mul-tiple causes which are not easily captured in one indicator (Stephenson et al. 2010; Wilson and Dowlatabadi 2007; Verhallen and Van Raaij 1981; Black et al. 1985; Nussbaumer et al. 2012). This is evident in the number of theories attrib-uted to energy poverty, yet they are limited in capturing the severity of the con-dition. The classic theory from Boardman implies a 'triad' of low incomes, high energy prices and poor household energy efficiency as causes of energy poverty (Boardman 1991). Energy poverty could also be aggravated by the absence of sav-ings and living in rental accommodation, which limits the ability of households to improve their homes (Boardman 2010). Recent years have seen more complex and nuanced aspects begin to emerge. Energy poverty has been linked to having high energy needs caused by disability or health condition which requires addi-tional energy (Snell et al. 2014). Bouzarovski and Petrova (2015) also highlight the degree of built environment flexibility and the extent to which households are able to access alternative energy carriers as additional factors that can influ-ence vulnerability to energy poverty. Vulnerability theory stresses that different households will have different degrees of vulnerability to energy poverty, depend-ing on their exposure and sensitivity to the condition and their capacity to adapt

(Middlemiss and Gillard 2015). Research has found that there are growing challenges related to the reluctance of some households, often the most vulnerable, to apply for assistance through subsidised programmes to help with burdens of energy poverty (Boardman 2010). Issues of stigma, concerns about the disruptions associated with heating and insulation being installed and distrust of authorities are key factors in this challenge (Lawson and Williams 2012; Boardman 2010). Despite these advances, in many policy discourses the dominant understanding of the causes of energy poverty remains limited to the triad of incomes, efficiency and energy prices.

It is difficult to target interventions for energy poor households by focusing on one aspect of the problem (Heffner and Campbell 2011). An example is the Winter Fuel Payment Programme in the UK, where the solutions of energy poverty are based on one of the causes – low income. A Winter Fuel Payment was given to all pensioner households regardless of circumstances, and it has been estimated that as a result about three-quarters of these fuel assistance payments went to households that were not energy poor (Boardman 2012). While blanket interventions such as these are often cheaper to administer than a targeted approach, the downside is that some affected households miss out. Moreover, as Robić et al. argue in Chapter 12 of this book, focusing only on income support can be a short-term measure that does little to improve the living conditions of households. Another example is from New Zealand, where interventions were framed solely around technical causes of energy poverty. An evaluation of a national-wide government insulation project in New Zealand showed that 77% of residents in New Zealand who received upgraded heating systems were not using them efficiently, showing the importance of interventions also considering factors such as the behaviour and practices of householders (Isaacs et al. 2010).

These various challenges point to the need for a comprehensive understanding of energy poverty, one that moves beyond the narrow 'triad' of income, housing and energy appliances. It is here that we argue the energy cultures framework, which conceptualises energy poverty through the interplay between technical factors, social norms and household practices, can be of value.

Energy cultures framework

Leading researchers in the energy field have called for a multidimensional view that encompasses the larger systems that influences energy consumption (Osbaldeston 1984; Stern 1986; Hards 2013; Sovacool 2014; Lutzenhiser 1993; Patterson 1996; Stephenson et al. 2010). A combination of economic, built environment and social and behavioural factors should be amalgamated, it is argued, to adequately understand the dynamics of household consumption (Pachauri and Spreng 2011; Shove 2003; Stern 1984).

The energy cultures framework provides an integrative approach that bridges the gap between theories of energy consumption focused on the individual and those centred on structural factors (Stephenson et al. 2015), supporting existing theories of energy poverty while strengthening what they each offer. The term 'culture' here refers to a cluster of similar 'knowledge, beliefs, behaviour and material objects' which affect energy consumption, both at an individual and household level (Stephenson et al. 2010, 6123). The framework offers a holistic outlook that factors in the broad range of variables that influence energy poverty – the material conditions of the house, values, beliefs and knowledge of consumers, and the wider social and cultural systems that impact on energy decisions – and importantly the way these variables *interact* (Stephenson et al. 2010). Figure 3.1 illustrates the energy cultures framework.

At the core of the framework are three key components that impact on energy consumption, or the level of energy services that a household is able to attain – norms, practices and material culture (see Figure 3.1). Norms are householder's expectations and knowledge regarding their energy use, practices are what they actually do in terms of energy usage, and material culture is their surrounding house and appliances that impact on how much energy is consumed. The framework's underlying principle is that these different components interact with and influence one another. A change in one of these elements impacts on another, while the interactions between these elements reinforces certain energy consumption patterns, resulting in a distinct 'energy culture'. To understand energy poverty through the energy cultures lens, energy consumption is seen as an interaction between norms, practices and material cultures, as well as the external influences that form the context in which these interactions occur. A household's ability to change their energy culture is affected by the particular 'barriers' and 'support' available to occupants, both internally within the household and

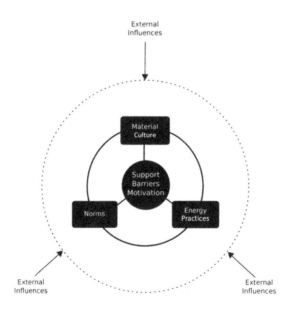

Figure 3.1 The energy cultures framework

Source: Adapted from Stephenson et al. (2016)

from external factors outside of it (Sweeney et al. 2013). The different elements of the framework are presented in more detail below.

Norms

Norms are shared believes about how individuals behave in a given context (Giddens 1991). In the energy cultures framework, norms are a household's expectations and aspirations in relation to energy consumption in a given context, with 'expectations' their beliefs and assessments about their current practices and material culture and 'aspirations' the practices and material culture that they consider desirable but have not yet achieved (Stephenson et al. 2015). A household's expectations and aspirations shape how they consume energy and how they perceive the situation that they live in and so are useful in understanding energy poverty. For example, norms shape how warm people expect their living space to be, their perceptions of different methods of keeping warm and the value that they place on having energy-efficient technologies – which can all affect how an energy poor household experiences their situation and whether they feel it is worthwhile attempting to make changes.

Material cultures

Material culture is a household's physical assets, includes the surrounding infrastructures, appliances and technologies that play a role in how energy is used. Material culture acts as a significant driver of energy poverty. A low level of insulation in a house and energy-inefficient appliances increase energy consumption and make it harder to warm the house or retain the warmth inside. Material culture should be one of the first components to tackle in measures to address energy poverty as it has one of the most direct impacts on the level of thermal comfort in the house. The energy cultures framework also recognises the interaction between material culture and norms – householders have expectations and aspirations regarding the material of their home, and these play a role in how they interact with their physical environment culture and how willing they are to make alterations to their home.

Practices

Practices refer to the actions of households – both their routinised, everyday activities and their relatively infrequent actions (Stephenson et al. 2015). Householder practices are strongly influenced by their norms, as these shape how people react to situations and what they consider appropriate activities. For example, the practice of putting the lid on pots when cooking to decrease moisture in the house, or closing the curtains to retain heat, may come from norms about preventing mould growth and retaining heat. Practices are also influenced by a household's material culture. For instance, the availability of an open fire, coupled with a preference for ambient warmth from fires, could see a household adopt very different heating methods compared to a household with only gas central heating.

External influences

External influences are those factors that are largely beyond the immediate agency or scope of control of an actor or household but which shape their norms, practices and material culture. The boundary of what constitutes an 'external' influence can vary between households. For example, whilst a homeowner has certain legal rights over the physical aspects of a house (and thus could decide to make changes to make the house warmer or more efficient), a renter often has limited agency to make such changes (these issues being controlled by a landlord instead), and so much of the infrastructure of the home form part of their external influences. External forces shared by both groups include market mechanisms, energy prices, subsidies, wider social norms, information campaigns and policies or regulations that impact on energy usage. External influence are important because they can lock-in current energy cultures and so act as 'barriers to change' (see below) or they can facilitate new energy cultures. For example, subsidies available for low-income renters towards insulation could motivate landlords to alter the material culture of their rental properties by installing insulation, thus aiding the situation of energy poor households living in such homes. The level of insulation installed in a house may also depend on other external influences, such as government building codes.

Motivation, barriers and support

In addition to the core elements and the external influences of the energy cultures framework, three additional factors are important to consider in relation to energy poverty – motivation, barriers and support available to the households.

Motivation plays an important role in changing habitual patterns; for example, if a grant is available for new insulation that will improve the energy efficiency of the home and lift a household out of energy poverty, a household must still be motivated to take up this offer. Motivation to change consumption habits may be influenced by norms, such as awareness about the health impacts of living in a cold, damp house or the high cost of electricity. At the same time, whilst a household might be motivated to change their energy culture, factors such as material culture (e.g. a difficult to insulate home) or external influences (e.g. a lack of adequate information or funding) might prevent such changes. This stresses the point that energy cultures framework highlights – energy poverty is influenced by not one element, but the interaction of different factors, and so solutions to energy poverty must consider the broader variables.

Barriers are limitations on deviations from current energy cultures. The different elements of an energy culture (material culture, norms, practices and external elements) can all act as barriers. For example, norms such as limited awareness about efficient energy appliances could prevent households adopting energy efficiency. External influences could also act as barriers, for example a lack of subsidies for home retrofits, low wages or inadequate regulation of the private rented sector can prevent households making changes to the material culture of their home.

While barriers are a limiting factor, support systems available to the household could aid them in changing their energy culture. Financial support from family or friends, or providing new information to a household, may help overcome the barriers that prevent a shift in energy culture. For example, an effective awareness campaign about energy poverty might provide households information about government subsidies or low-cost options that can change their material culture. Likewise, a well-informed friend might provide advice needed to change the norms of households.

Energy poverty through the energy cultures lens

This section presents two case studies to illustrate how the energy cultures framework can be applied to better understand the causes of energy poverty. These cases studies are drawn from an energy consumption study conducted in New Zealand, in which the framework was used to guide the research design and analyse the findings. Full details of the methodology of this study can be found in McKague et al. (2016). In both case studies, the names of respondents have been changed in order to protect identity.

Case study 1

Norma is a 39-year-old mother of two who lives in Dunedin, New Zealand. She lives in a rental house in the north side of the city with her partner and two children. During winter she finds it really cold in her house.

> I've lived here for a year and a half. During the winter it's not that great, because the sun's gone by two or three o'clock in the afternoon. . . . When we first shifted in it was so cold . . . you can smell the cold, you can smell the mildew. . . . I had to actually ask to get some ceiling insulation and also seals around the windows which they (landlord) didn't do. . . . I didn't qualify for the government grants. . . . I just went and did it myself . . . because there was a lot of draught . . . it was very cold . . . but that is not enough, I need more insulation to make it weather-tight.

Norma uses portable heaters in her bedroom and living room. She is very aware about retaining heat and about the level of moisture inside her house.

> Heating is very important cos you know you don't want your kids to get sick . . . and you know when we cook and what not lots of steam builds up

and even that produces mould and mildew . . . we move around a lot less in winter . . . we pull out blankets and just hunker down.

Norma is conscious about saving energy but ensures she keeps the house comfortable for her children.

> I try to turn the heater on just before 4 o'clock . . . just before the kids get home so you know it's starting to warm up and I keep it that way . . . I turn the heater off at night before we go to bed. . . . The power bill it's not unmanageable but it's sort of getting up there. . . . You've got to conserve power at the end of the day, unless you want to either have your power disconnected or have a massive power bill at the end of the month which you just can't afford. . . . At the end of the day I think if we don't conserve our power we are going to end up with nothing. . . . Power is becoming too expensive and unaffordable.

Using the energy cultures framework to analyse Norma's energy poverty outlines the circumstances underpin her situation. In Norma's case, the material culture is the main cause of her energy poverty. The position of her house that does not capture adequate passive heat from the sun in winter, the lack of thermal insulation in the walls and loft leading to the heat escaping quickly and the inefficiency of heating systems, all of which means using the heating is expensive. Her material culture is further inhabited by the external influences, such as an inability to access subsidies for insulation and the high electricity prices. The material culture and external influences acts as barriers for Norma to move out of energy poverty.

Norma's practices of moving around less inside the house during winter, putting on extra clothes and putting lids on pots when cooking to reduce moisture all indicate that she is very energy aware. Her practices are driven by the material culture around her and the strong norms and awareness around energy. Norma is energy conscious and is careful about her energy spending. She confines heating to one space to conserve power and prefers extra clothing to stay warm over turning the heating up. When practices and material culture are aligned with norms, it embeds the behaviour, forming habits.

For a change in energy culture to occur, one of the elements must change. In Norma's case, it is clear that the change must originate from the material culture. As Norma is already energy conscious; has aspirations for her home to be warmer and better insulated; and carries out a lot of activities to prevent moisture, contain heat and warm her house, it is the level of insulation in her house and the energy efficiency of her appliances that needs to be changed for her to move out of energy poverty. External factors such as regulations impacting on building standards or subsidies for low-income families towards energy-efficient appliances and insulation, could lift her out of energy poverty. However, while this may be the case for Norma, other situations might demand interventions driven by practices or focused on norms.

Case study 2

Eric is a single father of a 4-year-old son, living in his own property in South Dunedin, New Zealand. Eric has made some changes to the house, including installing insulation.

> The original part of this house is very thin and has no cavity available for insulation. . . . It's weatherboard on the outside. . . . The cold air just rushes up the floor. . . . There's a lot of springs in the area which makes it very cold. . . . I have insulated everything I can, with the assistance of grants. . . . It's a two story house, and I can't put any insulation on [the ceiling] because of the way the house is built. . . . The only way I can do that is to re-roof the house and I can't afford to do that.

Eric relies on a wood burner to keep warm in winter. He spends a lot of time acquiring wood to keep the burner going.

> Winter here is very cold. . . . This house is kept warm by a fire. . . . I don't use heaters. . . . I just go out and cut firewood. . . . Anytime I go anywhere outside of the city I have trailer, I have some saws and I bring the wood. . . . [My wife and I] have recently separated. . . . [My ex-wife] had the fire going all year, that's why we go through so much wood. . . . I'm out chopping firewood all the time so she can keep it warm to her standards.

Eric has expectations in which he accepts living in a cold home, and these expectations then shape how he deals with the cold and his aspirations to change his situation:

> I've always lived in cold flats as a student so I'm used to piling on clothes instead of turning on the heater. When I was flatting many of my flat-mates came from hot climates and they had the heaters up all the time. . . . You don't need to have the house that warm, just put some clothes on for god's sake. . . . My son has gotten used to being in this cold house, [but] my ex-wife and I had arguments about heating . . . it caused a lot of stress in our relationship. . . . Electricity bills and trying to rationalise why I don't want to spend so much on it. . . . Is it really necessary to have a hot shower every day? From a male point of view, no it's not!
>
> In Dunedin, in winter it's very hard for people to stay psychologically well . . . it's a cold, depressing place and the climate is very cold . . . but that's just the way it is . . . it's the situation . . . it's the geography of this place . . . you've just got to adjust your attitude. . . . Ana found it very hard and that's one of the reasons why we separated.

Using the energy cultures framework to help understand Eric's situation unveils his norms – encompassing expectations and aspirations – that drive his practices and act as barriers to change. As Eric grew up in a cold house, cooler indoor climate is the norm for him, and he sees little value in warming up the house, instead preferring to put on extra clothing. A conflict in attitudes to warmth might lead to disagreements amongst household members – as Eric pointed out, the mis-match of energy consumption values and priorities was one of the reasons for his separation from his ex-wife. Eric's norms and values could be acting as a barrier to him making the necessary changes to move out of energy poverty.

In order to tackle Eric's energy poverty, his norms and practices need to be targeted. Deep-set belief systems are hard to change instantly. An intervention based on explaining the health impacts of living in cold houses, how the cooler indoor temperatures may be affecting his son or showing how other households live and keep warm, might help drive change in Eric's energy habits.

An integrated energy poverty framework: implications for policy and research

The energy cultures framework provides a holistic understanding of the causes of energy poverty by bringing together the norms, practices and material cultures of households. A household's energy culture shapes their vulnerability to energy poverty, and the barriers and support systems available to them determine their potential pathways out of the condition. For effective policy development, it is important to have an integrated system of understanding the complex drivers of energy poverty, which the energy cultures framework provides.

The framework also helps identify different categories of energy poor households that require distinct policy interventions. Indicators such as perceived energy needs, conditions of the house or coping mechanisms occupants adopt to deal with energy poverty could be used to efficiently target households. Better understanding of the different norms, behaviours and material settings of households helps in capturing segments of users who may be demographically similar but have very different energy cultures (Bouzarovski et al. 2012; Lawson and Williams 2012). For example, people who spend extended amounts of time in the home, such as elderly people and families with young children, would require extra energy for their day-to-day needs. This group would benefit from direct interventions focused on the material cultures, such as continuing subsidies for heating and insulation. Those who do not use energy as efficiently as they could may benefit from programs to help alter their energy practices, such as customised home energy advice. It would also be useful to link this group up with services in the community which may help them cope with the financial hardship of increased power bills.

Energy poverty is complex and has wide-ranging consequences for family and society. Looking at energy poverty through the energy cultures lens provides a useful analytical structure to understand the complex drivers of energy poverty, how habits are formed and what external influences impact on energy consumption or non-consumption. The framework will enable better informed policy-making and add significant value to expanding energy poverty research. The energy cultures framework is transferable to different contexts and agents as well. For example, future studies could compare the drivers of energy poverty between two contrasting geographical contexts, such as a cooler country and a warmer one, or between households and businesses. A better understanding of the complex energy consumption patterns of the energy poor, and using this understanding to help drive change, will help the transition towards a sustainable and secure energy future for all.

Acknowledgements

This research has been generously supported by a Todd Foundation Scholarship in Energy Research grant and aided by the Centre for Sustainability Energy Cultures Project at the University of Otago, New Zealand.

References

AGECC. (2010). *Energy for sustainable future*. New York: The Secretary-General's Advisory group on Energy and Climate Change.

Barton, B., Blackwell, S., Carrington, G., Ford, R., Lawson, R., Stephenson, S., Thorsnes, P. and Williams, J. (2013). *Energy cultures: Implications for policymakers*. Technical report, Centre for Sustainability. Dunedin, New Zealand: University of Otago.

Bell, M., Carrington, G., Lawson, R. and Stephenson, J. (2013). Socio-technical barriers to the use of energy-efficient timber drying technology in New Zealand. *Energy Policy*, 67, 747–755.

Black, J., Stern, P. and Elworth, J. (1985). Personal and contextual influences on household energy adaptations. *Journal of Applied Psychology*, 70, 3–21.

Boardman, B. (1991). *Fuel poverty: From cold homes to affordable warmth*. London: Belhaven Press.

Boardman, B. (2010). *Fixing fuel poverty: Challenges and solutions*. London: Earthscan.

Boardman, B. (2012). Fuel poverty synthesis: Lessons learnt, actions needed. *Energy Policy*, 49, 143–148.

Bouzarovski, S. and Petrova, S. (2015). A global perspective on domestic energy deprivation: Overcoming the energy poverty-fuel poverty binary. *Energy Research and Social Sciences*, 10, 31–40.

Bouzarovski, S., Petrova, S. and Sarlamanov, R. (2012). Energy poverty policies in the EU: A critical perspective. *Energy Policy*, 49.

Bruce, N., Perez-Padilla, R. and Albalak, R. (2000). Indoor air pollution in developing countries: A major environmental and public health challenge. *Bulletin of the World Health Organization*, 78, 1078–1092.

Clinch, J. and Healy, J. (2001). Cost-benefit analysis of domestic energy efficiency. *Energy Policy*, 29(2), 113–124.

Day, R., Walker, G. and Simcock, N. (2016). Conceptualising energy use and energy poverty using a capabilities framework. *Energy Policy*, 93, 255–264.

DECC. (2015). *Annual report on fuel poverty statistics*. London: Department of Energy and Climate Change.

Geller, H. (2003). *Energy revolution: Policies for a sustainable future*. New York: Island Press.

Giddens, A. (1991). *Modernity and self-identity: Self and society in the late modern age*. Stanford, CA: Stanford University Press.

Goldthau, A. and Sovacool, B. (2012). The uniqueness of the energy security, justice, and governance problem. *Energy Policy*, 41, 232–240.

Hards, S. (2013). Status, stigma and energy practices in the home. *Local Environment*, 18(4), 438–454.

Harrington, B. E., Heyman, B., Merleau-Ponty, N., Stockton, H., Ritchie, N. and Heyman, A. (2005). Keeping warm and staying well: Findings from the qualitative arm of the warm homes project. *Health and Social Care in the Community*, 13(3), 259–267.

Heffner, G. and Campbell, N. (2011). *Evaluating the co-benefits of low-income energy-efficiency programmes*. Paris: International Energy Agency.

Hills, J. (2012). *Getting the measures of fuel poverty: Final report of the fuel poverty review*. London: Centre for Analysis of Exclusion.

Hoica, C. (2012). *Understanding pro-environmental behaviour as process: Assessing the importance of program structure*. PhD thesis, University of Waterloo.

Hopkins, D. and McCarthy, A. (2016). Change trends in urban freight delivery: A qualitative inquiry. *Geoforum*, 74, 158–170.

Howden-Chapman, P., Viggers, H., Chapman, R., O'Sullivan, K., Telfar-Barnard, L. and Lloyd, B. (2012). Tackling cold housing and fuel poverty in New Zealand: A review of policies, research, and health impacts. *Energy Policy*, 49, 134–142.

Intelligent Energy Europe. (2009). *European fuel poverty and energy efficiency*. Brussels: Intelligent Energy Europe.

Isaacs, N., Camilleri, M., Burrough, L., Pollard, A., Saville-Smith, K., Fraser, R., Rossouw, P. and Jowett, J. (2010). *Energy use in New Zealand households: Final report on the household energy end-use*. Wellington: HEEP Technical report, BRANZ.

Jansen, J. C. and Seebregts, A. J. (2010). Long-term energy services security: What is it and how can it be measured and valued? *Energy Policy*, 38(4), 1654–1664.

Lawson, R., Robertson, K. and Wooliscroft, B. (2016). Health, vulnerability, and energy: Assessing energy markets and consumer agency in New Zealand. *Energy Research & Social Science*, 19, 119–123.

Lawson, R. and Williams, J. (2012). *The nature of fuel poverty in New Zealand*. Australia and New Zealand Academy of Marketing, University of Otago, Dunedin.

Lawson, R., Williams, J. and Wooliscroft, B. (2015). Contrasting approaches to fuel poverty in New Zealand. *Energy Policy*, 81, 38–42.

Liddell, C. (2010). Fuel poverty and human health: A review of recent evidence. *Energy Policy*, 38(6), 2987–2997.

Liddell, C. (2012). The missed exam: Conversations with Brenda Boardman. *Energy Policy*, 49, 12–18.

Lloyd, B. (2006). Fuel poverty in New Zealand. *Social Policy Journal of New Zealand*, 27, 142.

Lutzenhiser, L. (1993). Social and behavioural aspects of energy use. *Annual Review of Energy and Environment*, 18(1), 247–289.

McKague, F., Lawson, R., Scott, M. and Wooliscroft, B. (2016). Understanding the energy consumption choices and coping mechanisms of fuel poor households in New Zealand. *New Zealand Sociology*, 31(1), 106.

Middlemiss, L. and Gillard, R. (2015). Fuel poverty from the bottom-up: Characterising household energy vulnerability through lived experiences of the fuel poor. *Energy Research and Social Sciences*, 6, 146–154.

New Zealand Government. (2013). *New Zealand energy efficiency and conservation strategy*. Wellington: New Zealand Government.

Nussbaumer, P., Bazilian, M. and Modi, V. (2012). Measuring energy poverty: Focusing on what matters. *Renewable and Sustainable Energy Reviews*, 16(1), 231–243.

Osbaldeston, J. (1984). Fuel poverty in UK cities. *Cities*, 1.

Pachauri, S. and Spreng, D. (2004). Energy use and energy access in relation to poverty. *Economic and Political Weekly*, 271–278.

Pachauri, S. and Spreng, D. (2011). Measuring and monitoring energy poverty. *Energy Policy*, 39(12), 7497–7504.

Patterson, M. (1996). What is energy efficiency? Concepts, indicators and methodological issues. *Energy Policy*, 25(5), 377–390.

Petrova, S., Gentile, M., Mäkinen, I. and Bouzarovski, S. (2013). Perceptions of thermal comfort and housing quality: Exploring the microgeographies of energy poverty in Stakhanov, Ukraine. *Environment and Planning A*, 45(5), 1240–1257.

Shove, E. (2003). *Comfort, cleanliness and convenience*. Oxford: Berg.

Snell, C., Bevan, M. and Thomson, H. (2014). *Fuel poverty and disabled people: The impact of policy change*. York: University of York.

Sovacool, B. (2014). What are we doing? Analyzing fifteen years of energy scholarship and proposing a social science research agenda. *Energy Research and Social Sciences*, 1, 1–29.

Sovacool, B., Cooper, C. and Bazillian, M. (2012). What moves and works: broadening the consideration of energy poverty. *Energy Policy*, 42, 715–719.

Stephenson, J., Barton, B., Carrington, G., Doering, A., Ford, R., Hopkins, D., Lawson, R., McCarthy, A., Rees, D., Scott, M. and Thorsnes, P. (2015). The energy cultures framework: Exploring the role of norms, practices and material culture in shaping energy behaviour in New Zealand. *Energy Research & Social Science*, 7, 117–123.

Stephenson, J., Barton, B., Carrington, G., Gnoth, D., Lawson, R. and Thorsnes, P. (2010). Energy cultures: A framework for understanding energy behaviours. *Energy Policy*, 38(10), 6120–6129.

Stern, P. (1984). *Energy use: The human dimension*. Washington, DC: National Academic Press.

Stern, P. (1986). Blind spots in policy analysis: What economics don't' say about energy use. *Journal of Policy*, 5, 200–227.

Stern, P. (2014). Individual and household interactions with energy systems: Towards integrated understanding. *Energy and Social Sciences*, 1, 41–48.

Sweeney, J. C., Kresling, J., Webb, D., Soutar, G. N. and Mazzarol, T. (2013). Energy saving behaviour: Development of a practice-based model. *Energy Policy*, 61, 371–381.

United Nations. (2016). *Sustainable development goals*. Geneva: United Nations.

Verhallen, T. M. and Van Raaij, W. F. (1981). Household behaviour and the use of natural gas for home heating. *Journal of Consumer Research*, 8, 253–257.

Walker, G. (2014). The dynamics of energy demand: Change, rhythm and synchronicity. *Energy Research & Social Sciences*, 1, 49–55.

WHO. (2007). *Housing, energy and thermal comfort: A review of 10 countries within the WHO European region*. Copenhagen: World Health Organisation.

Wilkinson, P., Smith, K., Beevers, S., Tonne, T. and Oreszczyn, T. (2007). Energy, energy efficiency, and the built environment. *The Lancet*, 370(9593), 1175–1187.

Wilson, C. and Dowlatabadi, H. (2007). Models of decision making and residential energy use. *Annual Review of Environment and Resources*, 32, 169–203.

4 Transcending the triad

Political distrust, local cultural norms and reconceptualising the drivers of domestic energy poverty in the UK

Irena L.C. Connon

Introduction

Energy poverty, defined as 'a measure of a household's ability to pay for energy services in the home to provide heating, lighting, cooking and appliance use to meet daily needs' (Boardman 2010, in Thomson et al. 2016: 10), is a relatively understudied area within the field of policy-relevant research. The majority of policy-based research in the UK continues to conceptualise the causes of energy poverty as a combination of energy-inefficient dwelling and appliances, low incomes and high energy costs (Hills 2011; Sutton and Hill 2012, The Energy and Utilities Alliance 2017) – what can be termed the 'triad' approach. However, this approach results in the analysis of a complex situation in a way that aligns with policy categories, rather than one that conceptualises the experience from the perspectives of those affected. Furthermore, it has been argued that it oversimplifies the causes and experience of domestic energy deprivation (Bouzarovski and Petrova 2015).

More recent scholarship has examined the dynamic experience of energy poverty, using this to highlight a much wider range of locally-contextualised contingencies that are implicated in causing the condition (Bouzarovski et al. 2013, Middlemiss and Gillard 2015). This includes studies that highlight the role played by socio-cultural meanings and norms (Cupples et al. 2007; Day and Hitchings 2011; Hards 2013; Hitchings et al. 2015; Petrova et al. 2013), but this continues to remain a relatively underexplored area. To address this limitation, this chapter draws upon in-depth qualitative research conducted within four communities in the UK and argues that domestic energy poverty needs to be understood as being driven, in part, by locally-embedded cultural norms that intersect and interrelate with material and political factors. The study makes the claim that local cultural and political geographies, in both the UK and in wider international settings, need to be acknowledged and considered in conceptualisations of energy poverty and in the development of energy poverty alleviation schemes. The study also lends support to theories of 'justice as recognition' by highlighting how patterns of geographically-situated socio-cultural stigma shape the experience and persistence of energy poverty in specific localities (Snell et al. 2015; Walker and Day 2012).

The empirical evidence presented in this chapter was collected between November 2014 and May 2015, from a study designed to explore personal experiences of fuel poverty across selected case study sites in the UK. Information was collected through: 1) a total of 13 personal oral histories of experiences of energy poverty and 2) a total of 33 semi-structured interviews. The study design was based upon the body of scholarship that values the agency of local actors and seeks to understand the experiences of energy poverty from the perspective of those affected (Bouzarovski et al. 2013; Middlemiss and Gillard 2015).

Participants were recruited from urban and rural locations in Scotland and England. Urban Scottish participants came from the town of Fort William, in the West Highlands. With a population of 10,437 and a 73% employment rate amongst residents of working age, it is the second largest town in the Highlands of Scotland and has a similar employment rate to the 69% Scottish average (Smith et al. 2014). The Scottish rural participants came from the villages of An-Aird, Banavie, Caol, Claggan, Corpach, Inverlochy and Lochyside that surround the town of Fort William. In Scotland, with the exception of five large cities, much of the geographic landscape continues to be characterised by towns similar in size to Fort William, with rural areas consisting of clusters of villages surrounding each town. While each small town and surrounding rural area is unique, the sites can be considered to be relatively representative of a typical small urban and rural area present in contemporary Scotland. In England, urban participants were selected from Slough, a large ethnically-diverse town in East Berkshire with a population of 140,200. 71% of residents were in employment, compared to a UK average of 72.7% (Bourner 2012). Rural English residents came from the villages of Blackheath, Bramley, Chilworth, Elstead, Milford, Peasmarsh and Shackleford that surround the market town of Godalming in Surrey. An area of wealth, the rural area is known for its high property prices and prosperity; however, concerns have been raised in recent years that the needs of those within the area who do not enjoy the same level of living standards are going unnoticed because of the focus on the area's prosperity (Personal communication 2014, representative from Age UK, Surrey).

Participants were identified from their involvement in a larger project exploring local responses to weather-related hazards and who had indicated that they had previously struggled to heat their homes or afford energy bills. Eight interviews and three oral history accounts were collected in Fort William, and seven interviews and four oral histories from the surrounding rural area. Ten interviews and three oral histories were undertaken in Slough, with eight interviews and three oral histories in the English rural site. Participants consisted of those of working age, referred to as 'younger adults' in chapter, and those aged 60 years and over, referred to as 'older adults'. Interview data were transcribed and analysed for words, phrases and nuances associated with stigma and cultural norms, including shame, discomfort, worry, distrust and isolation. Descriptions of changes to energy use and perceptions of shame over time where highlighted from the oral history data, before being organised and verified using NVivo software. All presented data has been anonymised.

Contextual background

While the vast majority of previous studies on energy poverty focus on inefficient housing structures and equipment, high energy costs and low household incomes, in what is known as a 'triad' approach to analysing its causes (Thomson et al. 2016, 3), others have taken a more expansive view by drawing attention to additional drivers. For example, as Boardman (2010) and Snell et al. (2015) note, increases in disability rates, elderly people and the numbers of people living in private short-term rented accommodation have contributed to increases in the numbers affected by energy poverty in the UK. Yet, despite recognition of the hardships that arise, the majority of policy-makers contend that energy poverty is distinct from general income poverty and is driven by 'poor energy efficiency and affordable energy carriers' (Thomson et al. 2016, 10, also see Boardman 2010; Hill 2012).

A more recent body of scholarship focuses upon subjective experiences of fuel poverty. These studies argue that traditional triadic approaches to energy poverty lack coherence in providing a holistic picture of the energy poverty experience (Bouzarovski et al. 2013, 2014; Middlemiss and Gillard 2015). The ways in which households experience energy poverty do not always correspond to official definitions and several studies have provided a more situated representation by taking a ground-up approach (See Anderson et al. 2012; Bouzarovski et al. 2013; Brunner et al. 2012; Gibbons and Singler 2008; Harrington et al. 2005; Hitchings and Day 2011; Middlemiss and Gillard 2015). These studies stress that experiences of energy poverty represent a subjective experience within a particular situation at a particular moment in time. Other studies reveal how the amount of energy consumption deemed necessary in order to achieve a decent standard of living is materially and culturally conditioned (Boardman 2010; Bouzarovski et al. 2013; Davis et al. 2015; Day et al. 2016; Hitchings and Day 2011; Walker et al. 2016). These approaches also reveal an overlap between energy poverty and general income poverty (Bouzarovski et al. 2014).

Middlemiss and Gillard (2015) developed an approach that suggests that the complexities of experiences could be conceptualised by adapting Spiers' (2000, in Middlemiss and Gillard 2015) framework of vulnerability to define specific risk factors associated with energy poverty. The approach asserts that a person becomes more or less vulnerable depending on the extent to which they are able to: 1) keep warm, 2) respond to challenges, 3) cope with change and 4) have power to challenge situations (Middlemiss and Gillard 2015, 147). Individuals become more or less vulnerable depending on the extent to which they can accommodate several identifiable challenges driven by external forces outwith their immediate control that impact upon their lives, including tenancy relations and ill health (ibid: 149). This represents a much broader approach to the dynamic drivers of energy poverty than the classic 'triad' approach.

Bouzarovski and Petrova (2014, 2015, 9), similarly, acknowledge that established social practices – locally embedded customs, norms and conventions (Edgerton 2000 and Patterson 2001) – can play a role in shaping whether households can access required energy services. These customs and norms are not statically fixed but can persist over time (Edgerton 2000). Yet, whilst the role of cultural factors have begun to be acknowledged as an important contingency in the emergence of energy poverty, empirical studies that examine such issues remain limited.

The few studies available that do examine this issue present some intriguing findings. Cupples et al. (2007) focuses on how individual preferences for heating homes in New Zealand is tied to cultural identities ground upon colonial heritage, notions of masculinity and national identity. Day and Hitchings (2011) explore how practices to keep warm during winter amongst older people in the UK are shaped by the stigma associated with older age. Meanwhile Hards (2013) explores how energy use in different areas of the world is shaped by socio-cultural ideas of status, and she also highlights the need for more comprehensive work to be undertaken to explore how status and stigma reflect and reinforce inequalities. Similarly, a study by Hitchings et al. (2015) focusing on how local perceptions of cold discomfort during winter in Australia were affected by a cultural focus on the summer season, concluded that there is a need for greater engagement with local cultural geographies to effectively understand issues of domestic heat.

This study provides an in-depth qualitative investigation into how local cultural norms influence the experience and generation of energy poverty in the UK. It builds upon previous research by exploring how such norms intersect with other economic and political drivers.

Findings

The shame of being cold

Participants in all four case study sites described experiences of energy poverty as one of 'shame' and 'social isolation'. Participants explained that not having the means to heat their homes to the extent required to live a socially inclusive life was associated with negative self-perceptions of irresponsibility and concerns about being seen as a failure or morally corrupt by others. Although previous scholarship has suggested that energy poverty and income poverty are distinct (Thomson et al. 2016, 10; Hills 2012), participants characterised social isolation as the hallmark of 'poverty' in general and did not make a distinction between income poverty and energy poverty. A total of 21 out of the 33 participants suggested that not being able to provide heating for oneself or one's household was something that they felt ashamed of. As a result, those affected often tried to conceal their hardship to avoid feeling embarrassed amongst their wider social network.

These actions were underpinned by cultural attitudes that placed significant emphasis on personal responsibility for avoiding financial hardship and for ensuring the comfort of family members. Furthermore, subtle differences were found in attitudes across the four case study sites. For example, in Fort William, participants explained that they took action to try to mask hardship by spending beyond their means to heat their homes when guests were arriving to avoid the shame associated with being seen to be financially struggling. One participant, a lady age 30, now employed as a Care Assistant for the elderly but who had previously experienced several years of unemployment, explained how in the past she:

> Spent what little money [she] had on electricity to make the house warm and to have food in when I knew I was getting visitors. I couldn't afford to have the heating on all day, but I wanted to show everyone I was getting by and getting on as normal.

She then explained that her motivations for masking her hardship resulted from feelings of shame:

> It was like it was really embarrassing, so I'd be like wanting to show that it was okay so they wouldn't look down on me. . . . They probably wouldn't think as harsh as that, but just the thought that they might makes you not want to say anything.

In Slough, participants emphasised that they tried to mask hardships because they felt a responsibility not to let others down because of 'a personal failing'. This was explained by a construction worker in his 30s, who was living with his partner and three children, who explained why he spent money on heating rather than bus fares for the week:

> I couldn't afford much and heating was a big part of that. But it was important to make sure that others were comfortable. I could have afforded the bus if I'd let the place go cold, but I didn't want people to stop coming round. . . . I didn't want to feel like some sort of failure and putting them off coming round here by moaning all the time.

Another participant – unemployed, but with a young family, also from Slough – also noted spending more on heating to avoid feelings of moral failings, stating:

> I was broke when they stopped my benefits those weeks. I had some money left and I thought keep the place warm so at least my kids are inside. If the house is too cold the kids won't want to stay in and I'm trying to keep them out of the streets. They don't need to get caught up in more fights with the neighbours. That gives them [the neighbours] an excuse to come round here and an excuse to think we're bad parents.

In the rural villages surrounding Fort William in Scotland and in the rural town of Godalming in England, participants spoke about how long-standing negative attitudes towards debt led to self-imposed isolation through not having the means to heat their homes and the perceptions of shame that this incurred. While desires to isolate were evident in the urban areas, they were more pronounced in the rural areas due to concerns that in a smaller area their hardships would be more likely to be visible to other residents. This was particularly true for elderly residents who perceived both debt and poverty as a marker of personal failure. Two participants described how they isolated themselves within their cold homes out of concern that 'others would see them as weak'. In the Scottish rural context, participants described how attitudes transmitted from their parents about the equation of debt with irresponsibility directly led to feelings of shame and guilt that they had let their parents (or memories of their late parents) down by not being able to meet the high moral standards that they had been raised with. In the English rural context, people spoke more often about not wanting to be seen as 'a charity case' by the wider community rather than being concerned that they had let their family members down, but which nevertheless contributed to feelings of low self-worth.

In both the Scottish urban and rural contexts, some participants attributed the origins of these stigmas surrounding poverty to historic Protestant church teachings that emphasised hard work as a marker of 'good moral character'. Others attributed the origins to particular localities, stating that these attitudes are more rigidly embedded in areas once dominated by the fishing industry and in working class communities, where the importance of being seen by others to be a good provider for one's family was emphasised as being a positive character trait. In contrast, areas once predominated by agriculture were viewed as being more 'forgiving' of hardship, where hardship was seen as less of a personal moral failing and more of an outcome of external circumstances. This was explained by an older participant now living in Fort William, but who had previously lived in various other locations in Scotland:

> I grew up in the country and we were all poor. If someone needed helped, folk helped. It was accepted that you'd struggle. There wasn't the judgement I saw when I moved to Aberdeen where it was your own hard luck and people, well their attitude was more it 'sort it out yourself' like it was your problem, your fault, you caused it. Here it's not as bad. . . . I think it's to do with the history of the place . . . tolerance is sort of built-in with the way of farming.

In the English sites, the stigma surrounding poverty was associated with social class and notions that aspirations to improve social standing were positive character traits. Participants spoke of how they learnt these attitudes and ideas from their parents and grandparents, which they generally accepted without much questioning. This reveals that these ideas were deeply ingrained within the fabric of society and persistent over a long period of time, as described by an older male resident, who was previously employed as a Gardener:

> You're taught this through your life; to work hard, improve yourself and if you don't make money, get a good home, decent living, that's you, a failure. You get it as you grow up, 'You need to go to school, get a good job'. . . . the

world doesn't respect you if you don't make it. You're brought up to try to get to being middle class. . . . you don't question when you hear it all the time. You try to live up to these standards and then feel bad when you can't.

Deeply-embedded cultural norms also influenced views about acceptable levels of warmth. Again, these ideas varied across each locality, with the lowest standards reported in rural Scotland where minimum expectations were to be able to heat the main living area with a gas, electric, solid fuel or log fire and have enough electricity or gas to take one bath or shower per day and be able to cook meals. In Fort William, participants described an acceptable level of warmth as being warm enough for each member of the household to feel comfortable and with enough supply to be able to use technological, cooking and washing facilities as often as they needed. In both English sites, minimum standards were defined as being warm enough to avoid any negative health effects. In all sites however, not being able to meet the minimum expectations was viewed as shameful.

In addition to influencing energy consumption, locally-embedded cultural norms impacted upon the ways that participants could obtain help to avoid hardship associated with energy poverty. In all four sites, participants spoke of local expectations relating to the disclosure of personal matters, including health and finance, as influencing abilities to cope with the hardship. Again, these norms were similar in each case study site. In rural Scotland, participants described how matters relating to personal finances were generally not regarded as suitable topics for discussion outwith immediate circles of family and friends, as one 41-year-old female participant explained:

It's just seen as something not done. It's too personal. You'd be sharing too much. It'd be seen as bad manners.

In the English sites, such restrictive views resonated more strongly with older residents, whereas younger residents in the urban Scottish and both the English sites expressed greater willingness to share this information beyond immediate social circles, but only when it was deemed absolutely necessary to do so, such as when the health of a member of the household, other than themselves, was at immediate risk, illustrated by a 25-year-old male participant from Slough:

It's not the sort of thing you'd want to hype about, but you gotta give information to get the help you need. You don't want to tell people you don't know that can't afford it, but if your Mum's ill and needs to be warm or if there's kids in the house, cold gets dangerous and you'd do it then.

Furthermore, even in cases where it was deemed to be an appropriate, general rules applied for with whom this information could be shared with, such as more distant friends or acquaintances who had personal experience of having been through similar hardships and could be trusted to keep the information confidential. Certain appropriate professionals, such as the family general practitioner, were deemed more acceptable to share information with than a Social Worker or a teacher from their children's school. Information could be shared with personnel from the Job Centre or from local branches of the Department for Work and Pensions only if it was absolutely necessary to disclose this information to secure an income. Participants over 60 years old in both urban sites expressed more reluctance to disclose this information to anyone they did not personally know than their younger counterparts.

The main reason that younger adults below the age of 60 gave for increased flexibility of disclosing financial information in the urban settings was that they had fewer strong close personal connections within their immediate community who they could turn to for help, as a result of having moved away from close friends and family in pursuit of employment. However, even for the younger adults, disclosures of hardship often resulted in entrenching feelings of shame and self-loathing, as described by one particular participant from the Scottish urban site:

> You feel like you are a failure. You hope others don't think that, but by speaking it, it's kind of like you're admitting it, when you shouldn't want to admit because it makes you look bad like you've got no standards. . . . You don't want to say to your folks you've no money for heating so they think you can't cope moving away from them.

Similar stories were echoed by participants from the English case study sites, with one subtle difference being that information could only be disclosed in such a way as to show that the person was taking personal responsibility for trying to improve their situation:

> You have to do it in a way that you're asking for help but not begging. You got to do it in a way that you are showing that you are serious about changing things for the better and not just trying to get money.

These deeply-rooted local expectations about disclosing information help reproduce energy poverty, as they impact upon people's abilities and willingness to seek help from social networks and professional organisations to avoid the ill health, discomfort and social isolation that results from not being able to heat their homes. In addition, if people are unwilling to directly disclose information about their hardships, this places greater emphasis on a person's social connections to notice the hardships of another via observation and to attend to the problem in ways that do not add to the person's sense of shame by asking invasive questions about personal circumstances. This also raises concern about how the energy needs of residents who are more socially isolated can be adequately met. Further, as the shame associated with experiencing inability to heat one's home results in self-imposed isolation or efforts to mask the true reality of one's situation by adjusting energy consumption behaviours and/or by getting into debt, the abilities of social contacts to become aware of the reality of the situation without asking directly becomes further impaired.

The relationship between cultural norms and wider processes of political and economic change in shaping experiences of energy poverty

These findings from the interviews were supplemented by additional information from the personal life histories collected during this study. These provide a holistic picture as to how prevailing cultural norms intersect with changing economic and political geographies of place to drive local experiences of energy poverty.

Participants' recollections illustrated how changes to the market economy during the 1980s and 1990s resulted in changes to local industry, property prices and social attitudes, which affected community demographics, employment opportunities, housing arrangements and social relationships within communities (see Berry 2011; Clements et al. 2008; Keating 2007; Mackenzie et al. 2004; McCrone 2001 for further information about socio-economic and political change). In combination with the deregulation of the energy supply industry, these wider impacts led to changes in households' ability to access energy and to ameliorate hardships. While participants mentioned how the sale of social housing and the rise of private tenancy agreements presented increased difficulties in choosing energy suppliers and preferred payment methods and in negotiating structural upgrades to building fabrics and household appliances, these were not seen on their own to contribute to their experiences of energy hardship. Instead, they were felt to coexist alongside changes in general social attitudes in creating exacerbations of energy vulnerability. For example, one female participant from Slough described how private landlords lacked the incentive to upgrade the building fabric to provide more adequate insulation, while tenants became increasingly reluctant to raise the issue for fear of rent rises and homelessness:

> Nowadays it's easier to get evicted. There's a shortage [of housing], so you dare not complain. If it's too cold you have to put up with it. You don't want to mention it.

She also explained that with recent government austerity agendas, attitudes towards those experiencing hardship have hardened. As a result, people are now even more reluctant to seek assistance and go to greater efforts to mask their hardships:

> People are harder on poorer people nowadays. Very negative. The Government . . . they want you to feel ashamed and people are now more judging and you think they look down at you more now. . . . You think if I complain they will judge more, so you don't talk about it.

However, with the growth of short-term and zero-hours employment contracts and higher risks of unemployment, people also became increasingly unable to mask their lack of ability to afford heating costs, leading to even greater risks of isolation, as noted by another participant from the same site:

> I asked at the job centre for emergency electricity money to get a shower before my interview. They didn't help me. You've no choice, you can't go

around stinky. People think bad of you. Or you shower, you can't eat and you need food to survive. I like being clean. If I can't shower, I don't want to go out. I have my pride.

Another participant described how changes to the demographic makeup of their rural English community led to increased isolation and feelings of shame, coupled with decreasing abilities to source out assistance via local social contacts. He explained that as increasing numbers of wealthy residents moved into rural areas, property prices increased to such an extent that many local residents were priced out of the local markets. With the decline in traditional rural employment opportunities, many local residents had little choice but to move away to seek out employment. For those who stayed behind, being surrounded by wealth and decreasing employment opportunities and shrinkages in traditional rural social networks, led to increased social isolation and heightened awareness of their hardships. With tenancies often being tied to employment, downturns in rural industries meant that residents were reluctant to complain about low wages or poor building quality over concerns about job losses and homelessness. Statements were also made that the wealthy incomers were more likely to be unsympathetic towards poorer people. One participant stated that those who did try to show sympathy were viewed as patronising because, although they tried to be sympathetic,

> [T]hey offer advice like you're a child and tell you what to do when you've tried everything before and they look at you like you must be stupid. They don't mean harm; it's more they haven't got a clue what it's like if you don't have the cash.

The Scottish life histories illustrated how recent political movements also influenced how socio-cultural norms played out in shaping experiences of energy poverty. Participants described how the build-up to the recent independence referendum in Scotland resulted in extroversion of the normally publicly hidden dimensions of discomfort associated with living in cold homes. Several of the Scottish participants described that, during this period, abilities to tolerate cold temperatures became celebrated as symbolically representative of Scottish identity. As a result, people began to speak with a sense of pride in being able to live frugally and endure the discomforts associated with cold temperatures, particularly in rural areas, as noted by a 43-year-old male participant from the Scottish rural site:

> It seemed strange. You sort of celebrate your hardship. Show you're tough and hardy. Saying it's how a tough Highlander should be. Folk's been saying 'Where the Scotsman in you if you canna take the cold?' . . . Maybe you should be proud of the cold; not moan about it. Made you moan less and think worse of yourself for thinking it shouldn't be like this to be putting up with the cold because you've no money.

While this appears rather far removed from the Scottish independence debate, it resulted in a situation whereby fuel-poor households were somewhat lessened of their need to mask their situation. However, as noted above, this also created in a situation whereby local people who were struggling to cope with hardships became even more reluctant to seek help. Similarly, those not local to the area were reported as going to increased lengths to mask the visibility of their suffering for fear of contributing to local socio-political tensions through the enhancement of an 'us' versus 'them' divide.

In both the English and Scottish case study sites, participants also revealed how memories of the impacts of the privatisation of industry in local areas and the move to financial and knowledge-based economies during previous decades resulted in creating a deeply-engrained, collectively-shared distrust of both central Government organisations and of energy companies. This was evident amongst both older and younger participants, as exemplified by a 70-year-old resident from Slough:

> I'd find it hard to trust any Government that supports putting the interests of people in the hands of markets. . . . That's what left us without jobs in the first place. Now if they really cared about helping people with their bills they would do something so that people have a decent standard of living without the need for any of these sticking plaster-type remedies that they can use as an excuse so they don't have to do anything to sort the real causes.

Similar attitudes were shown in Scotland, in both the rural and urban case study sites, which had been previously affected by the decline of the fishing and agricultural industries. Similar findings were also present in the English rural case study site, where the area was affected by the rise of the financial economy and the decline of the agricultural industry. This also revealed that the increased wealth brought to the Godalming area in the 1980s and 1990s did not benefit all residents within the area. Furthermore, this distrust towards National Government can be seen to help perpetuate energy poverty, as the distrust creates additional resistance to taking steps towards trying to ameliorate the situation energy through engagement with official fuel poverty alleviation schemes, such as the Home Energy Efficiency Programme for Scotland and The Affordable Warmth Scheme in England. These schemes aim to provide grants to enable householders and landlords to undertake structural improvements to properties and to provide energy-saving appliances to cut down costs of fuel bills (see Scottish Government 2014 and National Energy Action 2017 for details of these schemes). However, over two thirds of participants explained that they would be extremely wary of actually taking up such an offer, citing distrust of government intentions and fears that this would result in higher future energy costs, as it would give the National UK Government no incentive to regulate the energy industry. Twenty-one respondents were concerned as to how their personal data would be used, citing concerns about personal finances being passed to other parties. While participant concerns were based on subjective opinion rather than fact, their concerns nevertheless created a genuine reluctance to engage with these initiatives at the expense of personal warmth. For example, eight participants in the English case study sites explained that they wouldn't trust governments to continue the scheme, believing that such schemes are brought in with the intention of providing a quick fix to a complex problem, or, as one participant put, 'to win votes and make the Government appear popular'. In Scotland, all but one participant expressed distrust concerning Government motives. Five participants were concerned that any immediate success of the scheme in reducing energy bills would provide the UK Government with the impression that the problem could be resolved without energy regulation. A total of 20 participants across all case study sites also expressed concern about becoming involved in these schemes simply because they were initiated by the Government, with Government initiatives being immediately viewed with suspicion. This was highlighted by a 23-year-old participant from Fort William:

> When any of these things come out you think where's it coming from? When you find out it's the Government, you just know don't trust it. UK, Scottish [Government], it's always about them and not us. . . . It's because this sort of thing's been happening for years. Things meant to help, but don't. And now people are like 'oh yeah' what they up to now? And that's everybody round here. I was brought up with it, hearing it from everybody. It's become part of the way life to second guess what's behind it if it's a Government thing.

Discussion and implications for policy development

The study highlights two key points: 1) the significance that cultural norms have in driving experiences of energy poverty in different UK settings and 2) that these norms combine with wider processes of economic and political change to help perpetuate energy poverty. The findings also reveal that these locally-embedded cultural norms, along with distrust in central Governments, generate barriers to engagement with policy-driven alleviation schemes. Perceptions of shame and moral failure were associated with energy poverty in all case study sites, revealing the prevalence of these perceptions throughout the UK. However, subtle differences emerged in participant perceptions of the origins of these ideas and in how they were articulated in the Scottish and English sites. Similarly, while prevailing cultural norms influence how, when and to whom participants were willing to share information about energy hardship, these were found to operate on a stronger basis among all participants in rural Scotland and amongst older participants in the other three sites. The findings also reveal how prevailing cultural norms intersect with changing economic and political geographies of place in driving local experiences of energy poverty, with changes to property prices and community demographics in the rural English case study site enhancing perceptions of shame amongst participants from this area. Changes to local industry, housing arrangements and social attitudes affected residents in both urban sites in the production of feelings of shame and self-isolating behaviour. Changes in the political landscape, from the growth of the free-market economy in the 1980s and the recent independence movement in Scotland, also impacted upon resident perceptions of shame in the respective locations.

These findings reinforce the suggestion that the drivers of energy poverty go beyond the traditional conceptualisation of energy-inefficient dwellings, low incomes and high energy costs. Instead, the findings lend support to the additional importance of socio-cultural norms and meanings – particularly those related to stigma, shame and (mis)recognition (Cupples et al. 2007; Day and Hitchings 2011; Hards 2013; Hitchings et al. 2015; Walker and Day 2012) – and the role that changing economic and political processes have on experiences of energy poverty within particular local contexts. They also lend support to calls to understand and examine the experience of energy poverty from the perspective of those affected by it (Anderson et al. 2012; Bouzarovski et al. 2013; Brunner et al. 2012; Middlemiss and Gillard 2015).

The findings have significant implications for policy development that aims to address energy poverty, both within the UK and in the wider international context. While policy developments in the UK aim to address the issue via the material causes of hardship, greater consideration should be given to cultural stigma and norms and processes of socio-political change that may shape their uptake in specific local contexts. While the actual study findings are particular to UK local context, they suggest that, while specific cultural norms may vary from place-to-place, their influence in shaping local experiences of energy poverty indicate a need for the acknowledgement and harnessing of local cultural and political geographies in developing effective, locally-responsive policy and alleviation initiatives. Possible ways that greater uptake of alleviation schemes in the UK may be achieved may therefore include moving towards more localised approaches to engagement.

Conclusion

While recent scholarship has given more attention to the significance of socio-cultural drivers in the experience and perpetuation of energy poverty, it continues to remain a relatively underexplored area. This study presents a novel contribution to this emerging body of scholarship, not only by exploring the role that cultural norms play in shaping local experiences of energy poverty in the UK, but by highlighting how such norms intersect with wider processes of economic and political change that impact upon local contexts. The findings raise considerations applicable to the wider international context as they assert the need for the acknowledgement of local cultural and political geographies of place to be recognised and addressed within policy development. In asserting the need to move beyond traditional triadic theorisations of the drivers of energy poverty, this study lends support to theories of 'justice as recognition' by highlighting of how patterns of geographically-located socio-cultural norms (re)produce energy poverty within specific localities.

References

Anderson, W., While, V. and Finney, A. (2012). Coping with low incomes and cold homes. *Energy Policy*, 49, 40–52.

Berry, C. (2011). *Globalisation and ideology in Britain: Neoliberalism, free trade and the global economy*. Manchester: Manchester University Press.

Boardman, B. (2010). *Fixing fuel poverty: Challenges and solutions*. London: Earthscan.

Bourner, R. (2012). *2011 Census, key statistics for local authorities in England and Wales: Slough Borough*. Slough: Slough Borough Council.

Bouzarovski, S. and Petrova, S. (2015). A global perspective on domestic energy deprivation: Overcoming the energy poverty-fuel poverty binary. *Energy Research and Social Science*, 10, 31–40.

Bouzarovski, S., Petrova, S. and Tirado-Herrero, S. (2014). From fuel poverty to energy vulnerability: The importance of services, needs and practices. Brighton: University of Sussex, Science Policy Research Unit, *Working Paper Series 2014–15*.

Bouzarovski, S., Petrova, S., Kitching, M. and Baldwick, J. (2013). Precarious domesticities: Energy vulnerability among young adults. In Bickerstaff, J., Walker, G. and Bulkeley, H. (eds.) *Energy justice in a changing climate*. London: Zed Books.

Brunner, K. M., Spitzer, M. and Christanell, A. (2012). Experiencing fuel poverty, coping strategies of low income households in Vienna/Austria. *Energy Policy*, 49, 53–59.

Clements, D., Donald, A., Earnshaw, M. and Williams, A. (2008). *The future of community: Reports of a death greatly exaggerated*. London: Pluto Press.

Cupples, J., Guyatt, V. and Pearce, J. (2007). 'Put on a jacket, you Wuss': Cultural identities, home heating and air pollution in Christchurch, New Zealand. *Environment and Planning A*, 39, 2883–2898.

Davis, A., Hirsch, D., Padley, M. and Marshall, L. (2015). *How much is enough? Researching consensus on minimum household needs*. Loughborough: Loughborough University, Centre for Research in Social Policy.

Day, R. and Hitchings, R. (2011). 'Only old ladies would do that': Age stigma and older people's Strategies for dealing with winter cold. *Health and Place*, 17, 885–894.

Day, R., Walker, G. and Simcock, N. (2016). Conceptualising energy use and energy poverty using a capabilities framework. *Energy Policy*, 93, 255–264.

Edgerton, R. (2000). Traditional beliefs and practices: Are some better than others? In Harrison, L. and Huntington, S. (eds.) *Culture matters: How values shape human progress*. New York: Basic Books, pp. 126–140.

The Energy and Utilities Alliance. (2017). *Fuel poverty: A connected solution*. Kenilworth Warwickshire: The Energy and Utilities Alliance.

Gibbons, D. and Singler, R. (2008). *Cold comfort: A review of coping strategies employed by households in fuel poverty*. London: Centre for Economic and Social Inclusion.

Hards, S. (2013). Status, stigma and energy practices in the home. *Local Environment*, 18, 438–454.

Harrington, B. E., Heyman, B., Merleau-Ponty, N., Stockton, H., Ritchie, N. and Heyman, A. (2005). Keeping warm and staying well: Findings from the qualitative arm of the Warm Homes Project. *Health and Social Care in the Community*, 13, 259–267.

Hills, J. (2011). *Fuel poverty: The problem and its measurements: Interim report of the fuel poverty review*, Case Report 69. London: Department of Energy and Climate Change/ Centre for Action on Social Exclusion, Crown Copyright.

Hills, J. (2012). *Getting the measure of fuel poverty: Final report of the fuel poverty review*, Report 72. London: Centre for Analysis of Social Exclusion.

Hitchings, R. and Day, R. (2011). How older people related to the private winter warmth practices of their peers and why we should be Interested. *Environmental Planning Part 1*, 43, 24–52.

Hitchings, R., Waitt, G., Roggeveen, K. and Chisholm, C. (2015). Winter cold in a summer place: Perceived norms of seasonal adaptation and cultures of home heating in Australia. *Energy Research and Social Science*, 8, 162–172.

Keating, M. (2007). *Scottish social democracy: Progressive ideas for public policy*. Pieterlen and Bern: Peter Lang Publishing Group.

Mackenzie, A. F. D., MacAskill, J., Munro, G. and Seki, E. (2004). Contesting land, creating community in the Highlands and Islands, Scotland. *Scottish Geographical Journal*, 120(3), 159–180.

McCrone, D. (2001). *Understanding Scotland: The sociology of a nation*. London: Routledge.

Middlemiss, L. and Gillard, R. (2015). Fuel poverty from the bottom-up: Characterising household energy vulnerability through the lived experience of the fuel poor. *Energy Research and Social Science*, 6, 146–154.

National Energy Action. (2017). *A Prospectus for Universal Affordable Warmth*. Newcastle Upon Tyne: The All-Party Parliamentary Fuel Poverty and Energy Efficiency Group.

Patterson, O. (2001). Taking culture seriously: A framework and an Afro-American illustration. In Harrison, L. E. and Huntington, S. P. (eds.) *Culture matters: How values shape human progress*. New York: Basic Books.

Petrova, S., Gentile, M., Bouzarovski, S. and Makinen, I. (2013). Perceptions of thermal comfort and housing quality: Exploring the microgeographies of energy poverty in Stakhanov, Ukraine. *Environment and Planning A*, 45(5), 1240–1257.

Scottish Government. (2014). Home energy efficiency programmes for Scotland. *Summary Delivery Report 2013/14*, The Scottish Government, Edinburgh.

Smith, H., Sobey, N. and Ross, C. (2014). *Fort William profile*. Inverness: The Highlands and Islands Enterprise.

Snell, C., Bevan, M. and Thomson, H. (2015). Justice, fuel poverty and disabled people in England. *Energy Research and Social Science*, 10, 123–132.

Sutton, L. and Hill, K. (2012). *Mediating the risk of fuel poverty in pensioner households*. Loughborough: Loughborough University Centre for Research in Social Policy.

Thomson, H., Snell, C. and Liddell, C. (2016). Fuel poverty in the European Union: A concept in need of definition? *People, Place and Policy*, 10(1), 5–24.

Walker, G. and Day, R. (2012). Fuel poverty as injustice: Integrating distribution, recognition and procedure in the struggle for affordable warmth. *Energy Policy*, 49, 69–75.

Walker, G., Simcock, N. and Day, R. (2016). Necessary energy uses and a minimum standard of living in the United Kingdom: Energy justice or escalating expectations? *Energy Research and Social Science*, 18, 129–138.

5 Post-apartheid spatial inequalities and the built environment

Drivers of energy vulnerability for the urban poor in South Africa

Abigail J. Knox, Jiska R. de Groot, and Nthabiseng Mohlakoana

Introduction

This chapter will explore the ways in which the legacy of apartheid spatial seg-regation, post-apartheid housing policy and energy service provision remain sys-temic drivers of energy vulnerability in South African townships. Wolpe and Reddy (Chapter 14) provide further context at a national level and examine policy frameworks that attempt to address energy poverty in South Africa. Energy poverty and vulnerability are prevalent in South Africa with nearly half (43%) of South Africans spending more than 10% of their net income on energy (DoE 2013). An early and poignant description of what it means to experience energy poverty in South Africa was captured by Wendy Annecke in the late 1990s:

> [B]eing without wood for two days during the rain meant two days without cooking, which in turn, means being without food. There is no bread in these households, no fast foods or cookies or anything other than salt and mealie meal and tea leaves and sugar.
>
> (Annecke 1999)

In the above example, the household depends on fuelwood for cooking and does not have access to other energy options or appliances or even an undercover space for cooking and storing fuelwood when it rains. Underlying this display of energy poverty are conditions and systemic pathways that increase household vulnerability to energy deprivation. Conditions, such as insufficient energy for cooking, are factors that describe a household's vulnerability to energy depriva-tion whereas systemic pathways are factors that lead to or cause energy depriva-tion, such as no alternative sources of energy for cooking indoors or unsuitable housing structure to store and cook with fuelwood undercover.

Mainstream energy poverty frameworks have focused on quantifiable indica-tors such as level of access, affordability, reliability, quality and safety of energy sources for basic energy needs. Beyond basic energy needs, however, the literature on energy poverty recognises that households not only require energy for cooking, heating and lighting but also for mobility and productive uses and to participate in modern society (Clancy et al. 2013; Kohler et al. 2009); this includes access to mechanical power, refrigeration, space cooling, drying, media, IT, cellular technology and public transport (Bouzarovski and Petrova 2015; Cabraal et al. 2005; Kimemia and Annegarn 2012; Kohler et al. 2009; Kooijman-van Dijk and Clancy 2010; Lues et al. 2006; Mills et al. 2014; Sovacool 2012). These studies highlight the need to understand the systemic pathways and contingencies that render households vulnerable to energy poverty. What economic, social, spatial and governance systems and conditions render households and individuals vulnerable to energy poverty? For example, how does rural living or housing policy or centralised electricity networks coupled with low incomes lead to problems of energy access, affordability, reliability, quality or safety of energy sources for basic energy needs?

This chapter investigates the extent to which post-apartheid spatial inequalities and the built environment (re)produce energy vulnerability in South African cities. We will employ an energy vulnerability lens, which 'emphasises the systemic pathways and conditions that lead to the rise of material deprivation in the home' (Bouzarovski et al. 2015; Hodbod and Adger 2014) rather than the 'relatively static and reductionist perspectives embodied in mainstream fuel and energy poverty frameworks' (Bouzarovski et al. 2015). This will facilitate understanding how geographical contingencies drive energy vulnerability among the urban poor in South Africa. In particular, we explore how the urban poor are rendered vulnerable to energy poverty through: 1) transportation costs and restricted mobility, 2) the layout and material aspects of the built environment in townships and 3) a shortage of affordable housing.

The following section will discuss the systemic factors that drive energy poverty. The next section will discuss urban planning under apartheid and provide background to South Africa's current spatial inequality. The sections after that will then discuss mobility-induced energy vulnerability, followed by energy vulnerability caused by the built environment in townships focusing on the provision of electricity and energy efficiency. The final section will bring together the main findings from this chapter.

Understanding systemic factors that drive energy vulnerability

Energy poverty literature highlights that a full range of affordable, clean, safe and reliable energy services is required to participate in modern society and to provide economic development in terms of livelihood opportunities. Low incomes and high energy costs have been highlighted as important causes of energy deprivation. High costs of mobility due to fuel costs or long travel distances and a lack of affordable transport can also exclude households from economic opportunities and induce vulnerability to poverty (Sovacool et al. 2012).

At the individual and household level, research into energy strategies explores how people cope with high costs of energy, low incomes, unreliable supply or limited access to energy for various energy services. Energy-stacking and multi-fuel use strategies in households have been observed commonly in the literature, in which modern and traditional energy sources are used interchangeably for various reasons, including accessibility, affordability, reliability, quality and safety, as well as habit, familiarity, culture and traditions (Masera et al. 2000; Sovacool et al. 2012; van der Kroon et al. 2013). Bouzarovski et al. (2015), for example, explored the socio-technical legacies and state policies that drive energy vulnerability in Hungary and observed that some households switch from modern energy sources to traditional biomass (firewood) as a strategy to reduce energy expenditures. This trend was dominant in rural areas due to easily available firewood at low cost and more common in single-family houses than in multi-family apartment blocks, which tend not to have the storage, chimneys and other suitable infrastructure. Understanding these coping mechanisms provides insight into the conditions and pathways that render households vulnerable to energy poverty.

In addition, there is a range of socio-technical, financial and spatial conditions that drive vulnerability to energy poverty. The literature on socio-technical transitions, for example, recognises that energy systems are socio-technical systems consisting of physical infrastructure, such as pipes, distribution networks and generation plants as well as 'financial networks, workforces and the schools necessary to train them, institutions for trading in energy, roads, regulatory commissions, land-use rules, city neighbourhoods, and companies as well as social norms and values that assure their proper functioning' (Miller et al. 2013). Thus, to understand energy vulnerability, there is a need to understand the conditions and systemic factors that drive energy poverty. Yet, few studies have sought to understand the role of housing policy in shaping energy vulnerability among the urban poor. Exceptions to this are Buzar (2007a), who examined how national housing and social welfare policies have an impact on the material quality and thermal efficiency of housing and the ability and willingness of households to invest in energy efficiency measures in Czech Republic and Macedonia. The study reported that 'the demographic profiles of energy poverty are not entirely consistent with the more general pattern of income poverty' (Buzar 2007a) but that material quality and thermal efficiency of housing, over and above affordability, contribute to energy vulnerability. In the UK context, Cauvain and Bouzarovski (2016) also examine how a negative cultural perception of housing in multiple occupancy (HMO) undermines the recognition of energy deprivation in HMO as a serious policy issue.

In South Africa, there is some technical information about low-cost state-subsidised housing, including an assessment of the thermal performance of such housing compared to traditional style housing (Makaka and Meyer 2006); the effect of low-cost housing on health (Govender et al. 2011); and the costs and benefits of energy efficiency measures in low-cost housing (Winkler et al. 2002). Such studies suggest that the provision of low-cost housing may have a direct impact upon energy strategies and the energy expenditure burden of households. However, efforts directed at assessing energy poverty and monitoring the impact of various policies and programmes are output oriented and tend to measure the level of dissemination of energy access and consumption (Chen et al. 2015; Pachauri and Spreng 2011) whilst affordability of energy is generally measured by identifying the portion of household disposable income spent on energy (Winkler et al. 2011). Although these studies provide important insights into energy poverty strategies, they do not explore how deeper spatial patterns and configurations of marginalisation and structural inequality induce energy deprivation among the urban poor.

There is growing interest in the role of energy in shaping material infrastructure, uneven geographies of mobility and socio-political production of space, linked to geopolitics, urbanisation and consumption (Huber 2015), which may assist in understanding energy vulnerability. This study will contribute to this body of literature and will explore the ways in which the legacy of apartheid spatial segregation, housing policy and energy service provision remain systemic drivers of energy vulnerability in the case of South Africa.

Post-apartheid spatial inequalities shaping South Africa's cities

Spatial drivers of energy poverty and vulnerability, such as housing, infrastructure and location are important but under-theorised factors influencing people's ability to access energy infrastructure and households' energy expenditure burden. South Africa has a long history of spatial inequality, exclusion and marginalisation during colonial and apartheid regimes (Beall et al. 2000). During apartheid, neighbourhoods were designed to spatially separate 'Black, Indian, and Coloured' households from white neighbourhoods, restricting movement between areas (Turok 2014). The areas designated for non-white South Africans during apartheid are known colloquially as 'townships' or 'locations', and there is much empirical research about how these residential areas have been excluded and marginalised (Crankshaw et al. 2000, Lemanski 2009). For the purposes of this chapter, it is important to note that these non-white residential areas were not provided with electricity or any modern energy services compared to the white areas. Marquard (2006) states, 'white households were almost entirely electrified, whereas black households were largely not' (Marquard 2006). Figure 5.1 presents the radial model of apartheid-style planning, showing how physical infrastructure and geographical boundaries were used to racially and economically separate residential areas and industrial areas, giving prime and centrally located areas to its white population. Black, Indian and coloured people were designated much smaller areas in townships or locations on the urban peripheries.

This disproportionate allocation of land and the high demand for housing in South African cities resulted in high population densities in black townships. The 1918 Natives in Urban Areas Bill and subsequent Urban Areas Act in 1923 formalised townships to contain black urban migration and manage settlement growth more efficiently (Turok 2015). The 1934 Slums Act and eventually the 1950 Group Areas Act reinforced this racial segregation, and people were prevented from moving freely between different areas, resulting

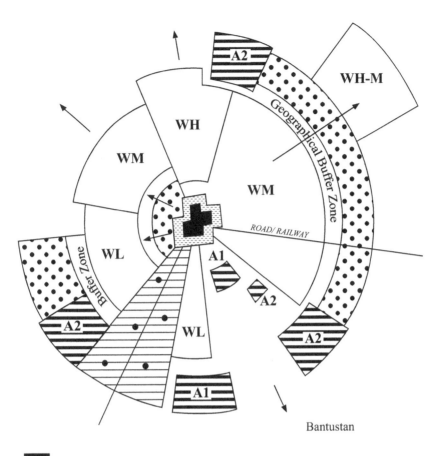

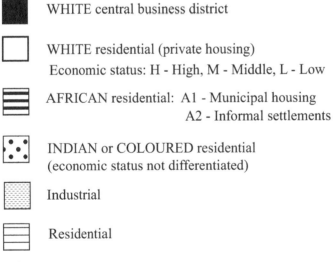

Figure 5.1 The spatial organisation of the Apartheid City

Source: Adapted from Davies (1981)

in high demand for accommodation in areas restricted to non-white people. The apartheid government actively prohibited black people from owning and building their own properties even in the townships, which resulted in a serious shortage of formal housing. Almost all black people permitted to live in the city were forced to rent accommodation in a hostel (consisting of dormitory-style housing built by private companies for their workers) or a state-owned council house (Crankshaw et al. 2000). Eventually, in 1986 under the rule of apartheid, the Abolition of Influx Control Act of 1986 lifted restrictions on urban migration to the cities. The unintended consequence of this act was the overpopulation of townships as citizens who were previously not allowed to move freely, now had an opportunity to go to the urban areas and look for work. The demand for accommodation in the black townships, however, was very high as the Group Areas Act of 1950 still prevented black people from living in the white, coloured or Indian areas. The scarcity of accommodation led to an increase of backyard dwellers as well as building of informal structures in the townships and on vacant land. The Group Areas Act was only repealed 5 years later in 1991.

The end of apartheid in 1994 brought a strong focus on the provision of housing, and programmes were designed to provide formal housing and title deeds to as many previously disadvantaged people as possible (Newton and Schuermans 2013). Between 1994 and 2007, the National Housing and Human Settlements programmes provided subsidies to local governments to build 2.3 million houses for indigent households (earning less than R3500/month) (Lemanski 2009) as part of the Reconstruction and Development Plan (RDP). These houses are often referred to as RDP homes and are typically 40m^2 stand-alone homes with a sub-division of up to 3 rooms depending on the specifications to the building contractor. The homes are on a single plot with some yard space, which allows homeowners to extend their houses with more rooms or build backyard dwellings (see section on backyard dwellings below) for income generation purposes and to accommodate extended family members. Unlike the typical township houses built during apartheid, RDP homes are fitted with electricity, water and sanitation systems to provide access to basic services.

Because the majority of state-subsidised houses were erected in or near townships or on undeveloped state land on the urban periphery, the implementation and roll out of state-subsidised housing in post-apartheid South Africa entrenched the sprawling segregation that characterises South African cities (Mabin et al. 2013; Seekings 2000; Turok 2015). Furthermore, the focus of the program did not include development of affordable rental accommodation in the main city centres to cope with urban migration, especially for temporary workers and many women – who for various reasons would prefer rental accommodation closer to economic opportunities and for impermanent periods of time (Crankshaw 1993; Goebel 2007). As a consequence, beneficiaries of RDP houses are known to rent out or sell their houses and move back to informal settlements closer to economic opportunities and places of work. Major reasons for this are the long travel distances, long travel times and higher costs of transport from these new locations (Goebel 2007; Huchzermeyer 2001).

The 'energy cost of exclusion': urban development and mobility

Energy enables the functioning of many modern transport systems and as such is often a crucial precondition for much everyday mobility. Mobility is therefore one of the important 'services' that energy provides, and an inability to attain contemporary mobility standards or expectations can exclude people from participating in society (Simcock and Mullen 2016). Yet mobility has received little attention in the energy poverty literature (Sovacool et al. 2012). Rode et al. (2014) review the path-dependency of urban from and transport upon human development and environmental sustainability in cities around the globe. Sprawling urban development leads to higher infrastructure, maintenance and operating costs than compact smart cities. Inadequate investment in public and non-motorised transport with an over-emphasis on private motorised transport results in restricted mobility, which negatively affects access to people, goods, services and information. Residing in townships, which are zoned residential and far from economic centres, reduces opportunities for the poor to increase their earning potential or shop for cheaper goods (Sovacool 2012).

In South Africa, the legacy of apartheid-style spatial planning is still evident in the presence of natural geographical features, green buffer zones and cemeteries, as well as infrastructure, bounded roads, highways and railway lines segregating neighbourhoods from one another. These geographical boundaries still very clearly prevent integration as can be seen in Figure 5.2, which shows how the

Figure 5.2 Manenberg and Phola Park separated by the railway line in Cape Town
Source: Johnny Miller 2016

dividing boundaries between Manenberg and Phola Park (Cape Town) separates 'formal' areas, on the left, and informal poverty-stricken areas, on the right.

Although racial segregation is slowly being replaced with class divisions and 'economic segregation' (Geyer and Mohammed 2015; Mbatha and Mchunu 2016), the geographic boundaries and buffer zones used by apartheid spatial planning still make it difficult for people to move through and from one area to the next and thus increases mobility-induced energy vulnerability. Post-apartheid urban housing programmes are widely criticised for perpetuating the spatial inequalities inherent in the former design of townships (Turok 2015). As extensions of townships in most cases, newly built state-subsidised housing projects force the urban poor to live further away from central business districts, economic opportunities and opportunities for social integration (Goebel 2007; Mabin et al. 2013; SACN 2016; Turok 2015). Without overcoming the geographical barriers and boundaries of apartheid planning, the urban poor now suffer from longer distances, higher transport costs and restricted mobility. The National Development Plan (NDP) and the draft White Paper (Towards a Policy Foundation for the Development of Human Settlements Legislation 2016) acknowledge these criticisms and the need to design inclusive cities and 'systematically respond to entrenched spatial patterns across all geographical scales that exacerbate social inequality and economic inefficiency'.

In addition to the establishment of buffer zones and geographic boundaries in urban spatial planning, the apartheid government purposefully limited public transport services to restrict movement between racially segregated areas (Barrett 2003). This is illustrated by the statement of an official involved with the implementation of Johannesburg's Rea Vaya:

> Compare Johannesburg with other major cities of the world and it becomes glaringly obvious that we don't have a public transport system. That is a direct legacy of apartheid. That was by design. It wasn't just that they forgot.
>
> (Wood 2014)

Despite pro-passenger transport policies post 1994, the long distances between places of work and people's residences have only been reinforced by post-apartheid urban settlement growth, which has further decentralised the city (Wood 2014) and increased the cost of transport. On average, the distances that South Africans commute is higher than most OECD countries (Kerr 2015). As a result, transport makes up approximately 17.1% of total household consumption expenditure (according to the StatSA Income and Expenditure Survey (IES) 2011). If the time cost of commuting is added to the total cost to households, the average proportion of income spent on public transport is 30% for commuters using minibus taxis, 40% for buses and 22% for trains (Kerr 2015). These are significant costs when considered under mobility-induced energy expenses. 'In Cape Town, commuters from peripheral locations spend around 50% more time travelling to work than more centrally located commuters within the same income bands' ((Behrens and Wilkinson 2003) cited in (Venter et al. 2007).

Along these lines, Czeglédy (2004) shows that there is a clear class distinction between commuters and the mode of transport that they can afford or which is available in their neighbourhood. For example, in newer, wealthier suburbs where rail infrastructure does not reach, wealthier commuters rely on private vehicles, and poorer commuters rely on minibus taxis and in some cases buses. These modes of transport are energy intensive, which result in high usage costs for individuals and households (Venter 2013).

The development of South Africa's post-apartheid city and the perpetuation of apartheid-style planning can, therefore, contribute significantly to energy vulnerability of those residing in townships. By increasing the costs of transportation-related energy costs, the urban form and growth-patterns of cities can reduce the disposable income of poor households even further, deepening patterns of poverty and inequality and rising material deprivation in the home. The next section will focus on the material aspects of the built environment in townships and how this is also a driver of energy vulnerability among the urban poor.

The provision of energy services in townships

The built environment in old and new townships has been heavily shaped by the implementation of national housing policies. The layout, poor-quality buildings, distance from economic opportunities and unmet demand for housing in townships all contribute to the vulnerability of households to energy poverty. This section will discuss material aspects of the built environment in townships with reference to case studies in the literature. We will first examine the recent history of electrification in townships. Thereafter, the energy and thermal efficiency of low-cost housing will be discussed, highlighting how the rollout of state-subsidised housing is a systemic factor driving energy vulnerability among the urban poor in South Africa.

Electrification

Prior to 1994, due to the exclusionary apartheid policies, less than a third of self-built housing and informal settlements in townships had electricity connections (Beall et al. 2000; Lloyd et al. 2004; Louw et al. 2008). As a result, most South Africans were forced to rely on polluting and inefficient fuels to meet their energy needs. Gaunt (2003) gives a brief history of energy provision in Khayelitsha (a location initially established in 1983 for black migrants to the city of Cape Town): grid electricity was only 'supplied to businesses, high mast area lighting and institutions like schools and community centres, but fees were too high for household connections' (Gaunt 2003). Although the initial intention was to provide fully serviced core housing, the government in an effort to keep pace with demand from in-migrants and reduce costs, built smaller houses with only water and sanitation services. To satisfy energy needs, households were expected to rely on local forests for firewood, supplemented by paraffin, liquefied petroleum gas (LPG) and candles. High urban concentrations and unsustainable harvesting caused a steep decline in local wood availability.

In the transition to democracy, numerous efforts were made to accommodate demand for affordable housing and provide basic services. Working independently of the housing programme, the Department of Energy (previously DME), Eskom and local municipalities were responsible for electrification. From 1994–2001, more than 3.4 million households were electrified (Winkler et al. 2011), and since 2002, the percentage of households connected to grid electricity has grown from 77% in 2002 to 86% in 2015 (StatsSA 2016). Table 5.1 provides a comparison of selected townships and the percentage of households with access to electricity in South Africa.

With a few exceptions, more than 90% of informal and formal households in the selected townships are electrified. The exceptions to this (Joe Slovo and Cato Manor) have the greatest percentage of informal dwellings (30.7% and 29% respectively), a number that is much higher than the country average (13.6%). Many informal dwellings cannot be electrified according to the National Guidelines for the Electrification of Unproclaimed Areas, which stipulates that informal dwellings located on private, unstable land, within zones prohibited for development (such as flood plains and road or rail reserves), cannot be electrified. To charge cellphones, power TVs and basic appliances such as irons and fans, unelectrified informal households make arrangements with formal neighbours to share electricity via an extension cord. Alternatively, they may pay for illegal connections albeit at their own risk.

Although South Africa's national electrification programme made significant improvements in providing access to electricity, many studies found that households cannot afford to use electricity or electrical appliances for all their cooking, lighting and heating needs, and instead they rely on multiple sources of energy (Mehlwana 1997; Musango 2014; White et al. 1997). Table 5.1 shows that households do not use electricity to satisfy all energy needs. At face value, the high rate of access to electricity in most townships (Table 5.1) suggests that the majority of households are not excluded from access to infrastructure. However, high electrification rates in these areas often do not equate to high usage of electricity services, mainly because many low-income households cannot afford the costs of electricity and are often disconnected or have irregular access. Energy poverty is therefore closely linked to income and affordability, whereby the energy expenditure burden for a poor rural or urban household can be as much as 18% of their household income (Winkler et al. 2011) compared to the norm of 10% established by the National Department of Energy (Kohler et al. 2009).

In an attempt to overcome energy deprivation in poor households, the Department of Energy introduced the Free Basic Energy (FBE) policy in 2003, which affords low-income households up to 50kWh of free electricity per month. This FBE allowance is allocated via electricity meters, which are installed in most houses. Households consuming more than 600kWh per month are assumed to be above the low-income bracket and do not receive this subsidy. However, although eligible for FBE, many households do not benefit from the policy because they share an electricity meter with one or more households, and as a result, they collectively consume more than 600kWh per month. It is common for a household

Table 5.1 Percentage of households with access to basic services in selected townships in South Africa

		% electrified	% use electricity for everything	% only use electricity for some things	Google maps distance from township centre to city hall
South Africa		85.3%	56%	29%	
Khayelitsha	Ward 92	99.6%	28%	71%	±30 min 32.3km from
	Ward 94	99.9%	25%	75%	Cape Town
Westlake	Ward 71	99.8%	68%	32%	±25 min 23.4km from Cape Town
Freedom	Ward 6	90.9%	41%	49%	±30 min 17.5km from
Square	Ward 7	91.6%	41%	51%	Bloemfontein
Joe Slovo	Ward 41	70.1%	47%	23%	±25 min 20.2km from Port Elizabeth
Alexandra	Ward 116	96.7%	90%	6%	±25 min 23.4km from Johannesburg
Cato Manor	Ward 29	75.1%	61%	14%	±16 min 8.1km from Durban
Adams Mission	Ward 67	92.8%	62%	31%	±37 min 36.4km from Durban

Source: 2011 Census data from wazimap.co.za

with a formal electricity meter to share electricity with informal neighbouring households and backyard tenants via an extension cord (Lemanski 2009). In addition, electricity tariffs are set using a block-tariff structure, meaning that the first 350kWh consumed in the month is cheaper (104c per kWh) than the next 250kWh (118c per kWh). As a consequence, the provision of electricity to other households via the formal dwelling's meter generally increases the monthly cost of energy. Households that consume more than 600kWh/month not only lose the right to the FBE subsidy, they also pay an increased rate due to a block-tariff structure. The high occurrence of informality is a key issue that inhibits such households from benefiting from FBE policy and constrains their access to energy.

Urban planning, rapid growth of cities and the lack of affordable rental housing have resulted in an increase in informal settlements and shacks erected in the backyards of formal houses. Although some informal settlements have access to electricity, many do not because municipalities are unable to keep pace with the demand for electricity in new settlements and are reluctant to electrify those that are not recognised in spatial planning. Huber (2015) warns that 'electricity networks not only reflect the uneven geographies of cities but actively reproduce them'. In practice, this means that many in South Africa's townships remain highly vulnerable to energy poverty. Depending on the location and plans to formalise the informal areas, people living in these areas may have to rely on other energy sources such as paraffin, kerosene, coal and biomass, which often bring significant costs for households, and will not allow them to benefit from FBE policies. Although policy has been made for Free Basic Alternative Energy

(FBAE), this policy is difficult to implement in practice, especially in urban informal areas. Therefore, understanding energy vulnerability requires consideration of the affordability of electricity for the poor and the opportunities they have to benefit from energy access policies. The following section will use the example of informal backyard dwellings, to explain how the unmet demand for the housing increases informality and excludes low-income households from the benefits of FBE.

Backyard dwellings – a response to the shortage of affordable housing

A further factor causing energy vulnerability in townships is the existence of backyard dwellings. In response to the housing shortage for coloured and black people in South Africa pre- and post-1994, and facilitated by the yard space of typical RDP houses, homeowners and occupiers in the backyards of formal plots erected informal backyard dwellings. About half of the houses in townships, especially those well located near the city centre, transport routes or employment opportunities, accommodated tenants in backyard dwellings (Lemanski 2009). Backyard dwellings are similar in construction quality to shacks in informal settlements, with the exception that they are situated on a demarcated plot within a formal, fully serviced housing area. 'Some backyards host multiple shacks, and landlords typically share electricity, water, sanitation and refuse collection with backyard tenants, in return for rent' (Lemanski 2009). Many backyard tenants feel that they have better access to infrastructure and greater tenure security in a backyard dwelling than in an informal settlement, which could face forced removals (Shapurjee and Charlton 2013). Because of this, Shapurjee and Charlton (2013) consider the phenomenon of backyard dwellings in state-subsidised housing programme as an opportunity rather than 'failed modernity' and emphasise that backyard dwellings are an entrepreneurial response of households to the demand for rental accommodation. However, the various arrangements for sharing electricity, water and use of the only toilet in the main house are challenging (Govender et al. 2011). In addition to health issues for both landlords and tenants caused by overcrowding, the backyard dwelling 'system' can increase vulnerability to energy poverty for those residing in the shacks.

Electricity is usually provided to backyard dwellers via an extension cord from the prepaid meter installed in the main house of a formal plot. Formal households function as the 'middle men' and supply electricity to informal backyard dwelling units or informal neighbouring households. Although the system enables 'cash-poor' landlords to earn a small income in rent and resale of services such as electricity and water (Lemanski 2009; Franks and Prasad 2014), there are significant issues associated with this system of energy provision, including an often unreliable connection, higher costs per unit of electricity and conflict. One issue is that, despite the existence of policies addressed at reducing energy poverty (the FBE and FBAE), there is no mechanism that allows the poor residing in backyard dwellings to benefit. Because the FBE guarantees 50kWh of electricity for free every month for *each household with a formal electricity meter*, the recipient of the FBE in the formal dwelling effectively shares the 50kWh with those in the backyard shack. As a consequence, in many cases, the 50kWh/month electricity subsidies (and the alternative energy subsidies) do not benefit the poorest households (Franks and Prasad 2014; Wolpe and Reddy 2010).

A second issue is that the lack of a mechanism for either tenant or landlord to accurately measure consumption rates between the house and backyard dwelling often results in tensions regarding over-consumption and under-payment. Because the landlords are the electricity provider, tenants are at the mercy of the landlords or formal households that control the electricity meter. In case of a conflict, landlords are able to curtail access to electricity (although at the risk of losing rental income), thereby rendering those residing the backyard shacks vulnerable to energy poverty (Lemanski 2009).

A third issue, like informal 'shacks', backyard dwellings are typically made of thermally inefficient building materials such as tin sheeting and thin Masonite boards. A survey conducted by DoE (2013) found that those living in informal dwellings or shacks tend to report higher or a moderately higher energy expenditure share on average than formal urban areas.

Energy efficiency

Electricity provision is not the sole contributor to energy vulnerability in a township setting. The built environment of townships in terms of energy efficiency and material quality of buildings can also be a key factor. The following two sections will discuss this issue.

'One house, one plot' – an aspiration and energy expenditure burden

Mbatha and Mchunu (2016) demonstrate that the black middle-class demand for stand-alone homes and yard space for traditional and cultural practices is in line with the 'American dream'-inspired notion of middle-class suburbia, where people can afford to invest in the quality of their homes. In an effort to redress the former exclusionary policies of apartheid, state-subsidised housing typically comprises single-story, freestanding dwellings with one or two rooms and a wash area, each on a single plot. The houses are small in size (varying from 27–45m² on plots that range between 65–250m²), and Huchzermeyer (2001) found that recipients were often disappointed with the size of the houses. The 'one house, one plot' approach of social housing in South Africa contributes to urban sprawl and is at odds with the development objectives of accessibility and compact cities (Rode et al. 2014). However, dense social housing options are typically associated with public housing and the hostels provided for black South Africans during apartheid and, for many, are a negative reminder of the apartheid era and are therefore unpopular. In contrast, freestanding houses represent land ownership and self-determination, a status which the majority of non-whites had no right to during apartheid (Winkler et al. 2002).

Freestanding houses, although preferred, are less thermally efficient than row housing (terraced or semi-detached homes), which share a common wall. Winkler et al. (2002) undertook a cost-benefit analysis of energy efficiency in low-cost social housing in South Africa and found that row housing and selected thermal improvements (such as ceilings) could result in significant economic and energy savings for beneficiaries and developers. However, most social housing projects in townships consist of freestanding houses (known as RDP houses). Beneficiaries of social housing therefore have a higher energy burden they would have if they were provided with semi-detached homes. The cost per metre of infrastructure supplied to freestanding homes is also more expensive than row housing due to the increased distances between houses. Despite the preference for freestanding homes, the 'one house, one plot' approach to social housing poses significant difficulties for the cost-effective provision of electricity to residents.

Energy efficiency in state-subsidised buildings

As explained above, the typical design of RDP homes can also lead to structural energy vulnerability. Energy inefficiency of buildings is an important contributor to this. Approximately 2.6 million housing units were built between 1994 and 2008 (Treasury 2012), and approximately 3.7 million housing opportunities have been created between 1994 and 2014, consisting of freestanding houses, social and rental housing (SACN 2016). Post-apartheid housing policy provided three options for beneficiaries earning less than R3500 per month to build a new house: 1) participate in the building of your own house, 2) receive a standard house built by contractors or 3) receive the equivalent value of a standard house as a contribution to buy an existing house. The most popular option was to receive a standard low-cost house (Huchzermeyer 2006; Newton and Schuermans 2013). Because the housing programme focused on providing low-cost accommodation for a large number of households, the new houses and associated infrastructure were of poor quality and require significant maintenance (Huchzermeyer 2001).

Most state-subsidised RDP houses are likely to have substandard thermal performance. For example, a study on the thermal performance of a selection of typical low-cost RDP houses in Alice Town in the Eastern Cape identified poor thermal performance, requiring higher energy consumption compared to traditional houses made of clay, grass or stone (Makaka and Meyer 2006). Marais and Ntema (2013) surveyed beneficiaries of subsidised housing and found low levels of satisfaction with the quality of building material, declining from 41% in 1998 to 35% in 2008, and quality of building work, declining from 76% in 1993 to 39% in 2008. Govender et al. (2011) investigated the poor quality of building materials and workmanship in Cape Town and found that almost 80% of formal RDP houses had leaking roofs, 68% had cracked walls, 60% had doors that did not fit well, 25% had broken windows and around half of the inside and outside walls were not painted. Based on evidence from a cost-benefit analysis of retrofitting houses in New Zealand with better insulation, Chapman et al. (2009) suggests that the value for money in improving housing quality and the associated environmental, energy and health benefits is high. Poor thermal performance, and the higher energy costs associated with it, can therefore render households vulnerable to energy poverty.

Table 5.2 Requirements to improve construction of RDP houses set out in the National Housing Code 2013

Thermal performance	The installation of a ceiling with the prescribed air gap for the entire dwelling
	The installation of above-ceiling insulation comprising of a 130 mm mineral fibreglass blanket for the entire house
	Plastering of all internal walls
	Rendering on external walls
	Smaller size windows
	Special low E clear and E opaque safety glass for all windows
Electrical installation requirements	Lights and plugs in all living areas of the house

To overcome the poor thermal performance of low-cost housing the National Housing Code was revised in 2013 for new builds and retrofitting existing RDP houses. The key requirements are shown in Table 5.2.

In addition to the range of thermal performance requirements set out in Table 5.2, the contractors are also required to adhere to basic electrical installation requirements, comprising of lights and plugs to all living areas of the house. Previously, contractors were only expected to install a pre-paid metering board. Although these measures improve energy efficiency and hereby may reduce energy vulnerability, it is also possible that they have some negative externalities. For example, there is an inherent risk that the revised standards would cause the house to be too expensive to subsidise or maintain for beneficiaries (SACN 2016). This is illustrated by Winkler et al. (2002), who estimate that investments to retrofit low-cost RDP houses with ceilings, wall insulation and smaller windows range from R1000–R2000 per household. Although this offers substantial benefits to households and considerable energy savings over the lifetime of the house, thereby reducing energy vulnerability, many struggle afford these investments or are not interested in taking a loan (Lemanski 2009). As a consequence, energy vulnerability persists.

Conclusion

This chapter has explored how spatial inequality in urban design and the implementation of housing policy and energy service provision in post-apartheid South Africa are systemic drivers of energy vulnerability among the urban poor. Persistent energy poverty and vulnerability has been shown to result from a number of factors, including:

1   The continuation of the planning patterns adopted under the apartheid regime has resulted in spatial inequality and perpetuated residential segregation. The peripheral locations of many townships contribute to energy vulnerability for the urban poor, as it leads to high transportation costs and restricted mobility.

2   The sprawling urban patterns characterised by low-density housing increase energy infrastructure costs. The desire for freestanding housing to restore pre-apartheid traditions, culture and dignity, as well as aspirations for housing resembling that of affluent suburbs, reduces the thermal efficiency of freestanding dwellings.
3   Persisting patterns of informality, resulting from insufficient affordable housing, increase energy prices for the poor. Furthermore, dependence on 'middlemen' for electricity provision renders them vulnerable to conflict and unreliable connection and hinders the effective implementation of policies aimed at addressing lack of energy access for the poor.
4   The enormous challenges of providing low-cost housing for its poorest citizens have caused the government to adopt a 'quantity over quality' approach in its state-subsidised housing programme. This approach has resulted in houses that have poor thermal performance, dramatically increasing the cost of energy for poor households.

This chapter has shown how post-apartheid spatial inequalities and conditions of the built environment may lead to the rise of material deprivation in the home and are systemic drivers of energy vulnerability among the urban poor in South Africa. This resembles spatial patterns of inequality and energy deprivation related to state housing programmes and policies identified in Hungary (Bouzarovski et al. 2015), in Eastern and Central Europe (Buzar 2007b; Buzar 2007a) and in the UK (Bouzarovski and Cauvain 2016), but the drivers of energy poverty in South Africa are also deeply embedded in the country's particular historical, political, spatial, social and cultural context. Breaking down spatial inequalities together with economic, racial and gender inequalities (as discussed by Großmann and Kahlheber in Chapter 2) and addressing energy vulnerability require a holistic approach involving town planning and housing programmes, as well as the transport and energy sectors. The potential of pro-poor energy policy in South Africa, and the challenges associated with its implementation, is discussed in detail by Wolpe and Reddy in Chapter 14.

References

Annecke, W. (1999). *Non-economic determinants of energy use in rural areas of South Africa.* Springfield, VA: Energy and Development Research Centre, University of Cape Town.
Barrett, J. (2003). *Organizing in the informal economy: A case study of the minibus taxi industry in South Africa.* Geneva: International Labour Office.
Beall, J., Crankshaw, O. and Parnell, S. (2000). Local government, poverty reduction and inequality in Johannesburg. *Environment and Urbanization,* 12, 107–122.
Behrens, R. and Wilkinson, P. (2003). *Housing and urban passenger transport policy and planning in South African cities: A problematic relationship.* Cape Town: UCT Press.
Bouzarovski, S. and Cauvain, J. (2016). *Spaces of exception: Governing fuel poverty in England's multiple occupancy housing sector.* Available at: http://dx.doi.org.ezproxy.uct.ac.za/10.1080/13562576.2016.1228194.
Bouzarovski, S. and Petrova, S. (2015). A global perspective on domestic energy deprivation: Overcoming the energy poverty – fuel poverty binary. *Energy Research & Social Science,* 10, 31–40.

Bouzarovski, S., Tirado herrero, S., Petrova, S. and Ürge-vorsatz, D. (2015). Unpacking the spaces and politics of energy poverty: Path-dependencies, deprivation and fuel switching in post-communist Hungary. *Local Environment*, 1–20.

Buzar, S. (2007a). The 'hidden' geographies of energy poverty in post-socialism: Between institutions and households. *Geoforum*, 38, 224–240.

Buzar, S. (2007b). When homes become prisons: The relational spaces of postsocialist energy poverty. *Environment and Planning A*, 39, 1908–1925.

Cabraal, R. A., Barnes, D. F. and Agarwal, S. G. (2005). Productive uses of energy for rural development. *Annual Review of Environment and Resources*, 30, 117–144.

Cauvain, J. and Bouzarovski, S. (2016). Energy vulnerability in multiple occupancy housing: A problem that policy forgot. *People, Place and Policy*, 10, 88–106.

Chapman, R., Howden-Chapman, P., Viggers, H., O'dea, D. and Kennedy, M. (2009). Retrofitting houses with insulation: A cost – benefit analysis of a randomised community trial. *Journal of Epidemiology and Community Health*, 63, 271–277.

Chen, X., Narkeviciute, R., Haselip, J. and Mackenzie, G. A. (2015). Developing and testing a best practice framework for energy access interventions. *Sustainable Development*, 23, 257–272.

Clancy, J., Mohlakoana, N. and Matinga, M. (2013). *Energy poverty: Have we got the measure of it?* UK Development Studies Association Conference 2013, 2013/11/16/ 2013, University of Birmingham.

Crankshaw, O. (1993). Squatting, apartheid and urbanisation on the Southern Witwatersrand. *African Affairs*, 92, 31–51.

Crankshaw, O., Gilbert, A. and Morris, A. (2000). Backyard Soweto. *International Journal of Urban and Regional Research*, 24, 841–857.

Czeglédy, A. P. (2004). Getting around town: Transportation and the built environment in post-apartheid South Africa. *City & Society*, 16, 63–92.

Davies, R. J. (1981). The spatial formation of the South African city. *GeoJournal Supplementary*, 59–72.

DOE. (2013). *Survey of energy related behaviour and perceptions in South Africa: The residential sector*. Pretoria, South Africa: RSA, Department of Energy.

Franks, L. and Prasad, G. (2014). *Informal electricity re-selling: Entrepreneurship or exploitation? Energy Research Centre*. South Africa: University of Cape Town.

Gaunt, T. (2003). *Electrification technology and processes to meet economic and social objectives in Southern Africa*. PhD thesis, University of Cape Town, Department of Electrical Engineering.

Geyer, H. S. and Mohammed, F. (2015). Hypersegregation and class-based segregation processes in Cape Town 2001–2011. *Urban Forum*, 27, 35–58.

Goebel, A. (2007). Sustainable urban development? Low-cost housing challenges in South Africa. *Habitat International*, 31, 291–302.

Govender, T., Barnes, J. M. and Pieper, C. H. (2011). Housing conditions, sanitation status and associated health risks in selected subsidized low-cost housing settlements in Cape Town, South Africa. *Habitat International*, 35, 335–342.

Hodbod, J. and Adger, W. N. (2014). Integrating social-ecological dynamics and resilience into energy systems research. *Energy Research & Social Science*, 1, 226–231.

Huber, M. (2015). Theorizing energy geographies. *Geography Compass*, 9, 327–338.

Huchzermeyer, M. (2001). Housing for the poor? Negotiated housing policy in South Africa. *Habitat International*, 25, 303–331.

Huchzermeyer, M. (2006). Challenges facing people-driven development in the context of a strong, delivery-oriented state: Joe Slovo village, Port Elizabeth. *Urban Forum*, 17, 25–53.

Kerr, A. (2015). Tax(i)ing the poor? Commuting costs in South Africa. Working Paper 156. Cape Town: South African Labour & Development Research Unit (SALDRU), University of Cape Town.

Kimemia, D. K. and Annegarn, H. J. (2012). Productive uses of basic energy and fuel transitions in Urban South Africa. *Energy and Environment Research*, 2.

Kohler, M., Rhodes, B. and Vermaak, C. (2009). Developing an energy-based poverty line for South Africa. *Journal of Interdisciplinary Economics*.

Kooijman-Van Dijk, A. L. and Clancy, J. (2010). Impacts of electricity access to rural enterprises in Bolivia, Tanzania and Vietnam. *Energy for Sustainable Development*, 14, 14–21.

Lemanski, C. (2009). Augmented informality: South Africa's backyard dwellings as a by-product of formal housing policies. *Habitat International*, 33, 472–484.

Lloyd, P., Cowan, B. and Mohlakoana, N. (2004). Improving access to electricity and stimulation of economic growth and social upliftment. *ResearchGate*. Available at: https://www.researchgate.net/publication/237453756_Improving_access_to_electricity_and_stimulation_of_economic_growth_and_social_upliftment.

Louw, K., Conradie, B., Howells, M. and Dekenah, M. (2008). Determinants of electricity demand for newly electrified low-income African households. *Energy Policy*, 36, 2812–2818.

Lues, J. F. R., Rasephei, M. R., Venter, P. and Theron, M. M. (2006). Assessing food safety and associated food handling practices in street food vending. *International Journal of Environmental Health Research*, 16, 319–328.

Mabin, A., Butcher, S. and Bloch, R. (2013). Peripheries, suburbanisms and change in sub-Saharan African cities. *Social Dynamics*, 39, 167–190.

Makaka, G. and Meyer, E. (2006). Temperature stability of traditional and low-cost modern housing in the Eastern Cape, South Africa. *Journal of Building Physics*, 30, 71–86.

Marais, L. and Ntema, J. (2013). The upgrading of an informal settlement in South Africa: Two decades onwards. *Habitat International*, 39, 85–95.

Marquard, A. (2006). *The origins and development of South African energy policy*. PhD thesis, University of Cape Town.

Masera, O. R., Saatkamp, B. D. and Kammen, D. M. (2000). From linear fuel switching to multiple cooking strategies: A critique and alternative to the energy ladder model. *World Development*, 28, 2083–2103.

Mbatha, S. and Mchunu, K. (2016). Tracking peri-urban changes in eThekwini Municipality – beyond the 'poor – rich' dichotomy. *Urban Research & Practice*, 1–15.

Mehlwana, A. M. (1997). The anthropology of fuels: Situational analysis and energy use in urban low-income townships of South Africa. *Energy for Sustainable Development*, 3, 5–15.

Miller, C. A., Iles, A. and Jones, C. F. (2013). The social dimensions of energy transitions. *Science as Culture*, 22, 135–148.

Mills, E., Gengnagel, T. and Wollburg, P. (2014). Solar-LED alternatives to fuel-based Lighting for night fishing. *Energy for Sustainable Development*, 21, 30–41.

Musango, J. K. (2014). Household electricity access and consumption behaviour in an urban environment: The case of Gauteng in South Africa. *Energy for Sustainable Development*.

Newton, C. and Schuermans, N. (2013). More than twenty years after the repeal of the Group Areas Act: Housing, spatial planning and urban development in post-apartheid South Africa. *Journal of Housing and the Built Environment*, 28, 579–587.

Pachauri, S. and Spreng, D. (2011). Measuring and monitoring energy poverty. *Energy Policy*, 39, 7497–7504.

Rode, P., Floater, G., Thomopoulos, N., Docherty, J., Schwinger, P., Mahendra, A. and Fang, W. (2014). *Accessibility in cities: Transport and urban form* New Climate

Economy (NCE) Cities Paper: 03. London: LSE Cities. Available at: https://lsecities.net/publications/reports/the-new-climate-economy-report/?/files/1022/60477.html.

SACN. (2016). *State of South African cities Report 2016*. Johannesburg: SACN.

Seekings, J. (2000). Introduction: Urban studies in South Africa after Apartheid. *International Journal of Urban and Regional Research*, 24, 832–840.

Shapurjee, Y. and Charlton, S. (2013). Transforming South Africa's low-income housing projects through backyard dwellings: Intersections with households and the state in Alexandra, Johannesburg. *Journal of Housing and the Built Environment*, 28, 653–666.

Simcock, N. and Mullen, C. (2016). Energy demand for everyday mobility and domestic life: Exploring the justice implications. *Energy Research & Social Science*, 18, 1–6.

Sovacool, B. K. (2012). The political economy of energy poverty: A review of key challenges. *Energy for Sustainable Development*, 16, 272–282.

Sovacool, B. K., Cooper, C., Bazilian, M., Johnson, K., Zoppo, D., Clarke, S., Eidsness, J., Crafton, M., Velumail, T. and Raza, H. A. (2012). What moves and works: Broadening the consideration of energy poverty. *Energy Policy*, 42, 715–719.

StatsSA. (2016). Housing from a human settlement perspective, in-depth analysis of the General Household Survey data 2002–2014. In *GHS Series Volume VII*. Pretoria: Statistics South Africa.

Treasury, R. S. A. (2012). *Chapter 6 – Human settlements*. Pretoria: National Treasury, RSA.

Turok, I. (2014). South Africa's tortured urbanisation and the complications of reconstruction. In McGranahan, G. and Martine, G. (eds.) *Urban growth in emerging economies: Lessons from the BRICS*. London: Earthscan, pp. 143–189.

Turok, I. (2015). South Africa's new urban agenda: Transformation or compensation? *Local Economy*, 0269-094215614259.

Van Der Kroon, B., Brouwer, R. and Van Beukering, P. J. H. (2013). The energy ladder: Theoretical myth or empirical truth? Results from a meta-analysis. *Renewable and Sustainable Energy Reviews*, 20, 504–513.

Venter, C. (2013). The lurch towards formalisation: Lessons from the implementation of BRT in Johannesburg, South Africa. *Research in Transportation Economics*, 39, 114–120.

Venter, C., Vokolkova, V. and Michalek, J. (2007). Gender, residential location, and household travel: Empirical findings from low-income urban settlements in Durban, South Africa. *Transport Reviews*, 27, 653–677.

White, C., Bank, L., Jones, S. and Mehlwana, M. (1997). Restricted electricity use among poor urban households. *Development Southern Africa*, 14, 413–423.

Winkler, H., Simões, A. F., Rovere, E. L. L., Alam, M., Rahman, A. and Mwakasonda, S. (2011). Access and affordability of electricity in developing countries. *World Development*, 39, 1037–1050.

Winkler, H., Spalding-Fecher, R., Tyani, L. and Matibe, K. (2002). Cost-benefit analysis of energy efficiency in urban low-cost housing. *Development Southern Africa*, 19, 593–614.

Wolpe, P. and Reddy, Y. (2010). *Alleviating energy poverty in the informal sector: The role for local government*. Overcoming inequality structural poverty in South Africa: Towards inclusive growth and development, Sustainable Energy Africa.

Wood, D. A. (2014). *Transforming the postapartheid city through bus rapid transit*. Available at: http://eprints.ncl.ac.uk.

6 Water-energy nexus vulnerabilities in China

Infrastructures, policies, practices

Alison Browne, Saska Petrova, and Beth Brockett

Introduction: the water-energy nexus in China

In recent years, driven by the three imperatives of security of supply, environmental sustainability and economic efficiency, the water and energy (WE) sectors have undergone rapid reform in many countries. Most developed countries have seen the introduction of highly developed management strategies in the energy sector that have affected the structure, ownership and regulatory arrangements of that sector (Marsh and Deepak 2007). The 'nexus approach' has been rendered a 'new kid on the block' for policy and academic discourse (Allouche et al. 2015; Cairns and Krzywoszynska 2016) that has been linked to modes of participatory decision-making (Wilson and Swyngedouw 2014). The benefits of addressing the interconnectivities (nexus) between WE resource and other environmental issues have increasingly been identified within international research and policy circles (Scott et al. 2011).[1] Specific aspects of the nexus of WE such as the national and regional security of supply (Bizikova et al. 2013; Hoff 2011; World Economic Forum 2011) have received ample academic and policy attention (Allan et al. 2015).

However, by offering managerial market security via technological innovations, this approach undermines and obscures its politics (Williams et al. 2014; Allouche et al. 2015), rendering it what we might call 'post-political' (Wilson and Swyngedouw 2014). The politicised tensions, socio-ecological processes and technologies that characterise the WE nexus, as revealed by studies in global political ecology (Peet et al. 2010), are a scarce minority in international literature (Kenway et al. 2011). The debate about the nexus also strongly misses any deep discussion of how vulnerabilities are produced and maintained through WE infrastructural and governance developments and how homes – and by extension their social, political and material interconnectivities – are key sites of reproduction, transformation and innovation of water and energy use (Fam et al. 2015).

China has witnessed unprecedented economic, social and environmental transformations – particularly in regards to the built landscape and domestic life – which have fundamentally altered the provision and use of WE resources. There are multiple resource crises emerging across China related to water scarcity and water quality, energy efficiency and low-carbon development (Liu and Yang

2012; Harvey 2014; Liu et al. 2013). Numerous interdependencies have been identified between these WE crises. At a fundamental level, energy generation requires water and energy for water treatment and transportation. In the residential sector, everyday practices related to various energy services such as heating, cooking and showering also depend on both energy and water resources. Still, WE resources and services are often framed separately within the technical and governance literatures (Harvey 2014; Liu et al. 2015). In China, recent efforts to expand research on the WE nexus have focused on city-level changes and a push towards quantification of the inputs and outputs of water, energy and food across multiple regions (Liu et al. 2015). The interconnectivities between WE resource use in the residential sector and wider infrastructural developments have remained largely unpacked, as have any reflections on WE nexus vulnerabilities.

Infrastructures, practices and politics of the WE nexus in China are 'on the move' due to large-scale regional transformations and changing economic, social and cultural contexts (e.g. Hubacek et al. 2009). Examples of these dynamics include: rural to urban migration, public to private provisioning of resource services, increased inequalities between rich and poor within and across regions and rapid urbanisation. Energy consumption in China has increased with economic growth and urban transformation (Zhu et al. 2014). Domestic water and energy consumption in China is expected to at least double by 2020 (Finlayson et al. 2013; Jiang 2009; Seckler et al. 1999). This is partly explained by improved resource provisioning and changing practices for clothes and dish washing, heating homes, personal hygiene and cooking (Plappally and Lienhard 2012). Existing research on energy and water demand in China retreats into a familiar focus on changing behaviour through individual motivational factors alone (such as conservation attitudes of urban householders, willingness to pay, price signalling and consumer choice) (Chang 2013; Wang et al. 2008) or technological and infrastructural development and efficiencies.

Mega-infrastructural developments – such as the South-to-North Water Transfer Project (SNWTP, Rogers et al. 2016) – are developed to support these exponential rises in demand of water and energy particularly in Chinese megacities. Such infrastructural developments are enacted with little consideration of what, how much and who is demanding these resources and resultant services (see for example Barnett et al. 2015). There is also little consideration of how such infrastructural developments are complicit in producing different spatial and temporal vulnerabilities and inequalities. While there are critical accounts emerging related to the governmentality and conduct of resource development (see Rogers et al. 2016), there remains an opportunity to critically reflect on the socio-material changes of water and energy systems across China.

Recognising a call from Liu et al. (2016) across the sustainable consumption and production literatures related to China, we attempt to bring a discussion of changing systems of provision for water and energy alongside a discussion of energy-water services and evolving practices. Connecting with the themes of the book identified in Chapter 1, within this chapter we use a number of examples from the grey and academic literatures to interrogate the interconnectivities between water and energy across various scales in China and elucidate the ways in which these interconnections produce multiple types of (spatially uneven) vulnerability. In this chapter, vulnerability is defined as the risks of people receiving inadequate levels of materially and socially necessitated WE resources and services as a result of transformations of infrastructure, governance and everyday life more broadly in China (based on Bouzarovski and Petrova 2015). We begin to conceptualise how vulnerabilities and spatial inequalities are produced and maintained at different spatial scales when considering the development of WE infrastructure and governance in a Chinese context.

China's spatially uneven WE challenges: exploring the regional WE nexus

Energy and water supply – and issues of rising resource demand – are serious issues for China. The country is facing one of the world's most severe water crises encompassing water shortages, water pollution and deterioration of aquatic ecosystems (Li et al. 2016; Liu and Yang 2012). China's available per capita water resources are only one quarter of the world average (Liu and Diamond 2005). Water use efficiency and water resource productivity (GDP output per unit water use) is low compared to other countries (Ali et al. 2016; Xie 2009), and China's water deficit is increasing year-on-year (Jiang and Ramaswami 2015). The dynamics of demand for water has changed in China over time – for example, residential demand has risen over time and residential wastewater discharge is now comparable to industrial and agricultural withdrawal (*Ibid.*). Populations in 630 Chinese cities are threatened by water pollution (WWF China 2016), and over 300 million rural people are without access to safe supplies of drinking water or sanitation (J. Liu et al. 2016; Zhang 2012). Despite reliable supply, water quality is major concern – for example, household residents often use varieties of bottled water (including large mounted bottled jugs) or have filtering systems fitted within kitchens to ameliorate the risk of tap water.

Regarding the interconnectivities between WE, the Chinese energy sector accounts for approximately 17% of total freshwater withdrawal, with the electricity generation sector having the fastest growing water demand (Jiang and Ramaswami 2015). Coal contributes more than 70% of China's electricity portfolio and electricity generation by coal is 'thirsty', especially the cooling process (Jiang and Ramaswami 2015). This is particularly a problem in water-scarce areas. For example, Shandong, a fast-growing city (its population grew 10% between 2013 and 2014; No author 2015) on the east coast of China, has a large number of coal-fired power stations but is a water-scarce province (Jiang and Ramaswami 2015). These WE infrastructural interconnectivities also reflect China's commitment to wide-scale hydropower development (Feng et al. 2014).

Water and energy resource planning and management have been undergoing major economic, governance and infrastructural reforms in China over the past few decades (Liu et al. 2015). Residential demand for electricity has an annual average growth rate of 12.35% (Zheng et al. 2014) and is linked to urbanisation and the rise in purchase and use of consumer goods such as 'air conditioners, computers, shower heaters and microwave ovens' (Zheng et al. 2014, 126). Electricity generation more than doubled between 2005 and 2015, and it is estimated that China's dependence on foreign oil will soar to 60% by 2020 (Downs et al. 2000), and despite the search for energy alternatives, oil imports continue to rise (see for example, Sun et al. 2014; Wu 2014; Zhang et al. 2013). In 2011, China became the world's largest energy consumer and generator with industrial consumption accounting for three quarters of China's electricity consumption; per capita consumption continues to rise fast too (Du et al. 2015).

In response to these challenges, various levels of the Chinese government are implementing strategies for creating water and energy efficiencies across Chinese society. For example, the Chinese Central Government initiated the 'Building a Water Saving Society' programme in 2002 (*Ibid.*). Energy reform also features in other policy announcements, such as China's first National Action Plan on Climate Change published in 2007 (National Development and Reform Commission 2007). In January 2011, the government's annual 'Number 1 Document,' which reflects its top priorities, outlined a plan to expedite water conservancy development and reform and to achieve sustainable use and management of water resources within a decade (Gu et al. 2016). National township and village electrification programmes began in 2001, and China's 12th Five Year Plan outlined that China would meet 11.4% of its primary energy requirements from non-fossil sources by 2015.[2] When announcing the draft 13th Five Year Plan in 2016 Premier Li Keqiang reported that China had met the environmental goals identified in the previous plan such as non-fossil-fuelled energy targets (Seligsohn and Hsu 2016). A number of other studies have also reported that availability of energy efficiency subsidies had helped many households to purchase more energy-efficient appliances in their homes (Zheng et al. 2014). While the reforms of WE systems focus on science and technology, and market-based policy solutions to address ever-increasing demands, transformative changes of 'end-use' practices have received comparatively less attention.

Modernisation and development of WE infrastructures have had uneven effects across China. This is particularly impactful as much of the country – for example Western and Central China – has yet to be fully urbanised (Wang 2014; Wang et al. 2015). However, unlike many other countries in the Global South, China has achieved near universal rural electrification through a state-sponsored but bottom-up approach to electricity development (Bhattacharyya and Ohiare 2012). However, electricity still plays a minor role in energy consumption in rural China – the large increase in rural energy consumption do not relate to electricity use but to higher demand for coal and non-commercial energy (*Ibid*). Bhattacharyya and Ohiare (2012) have also registered differences in consumption patterns of energy, particularly between the north and south. Water supply rates, and water demand, are also high. However, an understanding of access to water in China cannot be thought about as simply infrastructural access to any form of water but, given the serious issues with water quality across the country, as access to *safe* water (Tao and Xin 2014). While water access and supply may be improved, the vast contamination of various types of water (groundwater, river systems, reservoirs and contaminated tap/potable water) leaves many areas with water sources that are either undrinkable (Tao and Xin 2014) or are perceived by citizens to be so (Jianjun et al. 2016).

There are still large disparities in the quality and standards of WE supplies between urban and rural areas of China (Liu et al. 2013; Zheng et al. 2014). There is also an intersectionality (nexus) of energy and mobility related to energy transportation, which also produces various vulnerabilities. Specifically, internal transport capacity limitations affect consistency of energy supply. Coal needs to be moved from the coalfields of the north of China to power generation centres in central, eastern and southern China. Some regions experience regular electricity shortages due to increased heating demands and problems with coal delivery to power stations in winter (Cornot-Gandolphe 2014). In general, the rail system struggles to deliver the quantity of coal needed by power stations, especially during adverse weather conditions (Cornot-Gandolphe 2014).

Securing supply to meet WE demand in cities may further exacerbate insecurities of supply in rural areas (Zhang 2012; Wang 2014) and exacerbate already existing conflict between regions (He et al. 2014). For example, in the Beijing area (that is the evolving Jingjinji megalopolis which includes the cities of Beijing, Tianjin, Shandong and Hebei) per capita availability of water is well below the internationally-defined 1000m^3 per person per year extreme water scarcity threshold (Liu et al. 2012). The major water sources (Huang, Huai and Hai Rivers) already have use-availability ratios between 59%–123% (Jiang and Ramaswami 2015); above 40% is considered to be cause for alarm (Liu et al. 2012). The ever-growing WE demands of megalopolises like Jingjinji rely heavily on 'imported' resources. Such rising demands 'legitimise' the development of megaprojects such as the South-North Water Transfer Project (SNWTP), reallocating water from regional and agricultural areas and creating water resources and hydropower for thirsty and energy-hungry megacities. There are strong interregional vulnerabilities related to these developments – from the human impacts of forced resettlement, to the impacts on agricultural communities in terms of reduced water resource allocation. Critical questions about *whose* demand are being met, at what cost or how these WE services could be alternatively provisioned are rarely considered.

With many cities relying on long distance/inter-river basin water transfer (like the SNWTP), some regions are asked to bear the costs of storing and transferring water or to sacrifice their own water rights in the interests of other provinces (He et al. 2014). In relation to water, there are often conflicts during periods of drought with upstream areas overusing allocation quotas leaving less for downstream provinces, despite existing water licensing and trading schemes (*Ibid.*). Regarding energy, Mischke and Xiong (2015) highlight that there are major disparities in the energy system across China and that the future development of China's energy infrastructure needs to reflect and be linked with this (uneven) regional economic and infrastructural development. Given the amount of electricity and energy that major mega-cities import from other regions of China – for example Beijing imports 70% and Shanghai 33% of electricity – such interregional dynamics are significant for WE resource use (Liu et al. 2012).

WE resources are distributed unevenly across China and do not match well with centres of population, industry or agriculture (Liu et al. 2012). In general, water is 'abundant in the south and scarce in the north' (per capita possession of water resource in the north is one quarter of that in the south), and this is 'not in coincidence with the spatial distribution of [agricultural] land and mineral resources and [industrial] productivity' (Liu et al. 2012, 6). For example, China's fastest growing industrial areas are predominantly in the east (e.g. Shanghai-Zhejiang) and south of the country (e.g. Guangdong, Fujian) (Mischke and Xiong 2015). North of the Yangtze River also has 60% of China's electricity generation capacity but only 17% of the water resources (Jiang and Ramaswami 2015). China's coalfields are located in the north-east (Heilongjiang, Jilin, Liaoning); north-west (Inner Mongolia); and north (Shanxi, Shaanxi, Henan) regions of China, and the majority of China's hydropower capacity is situated in the south-west of China (Sichuan, Yunnan and Tibet).

Water resource availability is also variable by river basin with, for example, most resource concentrated in the Yangtze, Pearl and other basins in the south-east and south-west of China (Liu et al. 2012). However, resources in these basins are also adversely affected by unregulated abstraction, pollution and variation in climate. For example, the drought of spring 2011 led to water levels in the Yangtze Basin falling, and, as well as leading to water supply issues (quantity and quality) (Liu et al. 2012), electricity supply reliant on hydropower failed (Watts 2011). Such droughts are expected to become more frequent due to global climate change (exacerbated by over-abstraction), and there is already evidence that the north and north-east regions of China are becoming drier (Piao et al. 2010). In a country increasing its reliance on 'green energy' such as hydropower, the interdependencies between water and energy resource systems become more significant (Parkes 2015).

There are also significant interconnectivities between infrastructures and practices (albeit this example focuses on the nexus between energy and food in everyday practices). In their on-going research, W. Liu et al. (2013) have found that per capita energy use in rural areas is increasing year on year (with the majority coming from traditional biomass use) and that overall rural consumption of energy is out-pacing urban when different fuel sources are taken into account (see also Bhattacharyya and Ohiare 2012). There is a steady increase in household energy consumption in rural areas and a shortage of commercial energy and biomass provision in these regions in general (W. Liu et al. 2013). There has been a trend in rural China of using a greater diversity of energy sources (such as coal, non-commercial energy sources like biomass stoves, etc.), and these rural energy transitions are accompanied by an increase in carbon emissions – linked to the increased use of commercial energy consumption, plus continued use of diverse fuel sources in homes and rising energy intensity (Du et al. 2015). This story of rising energy consumption in rural areas is one of interconnectivities between infrastructural development and local preferences and practices. People in many rural areas still use (and prefer to use) coal stoves and biomass for cooking and space heating rather than using electrical or LPG appliances, even in areas that have been electrified – despite the potential to mitigate climate change, reduce local pollution and increase health outcomes through the reduction of biomass fuels. In relation to cooking, W. Liu et al. (2013, 136) explain

> This is because [householders] judge the resulting food [cooked on electric or LPG cookers] to be distasteful. They prefer to eat that kind of food when cooked on a traditional biomass stove. This is one reason why some households reserve stoves combusting firewood or corncob for cooking.

Such examples point to the fact that policies that aim to change WE infrastructures should not just focus on the technological or environmental performance of energy fuels but also how these fuels intersect with local cultural preferences and everyday practices.

In summary, WE resource crises in China are strongly interconnected and widely spatially variable. The rural-urban, North-South unevenness of resource provision, resource quality and preferences in consumption outlined in this section produces a range of interconnected vulnerabilities and inequalities from the household to regional levels. In this section, we have highlighted a few examples of the ways in which these local and national vulnerabilities interconnect between water, energy and other environmental issues. However, in highlighting these dynamics, we implore that WE nexus vulnerabilities and spatial inequalities should be taken forward as an essential area of research for China. Conceptualising, and finding evidence for, the ways in which current WE systems in China produce, perpetuate and maintain existing infrastructural and lived vulnerabilities should be a pressing research and policy priority. Increased focus should be paid to the way that WE infrastructures, policies and practices increase vulnerability *within* and *between* city regions (e.g. linked to Hukou and tenure; rising urban income inequalities etc.) and rural-urban disparities and vulnerabilities such as rising regional income inequalities (Xie and Zhou 2014) and interregional environmental and social effects of WE infrastructural development. Such research exploring these spatially uneven vulnerabilities produced through existing and emergent WE infrastructures, governance and policies will be essential if the future development of WE systems in China is to achieve both social and environmental sustainability.

So far, we have explored the wider socio-technical systems of WE and the ways in which spatial vulnerabilities are produced and maintained through WE infrastructures in China. In the next section, we investigate in more depth how these spatially uneven WE infrastructures are embedded in and maintain various demands for energy in homes. We will discuss how the commitments to historical ways of defining energy infrastructure provision across South-North China shape various vulnerabilities and spatial inequalities, creating real material effects on Chinese citizens' lives.

Unpacking the domestic WE nexus in China

The dynamics of consumption of WE in the home is fundamental to a holistic understanding of the nexus as a system of circulations underpinned by supply and distribution systems and wider patterns of demand.[3] The domestic scale is the key place where WE vulnerabilities linked to systems of provision are negotiated in related practices such as heating and cooking. The home is the fulcrum where WE resources are transformed and mediated in the coordination, reproduction, routines and rhythms of everyday life. In China, these routines and rhythms are strongly interwoven with historical ways of governing WE supply and demand. The following discussion of central heating in the North of China is representative of the ways that infrastructures produce different types of domestic vulnerabilities both within regions (for example, issues of payment and access, influence of heating on broader environmental pollution experiences and inequalities) and across regions (such as different access to central heating provision across different areas) of China. We will explore this through the example of the Heating Line and the continued effects of the Huai River policy in creating regional disparities in access to, and experiences of, thermal comfort. While this example superficially appears to just refer to heating policy, and negotiations of energy and thermal comfort in homes, we remind the reader of the previous section in which we outlined how WE in China are strongly interconnected through systems of supply.

'The Heating Line' – drawn along the Qin Mountains and the Huai River – is considered the traditional dividing line between north and south China, although the actual division is more sophisticated (see Xiao et al. 2015). Since the 1950s, this line has had performative policy and infrastructural effects and has produced a range of infrastructural legacies that remain visible and are still experienced today. In the 1950s China's Huai River policy divided the country in two in regards to thermal comfort provision: free winter heating for homes and offices in cities north of the Huai River (through provision of coal for fuel burners) as a basic right, but not for the regions south of the line due to budgetary constraints (Chen et al. 2013). This division, shown in Figure 6.1, persists today.

One of the effects of this policy is that there are strong intersections between the coal power stations that support the provision of centralised heating systems in the North and a rise in air pollution in Northern Chinese cities during winter (Chen et al. 2013; Xiao et al. 2015). In Northern China there are centralised heating systems, and residents have no to little control over the thermostat settings of their home/office, and the costs of the heating are subsidised. In Beijing for example residents can get subsidised rebates for the money they spend on heating their homes through their employers.[4] These central heating systems rely mostly on coal-fired energy generation, production of which ramps up from mid-November when the heating systems are generally activated as the cold weather sets in. Notably, the winter period is also one of the worst times of the year in terms of air quality and air pollution in the major northern cities like Beijing, Hebei and Tianjin (Jingjinji), and across regional Northern China, as the increased use of coal-fired power stations to support rising heating needs in these areas leads directly linked to air pollution. Water consumption also rises because as noted the production of coal into power is water intensive (Olsson 2015); even programmes intended to improve air pollution by changing the processing of coal to be less polluting create significant impacts on water supply (Luo and Shiao 2013).

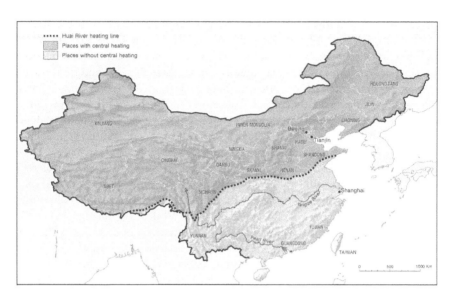

Figure 6.1 China's Huai River policy and heating system split between North and South China

The Heating Line and Huai River policy, and widespread heating services and thermal comfort for residents in Northern China, have thus had some significant detrimental impacts on the health of the population in Northern China (Chen et al. 2013). Chen et al.'s (2013) study has shown significant reductions in life expectancy linked to the health effects of air pollution produced by winter heating in Northern China. Ironically middle- to high-income earners in Northern China then consume even more energy to mitigate the health effects of pollution in homes and offices by purchasing and operating a range of air purifying systems.[5]

The example of claiming rebates for heating through employers also produces vulnerabilities for people who might not be in regular employment or in casual or precarious forms of labour and therefore are not in positions of claiming this rebate through their employers (Zheng et al. 2014). This leads to particular inequities in accessing a form of social welfare across Northern China – those who are employed have access, and those who do not have to pay for their own heating. These dynamics are also compounded for those who do not have 'hukou' (household registration) in the city in which they live and therefore have reduced status within a city such as limited access to social welfare and different rights to housing tenure (see Logan et al. 2009). People without hukou are also seen to be particularly disadvantaged through environmental inequalities as they are disproportionately exposed to pollution as a result of where they live and work in cities (Schoolman and Ma 2012).

As well as air pollution impacts, the Heating Line significantly shapes a diversity and unevenness in peoples' thermal comfort experiences across China.

In China there is a popular narrative of 'Hot North' and 'Cold South' reflecting the legacies of regional differences in central heating infrastructures described above. The North is characterised as having *over*-productive heating systems. Numerous Chinese cartoons depict people in the North of China sitting inside during winter next to central heating radiators, in very little clothes, eating ice cream and growing summer flowers with the windows cast open because the inside temperature is too hot, as they cannot control the central thermostats. Depictions of the thermal comfort experiences of the South reflects people with frozen windows in bed with numerous layers of winter clothes, hats and warm blankets on with hot water bottles to keep them warm. While characteristic of the pronounced jokes of the differences in culture between the North and the South that Chinese people often make, the cartoons also show significant differences in experiences of heating services across China and across social 'groups and classes'.[6]

The historical legacies of the Heating Line not only shapes public sentiment and media representation of regional differences but also has very real effects on thermal comfort experiences and adaptations. Due to the lack of heating and cooling policies for Southern China, people have been found to be both more tolerant of thermal discomfort and adept and active in changing their indoor environments to increase their living conditions (Li et al. 2012). People on higher incomes in the South tend to use distributed heating or cooling such as air conditioners and personal and portable electric heating devices (for example, Zheng et al. 2014). However, a range of lower-income groups – including college and university students in the south who are often not allowed to use heating or other electronic equipment in their dormitories due to fire risks – struggle with meeting their heating needs during cold and wet winters. There are also significant urban-rural gaps related to access to reliable thermal comfort in winter in zones where there is no heating policy (Zheng et al. 2014).

In China, the domestic vulnerabilities related to thermal comfort are a product of the legacies of the Heating Line and Huai River policy, and the vast differences in infrastructures to provide thermal comfort in winter across the north and south of the country. While extending the central heating to the south has been a matter of public debate and policy consideration, it is not seen to be economically or environmentally feasible (see Xiaoping 2015). This individuation of thermal comfort provision creates vulnerabilities in terms of access to thermal comfort services in the south of China particularly for those that are from lower socio-economic groups; those who do not have hukou; have insecure tenant rights; or live in dormitories (e.g. students, migrant workers). The Heating Line creates different vulnerabilities for those who live north of it. While people in the north have their thermal comfort needs met, this is at the cost of individual and population level health and increased morbidity. In the north, vulnerabilities are also revealed through how rebates are claimed (through employers) leaving those in precarious forms of labour particularly vulnerable.

In this discussion of the Heating Line policy, we have shown that domestic vulnerabilities in China depend largely on regional differences in infrastructural access (north/south; urban/rural) but is also compounded by a range of other

inequalities such as the socio-economic and hukou status. Greater consideration needs to be given to these historical legacies of infrastructures, policies and
practices and how with the emergence of new WE infrastructures – which aim
to address rising demand and climate insecurity – these lived and embodied vulnerabilities can be reproduced in new ways. Delivery of services such as heating
in China cannot be considered separately from a range of other environmental
risks and vulnerabilities – namely health and morbidity effects of winter air pollution and, linking to the examples in the previous section, water and energy quality. Energy- and water-related lifestyles and practices also change and shape the
meanings and importance of (transitioning) infrastructures. Therefore it is absolutely imperative that when we consider the 'nexus' of water and energy in China
(and elsewhere) we do so across a range of scales, as it is through these interconnectivities that the depths of nexus vulnerabilities and risks are revealed (POST
note 2016).

Conclusions

The research on WE vulnerabilities in the Global South suffers from a rather
limited conceptualisation of energy and water poverty as issues only of access (e.g.
access to electricity sources or access to regular service levels of water). When
considered solely from the perspective of access, China seems to be fulfilling its
international obligations – it has an almost universal electrification rate and a
higher access to water and sanitation than is seen across many other industrialis-
ing nations. However, the conceptualisation of water or energy poverty in the
Global South as being solely about increasing access has been disturbed by the
case studies and examples provided in this chapter. In China the crises of water
and energy, and experiences of water and energy poverty and wider socio-technical
vulnerabilities, emerge within the interconnectivities between WE *quality* (such
as water contamination and the effects of winter thermal comfort provision on
wider issues of air quality); WE *availability and access* (e.g. connectivity of WE
supply); and the wider *environmental and social effects* (for example, air pollution).

Questions also need to be raised about the ways in which historical, existing
and proposed WE infrastructural developments privilege 'needs' (of rural-urban
or North-South, or those with/without hukou registration or employment) as jus-
tifications for further infrastructural development. Arguably, the exponentially
increasing water and energy demand observed across Chinese cities facilitates a
political legitimacy for mega-project developments – such as the SNWTP outlined by Rogers et al. (2016) – which in turn produce a range of environmental
and societal vulnerabilities. There is a need to develop a much stronger account
of these socio-material dynamics of rapid infrastructural, social and everyday
practice landscapes related to the nexus of WE in China, in order to more systematically critique the vulnerabilities that are being produced at multiple scales.

With little understanding of the socio-material changes that have increased
WE demand across Chinese cities, and very limited imagining of new socio-
material futures that may influence water and energy consumption beyond technological efficiencies and end of product upgrading, such mega-projects remain

politically 'legitimate' and 'necessary' in order to meet increasing urban needs. This chapter represents a first step to begin to engage from within contemporary geographical and social science perspectives (for example for theories of practice, see Browne et al. 2014; Shove et al. 2012, or for social justice, see Walker and Day 2012; Petrova et al. 2013) to bring new reflections on how broad infrastructural change such as urban regeneration and infrastructural development, changing social norms and the politics of water/energy supply and demand co-evolve and change household/communal practices. There is an opportunity to develop this research and also to more explicitly consider the ways in which such developments produce vulnerabilities and inequalities across and within Chinese regions and cities.

Notes

1 It has been argued elsewhere that the evolving literature reflecting 'nexus thinking' renders invisible the politicised tensions, socio-ecological processes and technologies that characterise the water-energy nexus (Williams et al. 2014; Leck et al. 2015). Critique can be levelled at the etymology of buzzwords such as 'nexus' (Cairns and Krzywoszynska 2016), which tend to overemphasise managerial market security to solve resource crises via technological and infrastructural innovations. Nevertheless, we reflect in this chapter that there are still benefits in working across resource siloes and considering the ways that water and energy co-produce conditions of scarcity, crisis and vulnerability at various scales and temporalities. The importance of this has been highlighted within several international policy settings such as the World Economic Forum (World Economic Forum 2011).
2 A full version of the plan (in Chinese) is available at http://news.xinhuanet.com/politics/2011-03/16/c_121193916.htm or at www.chinacleanenergydb.com/general-strategic-plans/Five-Year-Plans/3-2011China12thFive-YearPlanonNationalEconomic andSocialDevelopment-Chinese.pdf?attredirects=0&d=1.
3 See for example the Nexus at Home project of which Browne is a part https://nexusathome.wordpress.com/.
4 Zhu Di, Chinese Academy of Social Sciences, Beijing, personal communication.
5 Qian Liu, Central University for Finance and Economics, Beijing, personal communication, October 2016.
6 See two examples of these cartoons in the *China Daily* newspaper www.chinadaily.com.cn/china/2015-01/30/content_19449162.htm and in the *Beijing Review* www.bjreview.com.cn/forum/txt/2013-01/28/content_514587.htm.

References

Ali, T. et al. (2016). Global footprints of water and land resources through China's food trade. *Global Food Security*. Available at: www.sciencedirect.com/science/article/pii/S2211912416300633.

Allan, T., Keulertz, M. and Woertz, E. (2015). The water – food – energy nexus: An introduction to nexus concepts and some conceptual and operational problems. *International Journal of Water Resources Development*, 31(3), 301–311.

Allouche, J., Middleton, C. and Gyawali, D. (2015). Technical veil, hidden politics: Interrogating the power linkages behind the nexus. *Water Alternatives*, 8(1), 610–626.

Barnett, J. et al. (2015). Sustainability: Transfer project cannot meet China's water needs. *Nature*, 527, 295–297.

Bhattacharyya, S. C. and Ohiare, S. (2012). The Chinese electricity access model for rural electrification: Approach, experience and lessons for others. *Energy Policy*, 49, 676–687.

Bizikova, L. et al. (2013). *The water-energy-food security nexus: Towards a practical planning and decision-support framework for landscape investment and risk management.* International Institute for Sustainable Development. Available at: http://empoderamiento.info/biblioteca/files/original/8e66ac686bf713f8c49a55d85db1e8fa.pdf.

Bouzarovski, S. and Petrova, S. (2015). A global perspective on domestic energy deprivation: Overcoming the energy poverty – fuel poverty binary. *Energy Research & Social Science*, 10, 31–40.

Browne, A. L. et al. (2014). Patterns of practice: A reflection on the development of quantitative/mixed methodologies capturing everyday life related to water consumption in the UK. *International Journal of Social Research Methodology*, 17(1), 27–43.

Cairns, R. and Krzywoszynska, A. (2016). Anatomy of a buzzword: The emergence of "the water-energy-food nexus" in UK natural resource debates. *Environmental Science & Policy*, 64, 164–170.

Chang, G. (2013). Factors influencing water conservation behavior among urban residents in China's arid areas. *Water Policy*, 15(5), 691–704.

Chen, Y. et al. (2013). Evidence on the impact of sustained exposure to air pollution on life expectancy from China's Huai River policy. *Proceedings of the National Academy of Sciences*, 110(32), 12936–12941.

Cornot-Gandolphe, S. (2014). *Gas strategy of China: Developing competition between national production and imports.* Available at: http://inis.iaea.org/Search/search.aspx?orig_q=RN:46034973 [Accessed 22 December 2016].

Downs, E. S. et al. (2000). *China's quest for energy security.* Santa Monica: Rand Corporation.

Du, G. et al. (2015). Residential electricity consumption after the reform of tiered pricing for household electricity in China. *Applied Energy*, 157, 276–283.

Fam, D., Lahiri-Dutt, K. and Sofoulis, Z. (2015). Scaling down: Researching household water practices. *ACME: An International Journal for Critical Geographies*, 14(3), pp. 639–651.

Feng, K. et al. (2014). The energy and water nexus in Chinese electricity production: A hybrid life cycle analysis. *Renewable and Sustainable Energy Reviews*, 39, 342–355.

Finlayson, B. L. et al. (2013). The drivers of risk to water security in Shanghai. *Regional Environmental Change*, 13(2), 329–340.

Gu, A., Teng, F. and Lv, Z. (2016). Exploring the nexus between water saving and energy conservation: Insights from industry sector during the 12th Five-Year Plan period in China. *Renewable and Sustainable Energy Reviews*, 59, 28–38.

Harvey, M. (2014). The food-energy-climate change trilemma: Toward a socio-economic analysis. *Theory, Culture & Society*, 31, 155–182.

He, S., Hipel, K. W. and Kilgour, D. M. (2014). Water diversion conflicts in China: A hierarchical perspective. *Water Resources Management*, 28(7), 1823–1837.

Hoff, H. (2011). Understanding the nexus. *Bonn2011 nexus conference: The water, energy and food security nexus.* Stockholm, Sweden: Stockholm Environment Institute (SEI). Available at: https://scholar.google.co.uk/scholar?q=Hoff+Understanding+the+nexus&btnG=&hl=en&as_sdt=0%2C5.

Hubacek, K. et al. (2009). Environmental implications of urbanization and lifestyle change in China: Ecological and Water Footprints. *Journal of Cleaner Production*, 17(14), 1241–1248.

Jiang, D. and Ramaswami, A. (2015). The "thirsty" water-electricity nexus: Field data on the scale and seasonality of thermoelectric power generation's water intensity in China. *Environmental Research Letters*, 10(2), 024015.

Jiang, Y. (2009). China's water scarcity. *Journal of Environmental Management*, 90(11), 3185–3196.

Jianjun, J. et al. (2016). Measuring the willingness to pay for drinking water quality improvements: Results of a contingent valuation survey in Songzi, China. *Journal of Water and Health*, 14(3), 504–512.

Kenway, S. J. et al. (2011). The connection between water and energy in cities: A review. *Water Science and Technology*, 63(9), 1983–1990.

Leck, H. et al. (2015). Tracing the water – energy – food Nexus: Description, theory and practice. *Geography Compass*, 9(8), 445–460.

Li, B. et al. (2012). The Chinese evaluation standard for the indoor thermal comfort environment in free-running buildings – Google Scholar. In *Proceedings of 7th Windsor Conference. The changing context of comfort in an unpredictable world.* Cumberland Lodge, Windsor: Network for Comfort and Energy Use in Buildings. Available at: https://scholar.google.co.uk/scholar?hl=en&q=Li+The+Chinese+evaluation+standard +for+the+indoor+thermal+comfort+environment+in+free-running+buildings&btnG =&as_sdt=1%2C5&as_sdtp=.

Li, G., Huang, D. and Li, Y. (2016). China's input-output efficiency of water-energy-food Nexus based on the Data Envelopment Analysis (DEA) Model. *Sustainability*, 8(9), 927.

Liu, J. and Diamond, J. (2005). China's environment in a globalizing world. *Nature*, 435(7046), 1179–1186.

Liu, J. and Yang, W. (2012). Water sustainability for China and beyond. *Science*, 337(6095), 649–650.

Liu, J. et al. (2016). Characteristics of pipe-scale in the pipes of an urban drinking water distribution system in eastern China. *Water Science and Technology: Water Supply*, 16(3), 715–726.

Liu, W. et al. (2013). Energy consumption practices of rural households in north China: Basic characteristics and potential for low carbon development. *Energy Policy*, 55, 128–138.

Liu, W., Oosterveer, P. and Spaargaren, G. (2015). Promoting sustainable consumption in China: A conceptual framework and research review. *Journal of Cleaner Production*, 134(Part A), 13–21.

Liu, W., Oosterveer, P. and Spaargaren, G. (2016). Promoting sustainable consumption in China: A conceptual framework and research review. *Journal of Cleaner Production*, 134 (Part A), 13–21.

Liu, Z. et al. (2012). Features, trajectories and driving forces for energy-related GHG emissions from Chinese mega cites: The case of Beijing, Tianjin, Shanghai and Chongqing. *Energy*, 37(1), 245–254.

Liu, Z. et al. (2013). Energy policy: A low-carbon road map for China. *Nature*, 500, 143–145.

Logan, J. R., Fang, Y. and Zhang, Z. (2009). Access to housing in Urban China. *International Journal of Urban and Regional Research*, 33(4), 914–935.

Luo, T. and Shiao, T. (2013). *China's response to air pollution poses threat to water.* WRI China. Available at: www.wri.org.cn/en/node/41128.

Marsh, D. S. and Deepak, S. (2007). Energy-water nexus: An integrated modeling approach. *International Energy Journal*, 8(4), 235–242.

Mischke, P. and Xiong, W. (2015). Mapping and benchmarking regional disparities in China's energy supply, transformation, and end-use in 2010. *Applied Energy*, 143, 359–369.

National Development and Reform Commission. (2007). *China's National Climate Change Programme.* Available at: http://en.ndrc.gov.cn/newsrelease/200706/P02007060456 1191006823.pdf.

No author. (2015). Qingdao's population soars to 9 million. *China Daily*, 13 February 2015. Available at: http://www.chinadaily.com.cn/m/shandong/e/2015-02/13/content_19582180.htm.

Olsson, E. (2015). *Water use in the Chinese coal industry*. Uppsala: Uppsala University. Available at: www.diva-portal.org/smash/get/diva2:816658/.

Parkes, R. (2015). Renewables market report on China: Eye of the tiger. *Renewable Energy Focus*, 16(4), 71–74.

Peet, R., Robbins, P. and Watts, M. (2010). *Global political ecology*. London and New York: Routledge.

Petrova, S. et al. (2013). Perceptions of thermal comfort and housing quality: Exploring the microgeographies of energy poverty in Stakhanov, Ukraine. *Environment and Planning A*, 45(5), 1240–1257.

Piao, S. et al. (2010). The impacts of climate change on water resources and agriculture in China. *Nature*, 467(7311), 43–51.

Plappally, A. K. and Lienhard, V. J. H. (2012). Energy requirements for water production, treatment, end use, reclamation, and disposal. *Renewable and Sustainable Energy Reviews*, 16(7), 4818–4848.

POSTnote. (2016). The water-energy-food nexus. No. 543.

Rogers, S. et al. (2016). Governmentality and the conduct of water: China's South – North Water Transfer Project. *Transactions of the Institute of British Geographers*, 41(4), 429–441.

Schoolman, E. D. and Ma, C. (2012). Migration, class and environmental inequality: Exposure to pollution in China's Jiangsu Province. *Ecological Economics*, 75, 140–151.

Scott, C. A. et al. (2011). Policy and institutional dimensions of the water – energy nexus. *Energy Policy*, 39(10), 6622–6630.

Seckler, D., Barker, R. and Amarasinghe, U. (1999). Water scarcity in the twenty-first century. *International Journal of Water Resources Development*, 15(1–2), 29–42.

Seligsohn, D. and Hsu, A. (2016). How China's 13th five-year plan addresses energy and the environment. *ChinaFile*. Available at: www.chinafile.com/reporting-opinion/environment/how-chinas-13th-five-year-plan-addresses-energy-and-environment.

Shove, E., Pantzar, M. and Watson, M. (2012). *The dynamics of social practice: Everyday life and how it changes*. London: Sage.

Sun, M., Gao, C. and Shen, B. (2014). Quantifying China's oil import risks and the impact on the national economy. *Energy Policy*, 67, 605–611.

Tao, T. and Xin, K. (2014). Public health: A sustainable plan for China's drinking water : Nature News & Comment. *Nature*, 511(7511), 527–528.

Walker, G. and Day, R. (2012). Fuel poverty as injustice: Integrating distribution, recognition and procedure in the struggle for affordable warmth. *Energy Policy*, doi:10.1016/j.bbr.2011.03.031

Wang, H., Xie, J. and Li, H. (2008). Domestic water pricing with household surveys: A study of acceptability and willingness to pay Chongqing, China. *Policy Research Working Paper 4690*.

Wang, Q. (2014). Effects of urbanisation on energy consumption in China. *Energy Policy*, 65, 332–339.

Wang, X-R. et al. (2015). The new urbanization policy in China: Which way forward? *Habitat International*, 47, 279–284.

Watts, J. (2011). China crisis over Yangtze River drought forces drastic dam measures. *The Guardian*, 25 May 2011. Available at: https://www.theguardian.com/environment/2011/may/25/china-drought-crisis-yangtze-dam.

Williams, J., Bouzarovski, S. and Swyngedouw, E. (2014). Politicizing the nexus: Nexus technologies, urban circulation, and the coproduction. *Nexus Network Think Piece Series Paper 1*, UK: ESRC.

Wilson, J. and Swyngedouw, E. (2014). *The post-political and its discontents: Spaces of depoliticization, spectres of radical politics*. Edinburgh: Edinburgh University Press.

World Economic Forum. (2011). *Water security: The water-food-energy-climate nexus*. Washington, DC: Island Press.

Wu, K. (2014). China's energy security: Oil and gas. *Energy Policy*, 73, 4–11.

WWF China. (2016). Available at: www.wwf.org.hk/en/news/press_release/?uNewsID= 9100.

Xiao, Q. et al. (2015). The impact of winter heating on air pollution in China. *PLOS ONE*, 10(1), e0117311.

Xiaoping, H. (2015). Central heating in south not a feasible idea. *China Daily*. Available at: www.chinadaily.com.cn/opinion/2015-11/19/content_22485383.htm.

Xie, J. (2009). *Addressing China's water scarcity: Recommendations for selected water resource management issues*. Washington, DC: World Bank Publications.

Xie, Y. and Zhou, X. (2014). Income inequality in today's China. *Proceedings of the National Academy of Sciences*, 111(19), 6928–6933.

Zhang, H-Y., Ji, Q. and Fan, Y. (2013). An evaluation framework for oil import security based on the supply chain with a case study focused on China. *Energy Economics*, 38, 87–95.

Zhang, J. (2012). The impact of water quality on health: Evidence from the drinking water infrastructure program in rural China. *Journal of Health Economics*, 31(1), 122–134.

Zheng, X. et al. (2014). Characteristics of residential energy consumption in China: Findings from a household survey. *Energy Policy*, 75, 126–135.

Zhu, S., Ding, J. and Zhuang, G. (2014). Analysis of energy base for developing a low carbon economy in Guangdong. *Chinese Journal of Urban and Environmental Studies*, 2(1), 1450007.

7 Rethinking energy deprivation in Athens

A spatial approach

Evangelia Chatzikonstantinou and
Fereniki Vatavali

Introduction: energy deprivation as a spatial phenomenon in Athens

The Greek debt crisis, marked by the entry of Greece in the European Mechanism of Support in 2010, has had a serious impact on the social and spatial characteristics of Greek cities. Austerity policies imposed as a remedy to the debt crisis included a shrinking of the welfare state, personnel and income cuts and significant tax increases – especially on property – that led to the increase of the unemployment rate and of poverty, as well as to a decline in living standards (Balabanides et al. 2013; Balourdos and Petraki 2012; ELSTAT 2016; Greek Ombudsman 2016; INE-GSEE 2017). Under these circumstances, the geography of Greek cities has been deeply affected at a range of spatial scales, and nearly all social and income groups have redefined their everyday practices and adjusted their locational decisions regarding housing, as well as their action areas, to the new conditions (Encounter Athens 2011).

In this context, and together with the international rise in fuel prices and the significant rise of taxes on heating oil, a distinctive form of poverty which is connected with inadequate access to energy at home has become a large-scale problem in Greek cities (Corovessis et al. 2017; Greek Ombudsman 2016; Greenpeace 2013; INE-GSEE 2017; Panas 2012; WWF Hellas and Public Issue 2013).[1] Inadequate access to energy formed the ground for the rise of discourse about energy poverty in both academic and policy-making circles, as well for the first – rather loose – attempts to define the phenomenon.[2] As more and more households cannot cover the cost for heating, cooling, lighting or cooking (ELSTAT 2016; INE-GSEE 2017), the use of energy has emerged as a highly contested terrain, especially in apartment buildings with central heating systems (Chatzikonstantinou and Vatavali 2016).

Until now, as in other European cities (Bouzarovski 2014; Bridge et al. 2013; Buzar 2007), the geographical aspects of energy deprivation in Greek cities have attracted little public and political attention, and they remain under-researched (Chatzikonstantinou and Vatavali 2016; Vatavali and Chatzikonstantinou 2016). In the relevant studies, inadequate access to energy is usually associated with technical and financial factors, such as fuel prices, household income and the energy efficiency of buildings, and is limited to the problems of individual households (Dagoumas and Kitsios 2014; Katsoulakos 2011; Papada and Kaliampakos 2016; Santamouris et al. 2013; Santamouris et al. 2014), while the solutions that are usually proposed to combat it are the same throughout the city (Atanasiu et al. 2014; Corovessi et al. 2017). Theoretical and empirical analysis on energy poverty in Greece does not cover the socio-spatial dimensions of the phenomenon nor the way spatial particularities are interrelated with households' energy vulnerability.

In this regard, the aim of this chapter is two-fold. First, we intend to investigate how the particularities of urban space are producing and reproducing energy vulnerability and energy poverty. Second, our approach attempts to highlight the significance of energy deprivation as an analytical tool for the study of urban space and the transformation of cities; something that is of the utmost importance for exploring the repercussions of the economic crisis and related austerity policies in Greek cities, but also in other cities around the world where austerity reforms have been implemented. Our intention is to discuss energy deprivation as a spatial phenomenon: a phenomenon that occurs in space and at the same time defines its own spatial frame. Also we intend to go beyond the household scale and investigate, not only the interdependences of housing quality, heating systems, social policies and everyday practices, but also the urban development processes as they have been formed in the long-term and redefined during the crisis.

Our approach is based on the idea that space is not an entity beyond society and social dynamics or something that has to be explored itself. On the contrary, we approach space – and therefore the spatial dimensions of energy deprivation – building on the theoretical discussion about the social production of space (Harvey 2006; Lefebvre 1991; Massey 2005) and the tripartite division of understanding space that has been introduced – through various but similar conceptual approaches – by several critical geographers (Harvey 1973, 2006; Lefebvre 1991). In particular, we build on Harvey's (1973, 2006) division of 'space' into absolute space (i.e. the fixed physical space with specific geometry and material features); relative space (for example, the complex topological relations and their understandings or mappings, the relative location of a site, its centrality and proximity to other places in terms of distance, cost and time, the flows and networks); and the space of social relations (i.e. the intangible relations between individuals and groups, the space of market forces, the experience people have of and in the space, their memories and expectations) in order to consider the spatial aspects of energy deprivation and analyze the spatial frame it creates.

Moreover, considering the multiplicity of social relations across all spatial scales (Massey 2005), we analyze energy deprivation in various interdependent spatial scales: the apartment (the private space of the households where access to energy is required for heating, cooking, lighting etc.); the apartment building (an entity with fixed structural features and common facilities that is managed under a specific set of rules); the neighborhood (a place with a particular identity and with fixed technical infrastructure); and the city (a territory with a particular historical, climate, institutional and social background). This approach gives us the chance to apply the tools used for analyzing the production of space in different scales to the analysis of energy deprivation in contemporary cities.

We focus on Athens, the capital of Greece, the city where the effects of the economic crisis and austerity policies became obvious in the most blatant and violent way (Encounter Athens 2011; Maloutas et al. 2013). Athens is a relatively new city, shaped mainly by rapid and unplanned urbanization of rural population between the 1950s and the 1970s. Small-scale ownership and especially homeownership have played a significant role in urban development and social integration processes (Leontidou 1990; Vaiou et al. 2000). The dominant housing typology in Athens is the apartment building (*polykatoikia*); a type of building that had a significant role in the shaping of the urban space, social relations and urban life (Maloutas and Karadimitriou 2001; Maloutas and Spirellis 2015). The apartment building combines flats of different size and characteristics, residential and commercial uses and households of different socio-economic and tenure status. On the scale of the city and despite the particularities of the neighborhoods of Athens, the apartment building contributed to the production of high-density and socially mixed areas and to a relatively coherent urban structure (Maloutas and Karadimitriou 2001).

We adopted a methodology capable of capturing the particularities of the city, as well as to the fluid state of energy deprivation itself. Therefore, we employed a mixed-method approach that combines quantitative and qualitative methods. In particular, we analyzed statistical data about the building stock and the infrastructure networks, household energy consumption, household income, as well as data about policies implemented against energy poverty in the City of Athens,[3] in order to produce a set of maps. As far as the qualitative approach is concerned, we focused on the apartment building and, in order to understand the impact of energy deprivation on the private and semi-private sphere, we conducted 23 open-ended semi-structured interviews with the inhabitants of 13 apartment buildings located in different neighborhoods of the City of Athens.[4] The first informant in each building was from our personal networks, and the rest were chosen via the snowball sampling method. We chose apartment buildings of various sizes which featured a wide range of heating technologies and which were located in neighborhoods with differing socio-economic characteristics. In each building, we interviewed people of different socio-economic backgrounds (age, sex, tenure status, educational backgrounds etc.). Fieldwork was conducted from autumn 2014 until summer 2016.

Energy deprivation and the space of buildings and infrastructures

Domestic use of energy, and also domestic energy deprivation, in Athens – just like in many other cities – is intertwined with the materiality of domestic and urban space, the characteristics of the building stock and the installed energy technologies. In the case of Athens, the majority of buildings are apartment buildings constructed between the 1950s and the 1970s, with low energy performance and lack of efficient insulation.[5] Their features, as well as the fact that just a few of them have been sufficiently maintained since their construction, form a relatively decaying building stock with serious functional problems. Most of the apartment buildings have a central heating system with an oil or gas burner located at the basement of the building and a network of vertical pipes that concurrently distribute hot water to the radiators of all the apartments. This heating system provides warmth to the whole interior of each building simultaneously, thus making individual choices regarding heating impossible.

Even though maintenance and functional problems are spread in urban space, it seems that there are significant differentiations from neighbourhood to neighbourhood considering the quality of construction and the availability of infrastructure. For example, in the central areas, the vast majority of the buildings have been constructed before 1979, when insulation became obligatory for the new constructions,[6] and so most of the apartment buildings do not have any insulation (Figure 7.1). Furthermore, the central neighborhoods are covered to a great extent by the natural gas network that provides cheaper energy for heating compared to oil, with the latter mainly used for heating in peripheral areas (Figure 7.2 and 7.3). These differentiations in material structures in the scale of the city form different conditions in relation to access and use of energy, which have played a significant role during the crisis.

The crisis has expanded the existing problems and created new ones in the material and functional features of the apartment buildings, mainly related to inadequate access to energy. There are severe consequences on a wide range of common facilities as, due to financial problems or ineffective management, the existing infrastructures are not maintained properly and there are delays on the payment of utility bills. In one of the apartment buildings we studied, the chimney of the central heating system collapsed due to inadequate maintenance, while the cut of the electricity supply due to debts put the elevator, the entryphone and the common area lights out of service. A flat owner of Albanian origin described the conditions formed due to lack of electricity as follows:

> [We did not have electricity in the common spaces] for more than two years. . . . The elevator was put out of service for four years and we were using the stairs, carrying our things in the dark with the help of a torch. Can you imagine that? Everybody had a torch. . . . I had always a torch in my bag, my husband and my son had too. Everybody had a torch, in order to go up and down the stairs.
>
> (V.K., 51, 08/07/2015)

Financial problems and the accumulation of debts related to shared utility costs meant that the inhabitants of many apartment buildings decided not to use the central heating system. Inadequate heating in wintertime, along with the fact that most of the apartment buildings are old, lacking insulation or inadequately

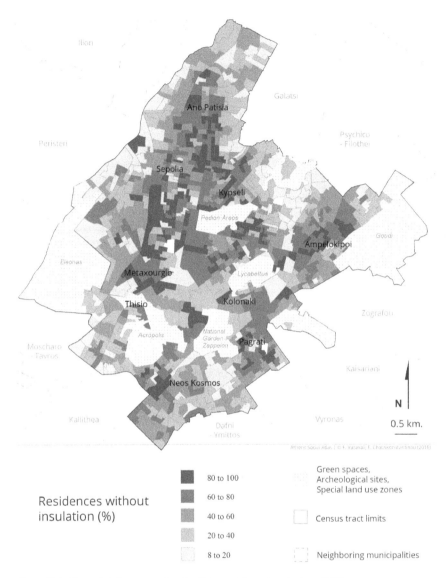

Figure 7.1 City of Athens: regular dwellings without insulation, 2011

Source: Data from ELSTAT (2011)

maintained, affected their structural characteristics and contributed to their dete-rioration. In particular, a lack of heating led to the increase of indoor damp and mold, to damage on wall paint, to the attraction of insects and the existence of unpleasant odors. As the manager of an apartment building commented, if there is no heating, the 'building suffers' and when a building suffers, its inhabitants

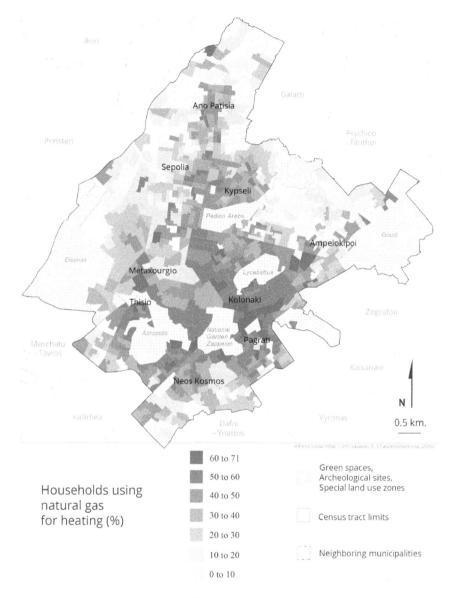

Households using
natural gas
for heating (%)

60 to 71
50 to 60
40 to 50
30 to 40
20 to 30
10 to 20
0 to 10

Green spaces,
Archeological sites,
Special land use zones

Census tract limits

Neighboring municipalities

N

0.5 km.

Figure 7.2 City of Athens: households using natural gas as the main energy resource for
heating, 2011

Source: Data from ELSTAT (2011)

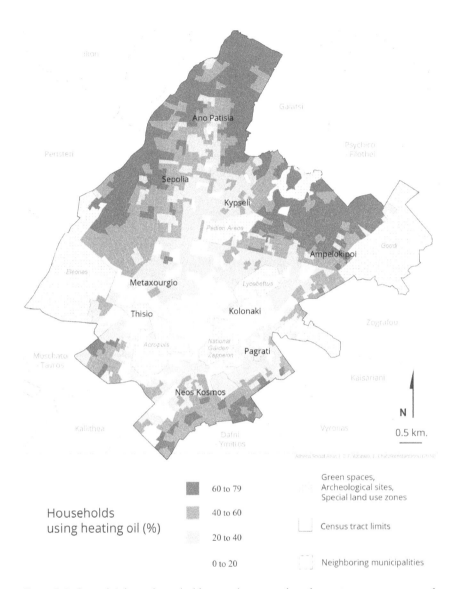

Figure 7.3 City of Athens: households using heating oil as the main energy resource for heating, 2011

Source: Data from ELSTAT (2011)

suffer too. This is described by a tenant of an apartment building where the central heating system has been off since 2012:

> Since we've decided to turn off the central heating system, there has been indoor damp all over the building. It was already vulnerable, but now it's full of problems. Paint is running off the walls. The plaster at balconies is

peeling. The bathroom is full of mould. The windows are covered with water. Clothes do not dry. . . . Sometimes we turn the air-conditioner on, in order to combat humidity. . . . This coincided with another problem. Due to smog,[7] we can't hang the laundry outside to dry at night, because in the morning they have an awful smell. So we hang it inside the flat and this has increased indoor damp.

(M.K., 40, 24/6/2015)

Energy deprivation and the space of policies: multiple interpretations and relations

Energy deprivation is a complex phenomenon with multiple manifestations and understandings. On the one hand, there are multiple intersecting processes from which to choose in order to discuss it and, on the other hand, its spatial frame depends crucially upon what is being analyzed and by whom, as well as upon existing power relations and interactions among various actors. The relative and relational nature of energy deprivation in space can be discussed – among others – in relation to the implemented policies for dealing with domestic energy needs.

Since the beginning of the Greek debt crisis, a wide range of policies and urgent measures have been applied by state agencies in order to meet the energy needs of specific social and income groups: subsidies for heating oil,[8] social tariffs for domestic electricity consumers,[9] free access to electricity for extremely poor households,[10] electricity reconnections for indebted households, favorable arrangements for debts and arrears on electricity bills and low electricity prices on days when weather conditions favor the creation of smog as well as discounts to electricity consumers who pay on time.

It can be claimed that the mapping of the spatial distribution of the beneficiaries of these policies in the scale of the city reveals various manifestations of energy deprivation and poverty. For example, considering that the main criterion of two programs – the 'Residential Social Tariff' (a program offering low electricity prices to vulnerable social groups since 2010) and 'Confrontation of the Humanitarian Crisis' (a program offering free electricity consumption and electricity reconnection for extremely poor households) – is low family income, the spatial distribution of the beneficiaries (Figure 7.4 and 7.5) reflects the concentrations of low-income and poor households (Figure 7.6),[11] although this does not correspond necessarily to other manifestations or indicators of domestic energy deprivation, such as reduction of energy consumption (Figure 7.7). As for the heating oil subsidy, the most popular among the implemented programs, its beneficiaries are spread across the city as the income and property criteria posed by the terms of the program are quite wide and, apart from the low-income households, include broader middle-income groups.[12] However, there is higher concentration of beneficiaries in the peripheral areas of the city (Figure 7.8) which are not covered by the gas network and therefore oil is used for the central heating system in most of the buildings (Figures 7.3 and 7.4).

But still, many conflicts and contradictions have emerged in relation to the heating oil subsidy that reflect institutional distinctions between citizens. For

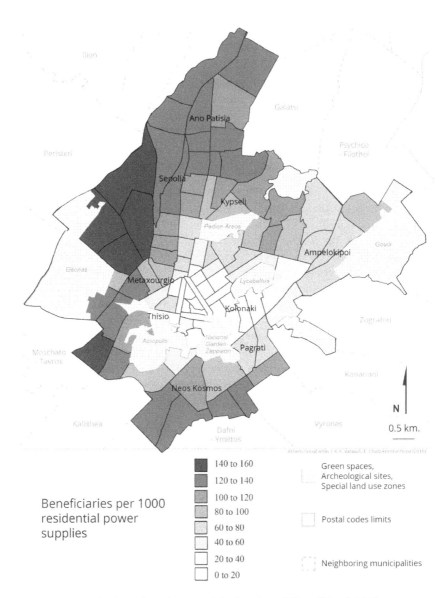

Figure 7.4 City of Athens: beneficiaries of the Residential Social Tariff, 2015

Source: Hellenic Electricity Distribution Network Operator S.A. (2016)

example, as one of our informants described, a couple of low-income immigrants living in an apartment building in a devaluated neighborhood of Athens was excluded from the subsidy because they did not have the required legal documents. Moreover, a businessman that faced energy affordability problems could not apply for the subsidy because the evaluation of his application was done on

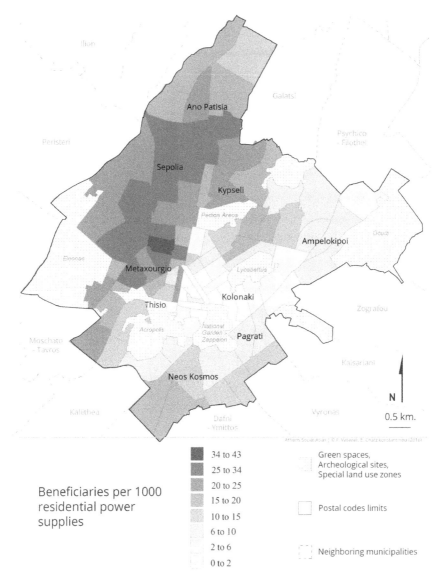

Beneficiaries per 1000
residential power
supplies

34 to 43	
25 to 34	
20 to 25	
15 to 20	
10 to 15	
6 to 10	
2 to 6	
0 to 2	

Green spaces,
Archeological sites,
Special land use zones

Postal codes limits

Neighboring municipalities

Figure 7.5 City of Athens: beneficiaries of the Program for Confronting the Humanitarian
Crisis for free electricity and reconnection to electricity network, 2015

Source: IDIKA (2016)

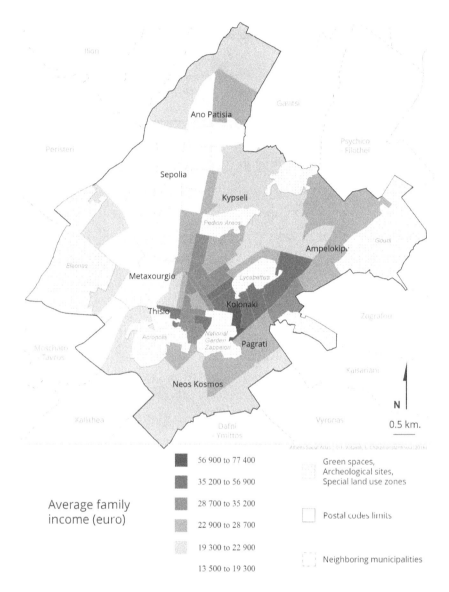

Figure 7.6 City of Athens: average family income, economic year 2011
Source: GSIS (2011)

the basis of the previous year's income – which was relatively high – and not on the current year's income. On the other hand, as a manager of a building reported, a relatively well-off household that is capable of affording its heating costs is among the beneficiaries of the subsidy, as it meets all the required income criteria.

Despite the poor targeting of the heating oil subsidy program, in the case of an apartment building in a middle-class area where the central heating system was off for 2 years due to the financial problems of its inhabitants, the fact that 20 out of 46 households – mainly low- and middle-income households – received the oil subsidy which allowed them to turn on the heating again. In other words, even though the oil subsidy is a policy that contributes mainly to the increase of the

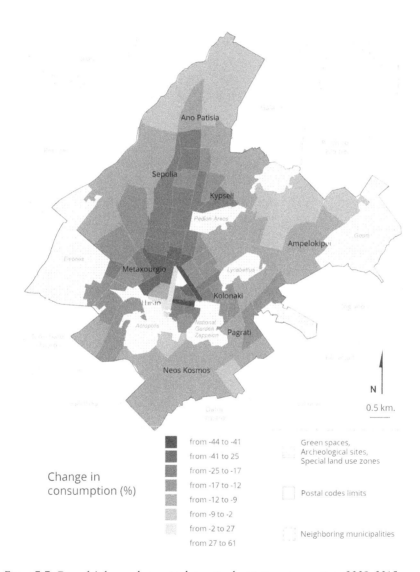

Figure 7.7 City of Athens: change in domestic electricity consumption, 2008–2015

Source: Hellenic Electricity Distribution Network Operator S.A. (2016)

households' income, in this apartment building, it led to the reuse of the common heating facilities.

> The last two years, we had a lot of grouch and grumble, because of the crisis. Mostly because some of the inhabitants wanted heating and others didn't. We had a lot of assemblies. But, it was difficult to take decisions. That's why we didn't have heating for two years. This year though, as they [the

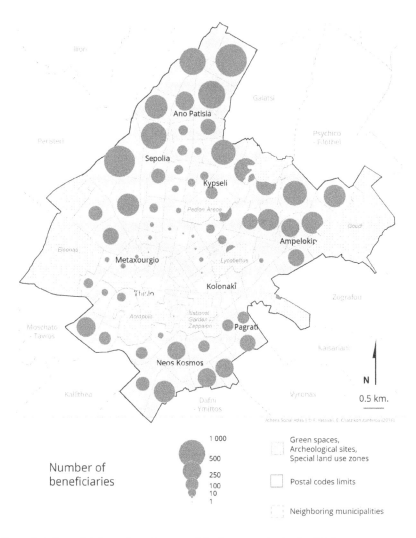

Figure 7.8 City of Athens: beneficiaries of the heating oil subsidy, 2014

Source: General Secretariat of Public Revenue (2016)

government] announced that they will give the oil subsidy, we thought about it again and we took our decision. Because most of us could be beneficiaries.

(D.G. 65, 30/3/2015)

In general, we could say that the terms and the eligibility criteria of the policies for combating energy deprivation reflect, apart from the existing power relations, the variety of understandings and interpretations of this social problem by decision-makers. This variety is reproduced on the maps of the beneficiaries of the programs (Figures 7.7 and 7.8), which, as with the maps about the characteristics of buildings and infrastructure (Figures 7.1, 7.2 and 7.3), present the relative locations of the concentration of energy deprivation and, in this sense, disrupt spatial continuities and reveal different topological relations.

The use of energy in apartment buildings: relations and practices

The Greek debt crisis and the subsequent increase in energy poverty has redefined the relations among the inhabitants of apartment buildings and the forms of interaction between the private and collective sphere (Chatzikonstantinou and Vatavali 2016). In general, the boundaries between private life and common duties in apartment buildings are defined by a set of regulations and are controlled by the decisions of the inhabitants' assembly, while the management of the building is run in shifts by one of the inhabitants. The same person is also responsible for the buildings' reserve fund – formed from inhabitants' contributions – in order to cover the costs of upkeep (electricity, water, cleaning, maintenance, heating etc.) or any unexpected costs. Apart from the 'formal' side of life at the apartment buildings, various relations among the inhabitants have been formed across time, making in many cases collective life and exchange practices rather diverse, varying from common social activities and cooperation for dealing with functional problems of the building to provision of help for those in need.

During the crisis, everyday life in apartment buildings has been deeply affected, mainly because the financial status of the inhabitants has changed and people have redefined their priorities, with direct impact on the relations with each other. Things and services that were taken for granted before the crisis, including the use of the central heating system or the access to electricity network, form now a contested field, and as one of our interviewees stated, 'people have to deal with the question whether they need heating or not' (L.T., 34, 30/3/2015).

In particular, during the crisis, many households cannot meet the cost of heating, fall into arrears and accumulate debts. It is estimated that more than 40% of the apartment buildings in Athens do not use the central heating at all,[13] while in the majority of the rest buildings the inhabitants have decided to use it for fewer hours every day. These decisions have seriously affected the comfort in the apartments. For example, in an apartment building of a middle-class area of Athens where the central heating system was off in winters of 2012–2013 and 2013–2014, a couple of immigrants of Albanian origin and their children facing serious economic problems, lived in the cold. In a totally different context as far as the financial capacity is concerned, a couple of middle-aged professors who live in the most expensive neighborhood of the centre of Athens also experienced a cold environment at home for several months.

The problems that have emerged concerning heating have posed new challenges for the management of the private and the common spaces and facilities. As a response to the inadequate heating in apartment buildings where the central heating system is off, households adopt a wide range of new practices in order to meet their heating needs. A variety of heating equipment is used – either exclusively or in combination – such as air-conditioners, gas heaters, halogen heaters, oil radiators, convectors, fan heaters, infrared radiators, pellet stoves, electric blankets, fireplaces etc. In many cases, though, the household's efforts to satisfy their heating needs individually do not succeed in reducing energy bills and are less effective compared to the use of the central heating system. The manager of an apartment building, who makes a living from designing and installing heating systems, told us about the rise in the cost for the households' budget:

> Many people spend money buying cheap air-conditioners, convectors or other heating appliances. But they were cheated. They bought cheap air-conditioners made in China. They thought that they would pay 200 euro for the air-conditioner, plus 100 euro for the cost of electricity and that they would solve their problem for a while. People continued to buy convectors, stoves, radiators, until they received the first electricity bills. . . . In 2012–2013, all these appliances have been selling like hot cakes. When people received the first electricity bills, they stopped buying.
>
> (A.P., 60, 2/12/2014)

Apart from the short-term solutions, during the last few years, some households permanently modified the heating systems in their flats in order to meet their heating needs. In particular, it is mainly homeowners who attempt to develop long-term strategies concerning the heating of their property. For example, in one of the apartment buildings we studied, the fact that the central heating system was off for more than 2 years and most of its inhabitants had serious problems with heating, led the assembly to 'reset the agenda' of problems and priorities for the common facilities management and so opened the way for giving permission to a flat-owner to disconnect his flat from the central heating system. This decision would not have been taken before the crisis when the heating system was operating regularly. After getting the permission of the inhabitants' assembly, this flat owner connected his apartment to the natural gas network, thus securing access to a relatively cheap form of energy for heating, cooking and hot water.

In contrast to the owners who try to find long-term solutions for heating and in general for energy in their flats, there are tenants who prefer to move to another apartment building that has regular heating. This means that flat owners, apart from been overburdened with significant property taxes (Bank of Greece 2012), are sometimes 'trapped' in inadequate living conditions in their property whilst tenants can make locational decisions by taking into consideration their heating needs and their income. For example, in the above-mentioned apartment building where the central heating system was off, an old couple of tenants with their grandchildren moved to another building where central heating was in operation, while a young tenant who was fed up with freezing in his flat and with the mold on the walls expressed his intention to do the same. Mobility of tenants for reasons related to heating is also encouraged by the changes in the housing market during the crisis.[14]

Complementary to the shift to individual solutions for covering energy needs is the adoption of informal or illegal practices that aim to reduce costs for the household. The main form of these practices – that in many cases are adopted by households that prior to the crisis paid their energy bills regularly – is illegal connections to the electricity supply network. This method basically transfers the cost of the consumed energy from the consumer to the provider. Such is the case of a young doctor who lives in a privileged central neighborhood of Athens with his wife and his baby. When the inhabitants of their apartment building decided to stop using the central heating system, he searched for a technician who could modify the electricity consumption meter of their flat in order to pay less than their real consumption. Explaining his choice, the doctor stresses the interaction of various factors that reduced his income, highlighting the burden of taxes:

> Our choice to do that is related to the huge increase of income taxation. In the past I had to pay 2,000, 3,000 or maximum 4,000 euro per year. Then [in 2012], I was obliged to pay a bit more than 12,000 for income tax, let's say almost half of my turnover. . . . In general, we are well-off in comparison with other people. We are not rich, but under these circumstances, we had to cut expenses.
>
> (M.K., 41, 24/6/2015)

Apart from individual responses to heating needs, many attempts to overcome heating issues involve reconfigurations of social relations at the level of the apartment building. One response is claiming money from the households that have debts; a practice adopted in apartment buildings both in low-income and high-income areas. The accumulation of debts from households that face serious economic problems has created a large private debt, which is the main reason for putting out of function the central heating system in many apartment buildings. In such cases, the actions that are taken include informal negotiations between the manager or the representatives of the inhabitants' assembly and the debtors, hiring a company to collect the money or taking legal action against the debtors. In most cases, the repayment of the debts is considered to be a precondition for turning on again the central heating system. Although inhabitants of some apartment buildings can work together to cope with private debts, such a situation can also create new tensions and social divides. For example, we encountered feelings of unfairness and resentment amongst those who paid their bills on time toward the inhabitants who had been unable or unwilling to pay, and thus they were affecting everyone in the building. As the manager of an apartment build-ing states:

> The hostage lasted two years. Two years without heating. . . . It is unaccep-table that inhabitants who pay are held hostages by a few inhabitants who don't pay. I live in an apartment building. All the inhabitants and I have chosen to live here, just because we want to benefit from specific ameni-ties. . . . But we are held hostage by two or three households, and it's very awful that 43 flats are held hostage by only 3 flats.
>
> (L.P., 60, 10/12/2014)

Another practice that is used in order to overcome heating problems at the apartment building level is the upgrading of the central heating system. This is a long-term solution chosen mainly in apartment buildings with few flats and with owners that have the financial capacity to cover the relevant costs. More specifically, in two of the apartment buildings we studied, the owners decided to convert the central heating system from oil to natural gas, given that natural gas is a cheaper fuel. Furthermore, they took advantage of the relevant funding programs provided by the state or by private energy companies.

In general, we could say that the crisis and austerity policies has increased the financial vulnerability of the households, has affected individual and collective practices and has made life and relations of the inhabitants in apartment build-ings even more instable and dynamic, as it is shown through the responses to energy issues.

Conclusions

Our analysis approached energy deprivation in Athens as a spatial phenomenon, a phenomenon that is related to physical conditions, multiple policy understand-ings and social relations. However, energy deprivation in space is neither abso-lute, relative or relational in itself, but it can become one or all simultaneously depending on the circumstances. The insights that come from such a dialectical approach could be significant, not only for analyzing modes of production and transformation of Athens during the crisis, but also for understanding how energy deprivation intersects various scales in urban space.

The analysis of energy deprivation in the City of Athens also revealed that poverty, devaluation, low energy efficiency of buildings and poor infrastructure and reduction in energy consumption are widespread in urban space. It seems that all neighborhoods and social groups have been affected by the crisis and austerity policies and that there is no clear or simple segregation connected with domestic energy deprivation, a finding that intersects with previous academic research about the social mixture of Athens' neighborhoods (Mantouvalou 1996; Maloutas et al. 2006). However, there are areas in the City of Athens where the living conditions are deteriorating and problems of energy poverty are especially acute. These problems have been generated or in some cases have expanded in the context of the crisis. But still, the broader picture is more complicated. In neighborhoods with severe problems, there are apartment buildings or flats in a relatively better condition, whereas enclaves of poverty, devaluation and deprivation are not a surprise in neighborhoods, apartment buildings and flats of the more privileged areas.

The study of energy deprivation in apartment buildings reveals that, in the context of the crisis, the established relations between rich and poor, immigrants and non-immigrants, owners and tenants, are redefined. For example, the tenants seem to be in a better position, as they can more easily leave their apartment in order to reduce their fixed costs – including the cost of heating – or move to other buildings in order to gain access to adequate heating. On the other hand, owners seem to be trapped in their property and, in many cases, have big debts. In fact, homeowners are less likely to leave their property, and this is the main reason why they often make long-term plans for the functioning and maintenance of the central heating system in their apartment buildings. This finding emphasizes the geographically embedded nature of energy poverty, as in other geographic contexts tenants are often seen as more vulnerable to energy deprivation (Cauvain and Bouzarovski 2016).

Furthermore, through the study of the impacts of the crisis on domestic energy consumption, we could say that apartment buildings function as one entity and their inhabitants seem to share a 'common fate'. In general, apartment buildings are at the same time fixed physical and legal entities, relative locations, in respect for example to places of employment, recreation and services, as well as places of social interaction. In recent years, there are cases of apartment buildings that have almost collapsed as a system of material and social relations. Through a process of a 'vicious circle', putting out of function the central heating system often provokes the further abandonment of the building and thus the further devaluation of household's living standards – even of those that have sufficient economic means. At the same time, there are vulnerable people that, despite their economic problems, have access to adequate heating due to the tolerance or even the support of the rest of the households in the apartment building, which in many cases functions as a safety net.

Moreover, policies for combating energy deprivation show that there are multiple means to understand and respond to the events occurring around us. All of this relativization does not necessarily reduce or eliminate the capacity for understanding energy deprivation, but it does indicate that special rules and laws are required for analyzing and combating it in different spatial contexts. Furthermore, the variety of interpretations of energy deprivation by policy-makers might form the ground for exclusions or inclusions of certain neighborhoods of the city or certain social groups. This is, for example, the case of poor and vulnerable households in Athens – consisting of undocumented immigrants and refugees, people without a bank account or people who owe money to the state – who do not satisfy the conditions of the relevant programs and they are excluded from the energy benefits.

All in all, we could say that in the case of Athens, the analysis of domestic energy deprivation as a spatial phenomenon can enrich the debate concerning the impact of austerity policies on urban space, at the level of the city, the neighborhood and the apartment building. This approach could be also useful for investigating energy deprivation in other cities that, although have a different historical and socio-economic background, might be affected in similar ways by austerity policies.

Reproduction of figures and acknowledgments

Figures 7.1 to 7.3 and 7.5 to 7.8 have been published in: Vatavali and Chatzikonstantinou (2016) 'Mapping energy poverty in Athens in the context of the crisis', in Maloutas T. and Spirellis S. (eds) *Athens Social Atlas, Digital compendium of texts and visual material* (www.athenssocialatlas.gr/en/article/energy-poverty). We would like to thank Dr. Stavros-Nikiforos Spyrellis, co-editor of *Athens Social Atlas*, for assistance with the editing of maps.

Notes

1 According to a survey by WWF Hellas and Public Issue (2013), 81% of the households surveyed have reduced their expenditure on heating and cooling, while 74% reduced their electricity consumption. A similar picture is described by the a survey conducted in the Northern Greece by the Athens University of Economics and Business, according to which 62.4% of households spend more than 10% of their total income on heating, 78.6% use less heating than they need because they cannot afford it and 64% declared they are unable to pay their heating bills (Panas 2012). Furthermore, a survey conducted by Santamouris et al. (2013) concluded that between winter 2010/2011 and winter 2011/2012 domestic energy consumption dropped by 15%, despite the fact that the second winter was colder, and the ratio of fuel-poor households increased from 11.1% to 11.7%. Also, according to the sample research of the Family Budgets of the Hellenic Statistical Authority, the use of central heating has fallen from 76% of the households in 2008 to 35.5% in 2014 (ELSTAT 2016), a percentage reduction of 46.7%. More specifically, the households using central heating systems reduced during the winters of 2008–2009, 2009–2010, 2011–2012 and 2013–2014 were 2.5%, 0.4%, 1%, 22.6% and 2.6% respectively (ELSTAT 2010, 2012a, 2012b, 2014, 2015). Finally, according to the annual report of INE-GSEE (2017), in 2010, 15.4% of the population could not afford the cost for adequate heating, while in 2015, this percentage raised to 29.2%.
2 According to Law 4001/2011 'For the function of the Energy Markets of Electricity and Natural Gas . . .', 'energy deprivation' is defined as 'the condition of the consumers that, due to low income, in combination with their employment condition, family status and specific health factors, cannot afford the cost for covering their needs for electrical power or natural gas, as the cost accounts for a large proportion of their income'.
3 The City of Athens (population 664,000 in 2011) is the largest among the 66 municipalities of the metropolitan area of Athens (population 3 million in 2011) (ELSTAT 2011), and it includes within its boundaries the center of Athens and some of the oldest neighborhoods of the city.
4 The interviews based on three sets of questions. The first set of questions focused on the main characteristics of each apartment building and the social profile of its inhabitants. The second set of questions intended to explore changes on housing prices,

rents and residential mobility. Finally, the third set of questions focused on individual and collective practices adopted as a response to energy deprivation and especially to problems with heating.

5 In the City of Athens, 256,153 out of 427,825 total dwellings do not have any insulation, i.e. 61% of the dwellings do not have insulation (ELSTAT 2011).

6 Presidential Decree 'On the approval of the regulation for the insulation of the buildings' (Official Gazette 362D'/1979).

7 Smog pollution has emerged as a serious problem in Athens since the outbreak of the crisis, as many households are forced to burn in their fireplaces and stoves any wood, paper as well as other inappropriate materials which come to hand, in order to reduce the cost of heating.

8 The Ministry of Finance implemented a series of heating oil subsidy programs from the winter of 2012–2013 until the winter of 2015–2016. At the national level, the number of the beneficiaries was 184,973 in the winter of 2013–2014, reaching 351,043 in the winter of 2014–2015 (Ministry of Finance 2014), while in the City of Athens the beneficiaries were 12,057 beneficiaries in 2013; 21,935 in 2014; and 23,012 in 2015 (General Secretariat of Public Revenues 2016).

9 Namely low-income consumers (annual family income less than 12,000 euro), families with three children, unemployed, people with disabilities, people who need mechanical support and consumers who do not have access to electricity due to debts (Ministerial Decision Δ5-ΗΛ/Β/Φ29/16027/ 6–8–2010 'Implementation of the Residential Social Tariff' (Official Gazette 1403B'/2010) and its amendments).

10 In 2015, the Ministry of Labor, Social Insurance and Social Solidarity announced a program for supporting the households living in extreme poverty which offers to the beneficiaries access to food and housing, as well as 300Kwh of free electricity consumption per month, free reconnection to the electricity network and favorable arrangements for households who have been disconnected from the electricity network due to debts. In 2015, 89,288 families had access to the subsidies in national level, a number that has been increasing during 2016. In the City of Athens, the beneficiaries of the free reconnection and access to electricity in 2015 were 7,849, i.e. 1.2% of the population (IDIKA 2016).

11 The map is based on the official data about annual family income of the economic year 2011, i.e. about income earned in 2010. We did not have access to more recent data, and so, we did not have the chance to map the effects of the austerity policies imposed after 2010 (salary cuts, staff reduction, tax increases etc.) on family incomes.

12 Ministerial Decisions 'Granting heating oil benefit and setting the amount of the beneficiary, the conditions and the procedure for granting this' (Official Gazette 3049B'/2012, 2656B'/2013, 2820B'/2014, 2677B'/2015 and 4076B'/2016). In 2012, the beneficiaries should have annual family income less than 35,000 euro and property of nominal land value less than 200,000 euro; in 2013 and 2014, annual family income less than 40,000 euro and property of nominal land value less than 300,000 euro; and in 2015, annual family income less than 20,000 euro and property of nominal land value less than 200,000 euro.

13 Kathimerini (2014). Without central heating 4 out of 10 apartment buildings in Athens, 12/2/2014.

14 In Athens, there was a steep decrease in rents the first years after the outburst of the crisis (Bank of Greece 2012).

References

Atanasiu, B., Kontonasiou, E. and Francesco, M. (2014). *Alleviating fuel poverty in the EU: Investing in home renovation, a sustainable and inclusive solution*. Brussels: Buildings Performance Institute Europe.

Balabanides, D., Patatouka, E. and Siatitsa, D. (2013). The right to housing within the crisis in Greece. *Geographies*, 22, 31–44.

Balourdos, D. and Petraki, M. (2012). *New poverty and social segregation*. Athens: Hellenic Parliament.

Bank of Greece. (2012). *Real estate market in the recent financial crisis*. Athens: Bank of Greece. Available at: www.bankofgreece.gr/BogEkdoseis/2012_AGORA_AKINHTON_II.pdf [Accessed 2 April 2017].

Bouzarovski, S. (2014). Energy poverty in the European Union: Landscapes of vulnerability. *WIREs Energy and Environment*, 3, 276–289.

Bridge, G., Bouzarovski, S., Bradshaw, M. and Eyre, N. (2013). Geographies of energy transition: Space, place and the low-carbon economy. *Energy Policy*, 53, 331–340.

Buzar, S. (2007). *Energy poverty in Eastern Europe: Hidden geographies of deprivation*. Aldershot: Ashgate.

Cauvain, J. and Bouzarovski, S. (2016). Energy vulnerability in multiple occupancy housing: a problem that policy forgot. *People Place and Policy*, 10(1), 88–106.

Chatzikonstantinou, E. and Vatavali, F. (2016). Energy deprivation and the spatial transformation of Athens in the context of the crisis: Challenges and conflicts in apartment buildings. In Großmann, K., Schaffrin, A. and Smigiel, C. (eds) *Energie und soziale Ungleichheit: Zurgesellschaftlichen Dimension der Energiewende in Deutschland und Europa*. Wiesbaden: Springer, pp. 185–207.

Corovessi, A., Metaxa, K., Touloupaki, E. and Chrysogelos, N. (2017). *Energy poverty in Greece: Social innovation proposals for combating the phenomenon*. Thessaloniki: Heinrich Böll Stiftung Greece.

Dagoumas, A. and Kitsios, F. (2014). Assessing the impact of the economic crisis on energy poverty in Greece. *Sustainable Cities and Society*, 13, 267–278.

ELSTAT. (2010). *Family budget report 2008*. Athens: Hellenic Statistical Authority.

ELSTAT. (2011). *Population – housing census*. Athens: Hellenic Statistical Authority.

ELSTAT. (2012a). *Family budget report 2009*. Athens: Hellenic Statistical Authority.

ELSTAT. (2012b). *Family budget report 2010*. Athens: Hellenic Statistical Authority.

ELSTAT. (2014). *Family budget report 2013*. Athens: Hellenic Statistical Authority.

ELSTAT. (2015). *Family budget report 2014*. Athens: Hellenic Statistical Authority.

ELSTAT. (2016). *Living conditions in Greece*. Athens: Hellenic Statistical Authority.

Encounter Athens. (2011). *What is the crisis at the centre of Athens? – A report about the public event*. Available at: https://encounterathens.wordpress.com/2011/06/01/enherwsh/ [Accessed 3 May 2017].

General Secretariat for Public Revenue. (2016). *Data about heating oil subsidy*. Athens: Ministry of Finance.

Greek Ombudsman. (2016). *Financial and humanitarian crisis in the neighborhoods of the city: Fieldwork results*. Available at: www.synigoros.gr/resources/160121-apotelesmata. pdf [Accessed 26 March 2017].

Greenpeace. (2013). *Are you freezing at home?* Available at: www.greenpeace.org/greece/ krioneis-spiti-sou/ [Accessed 5 May 2013].

GSIS. (2011). *Public data*. Available at: www.gsis.gr/gsis/info/gsis_site/PublicIssue/.

Harvey, D. (1973). *Social justice and the city*. Athens and Georgia: The University of Georgia Press.

Harvey, D. (2006). Space as a keyword. In Castree, N. and Gregory, D. (eds.) *David Harvey: A critical reader*. Oxford: Blackwell Publishing Ltd.

Hellenic Electricity Distribution Network Operator S.A. (2016). *Data about energy consumption*. Athens: Hellenic Electricity Distribution Network Operator S.A.

IDIKA. (2016). *Data about the program for confronting the humanitarian crisis*. Athens: Electronic Governance of Social Insurance S.A.

INE-GSEE. (2017). *The Greek economy and employment: Annual report 2017*. Athens: Institute of Employment GSEE.

Kathimerini. (2014). Without central heating 4 out of 10 apartment buildings in Athens. *Kathimerini*, 2 December.

Katsoulakos, N. (2011). Combating energy poverty in mountainous areas through energy-saving interventions. Insights from Metsovo, Greece. *Mountain Research and Development*, 31(4), 284–292.

Lefebvre, H. (1991). *The production of space*. Oxford: Blackwell.

Leontidou, L. (1990). *The Mediterranean city in transition: Social change and urban development*. Cambridge: Cambridge University Press.

Maloutas, T., Emmanouil, D. and Pantelidou-Malouta, M. (2006). *Athens: Social structures, practices and perceptions: New parameters and practices and patterns of change 1980–2000*. Athens: National Research for Social Science.

Maloutas, T., Kandilis, G., Petrou, M. and Souliotis, N. (eds.) (2013). *The centre of Athens as a political stake*. Athens: National Research for Social Science and Harokopio University.

Maloutas, T. and Karadimitriou, N. (2001). Vertical social differentiation in Athens: Alternative or complement to community segregation? *International Journal of Urban and Regional Research*, 25(4), 699–716.

Maloutas, T. and Spirellis, S. (2015). Vertical social segregation in Athenian apartment buildings. In Maloutas, T. and Spirellis, S. (eds.) *Athens social atlas, digital compendium of texts and visual material*. Available at: www.athenssocialatlas.gr/en/article/vertical-segregation/.

Mantouvalou, M. (1996). Urban land rent, land prices and processes of urban development II: Problematizing the analysis of space in Greece. *The Greek Review of Social Research*, 89–90, 53–80.

Massey, D. (2005). *For space*. London: Sage.

Ministerial Decision 'Granting heating oil benefit and setting the amount of the beneficiary, the conditions and the procedure for granting this' (Official Gazette 2656B'/2013).

Ministerial Decision 'Granting heating oil benefit and setting the amount of the beneficiary, the conditions and the procedure for granting this' (Official Gazette 2677B'/2015).

Ministerial Decision 'Granting heating oil benefit and setting the amount of the beneficiary, the conditions and the procedure for granting this' (Official Gazette 2820B'/2014).

Ministerial Decision 'Granting heating oil benefit and setting the amount of the beneficiary, the conditions and the procedure for granting this' (Official Gazette 3049B'/2012).

Ministerial Decision 'Granting heating oil benefit and setting the amount of the beneficiary, the conditions and the procedure for granting this' (Official Gazette 4076B'/2016).

Ministry of Finance. (2014). *Announcement for the heating oil subsidy*. Athens: Ministry of Finance, 24 November 2015.

Panas, E. (2012). *Research for the energy poverty in Greece*. Athens: National Technical Chamber of Greece.

Papada, L. and Kaliampakos, D. (2016). Measuring energy poverty in Greece. *Energy Policy*, 94, 157–165.

Santamouris, M., Alevizos, S. M., Aslanoglou, L., Mantzios, D., Milonas, P., Sarelli, I., Karatasou, S., Cartalis, K. and Paravantis, J. A. (2014). Freezing the poor – Indoor environmental quality in low and very low income households during the winter period in Athens. *Energy and Buildings*, 70, 61–70.

Santamouris, M., Paravantis, J., Founda, D., Kolokotsa, D., Michalakakou, P., Papadopoulos, A., Kontoulis, N., Tzavali, A., Stigka, E., Ioannidis, Z., Mehilli, A., Matthiessen, A.

and Servou, E. (2013). Financial crisis and energy consumption: A household survey in Greece. *Energy and Buildings*, 65, 477–487.

Vaiou, D., Mantouvalou, M. and Mavridou, M. (2000). Post war Greek urban planning between theory and juncture. *Proceedings of the 2nd Conference of the Society of the History of the City and City Planning: City Planning in Greece from 1949 to 1974*, 25–37.

Vatavali, F. and Chatzikonstantinou, E. (2016). Mapping energy poverty in Athens in the context of the crisis. In Maloutas, T. and Spirellis, S. (eds.) *Athens social atlas, digital compendium of texts and visual material*. Available at: www.athenssocialatlas.gr/en/article/energy-poverty.

WWF Hellas and Public Issue. (2013). *Research for the program 'Better life'*. WWF Hellas. Available at: www.wwf.gr/images/pdfs/publicIssue-graphs-better-life.pdf.

8 Location, location, location

What accounts for the regional variation of energy poverty in Poland?

Maciej Lis, Agata Miazga, and Katarzyna Sałach

Introduction

The regional variation in energy poverty has rarely been studied in detail, although it is important from a policy perspective. The effectiveness of instruments designed to reduce energy poverty depends, not only on the correct identification of the target group, but also on matching the type of aid to the characteristics of the poor in a given region (Roberts et al. 2015). Both country-level studies (e.g. Isherwood and Hancock 1979; Boardman 1991; Hills 2011; Walker et al. 2014; Legendre and Ricci 2015; Imbert et al. 2016) and international comparisons (Buzar 2007; Thomson and Snell 2013; Bouzarovski and Tirado-Herrero 2015) confirm the significance of the specific local conditions of energy poverty. Although several understandings of energy poverty are in use, in this chapter, we reduce this broad concept to two dimensions. Firstly, thermal comfort includes experiencing problems with maintaining an adequate indoor temperature in winter. And secondly, energy affordability comprises the reduction of spending on basic goods due to high energy bills (Boardman 1991; Hills 2011).

Previous research has shown that energy poverty is often concentrated in rural areas due to the lower income of their inhabitants and the lower energy efficiency of buildings in many countries (e.g. the United Kingdom, Baker et al. 2008; Scotland, Illsley et al. 2007; Northern Ireland, Rugkåsa et al. 2007 and Walker et al. 2012). In the United Kingdom, energy poverty in rural areas is related to the limited access to relatively cheap natural gas (Baker et al. 2008). The distance between villages and larger urban centres might hamper access not only to infrastructure, but also to thermal retrofitting and other resources improving the energy efficiency of buildings (Boardman 2010). The energy poor from rural areas are also, in some countries, more sensitive to increases in energy prices (Roberts et al. 2015). As a consequence, the volatility of energy prices results in an increased probability of remaining fuel poor amongst rural areas' inhabitants, relative to their urban counterparts (Roberts et al. 2015).

Regional analyses of energy poverty point to similar risk factors. Energy poverty in the United Kingdom is concentrated in Northern Ireland (44% of the inhabitants) and Scotland (33%), where the percentage of households connected to gas distribution networks is low (Illsley et al. 2007). The major cause of this regional variation is the differences in the level of household income (e.g. Boardman 2010; Walker et al. 2012). Differences in average temperatures and the energy efficiency of buildings, in turn, affect the energy costs needed to satisfy thermal comfort (Baker et al. 2008; Walker et al. 2012; Bouzarovski and Tirado-Herrero 2015). The indoor temperature required to satisfy thermal comfort varies by the type of household. For instance, the elderly face the highest risk of energy poverty in England as a consequence of their higher thermal comfort standard and the longer time spent at home (Baker et al. 2008).

The geographical location, both in terms of latitude and elevation, is an important determinant of the expenditure required for heating a dwelling. In Austria, Switzerland and Northern Italy, inhabitants of mountainous areas are more vulnerable to energy poverty than those living in the lowlands (Papada and Kaliampakos 2016a. A typical house in Switzerland, situated 1,200 m above sea level, is characterised by a demand for thermal energy that is twice as high as an identical house situated 200 m above sea level. This is due to lower outdoor temperatures and a heating season that is 5 months longer. Similar results were obtained for Greece (Papada and Kaliampakos 2016b), where the number of heating days had a strong positive correlation with altitude, and a much lower correlation with other geographical variables, such as latitude, the number of sunny days per year and distance from the sea.

Energy affordability and the lack of thermal comfort constitute separate dimensions of energy poverty and require different policy measures. These differences can also be observed at regional level (e.g. Fahmy et al. 2011; Papada and Kaliampakos 2016a). English households whose 'required' energy expenditure exceeds 10% of income only coincide with households declaring a lack of thermal comfort at the place of living to a small extent (Fahmy et al. 2011). Differences also arise depending on methodological choices regarding the equivalisation of income and energy expenditure (Baker et al. 2008).

Post-communist countries, including Poland, are in the lead when it comes to the number of people declaring that they live in inadequately warm houses compared to other European countries (Bouzarovski and Tirado Herrero 2016). Due to the climate conditions in Poland, we focus on dwellings that are insufficiently warm in winter, omitting those that are insufficiently cool in summer. The average annual number of days with air temperature below zero in 1981–2010 ranged from about 20 days in coastal areas to about 50 days in the eastern part of the country, whereas the number of days with air temperature exceeding 30 degrees Celsius gave an average of slightly more than 11 days a year in the hottest region (IMGW – PIB 2013a; IMGW – PIB 2013b). Although excessive heat can be as dangerous to human health as excessive cold, in this chapter, we focus on excessive cold only, considering it to be more problematic in Poland.

There are a few reasons for focusing on the regional dimension of energy poverty in Poland. In 2014 almost half (approx. 40%) of Poles lived in villages (CSO 2015). Disparities between rural and urban areas shape the regional differences of Poland. Out of the 16 voivodeships, the administrative subdivisions corresponding to NUTS2 statistical level (see Eurostat 2017 for a full explanation of the

NUTS statistical levels), the poorest are those with the highest ratio of rural area (CSO 2015). During the last 25 years, Poland has faced problems with regionally-concentrated unemployment and social polarisation in big cities (Bouzarovski and Tirado Herrero 2016).

Studies of energy poverty in Poland have focused on describing the structure of the poor and poverty determinants (Kurowski 2011; Stępniak and Tomaszewska 2014; Szamrej-Baran 2014; Miazga and Owczarek 2015; Szpor 2016; Lis et al. 2016a; Lis et al. 2016b) or mechanisms observed at local level (Frankowski and Tirado-Herrero 2015). The regional dimension of the phenomenon has not been the main focus. It has been analysed at the country level in international comparisons of post-communist countries (e.g. Bouzarovski and Tirado Herrero 2016). Eastern Poland is more vulnerable to energy poverty than the rest of the country (e.g. Bouzarovski and Tirado Herrero 2016).

We aim to focus on the regional variation concerning energy poverty in Poland by addressing the following questions:

1   What is the scale of regional variation concerning energy poverty in Poland, both in terms of energy affordability and lack of thermal comfort?
2   What is the scale of the regional variation in the five groups of energy poverty determinants: characteristics of buildings, household structure and income, level of urbanisation, level of energy prices and the local climate?
3   What is the role of region-specific factors in explaining the variation in energy poverty? Does the impact of the highlighted causes of energy poverty vary by region?
4   Can regional differences in climate and energy prices explain the regional variation in energy poverty, which cannot be attributed to the characteristics of households and buildings?

The chapter is organised as follows: first we introduce the methods and data that allow us to deal with the above questions, then we present the results of the logistic model of energy poverty risk and a statistical analysis of the relationships between the voivodeship effects that have not been explained by the model. The impact of climate and energy prices is also considered. Finally, we present the conclusions and policy implications.

Methods and data

Energy poverty measures

In order to cover the two dimensions of energy poverty – energy affordability and thermal comfort – we use two measures of incidence for energy poverty: the low income high cost measure (LIHC) and the subjective measure of thermal comfort. To be classified as energy poor according to the LIHC definition, a household must simultaneously meet two criteria: low income (LI) and high required energy costs (HC). The construction of the LIHC definition, which is based on two measurable values, household income and energy expenditure, results in the main feature of this measure: objectivity. The subjective measure of thermal comfort, on the other hand, is based on respondents' statements about the level to which their energy needs are met (or the difficulty in satisfying those needs). This measure corresponds best to the public understanding of energy poverty as an experience of insufficient thermal comfort. It is useful for monitoring the dynamics of energy poverty too (Hills 2011). The subjective energy poverty measure used in this study is based on the answers to the question in the Household Budget Survey (HBS): 'Is, in your opinion, the home you live in sufficiently warm in winter (with serviceable heating and/or sufficient thermal insulation of the building)?' A negative answer from a respondent means that she or he experiences energy poverty. The question in the HBS differs from the one in European Union Statistics on Income and Living Conditions (EU-SILC), which is 'Can your household afford to keep its home adequately warm?' The one asked in the HBS does not take affordability directly into account, and therefore, our results cannot be directly compared to the analysis based on EU-SILC.

Data

The Polish Household Budget Survey (HBS), carried out annually by the Central Statistical Office of Poland (CSO), provides data about the level and structure of household expenditure, as well as the level and sources of the income earned. It also contains variables regarding the household possession of durable goods and information about living conditions, a subjective assessment of the household financial situation as well as their demographic and social characteristics. The multidimensionality of the data and the sample size (37,215 households examined in 2014[1]) permits a regional analysis of energy poverty.

The LIHC indicator adopted in this study is based exclusively on the data obtained from the HBS both with respect to heating and electricity expenditure. The LIHC analyses previously published in Poland (Miazga and Owczarek 2015; Lis et al. 2016a) utilised data provided by the Polish National Energy Conservation Agency (KAPE) for calculating required heating expenditure. However, the required expenditure defined by KAPE differs considerably from the energy expenditure declared by households in the HBS. Particularly significant discrepancies are noticeable in the case of single-family houses. According to KAPE assumptions, the expenditure required to heat 1 m² should be 2–3 times higher for a detached house than for a dwelling in a block of flats, yet the HBS data shows evidence of an opposite relationship: the average monthly heat expenditure in blocks of flats amounts to PLN 4.10 per m², in a single-family terraced house it is PLN 2.70 per m², and in a single-family detached house – PLN 2.60 per m². This may be the effect of an inaccurate measurement of the energy efficiency of individual buildings in the HBS and differences in the level of thermal comfort between residents of various types of buildings. The qualitative studies on poverty in Poland also reveal a third reason for this discrepancy: the use of cheap heating fuels, such as brushwood, garbage and sawdust, by residents of single-family houses (Rakowski 2009).

Because of the aforementioned differences, only the HBS data was used to calculate the required energy expenditure. This was done by taking the average expenditure in these categories: the type of building, age of building and type of heating. The average energy expenditure calculated for each unique building-age-heating cell was then assigned to every household. Doing so allowed us to identify households that spent less on energy than they needed.

The adoption of the described methodology (see also Lis et al. 2016b) resulted in a drop in the energy poverty estimate from 17.1% of the population in 2013 to 11.7% in 2014, and with regards to households – 9.6%. This difference is purely due to a change in methodology. According to the previous method, the drop in LIHC in 2014 was 0.1 percentage point.

The data on the regional variation in energy prices was obtained from a CSO database called the Local Data Bank. The data on average temperatures was based on findings from the Institute of Meteorology and Water Management (CSO 2015). The average annual air temperature is reported for 32 meteorological stations in Poland. For regions with more than one meteorological station, we calculate the average of all available values.

Analysis of the energy poverty measure variance

We analyse the energy poverty variation using the analysis of variance (ANOVA) method, adapted to the logit model for the binary dependent variable. The analysis of variance allows for 1) an assessment of the significance and 2) of the power of individual groups of variables in explaining both the energy affordability and thermal comfort dimensions of energy poverty.

Based on the reviewed literature, we consider five factors that influence the energy poverty risk: the characteristics of buildings, characteristics of households (including income), degree of urbanisation, local climate and energy prices. The first three are directly covered by the variables available in HBS, while the last two are observable in other datasets at regional level only. Each of the factors is composed of several, both continuous and discrete, variables. The influence of the individual factors on energy poverty risk is not only direct, but also indirect. For example, the size and type of dwelling are influenced by household income. Apartments are concentrated particularly in larger cities, whereas detached houses are concentrated in villages. Voivodeships differ significantly in terms of their degree of urbanisation.

In order to account for the direct and indirect impact of each factor, the analysis of variance is carried out twofold. Firstly, the fit of the models with each group of variables is compared separately to the fit of the null model (with just the constant). Secondly, the fit of the model with all variables (saturated model) is compared to the fit of the model with all but selected variables included. The influence of a given variable or a set of variables is examined for its significance using the Wald test and their impact is measured by the change of the pseudo-R^2 measure of goodness-of-fit (McKelvey and Zavoina 1975; Veall and Zimmermann 1996) between appropriate models. We use pseudo-R^2 instead of the value of likelihood function due to the interpretability of the results.

The models are estimated separately for relative poverty and subjective poverty. Interactions between groups of variables and voivodeships are estimated separately by introducing the Cartesian product of those variables as a separate group of dummy variables. The same analysis (except for the inclusion of interaction terms) is repeated 16 times for each voivodeship in order to measure the impact of each factor at regional level.

Regional variation concerning energy poverty in Poland

Variation of energy poverty incidence

According to the HBS data for 2014, the affordability (LIHC) dimension of energy poverty was experienced by 9.6% of households in Poland (1.3 million households, i.e. 4.5 million people), and its incidence varied a lot amongst the

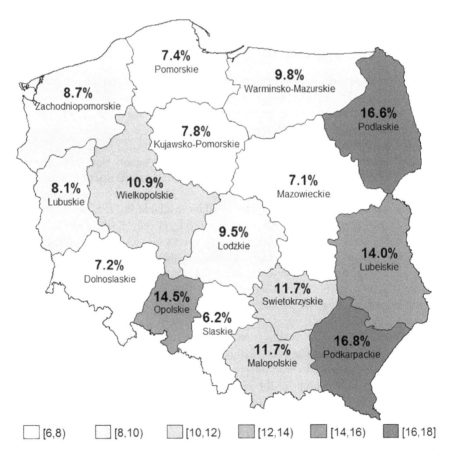

Figure 8.1 LIHC energy poverty rates in voivodeships in Poland in 2014 (%)

Source: Own calculations based on the 2014 Polish HBS data

regions. In accordance with the LIHC measure, energy poverty mainly concerned eastern voivodeships: Podkarpackie (17% of households), Podlaskie (17%) and Lubelskie (14%) as well as Opolskie (15%). The lowest levels were recorded in the richest regions: Śląskie (6%), Mazowieckie (7%), Dolnośląskie (7%) and Pomorskie (7%) (Figure 8.1). Hence, the difference in the risk of energy poverty between the extreme voivodeships was almost triple.

The subjective measure of energy poverty shows a similar scope, with 11.5% of households in Poland declaring that they live in under-heated accommodation in winter. As was the case with the LIHC measure, the regional variation of the subjective measure was almost triple: from 6.1% of energy poor households in Podkarpackie to 17.9% in Lubuskie (Figure 8.2). At the voivodeship level, the correlation between the affordability and subjective measures of energy poverty is negative, i.e. the higher the percentage of poor according to the LIHC, the lower the percentage of poor according to the subjective measure. Combining the two

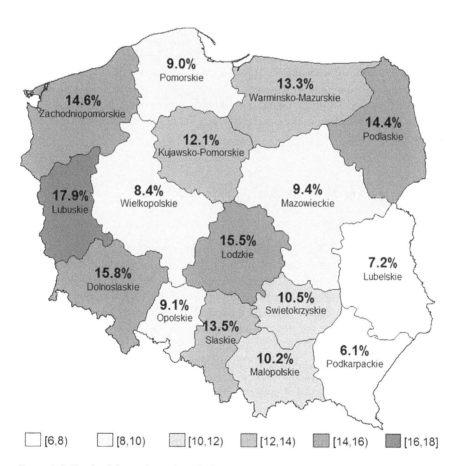

Figure 8.2 "Lack of thermal comfort" (subjective energy poverty) rates in voivodeships in Poland in 2014 (%)

Source: Own calculations based on the 2014 Polish HBS data

dimensions of energy poverty (energy affordability and lack of thermal comfort) allows us to distinguish four groups of voivodeships:

- The poorest (Podlaskie) – This voivodeship is characterised by a high percentage of energy poor according to both the LIHC and subjective measures. It is the voivodeship with the second highest indicator of relative income poverty – 24% (CSO 2015).
- Regions with a high score for the affordability dimension of energy poverty (Podkarpackie, Lubelskie, Opolskie, Wielkopolskie, Małopolskie and Świętokrzyskie) – These regions combine high scores on the LIHC with low scores on the subjective measure of energy poverty. The majority of these voivodeships are also characterised by a high percentage of relative income poverty.
- Regions with high prevalence of a lack of thermal comfort (Lubuskie, Dolnośląskie, Łódzkie, Zachodniopomorskie, Śląskie, Warmińsko-Mazurskie, Kujawsko-Pomorskie) – These regions have a high subjective poverty measure and low LIHC measure. Only two voivodeships from this group are also characterised by a high percentage of income poor: Warmińsko-Mazurskie and Kujawsko-Pomorskie.
- Regions with the lowest intensity of poverty (Mazowieckie and Pomorskie). These voivodeships are characterised by the lowest scale of both the LIHC and subjective measures of energy poverty. They also show low incidence of income poverty.

Variation of energy poverty factors

Characteristics of buildings

The characteristics of buildings differ a lot among regions, both in terms of thermal efficiency and energy carriers. In 2014, 56% of households in Poland lived in blocks of flats and 38% in detached houses. Detached houses prevail in the east and south of Poland, and the variation in the percentage of households in detached houses between individual voivodeships reaches 47 percentage points (Podkarpackie – 63% versus Zachodniopomorskie – 16%). Detached houses dominate in rural areas (78% of households in villages), where they are usually heated with solid fuel. According to the calculator for the cost of heating a standard house (Adgar EcoEnergia Serock 2016), heating with natural gas is twice as expensive as coal or wood and simultaneously twice as cheap as electricity. The use of solid-fuel stoves varies among voivodeships. The highest incidence is recorded in the Warmińsko-Mazurskie voivodeship – 19.3% of households, which is nearly three times more than in the Mazowieckie voivodeship – 7.3%.

The age structure of buildings in Poland shows high regional variation, as evidenced by the HBS data. The oldest buildings are located in the west and north of the country. In the Lubuskie voivodeship, 43% of households reside in pre-war buildings, and in the Dolnośląskie and Opolskie voivodeships – 41%, while the average for Poland is 20%. The highest percentage of buildings constructed after 1996 is recorded in voivodeships with large urban centres: Mazowieckie (22%), Małopolskie and Pomorskie (17%). The age of the building is a clear sign of its energy efficiency.

Characteristics of households

Household income is one of the major determinants of energy poverty (e.g. Boardman 2010; Walker 2012) despite the fact that energy and income poverty coincide only in approximately 30% of households in Poland (Miazga and Owczarek 2015). The median disposable income in Poland amounted to PLN 3,167 per month in 2014. The lowest average disposable income was disclosed by households in north-eastern, rural regions of Poland (Podlaskie – PLN 2,800 per month, Warmińsko-Mazurskie – PLN 2,811 per month) and eastern regions (Lubelskie – PLN 2,902 per month). North-eastern voivodeships are also characterised by a high percentage of income poverty (Warmińsko-Mazurskie – 18%, Podlaskie – 16%; Figure 8.3).

Energy poverty is also influenced also by the demographic structure of households as it determines thermal comfort preferences. Families with children, retirees and pensioners belong to the groups with the highest level of temperature standards. In 2014, as evidenced by the HBS data, the highest percentage of retiree households was recorded in the following voivodeships: Podlaskie (32% of households), Zachodniopomorskie (31%) and Dolnośląskie (30%). The lowest percentage of these households is present in voivodeships with large urban centres. The regional gap of the percentage of retiree households amounts to 8.7 percentage points.

Degree of urbanisation

Almost 40% of the Polish population lives in rural areas, although in the case of households, it is only 33% (CSO 2015). This is due to more children and more multi-generational families living in rural areas. The level of urbanisation varies along the east-west gradient (Figure 8.4). The highest percentage of rural households is recorded in eastern and south-eastern voivodeships (Podkarpackie – 54%, Lubelskie – 48%, Świętokrzyskie – 50%). In the west, the percentage is approximately 30%, while the lowest is noticed in the Śląskie voivodeship, which also shows the highest degree of urbanisation, with only 18% of the population living in rural areas. Big cities with a population of more than 500,000 are located in only 5 voivodeships: Mazowieckie, Małopolskie, Łódzkie, Dolnośląskie and Wielkopolskie.

Explaining the variance of energy poverty

Causes of energy poverty in Poland

In order to quantify the role of each aforementioned factor (buildings, households, urbanisation) in explaining the variation in energy poverty, we build two

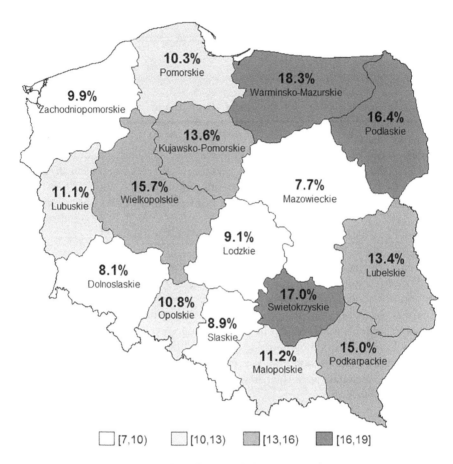

Figure 8.3 Income poverty incidence by voivodeships in Poland in 2014 (%)

Note: Relative measure of income poverty used.

Source: Own calculations based on the 2014 Polish HBS data

logistic regression models. In the first one, the affordability measure of energy poverty (LIHC) is a dependent variable whereas in the second one, the experienced lack of thermal comfort (the subjective measure of energy poverty) is modelled. All independent variables together are statistically significant in both models, but they explain the affordability dimension of energy poverty much better (pseudo-R^2 of 61%) than in the case of the lack of thermal comfort dimension (pseudo-R^2 of 19%). Hence, subjective energy poverty is a phenomenon that is more difficult to explain using the variables available via the HBS.

Starting with the interpretation of the estimates of the model for the LIHC measure, households of blue-collar workers, farmers and the self-employed face a greater risk of energy poverty than white-collar workers (see Appendix 8.1 for

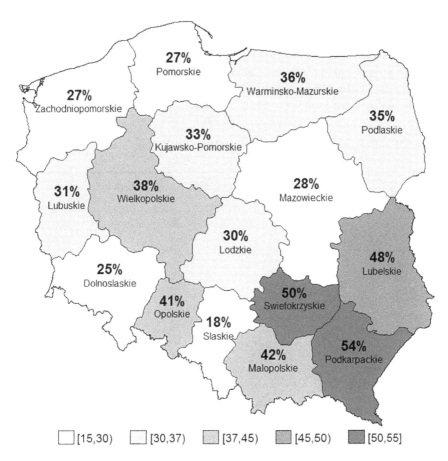

Figure 8.4 Percentage of households inhabiting rural areas by voivodeships in Poland in 2014 (%)

Source: Own calculations based on the 2014 Polish HBS data

full details of the logistic regression results). Lower income, larger floor area and more children significantly increase the risk of affordability dimension of energy poverty. The risk factors also include living in detached houses, old buildings (built before 1970) and rural areas.

According to the estimates in the model for the subjective energy poverty measure, the risk factors for experiencing a lack of thermal comfort are similar to those for affordability, although some differences are meaningful. Compared to central heating, gas and solid fuel stoves increase the risk of subjective measures of energy poverty and lower the risk of affordability. Other risk factors are similar.

The reasonable estimates of parameters allow us to continue with the analysis of the variance of energy poverty. Income and floor area are the key factors that explain the affordability dimension of energy poverty (Table 8.1). Socio-economic characteristics of households are the most crucial for explaining the LIHC measure variance (30% of total variance), and it is income that is almost exclusively responsible for this effect (27%). The size of household, the source of income or the number of children are definitely less important (4% in total). The characteristics of buildings explain 21% of the LIHC measure variance. Floor area is predominant in the group as it explains 17% of the general variance. The

Table 8.1 Influence of selected groups of variables on explaining energy poverty variation in Poland in general

Variable	Affordability measure (LIHC)		"Lack of thermal comfort" measure	
	Direct impact	Indirect and direct impact	Direct impact	Indirect and direct impact
Buildings characteristics	0.21***	0.24***	0.09***	0.16***
Floor area	0.17***	-	0.01***	-
Type of building	0.03***	-	0.001**	-
Type of heating	0.01***	-	0.01***	-
Building construction period	0.03***	-	0.03***	-
Socioeconomic characteristics	0.3***	0.3***	0.02***	0.07***
Number of children (under 14 years old)	0.01***	-	0.001***	-
Socioeconomic group	0.03***	-	0.002***	-
Disposable income of household [ln PLN]	0.27***	-	0.01***	-
Degree of urbanisation	0.02***	0.17***	0.002***	0.003***
Regional effect	0.003***	0.03***	0.02***	0.03***
Interactions between variables				
Voivodeship × Degree of urbanisation	0.015**	0.026***	0.021***	0.033***
Voivodeship × Buildings characteristics	0.008***	0.018***	0.004***	0.004***
Voivodeship × Socioeconomic characteristics	0.001***	0.003***	0.001***	0.001***

Note: The direct influence of the variable is calculated as a pseudo-R^2 decrease in the model after the removal of the variable in comparison to the base model. Pseudo-R^2 for the base model was 0.61 for the LIHC measure and 0.19 for the subjective measure. The direct and indirect influence was calculated as a pseudo-R^2 increase in comparison to the model just with the constant. In the case of models with interactions, the direct influence is calculated as a pseudo-R^2 increase in comparison to the base model, while the direct and indirect influence is the pseudo-R^2 increase in the model with two groups of variables and interactions in comparison to the model without interaction (only with two groups of variables). Significance levels: *** $p < 0.01$, ** $p < 0.05$, * $p < 0.1$.

Source: Own calculations based on the 2014 Polish HBS data

energy efficiency of buildings, approximated by the age, type and heating method of the building, only explains a total of 4% variance. The level of urbanisation and geographical location (voivodeships) have a significant influence on the phenomenon, although their contribution is considerably lower at 2% and 0.3%, respectively. The influence of the degree of urbanisation is largely indirect and occurs due to differences in income and the types of buildings between rural and urban areas. Therefore, when compared to the null model the effect of the degree of urbanisation rises more than eightfold to 17%. A similar effect is observed in the case of voivodeships – when there are no other variables, the influence of voivodeships on the goodness-of-fit of the model is significant and explains 3% of the variance, and when other variables are controlled, it drops below 1%.

In case of a lack of thermal comfort of energy poverty, all variables explain 19% of the variance. Contrary to the results of the LIHC measure, the characteristics of buildings are the dominant factor, explaining 9% of the variance. Within this factor, the year of construction is the most important (3%). Therefore, thermal comfort is much more linked to thermal efficiency (year of construction and type of building) than to the floor area. Socioeconomic characteristics, including income, account for merely 2% of the subjective measure of energy poverty variance. The income impact is indirect and appears mainly through the characteristics of buildings. Higher income allows better living conditions. For a model with no other socioeconomic variables, the significance of income in explaining the subjective energy poverty measure increases to 7%. The degree of urbanisation explains less than 1% of subjective energy poverty variance, no matter whether other factors are included. Compared to the LIHC measure, the regional factor (voivodeships) is more important and accounts for 2%, even after controlling all other factors.

Regional diversity

In order to assess the regional variation of the impact of selected factors on energy poverty in every region of Poland, we separately analyse the interactions between selected variables and regional dummies. All interactions were statistically significant, both for the affordability and subjective measures. However, a noticeable (more than 1%) influence on the goodness-of-fit of the models appears only in the case of interactions between dummies of voivodeships and the degree of urbanisation (Table 8.1). It means that, even after controlling for the characteristics of buildings and households, the difference in energy poverty incidence among large cities, small towns and villages varies between regions. On the contrary, the impact of energy efficiency and household characteristics is similar in each voivodeship.

In order to identify the regional differences in the relative role of the specific factors in explaining energy poverty, we conduct an analysis of variance for each region separately. The regional models differ a lot in terms of goodness-of-fit. The share of the LIHC measure variance explained by the households and buildings characteristics ranges from 52% in Śląskie to 88% in Lubuskie, whereas the share of the subjective measure variance explained ranges from 18% (Śląskie and Zachodniopomorskie) to 27% (Lubelskie, Łódzkie, Małopolskie and Podlaskie). In most cases, the regional models confirm the findings for Poland in general. There are, however, a few meaningful exceptions.

As far as the lack of thermal comfort dimension of energy poverty is concerned, the influence of socioeconomic characteristics in general is low (2%), yet the regional analysis revealed a high variation of the role of this group of characteristics between voivodeships (Figure 8.5). The influence of socioeconomic characteristics was most visible in the Małopolskie and Świętokrzyskie voivodeships (5% and 4% of the explained variance, respectively). These voivodeships belonged to the group of moderately rich (household median disposable monthly income in 2014: PLN 3,300 and PLN 3,200, respectively), which corresponded to the low rate of subjective energy poverty (10.2% and 10.5%).

There were only two voivodeships (Kujawsko-Pomorskie and Lubelskie) where the LIHC energy poverty rate is determined more by the characteristics of buildings than by socioeconomic characteristics (Figure 8.6). In the Lubelskie voivodeship, the high energy poverty rate stems from the fact that the inhabitants of this region have both low incomes and big houses. However, inhabitants of the Kujawsko-Pomorskie voivodeship have low income and small floor area on average. In the Lubelskie and Kujawsko-Pomorskie voivodeships, the influence of the level of urbanisation proved to be a few percentage points higher than the influence of the group of socioeconomic variables. In Kujawsko-Pomorskie, one can observe the highest percentage of subjectively energy poor households in cities with a population of 20,000–99,000 in Poland (34% compared to 12% in cities of this size in Poland in general).

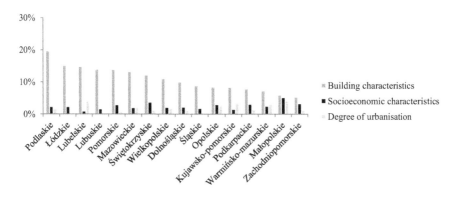

Figure 8.5 Direct influence of specific factors on subjective energy poverty measure ("lack of thermal comfort") in voivodeships

Note: Figure shows decrease in pseudo-R^2 in restricted logistic regression models in comparison to saturated logistic regression model.

Source: Own calculations based on the 2014 Polish HBS data

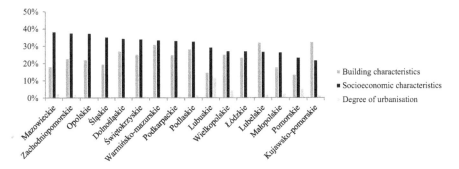

Figure 8.6 Direct influence of specific factors on the LIHC measure of energy poverty in voivodeships

Note: Figure shows decrease in pseudo-R^2 in restricted logistic regression models in comparison to saturated logistic regression model.

Source: Own calculations based on the 2014 Polish HBS data

Climate and energy prices

The characteristics of buildings, characteristics of households and the degree of urbanisation explain the majority of LIHC energy poverty variations between regions. The regional dummies add very little to the model fit (0.1%), and only some differences between voivodeship dummies are statistically significant. Parameter estimates indicate that, after factoring out the impact of buildings, households and degree of urbanisation, the affordability dimension of poverty risk is the highest in Podlaskie, Podkarpackie and Małopolskie and lowest in Mazowieckie, Pomorskie, Kujawsko-Pomorskie and Świętokrzyskie.

More than 2% of the variance in the subjective energy poverty measure is explained by regional dummies, even after the inclusion of other variables (Table 8.1), compared to 0.3% in the case of the LIHC measure. Consequently, the additional factors, such as climate and energy prices, could explain subjective energy poverty. In the case of the LIHC measure, the remaining regional differences are negligible.

Climate influences the outlay needed to maintain a comfortable temperature in buildings. The average annual outdoor temperatures vary to a limited extent between the Polish voivodeships. In 2014, the maximum difference was 3 degrees Celsius (7.9 degrees Celsius in Podlaskie compared to 10.8 degree Celsius in the Opolskie voivodeship). The coldest regions of Poland are located in the south (mountainous areas) and east of Poland (especially the Podlaskie voivodeship). In Białystok, the capital city of Podlaskie, the minimum average temperature in January for the period 1999–2013 was −10.2 degrees Celsius, in comparison to −5.9 degrees Celsius for the hottest provincial city – Wrocław (Dolnośląskie voivodeship; Dopke 2014). The correlation coefficient between the estimates of regional dummies in the model of subjective energy poverty measure, and the

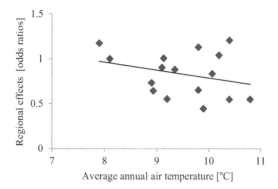

Figure 8.7 Correlation between regional effects of subjective energy poverty variation (odds ratios) and average annual air temperatures (degrees Celsius) by voivode-ships in Poland in 2014

Note: The figure uses the logistic regression results in the form of odds ratios. Values higher than 1 indicate that a given analysed phenomenon is more likely to occur (here: energy poverty), and values lower than 1, that it is less likely than for the reference level.

Source: Own calculations based on the 2014 Polish HBS and CSO 2015

average air temperatures in voivodeships is −0.29 and, although it is not statistically significant (due to the low sample size of 16), it indicates the influence of regional climate variation on the perceived thermal comfort (Figure 8.7). The high subjective poverty rate in the Podlaskie voivodeship could be partly attributed to lower outdoor temperatures. In the south of Poland, where average temperatures are lower due to the altitude (Podkarpackie and Małopolskie voivodeships in particular), the regional effects in the subjective poverty model are also notably high.

As far as prices of energy carriers are concerned (gas, power, central heating, coal), the greatest variation relates to the prices of district central heating. In 2014, the average price amounted to PLN 3.97 per 1m² and the variation between voivodeships reached 40% (Opolskie: PLN 3.18 per m², Podlaskie: PLN 5.27 per m²; own calculations based on Local Data Bank). The correlation coefficient between regional effects in the subjective energy poverty model and prices of central heating equals 0.57 and is statistically significant. The higher the price of central heating, the higher the subjective energy poverty rate (Figure 8.8). However, differences in central heating prices expressed in PLN per square metre are affected by the energy efficiency of buildings and air temperatures: the lower they are, the higher the energy requirement. Consequently, the identified statistically significant correlation is also due to the excessively crude energy efficiency measures of the buildings.

The prices of other energy carriers are less correlated with regional effects (correlation coefficient for electricity: 0.1, natural gas: −0.04, hard coal: 0.15) and show lower regional variation. In 2014, the cost of 1 m³ of methane-rich natural

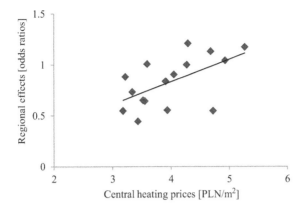

Figure 8.8 Correlation between regional effects of subjective energy poverty variation (odds ratios) and prices of central heating (PLN/m²) by voivodeships in Poland in 2014

Note: The chart uses the logistic regression results in the form of odds ratios. Values higher than 1 indicate that a given analysed phenomenon is more likely to occur (here: energy poverty), and values lower than 1, that it is less likely than for the reference level.

Source: Own calculations based on the 2014 Polish HBS and BDL (Local Data Bank) data

gas from the distribution network was approximately PLN 2.29, and regional differences were 12%. The regional variation in the price of hard coal was 17%, with the national average at PLN 802 per tonne. The price of electrical energy in Poland in 2014 amounted to PLN 0.64 per 1 kWh on average, and the level of differences between voivodeships was 10%.

Conclusions

The regional variation of energy poverty in Poland is significant in both dimensions: energy affordability (LIHC measure) and lack of thermal comfort (subjective measure). The high level of one dimension coincides with a low intensity of the other. The Podlaskie voivodeship is the only one that accumulated both dimensions of energy poverty. On the other hand, Mazowieckie and Pomorskie show a low risk of both dimensions of energy poverty. Other voivodeships are significantly exposed to either the subjective or affordability dimension of energy poverty.

The affordability dimension of energy poverty is mostly related to a household's income and dwelling area, whereas the lack of thermal comfort can be linked to energy efficiency. The energy efficiency of buildings and household income is highly related to the degree of urbanisation. Large detached houses predominate in rural areas, while blocks of flats (usually with a smaller floor area) are more common in urban areas. Income is also higher in cities. The consequence of this spatial sorting is the concentration of energy affordability difficulties in rural areas and the lack of thermal comfort in cities. Therefore, the instruments that aim to eradicate the affordability dimension of energy poverty should focus on income inequalities and the energy efficiency of detached houses. Decreasing income inequality requires an increase in the scope and precision of social transfers. In order to increase thermal comfort; in turn, it is crucial to improve the energy efficiency of old blocks of flats in cities. This is a matter of public investments outlays and creating incentives for private investment as well as improvements in regulations.

The characteristics of buildings, characteristics of households and the degree of urbanisation together explain the majority of the variation in the energy affordability dimension (LIHC measure) of energy poverty. The lack of thermal comfort (a subjective measure) is a more complex phenomenon, and it is more difficult to capture by aggregate variables. In order to improve the fit of the model for the subjective measure of energy poverty, more detailed data on the energy efficiency of buildings is needed than the data currently available in the HBS.[2]

There is a significant component of regional variation in the lack of thermal comfort that cannot be explained by the characteristics of buildings and households. This component is related to the differences in prices of central heating and average outdoor temperatures. Our results indicate the need for separate research into the influence of prices of energy carriers on energy poverty, using energy prices at household level. With regards to the understanding of the influence of regional climate variation on energy poverty, it is necessary to apply data at the sub-region or county level. Clearly, lower temperatures can be noticed along the southern border of Poland (mountainous areas) and in the north-east of Poland. Further work on the regional variation of potential energy expenditure could show a much more important role of regional factors in shaping the affordability dimension of energy poverty (LIHC).

The strategies to eradicate energy poverty should vary by region, due to the strong regional variation in the causes of energy poverty. Particular attention should to be paid to the Podlaskie voivodeship, which is characterised by the highest intensity of both energy affordability and lack of thermal comfort. It is a poor and rural region with a high prevalence of detached houses. Regional development strategies, which determine the structure of expenditure in the area of urban retrofit as well as development aid to rural areas should, as one of their goals, take eradicating energy poverty into account. Moreover, strategies and actions should consider the intensity of both poverty dimensions and their causes in each region.

Acknowledgements

We would like to thank Piotr Lewandowski for his many helpful suggestions during the research process. We would also like to thank the participants of 3rd ESPAnet Poland Conference for their insightful comments. The research was developed by a grant funded by the European Climate Foundation. The usual disclaimers apply. All errors are our own.

Notes

1 The sample used in the models amounted to 35,977 observations. It did not allow for households with more than one house and those living in unknown types of buildings or using unknown types of heating. After this cleaning procedure, the sample amounted to 36,626 households and all the descriptive statistics refer to this amount. However, before logistic regressions were carried out, people declaring that their houses were heated with an electric stove were also excluded from the sample, since for them, due to the impossibility of separating heat expenditure from electrical energy expenditure, the values for the LIHC fuel poverty were considered to be distorted. This impossibility resulted from a lack of knowledge, necessary in the construction of the LIHC measure used in this chapter, about which part of electrical energy expenditure was used to power electric heaters and which was used to meet other needs (e.g. lighting, cooking).

2 There is a module in the Polish HBS regarding energy consumption in households that contains, amongst other things, data on the energy performance of buildings. However, the relatively small sample size (4,576 observations) does not allow detailed studies.

References

Adgar EcoEnergia Serock. (2016). *Online calculators.* Available at: http://ag-dar.vaillant-partner.pl/kalkulatory-on-line.

Baker, W., White, V. and Preston, I. (2008). *Quantifying rural fuel poverty.* Report prepared by the Centre for Sustainable Energy to Eaga Partnership Charitable Trust, CSE, Bristol.

Boardman, B. (1991). *Fuel poverty: From cold homes to affordable warmth.* London: Belhaven Press.

Boardman, B. (2010). *Fixing fuel poverty: Challenges and solutions.* London: Earthscan.

Bouzarovski, S. and Tirado Herrero, S. (2015). The energy divide: Integrating energy transitions, regional inequalities and poverty trends in the European Union. *European Urban and Regional Studies,* 1–18.

Bouzarovski, S. and Tirado Herrero, S. (2016). Geographies of injustice: The socio-spatial determinants of energy poverty in Poland, the Czech Republic and Hungary. *Post-Communist Economies,* 1–24.

Buzar, S. (2007). *Energy poverty in Eastern Europe: Hidden geographies of deprivation.* Aldershot: Ashgate.

CSO. (2015). *Statistical yearbook of the regions – Poland.* Warszawa: Statistical Publishing Establishment.

Dopke, J. (2014). *Średnie miesięczne temperatury powietrza w I kw. 2014 r. w polskich miastach.* Available at: www.info-ogrzewanie.pl/artykul,id_m-100365,t-srednie_miesieczne_temperatury_powietrza_w_i_kw_2014_r_w_polskich_miastach.html.

Eurostat. (2017). *NUTS – Nomenclature of territorial units for statistics.* Available at: http://ec.europa.eu/eurostat/web/nuts/overview.

Fahmy, E., Gordon, D. and Patsios, D. (2011). Predicting fuel poverty at small-area level in England. *Energy Policy,* 39, 4370–4377.

Frankowski, J. and Tirado-Herrero, S. (2015). *Energy vulnerability of the urban areas in Gdańsk: First results of the EVALUATE project.* Presentation given at the workshop "Energy vulnerability of urban areas", Gdańsk.

Hills, J. (2011). *Fuel poverty: The problem and its measurement.* CASE Report, 69. London: Department of Energy and Climate Change.

Illsley, B., Jackson, T. and Lynch, B. (2007). Addressing Scottish rural fuel poverty through a regional industrial symbiosis strategy for the Scottish forest industries sector. *Geoforum,* 38, 21–32.

Imbert, I., Nogues, P. and Sevenet, M. (2016). Same but different: On the applicability of fuel poverty indicators across countries – insights from France. *Energy Research & Social Science*, 15, 75–85.

Institute of Meteorology and Water Management – National Research Institute (IMGW – PIB). (2013a). *Vademecum. Niebezpieczne zjawiska meteorologiczne – geneza, skutki, częstość występowania. Część pierwsza – wiosna, lato*, IMGW – PIB, Warsaw.

Institute of Meteorology and Water Management – National Research Institute (IMGW – PIB). (2013b). *Vademecum. Niebezpieczne zjawiska meteorologiczne – geneza, skutki, częstość występowania: Część druga – jesień, zima*, IMGW – PIB, Warsaw.

Isherwood, B. C. and Hancock, R. M. (1979). *Household expenditure on fuel: Distributional aspects*. London: Economic Adviser's Office, DHSS.

Kurowski, P. (2011). Ubóstwo energetyczne w Polsce na podstawie badań GUS z 2008 r. *Polityka Społeczna*, 27, 17–22.

Legendre, B. and Ricci, O. (2015). Measuring fuel poverty in France: Which households are the most fuel vulnerable? *Energy Economics*, 49, 620–628.

Lis, M., Miazga, A. and Ramsza, M. (2016a). Dynamiczne własności miar ubóstwa energetycznego. *IBS Research Report 01/2016*, Institute for Structural Research, Warsaw.

Lis, M., Sałach, K. and Święcicka, K. (2016b). Reasons for and symptoms of fuel poverty heterogeneity of the fuel poor in Poland – quantification and policy implications. *IBS Working Paper 08/2016*, Institute for Structural Research, Warsaw.

McKelvey, R. D. and Zavoina, W. (1975). A statistical model for the analysis of ordinal level dependent variables. *The Journal of Mathematical Sociology*, 4(1), 103–120.

Miazga, A. and Owczarek, D. (2015). It's cold inside – energy poverty in Poland. *IBS Working Paper 16/2015*, Institute for Structural Research, Warsaw.

Papada, L. and Kaliampakos, D. (2016a). Developing the energy profile of mountainous areas. *Energy*, 107, 205–214.

Papada, L. and Kaliampakos, D. (2016b). Measuring energy poverty in Greece. *Energy Policy*, 94, 157–165.

Rakowski, T. (2009). Łowcy, zbieracze, praktycy niemocy. *słowo/obraz/terytoria*, Gdańsk.

Roberts, D., Vera-Toscano, E. and Phimister, E. (2015). Fuel poverty in the UK: Is there a difference between rural and urban areas? *Energy Policy*, 87, 216–223.

Rugkåsa, J., Shortt, N. K. and Boydell, L. (2007). The right tool for the task: 'Boundary Spanners' in a partnership approach to tackle fuel poverty in rural Northern Ireland. *Health and Social Care in the Community*, 15(3), 221–230.

Stępniak, A. and Tomaszewska, A. (2014). Ubóstwo energetyczne a efektywność energetyczna: Analiza problemu i rekomendacje. *Instytut na Rzecz Ekorozwoju*, Warszawa.

Szamrej-Baran, I. (2014). Identyfikacja przyczyn ubóstwa energetycznego w Polsce przy wykorzystaniu modelowania miękkiego. *Research Papers of the Wroclaw University of Economics*, 328, 343–352.

Szpor, A. (2016). Energy poverty in Poland – buzzword or a real problem? *IBS Policy Paper 02/2016*, Institute for Structural Research, Warsaw.

Thomson, H. and Snell, C. (2013). Quantifying the prevalence of fuel poverty across the European Union. *Energy Policy*, 52, 563–572.

Veall, M. R. and Zimmermann, K. F. (1996). Pseudo R^2 measures for some common limited dependent variable models. *Journal of Economic Surveys*, 10(3), 241–259.

Walker, R., Liddell, C., McKenzie, P., Morris, C. and Lagdon, S. (2014). Fuel poverty in Northern Ireland: Humanizing the plight of vulnerable households. *Energy Research & Social Science*, 4, 89–99.

Walker, R., McKenzie, P., Liddell, C. and Morris, C. (2012). Area-based targeting of fuel poverty in Northern Ireland: An evidenced-based approach. *Applied Geography*, 34, 639–649.

Appendix 8.1

Logistic regression results (estimation of parameters)

		Dependent variable – energy poverty measured as:	
		Affordability (LIHC)	Lack of thermal comfort
Voivodeship	REF: Dolnośląskie		
	Kujawsko-pomorskie	−0.156	−0.428***
	Lubelskie	−0.0184	−0.441***
	Lubuskie	0.181	0.189*
	Łódzkie	−0.0177	0.123
	Małopolskie	0.199*	0.00731
	Mazowieckie	−0.192*	−0.126
	Opolskie	0.0450	−0.601***
	Podkarpackie	0.288**	−0.813***
	Podlaskie	0.423***	0.160
	Pomorskie	−0.122	−0.592***
	Śląskie	−0.265***	0.179**
	Świętokrzyskie	−0.144	−0.101
	Warmińsko-mazurskie	0.0866	−0.312***
	Wielkopolskie	−0.00735	−0.603***
	Zachodniopomorskie	0.0902	0.0413
Degree of urbanisation	REF: ≥ 500 thous. residents		
	200–499 thous. residents	−0.853***	−0.274***
	100–199 thous. residents	−0.318**	−0.0890
	20–99 thous. residents	−0.124	−0.0602
	< 20 thous. residents	0.194**	−0.364***
	rural areas	0.489***	−0.0782
Type of building	REF: block of flats		
	terraced house	2.030***	0.293
	detached house	2.012***	0.0749
	Floor area [m²]	0.0708***	−0.00117
Interactions	terraced house × floor area	−0.0436***	−0.00417*
	detached house × floor area	−0.0433***	−0.00336**

(Continued)

(Continued)

		Dependent variable – energy poverty measured as:	
		Affordability (LIHC)	Lack of thermal comfort
Type of heating	REF: central heating system		
	fuel stoves	−0.999***	0.914***
	electric stoves	−1.023***	0.692***
Building construction period	REF: 1961–1980		
	before 1946	−0.357***	0.748***
	1946–1960	0.449***	0.357***
	1981–1995	−0.183***	−0.0799
	1996–2006	−1.321***	−0.347***
	after 2006	−1.437***	−1.169***
	Disposable income [ln PLN]	−2.998***	−0.401***
Socioeconomic group	REF: White-collar workers		
	Blue-collar workers	0.593***	0.205***
	Retirees	−0.506***	−0.0360
	Pensioners	−0.211**	0.203***
	Farmers	0.521***	−0.0897
	Self-employed	0.382***	−0.0210
	Social beneficiaries	−0.859***	0.365***
	Beneficiaries of other non-income sources	−0.884***	0.105
	Number of children (under 14 years old)	0.289***	0.100***
	Constant	16.42***	1.078***
	No. of observations	35 977	35 977
	LR chi2 (41)	8719.53	2668.72
	McFadden's Pseudo-R^2	0.378	0.106
	Efron's Pseudo-R^2	0.332	0.091
	McKelvey and Zavoina's Pseudo-R^2	0.606	0.189

Source: Own calculations based on the 2014 Polish HBS data

9 Multiple vulnerabilities?

Interrogating the spatial distribution of energy poverty measures in England

Caitlin Robinson, Stefan Bouzarovski, and Sarah Lindley

Introduction

For researchers concerned with energy poverty (more commonly referred to as fuel poverty in the UK context), the unique spatial dynamics of the phenomenon are of increasing interest (Bouzarovksi et al. 2015). One way in which spatiality has become central to conversations about energy poverty is through mobilisation of the concept of vulnerability (Bouzarovski and Petrova 2015; Hall et al. 2013; Middlemiss and Gillard 2015). In comparison to theorising energy poverty as a combination of high energy prices, low incomes and domestic energy inefficiency, a vulnerability framework allows for an explicit focus upon the unique, and often complex, spatial patterns associated. The framing draws attention to how vulnerability dimensions, including access to energy, affordability, energy efficiency, needs and the flexibility to meet these needs, are unevenly distributed across space (Bouzarovksi and Petrova 2015). In England, the Department for Energy and Climate Change (DECC) recognises the importance of the spatial distribution of energy poverty, producing sub-regional estimates at a Lower Super Output Area (LSOA) scale (DECC 2014). However, despite the recent replacement of a 10% energy poverty indicator with a Low Income High Cost indicator (LIHC), both understand energy poverty as a combination of income, efficiency and price (Hills 2012).

This chapter aims to scrutinise the spatial distribution of energy poverty yielded by the 10% and LIHC indicators using a vulnerability framework. Sub-regional datasets representing wider vulnerability dimensions are integrated into the analysis using a global multiple regression methodology and Geographical Information Systems (GIS). This allows for consideration of whether the spatial distribution of energy poverty using the revised LIHC indicator reflects the increased understanding within research of the complexity of domestic energy deprivation, or whether the focus of existing indicators upon a narrow triad of drivers obscures particular socio-spatial vulnerabilities. The results suggest that, rather than succeeding in representing this complexity, the transition from a 10% indicator to a LIHC indicator has shifted the focus towards an alternative, narrow subset of vulnerabilities, from pensioners and households without gas central heating towards low-income families.

The findings encourage reflection about the role of different indicators used to measure and map energy poverty. Whilst existing national indicators can make the issue visible, providing a national estimate of energy poor households according to a specified threshold of income-efficiency-price, when disaggregated to more localised scales complex socio-spatial vulnerabilities are often overlooked. Within wider research there are several valuable examples of area-based targeting of energy poverty, however, they tend to be framed using more simplistic theorisations and assume that the relationship between energy poverty and wider vulnerability factors is spatially invariant. The development of spatially constituted indicators that move away from the narrow triad as a framing is encouraged if policy-makers are to succeed in 'finding the fuel poor' (Hills 2012, 70).

Energy poverty and vulnerability

The changing energy poverty landscape

The issue of energy poverty has been widely acknowledged amongst policy-makers, academics and practitioners in industrialised nations for several decades. This has been driven primarily by a concern about how energy poverty endangers different aspects of wellbeing including: reduced physical and mental health (Liddell and Morris 2010), strained family relations (Gilbertson et al. 2006), increased social isolation (Anderson et al. 2012) and reduced educational attainment (Barnes et al. 2008). Inspired by the influential work of Boardman, the end state of energy poverty is widely understood as the result of low incomes, high energy prices and domestic energy inefficiency (Boardman 1991; Boardman 2010; Hills 2012). Where national governments have sought to define energy poverty, they draw inspiration from this triad. In the United Kingdom (UK), the energy poor are defined as those 'on a lower income [living] in a home which cannot be kept warm at reasonable cost' (DECC 2015, 14). This understanding is echoed elsewhere in France's definition of energy precariousness (précarité énergétique) (Dubois 2012) and the Republic of Ireland's definition of energy poverty (DCENR, 2016).

Liddell et al., reflecting upon the development of energy poverty research, recognises that 'a new energy crisis more complex and wide ranging than ever before' (2012, 4) has unfolded, with implications for the energy poverty landscape. Significant increases in fuel prices have exceeded relatively modest energy poverty interventions (Boardman 2010). This has been enhanced by increased inequality and poverty following the Global Financial Crisis (Hall et al. 2013). The accompanying mantra of austerity has led to a reduction in spending on public services and the side-lining of spending on energy poverty (Jansz and Guertler 2012). In this context, Buzar (2007) offers a definition of energy poverty that builds upon work by Boardman (1991, 2010) and Bradshaw and Hutton (1983) to define the energy poor as those with an inability to attain the socially and materially necessitated level of domestic energy services. Additionally, alternative framings are increasingly mobilised that seek to understand how this state of energy poverty emerges, utilising concepts of justice (Walker and Day 2012), capabilities (Day et al. 2016) and vulnerability (Bouzarovski and Petrova 2015; Hall et al. 2013; Middlemiss and Gillard 2015) upon which this chapter will focus.

Vulnerability to energy poverty

As part of a wider ambition to explore the relations between energy and justice, equity and vulnerability, an embryonic vulnerability framework is increasingly advocated for exploring energy poverty (Hall et al. 2013). More widely, the concept of social vulnerability is used to explain the differential losses that result between diverse societal groups. It provides a means by which to identify and understand the characteristics of those most susceptible to harm from particular stressors and thus the opportunity to mitigate against these harms (Adger 2006). As a negative outcome of energy-society relations, energy poverty can be thought of in this way.

The vulnerability framework builds upon existing energy poverty discourses but challenges the reliance upon the triad of low income, energy efficiency and energy prices as narrow, considering them less able to capture the complex dynamics that give rise to energy poverty in the home. Rather than focusing upon the end state of energy poverty, vulnerability is understood as a set of conditions inherent within an individual, household or social group that renders them less likely to be able to access the socially and materially necessitated amount of affordable and reliable energy services. For Middlemiss and Gillard (2015), this determines the sensitivity of a household to energy poverty and its capacity to cope with and adapt to the condition.

Bouzarovski and Petrova (2015) outline a framework for understanding the often multifaceted pathways via which households become vulnerable to energy poverty. The framework identifies several interacting vulnerability dimensions within the system of provision of domestic energy services: affordability, access, energy inefficiency, specific household needs, energy-related practices and inflexibility. These dimensions include traditional energy poverty drivers but reach beyond the accessibility-affordability binary (Bouzarovksi 2013), capturing households in which available energy services do not match their needs (e.g. Snell et al. 2015), individuals whose practices within the home mean that they tend not to use energy efficiently (e.g. Day and Hitchings 2011) and households in which the built environment or tenancy relations prevent them from switching to more appropriate energy services (e.g. Bouzarovski and Cauvain 2016). Table 9.1 summarises the vulnerability factors that increase the likelihood of a household falling into energy poverty.

Complex spatial dynamics of vulnerability to energy poverty

When the concept of social vulnerability is combined with 'aspects of place' (Lindley et al. 2011, 7), socio-spatial vulnerability results in a geographical expression of the likelihood of a loss of wellbeing in the household. Given the diversity of

Table 9.1 Vulnerability dimensions and examples of vulnerability factors that increase the likelihood of a household falling into energy poverty

Vulnerability dimension	Example of vulnerability factor
Access	Inability to access cheaper fuel types
Affordability	Reliant on single low income
	Reliant on state pension
	Reliant on state security benefits
	Unemployed or in part-time employment
	Ineligible for financial support for heating
	High energy use per capita
	Income from state support reduced
Efficiency	Lack of capital to invest in efficiency
	Inefficient energy conversion by appliances
	Energy-inefficient property
	Limited eligibility for efficiency measures
Flexibility	Inability to switch to cheaper tariff
	Under-occupancy of the home
	Reduced autonomy over energy services
	Lack of control or choice over daily lives
	Precarious living arrangements
	Lack of housing rights
	Unaffordability of owner-occupancy
	Large proportion of time spent at home during the day
Needs	Physiological need for heat or energy services
	Under-representation in energy poverty policy
	Lack of awareness of support
Practices	Lack of social relations inside/outside the home
	Unhealthy warm-related practices

Source: Vulnerability dimensions column extracted from Bouzarovski and Petrova (2015)

vulnerability pathways and subsequent losses of wellbeing, vulnerability to energy poverty has a complex and uneven spatial distribution (Bouzarovksi and Petrova 2015). The following section explores some examples of the complex spatial distribution of socio-spatial vulnerabilities that enhance the likelihood of falling into energy poverty. Many of the examples drawn upon are from the UK context; however, there is evidence of these uneven spatial distributions across Europe, due to the unique socio-technical, political and institutional configurations that exist in different national contexts (Bouzarovski and Tirado Herrero 2015).

Regarding access, the networked infrastructure that provides energy to the home has a unique spatial distribution (Harrison and Popke 2011). Abandonment of universal tariff structures due to the privatisation of energy companies has led to social fragmentation, with fewer cross subsidies between urban and rural areas (Graham and Marvin 1994). Thus, households in rural areas or flat blocks in high-density urban areas without access to the gas network are disproportionately reliant upon high-cost fuels (Roberts et al. 2015). Fuel prices can also fluctuate considerably at a local level (Walker et al. 2015). In terms of energy efficiency, its relative importance as a driver varies with climatic exposure to colder conditions (Liddell et al. 2011). The efficiency of the building stock differs spatially as higher heating costs tend to be associated with older, solid wall properties in rural areas (Roberts et al. 2015) and inner-city, pre-1918 terraced housing (Rudge 2012). Walker et al. (2012) recognises that in rural areas the population is often more dispersed. Thus, rural populations tend to be more heterogeneous and targeting of measures to ensure their needs are met can become problematic. Concerning affordability, a 'postcode lottery' exists between regional energy prices that fluctuate with demand and the cost of local distribution networks (USwitch 2016). Reductions in public spending since the Global Financial Crisis have also disproportionately impacted particular areas. In England, the most disadvantaged Local Authorities have borne the brunt of public service cuts, impacting upon incomes, local services and infrastructure provision (Pearce 2013).

Specific vulnerability pathways are often associated with demographics with a particular need for energy that tend to concentrate in certain locales. Households with a physiological need for relatively higher temperatures include those with a disability (Snell et al. 2015) or limiting long-term illness (Liddell and Morris 2010), the elderly (Wright 2004) and families with young children (Liddell 2008). Alongside space heating, people with a disability or long-term illness can require energy-intensive medical equipment (Snell et al. 2015). The vulnerability of these groups also reaches beyond a need for greater levels of energy services, to affordability. Those with a disability or illness are far less likely to be employed or to have savings, whilst older people reliant on fixed pensions have little opportunity to increase their income. The issue of affordability also has significant influence upon the vulnerability of lone parent households (Druckman and Jackson 2008). In England, the spatial distribution of these households varies considerably. A higher proportion of pensioners live in rural communities, whilst families with young children are more concentrated in the suburbs of cities, those with a disability or illness tend to live in urban areas or coastal communities and lone parent families tend to concentrate in urban areas (ONS 2011a). Finally, households in the private rented sector, where properties are disproportionately inefficient and tenants often lack housing rights, tend to concentrate in inner-city areas (Ambrose 2015; Bouzarovksi and Cauvain 2016).

Acknowledgment of these complex spatial dynamics calls into question how energy poverty can be meaningfully measured and mapped. Fahmy et al. (2011) recognise that the spatial distribution of energy poverty varies considerably depending upon the chosen measurement approach. Those that rely upon a handful of indicators only succeed in capturing a selection of the socio-spatial vulnerabilities that contribute to energy poverty, leading to the over- and under-estimation of energy poverty and mis-targeting of alleviation measures (Boardman 2010; Dubois 2012; Liddell et al. 2012).

National energy poverty indicators in England

Since its conception, like many other multi-dimensional concepts including welfare and wellbeing, energy poverty has been measured using composite indicators that compile a series of individual indicators into a single index (OECD 2008). In England, these indicators have undergone considerable scrutiny since the Hills Review in 2012 (Hills 2012) and the introduction of a new energy poverty strategy in 2015 'Cutting the Cost of Keeping Warm' (DECC 2015). A 10% indicator, the most widely accepted definition of energy poverty used by the four devolved administrations in the UK, has been replaced in England by a LIHC indicator.

Using the 10% indicator a household is energy poor if 'they are required to spend more than 10% of their income to maintain an adequate standard of warmth' (DECC 2015, 8), building upon the work of Boardman (1991). Despite a focus upon affordable warmth, the indicator also incorporates domestic need for energy including lighting, heating water, appliance usage and cooking. A ratio of modelled fuel costs and income is calculated using a Before Housing Cost (BHC) definition of income. Modelled fuel costs are derived from energy price and a modelled figure of 'required' consumption that takes into account property size, the number of people in the household, energy efficiency and the mix of fuels used. Energy poor households are those with a ratio of greater than 0.1 (10%). In comparison to the 10% definition suggested by Boardman (1991), the DECC indicator is an absolute rather than relative measure.

The LIHC indicator is calculated using an income threshold and a fuel cost threshold to provide a relative measure of energy poverty (Hills 2012). The fuel cost threshold is an equivalised weighted median of the fuel costs of all households. Thus, half of all households exceed the fuel cost threshold and are considered 'high cost'. The income threshold is calculated as 60% of the weighted median for income After Housing Costs (AHC). The income figure for each household is equivalised and combined with the equivalised fuel costs of the household. Therefore, the income threshold is higher for those households that require a greater level of income to meet larger fuel bills.

Broadly, this represents a transition from a 10% indicator that is extremely sensitive to fluctuations in energy price (Moore 2012), towards a LIHC indicator that builds upon ideas of relative poverty and is largely irresponsive to fluctuations in energy price (Boardman 2012). Considerable examination and critique of both indicators exists (Boardman 2012; Middlemiss 2016; Moore 2012), not least because the introduction of the LIHC indicator has led to a considerable reduction in energy poor households. In 2012, 13.8% of households in England were energy poor using the 10% indicator whilst 10.5% were energy poor using the LIHC indicator (771,014 fewer households).

In this chapter we scrutinise the spatial distribution of energy poverty yielded by the DECC indicators. In England, DECC have begun to recognise the importance of the spatial distribution of energy poverty, producing sub-regional estimates of energy poverty. We seek to understand whether the new LIHC indicator succeeds in representing more complex socio-spatial vulnerabilities or whether these are obscured by the narrow framing of income-efficiency-price. The findings have implications for other national contexts seeking to measure energy poverty using a LIHC indicator (e.g. Strakova 2014).

The changing spatial distribution of energy poverty indicators in England

Sub-regional estimates of fuel poverty are available at the LSOA scale (neighbourhoods representing 400–1200 households) (ONS 2011b). The modelling used to derive the estimates is based on national data drawn from the English Housing Survey (DECC 2016). LSOA scale datasets for the 10% and LIHC indicators for 2012 are mapped in Figure 9.1 and Figure 9.2, using a relative scale,

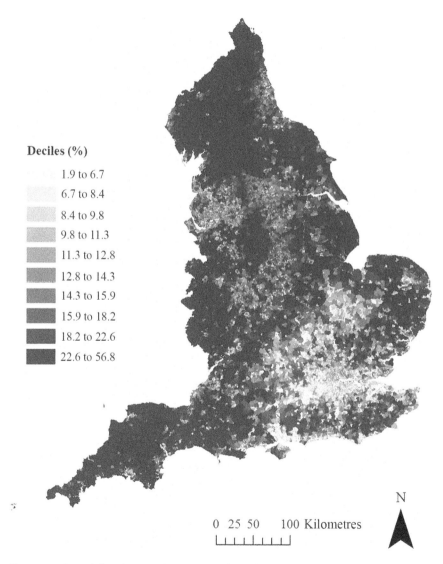

Deciles (%)

1.9 to 6.7
6.7 to 8.4
8.4 to 9.8
9.8 to 11.3
11.3 to 12.8
12.8 to 14.3
14.3 to 15.9
15.9 to 18.2
18.2 to 22.6
22.6 to 56.8

0 25 50   100 Kilometres

N

Figure 9.1 Spatial distribution of energy poor households using the 10% indicator
Source: Data from DECC (2014), ONS (2011a)

deciles. Figure 9.4 shows the difference in the spatial distribution of energy poverty in England with a transition from a 10% indicator to a LIHC indicator. Table 9.2 summarises the regional statistics for both indicators for each region. Several distinct spatial distributions are visible.

Using the 10% indicator, the regions of the South East and London have a considerably lower percentage of energy poor households compared to the rest

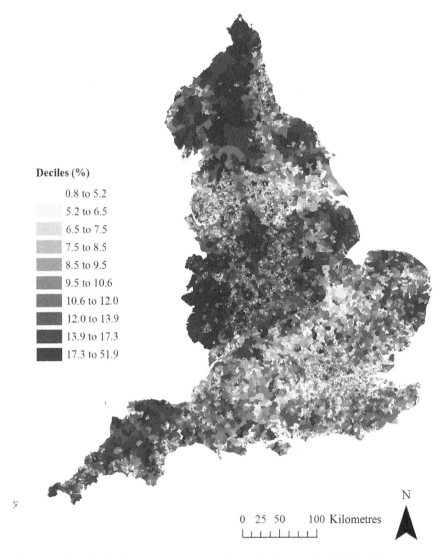

Deciles (%)

0.8 to 5.2
5.2 to 6.5
6.5 to 7.5
7.5 to 8.5
8.5 to 9.5
9.5 to 10.6
10.6 to 12.0
12.0 to 13.9
13.9 to 17.3
17.3 to 51.9

0 25 50   100 Kilometres

N

Figure 9.2 Spatial distribution of energy poor households using the LIHC indicator
Source: Data from DECC (2014), ONS (2011a)

of England (Figure 9.1). This spatial distribution is less distinct using the LIHC indicator (Figure 9.2) and can be explained by the difference in the method used within each indicator to calculate income. The LIHC indicator uses an AHC income measure, compared to the BHC income measure used in the 10% indicator. An AHC income measure accounts for the housing costs associated with rent and mortgage payments, thus better reflecting the higher property and rent prices in the South East and London.

Furthermore, using the 10% indicator, there is a higher percentage of energy poor households in rural LSOA compared to urban LSOA (see Figure 9.3 for

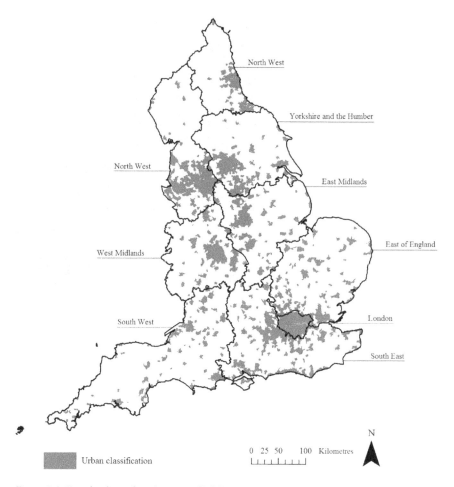

Figure 9.3 Rural-urban classification of LSOA in regions

Note: An area is defined as rural if they are outside settlements of more than 10,000 residents (ONS 2013).

Source: Data from DEFRA (2013), ONS (2011a)

context). In comparison, whilst on average there are 3.3% fewer energy poor households in each LSOA using the LIHC indicator (DECC 2014), this reduction is concentrated in rural areas (Figure 9.4). In urban areas there is on average a 0% difference in energy poor households between the two indicators, whilst in rural areas there is an average decrease of 8.1% in energy poor households using

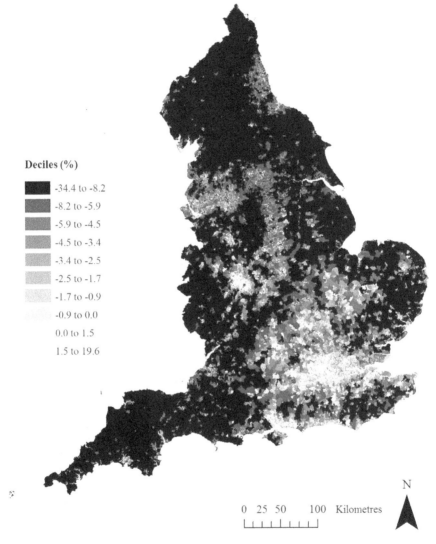

Deciles (%)

-34.4 to -8.2
-8.2 to -5.9
-5.9 to -4.5
-4.5 to -3.4
-3.4 to -2.5
-2.5 to -1.7
-1.7 to -0.9
-0.9 to 0.0
0.0 to 1.5
1.5 to 19.6

0 25 50   100 Kilometres

N

Figure 9.4 Difference between the percentage of energy poor households shifting from a 10% indicator to a LIHC indicator

Note: The grey scale represents LSOA that have experienced a decrease in the percentage of energy poor households with the introduction of the LIHC indicator. The white LSOA are those that have experienced an increase.

Source: DECC (2014), ONS (2011a)

Table 9.2 Regional data for 10% and LIHC energy poverty indicators

Region	10% indicator (count)	10% indicator (%)	LIHC indicator (count)	LIHC indicator (%)	Difference (%)
North East	197,889	17.8	128,971	11.6	−6.2
North West	467,214	15.7	335,344	11.3	−4.4
Yorkshire & Humber	394,776	17.4	244,850	10.8	−6.6
East Midlands	345,203	17.8	256,017	13.2	−4.6
West Midlands	373,783	16.7	340,226	15.2	−1.5
East of England	278,142	11.6	206,319	8.6	−3.0
London	296,165	9.5	276,782	8.9	−0.6
South East	315,568	8.9	276,860	7.8	−1.1
South West	384,853	16.5	217,210	9.3	−7.2

Source: Data from DECC (2014)

the LIHC indicator compared to the 10% indicator (DECC 2014). In particular, LSOA in the cities of London and Birmingham have a significantly higher percentage of energy poor households using an LIHC indicator relative to other LSOA. This can be partly attributed to the role that the driver of energy price plays within each indicator design (Moore 2012). The price of energy significantly affects the percentage of energy poor households using a 10% indicator, whilst fluctuations in energy price have little influence upon energy poverty using the LIHC indicator. The cost of heating the home to an adequate standard is considerably higher in rural areas, as properties are more likely to be off the gas grid and are subsequently reliant on more expensive fuel types (Roberts et al. 2015).

Multiple vulnerabilities: methods

To begin to understand whether the spatial distribution of the new LIHC indicator succeeds in representing more complex socio-spatial vulnerabilities, an Ordinary Least Squares (OLS) multiple regression technique is used (Hutcheson and Sofroniou 1999). The technique explores the relationships between each energy poverty indicator and a series of vulnerability variables.

Vulnerability variables

A selection of vulnerability variables are chosen to represent households with distinctive vulnerability pathways, that increase the likelihood of them falling into energy poverty. Each vulnerability variable represents a particular demographic, socio-economic or socio-technical characteristic of a household. The variables reach beyond the UK government definition of 'vulnerable', concerned with physiological need for heat (DECC 2015), to include vulnerability factors apparent within wider research. The variables that yield the most suitable multiple regression model are: households with a member with a long-term

Table 9.3 Vulnerability variables

Vulnerability variable (ONS 2011b)	Descriptor	Reference example
Household with disability or limiting long-term illness	DISABILITY	Snell et al. (2015)
All pensioner household (aged over 65 years)	PENSIONER	Wright (2004)
Household with young child(ren) (0–4 years)	CHILD	Liddell (2008)
Lone parent household	LONE PARENT	Brunner et al. (2012
Privately rented household	PRIVATE RENT	Ambrose (2015)
Household with non-gas central heating	NON GAS	Roberts et al. (2015)

disability or illness, all pensioner households, households with young children, lone parent households, private rented households and households with non-gas central heating (Table 9.3). Several additional vulnerability variables were considered but have been excluded due to a lack of appropriate data or fit within the model.

Sub-regional datasets representing each vulnerability variable at LSOA scale have been obtained from the 2011 Census at household scale. The variables have been transformed using a Box-Cox Power transformation to make them normally distributed and standardised using a range standardisation methodology (Wallace and Denham 1996). The vulnerability variables are mapped in Figures 9.5–9.10, helping to visualise some of the unique spatial distributions discussed.

Regarding the selection of vulnerability variables, it is recognised that it is impossible to identify the energy poor using any single criteria, as evidenced by the mis-targeting of the energy poor using the Winter Fuel Payment, a universal income support offered to pensioners (Boardman 2012). It should also not be assumed that all of the households within the demographics selected are vulnerable. For example, Boardman (2010) recognises that the UK government criteria of 'vulnerable', including older householders, families with children and householders who are disabled or suffering from a long-term illness, encompasses 72% of households. Furthermore, analyses of this nature that categorise people using particular demographic characteristics can risk underestimating the complexities associated with domestic energy deprivation (Walker and Day 2012). In spite of this, some simplification of these complexities is inevitable (Turner et al. 2003), and there is value in making certain groups visible for specific vulnerabilities to be recognised in policy (Walker and Day 2012).

Multiple vulnerabilities: results

Suitability of the multiple regression models

Before exploring the relationships between the vulnerability variables and the energy poverty indicators, the suitability of each model is assessed. The Adjusted

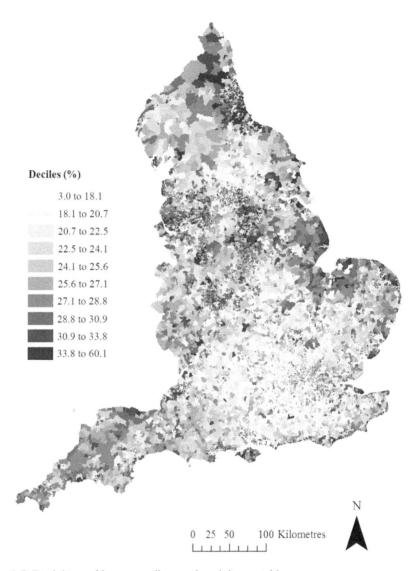

Deciles (%)

3.0 to 18.1
18.1 to 20.7
20.7 to 22.5
22.5 to 24.1
24.1 to 25.6
25.6 to 27.1
27.1 to 28.8
28.8 to 30.9
30.9 to 33.8
33.8 to 60.1

N

0   25   50   100 Kilometres

Figure 9.5 Disability and long-term illness vulnerability variable
Source: Data from ONS (2011a), ONS (2011b)

R-Squared value demonstrates that the 10% indicator model explains 32% of variance in energy poor households identified by the 10% indicator and the LIHC model explains 23% of variance in energy poor households identified by the LIHC indicator. These low values are not unusual for a regression model that seeks to understand social phenomena. The Variance Inflation Factor (VIF) statistic in Table 9.4 and Table 9.5 is below 7.5 for each vulnerability variable indicating that none of the variables are redundant. The t-test and associated p-value are statistically significant confirming that the coefficient estimates reflect the strength and the type of relationship between the vulnerability variables and each energy poverty indicator.

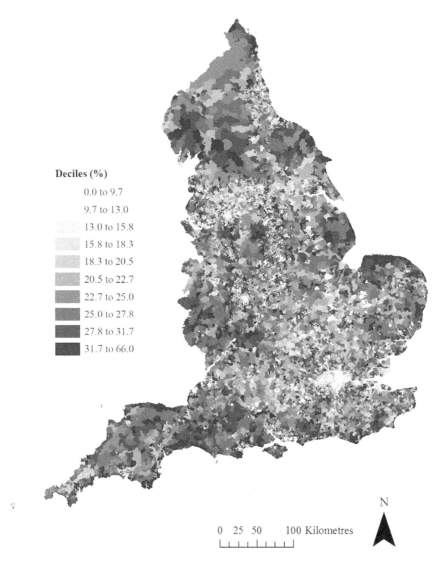

Deciles (%)
0.0 to 9.7
9.7 to 13.0
13.0 to 15.8
15.8 to 18.3
18.3 to 20.5
20.5 to 22.7
22.7 to 25.0
25.0 to 27.8
27.8 to 31.7
31.7 to 66.0

N

0   25   50   100 Kilometres

Figure 9.6 All pensioner households vulnerability variable
Source: Data from ONS (2011a), ONS (2011b)

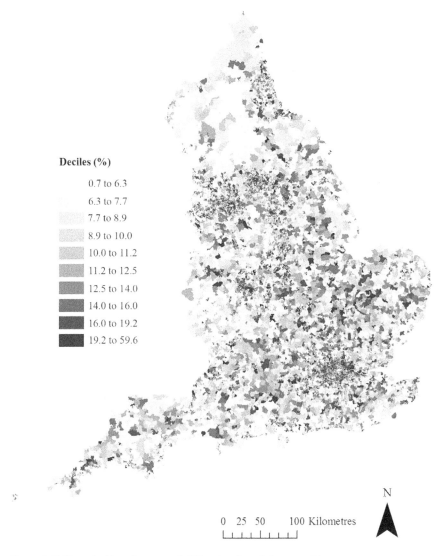

Deciles (%)

0.7 to 6.3
6.3 to 7.7
7.7 to 8.9
8.9 to 10.0
10.0 to 11.2
11.2 to 12.5
12.5 to 14.0
14.0 to 16.0
16.0 to 19.2
19.2 to 59.6

0 25 50   100 Kilometres

N

Figure 9.7 Household with young child(ren) vulnerability variable
Source: Data from ONS (2011a), ONS (2011b)

Relationships between the vulnerability variables and energy poverty indicators

Having determined model suitability, the multiple regression models can be used to explore the relationship between each vulnerability variable and energy poverty indicator. The estimate columns in Table 9.4 and Table 9.5 list the coefficient

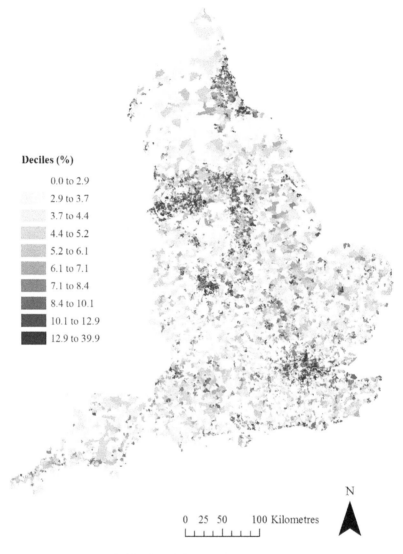

Figure 9.8 Lone parent household vulnerability variable
Source: Data from ONS (2011a), ONS (2011b)

estimates that reflect both the type and the strength of these relationships. They provide an indication of how much energy poverty increases using each indicator with a 1 percentage point increase in the vulnerability variable. For example, an average increase of 0.16% in energy poor households according to the 10% indicator in each LSOA is anticipated for every 1% increase in privately rented households.

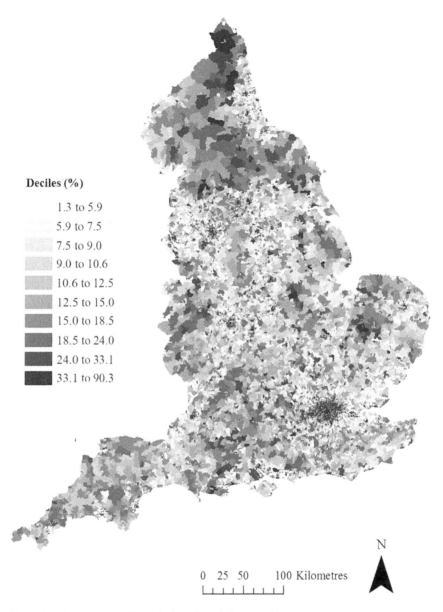

Deciles (%)

1.3 to 5.9
5.9 to 7.5
7.5 to 9.0
9.0 to 10.6
10.6 to 12.5
12.5 to 15.0
15.0 to 18.5
18.5 to 24.0
24.0 to 33.1
33.1 to 90.3

N

0 25 50   100 Kilometres

Figure 9.9 Private rented household vulnerability variable
Source: Data from ONS (2011a), ONS (2011b)

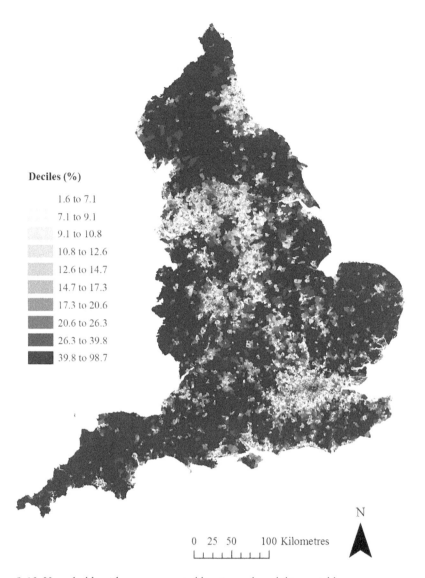

Figure 9.10 Households with non-gas central heating vulnerability variable

Source: Data from ONS (2011a), ONS (2011b)

The 10% indicator has a positive relationship (the percentage of energy poor households increases) with the DISABILITY (+0.29), PENSIONER (+0.06), PRIVATE RENT (+0.16) and NON GAS (+0.31) vulnerability variables, when controlling for the other vulnerability variables (Table 9.4). The 10% indicator has a negative relationship (the percentage of energy poor households decreases)

Table 9.4 Parameter estimates from the 10% indicator multiple regression model

Variable	Estimate	Std. error	t-Statistic	p-value	VIF
Intercept	0.340571	0.370015	0.920423	0.000000*	–
DISABILITY	0.294818	0.006499	45.364943	0.000000*	1.534838
PENSIONER	0.060302	0.007389	8.160738	0.000000*	2.442525
CHILD	−0.031796	0.007840	−4.055711	0.000000*	1.651629
LONE PARENT	−0.014179	0.007872	−1.81188	0.000000*	2.121714
PRIVATE RENT	0.163514	0.005253	31.127402	0.000000*	1.511060
NON GAS	0.312323	0.003155	99.002216	0.000000*	1.102838

Table 9.5 Parameter estimates from the LIHC indicator multiple regression model

Variable	Estimate	Std. error	t-Statistic	p-value	VIF
Intercept	0.094472	0.337705	0.279747	0.000000*	–
DISABILITY	0.3355458	0.005931	56.557118	0.000000*	1.534838
PENSIONER	−0.086398	0.006744	−12.811075	0.000000*	2.442525
CHILD	0.069810	0.007155	9.756461	0.000000*	1.651629
LONE PARENT	0.056805	0.007185	7.906306	0.000000*	2.121714
PRIVATE RENT	0.253467	0.004794	52.867880	0.000000*	1.511060
NON GAS	0.064383	0.002879	22.361189	0.000000*	1.102838

with the CHILD (−0.03) and LONE PARENT (−0.01) vulnerability variables, when controlling for other vulnerability variables.

The LIHC indicator has a positive relationship with the DISABILITY (+0.34), CHILD (+0.06), LONE PARENT (+0.05), PRIVATE RENT (+0.25) and NON GAS (+0.06) vulnerability variables (Table 9.5), when controlling for other vulnerability variables. The LIHC indicator has a negative relationship with the PENSIONER (−0.09) vulnerability variable, when controlling for other vulnerability variables. These relationships are summarised in Figure 9.11.

DECC energy poverty indicators: representative of socio-spatial vulnerabilities?

The 10% and LIHC indicators used to measure the percentage of energy poor households in England by DECC yield different spatial distributions. Our analysis suggests that the transition from a 10% indicator to a LIHC indicator has shifted focus towards an alternative subset of socio-spatial vulnerabilities, from pensioners and non-gas central heating towards low-income families with young children or lone parents. This implies a reprioritisation of the vulnerability of rural communities experiencing unique challenges associated with a lack of access to relatively affordable energy, instead drawing attention to groups who are more likely to have relatively lower incomes and higher housing costs. Seemingly, national

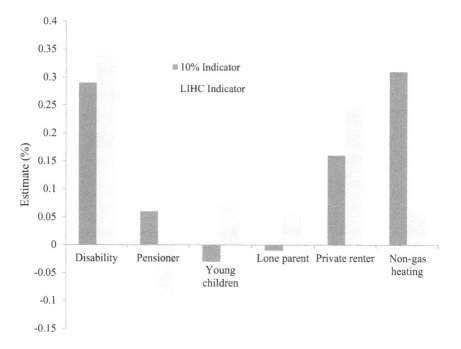

Figure 9.11 Summary of coefficient estimates from 10% indicator and LIHC indicator OLS regression models

measures of energy poverty are able to capture certain vulnerabilities, but neither the 10% nor the LIHC indicator succeeds in representing a wider range of socio-spatial vulnerabilities. This can be attributed in part to their reliance upon the narrow triad of drivers as a framing and to the difficulties associated with quantifying and mapping a complex, multidimensional, social vulnerability (Eakin and Luers 2006).

These findings are problematic, as they imply that national energy poverty indicators do not reflect those most in need, a disconnect that is reflected in wider research (Moore 2012). For example, Snell et al. (2015) considers the implementation of the LIHC indicator in England to contribute towards a lack of acknowledgment of energy poverty amongst the disabled. The indicator fails to recognise the higher energy needs of certain impairments whilst exaggerating household incomes. It is considered too simplistic and blunt to adequately represent the reality of living with a disability. Walker et al. (2014), in analysing the spatial distribution of home energy efficiency installations in Northern Ireland, identifies that government definitions tend to have only weak association with the level of need in a particular area. Subsequently the DECC indicators have little role in informing localised, practical action to alleviate energy poverty as the measures tend not to be used by practitioners to identify individual energy poor households. These findings encourage reflection upon the role of the different indicators used to measure energy poverty, specifically in terms of its spatial distribution.

Reflections on the purpose of the sub-regional DECC energy poverty indicators

Within its broader energy poverty agenda, DECC sets out the intended purpose of its sub-regional energy poverty estimates. Firstly, the datasets provide information about the characteristics and spatial distribution of energy poor households in England, with the accompanying policy documentation outlining the role of the statistics in enhancing 'understanding of the demography and geography of the fuel poor, and to indicate which groups are particularly susceptible to fuel poverty' (DECC 2015, 7). Secondly, the indicators provide a measure of progress in the alleviation of energy poverty nationally. Thirdly, the indicators inform the development and targeting of policy and alleviation measures, contributing towards a wider ambition of 'finding the most vulnerable' (DECC 2015) and 'finding the fuel poor' (Hills 2012, 70).

Despite these statements of intent, analysis by DECC explores the national-scale demography of energy poverty yielded by each measure but gives little consideration to the geography of energy poor households using the indicators. DECC cross tabulates key energy poverty statistics for England using the LIHC indicator with information about dwelling type and household characteristics from the English Housing Survey, illustrating some of the national-scale variations in energy poverty rates between different household types; for example, the high prevalence of energy poverty in poorer, larger and less-energy efficient properties and the high prevalence of energy poverty in households in which the youngest person is a child, in rural areas and in those using a pre-payment meter (Barton and Hough 2016). However, these analyses offer only a national picture of the characteristics of energy poor households using the indicators.

In fact, a review by DECC in conjunction with the Office for National Statistics (ONS) finds the sub-regional energy poverty datasets not to be robust at very low-level geographies (DECC 2015). It recommends that LSOA scale data should be used to highlight only general patterns in the spatial distribution of energy poverty. Despite the seemingly spatial ambitions of DECC, the primary purpose of the energy poverty indicators is to offer a national figure of total energy poverty around which government policy can centre. This reflects a wider erosion of spatial policy-making over the last decade. However, there is still a need for composite energy poverty indicators to reflect localised vulnerabilities and for policy-makers to 'think spatially, act spatially' (Wong et al. 2015, 1020).

Rethinking the measurement of the spatial distribution of energy poverty

The recognition of the unique spatial distribution of the socio-spatial vulnerabilities that give rise to energy poverty in the home, and evidence that these are missing from existing energy poverty indicators highlights the need for alternative indicators of energy poverty that place these unique spatial dynamics at their core. This concurs with Liddell et al. who call for composite indicators to better reflect the 'local realties' (2011, 9) of the energy poverty landscape. Therefore, we now seek to identify different types of composite indicators that play a role in the measurement of energy poverty and succeed in capturing the spatial to varying degrees. These range from indicators that increase the visibility of energy poverty at the policy level to those that understand the localised spatial dynamics of vulnerability to energy poverty. Three types of indicators are discussed: national composite indicators, area-based composite indicators and spatially constituted composite indicators (Table 9.6). Whilst recognising its value, here we do not deal with a consensual approach that uses subjective indicators, an approach that is useful for the comparison of different national contexts, for example, across Europe (Healy 2003; Thomson and Snell 2013).

National composite indicators

National energy poverty indicators have a role in the profiling of the issue of energy poverty, ensuring it is recognised in policy (Walker and Day 2012; Thomson et al. 2016). Yet the 10% and LIHC indicators, designed at the national scale using the income-efficiency-price triad, seemingly do not disaggregate to

Table 9.6 Composite energy poverty indicators

	Indicator	Scale	Description	Primary purpose
Aspatial ↑	Composite indicator	National	National figure of total energy poor households according to ratio based upon income-efficiency-price	Increasing visibility and recognition of the issue of energy poverty and providing a benchmark for statutory requirements to reduce energy poverty
	Area-based composite indicator	Regional, neighbourhood, household	Localised measure recognising wider range of vulnerable demographics	Finding those considered energy poor according to national indicators and better targeting alleviation measures
Spatial ↓	Spatially constituted composite indicator	Regional, neighbourhood, household	Localised measure capturing range of socio-spatial vulnerabilities and the complex spatial dynamics associated	Finding the energy poor, better targeting alleviation measures and improving understanding of localised socio-spatial vulnerabilities

provide a meaningful measure of more localised vulnerabilities and subsequent energy poverty. This concurs with Boardman (2012) who acknowledges that the LIHC indicator is intended for monitoring purposes and does not translate into appropriate criteria for the identification of energy poverty in individual households. Recognising these issues, attempts have been made to supplement national indicators using area-based approaches (Fahmy et al. 2011; Walker et al. 2012).

Area-based composite indicators

The rationale for area-based targeting is founded upon how deprivation tends to be spatially concentrated, which can have a cumulative effect upon individuals and particular areas (Smith 1999). By targeting energy poverty alleviation resources geographically, a greater number of vulnerable households are captured than if resources were evenly spread, reflecting principles of geographic equity and distributional justice (Walker and Day 2012). Walker et al. (2012) recognises that alleviation programmes are often poorly targeted, citing the example of the Warm Front scheme in England, thus a need for area-based targeting.

Area-based composite indicators seek to reflect the severity of energy poverty in different areas, within the boundaries of existing energy poverty definitions. Typically, they focus upon how a selection of environmental and socio-economic variables, that enhance the risk of experiencing energy poverty, spatially coincide in a particular neighbourhood. The strength of these area-based approaches is that, unlike national energy poverty indicators, they are designed at a higher spatial resolution using neighbourhood units. This allows for further exploration of the composition and spatial distribution of those considered energy poor by national energy poverty indicators. Several valuable examples exist across the UK of research that fulfils this need (Baker et al. 2003; Fahmy et al. 2011; Walker et al. 2012, 2013, 2014).

In England, the Centre for Sustainable Energy (CSE) have developed a small-area 'fuel poverty indicator' (FPI) for predicting the incidence of energy poverty in Census Output Areas (OA) and informing the localised targeting of affordable warmth policies (Baker et al. 2003; Fahmy et al. 2011). A series of variables considered 'predictors' of energy poverty are derived from the Census including lone parent households, single pensioner households, households without a car, non-earners, private and social renter, households without central heating, large families, households of a lower social class and properties that are overcrowded. These variables are weighted using the English Housing Condition Survey and the 10% definition of energy poverty.

In Northern Ireland, a team led by Christine Liddell use a risk index designed to identify geographic clusters of OA where there is a greater likelihood of households being considered energy poor using the 10% definition (Liddell and Lagdon 2013; Walker et al. 2012). The index is composed of three factors: heating burden (outdoor temperature and oil price); built environment vulnerability (floor space as a proxy for energy efficiency); and social vulnerability (including Pension Credit, Child Benefit, the Disability Living Allowance to satisfy the government's criteria for 'vulnerable' households and Income Support and Job-seekers Allowance to represent low-income households). The components are weighted: 40% for heating burden, 20% for built environment vulnerability and 40% for social vulnerability.

Each of these examples of an area-based approach supplements the national 10% energy poverty indicator in some way (Fahmy et al. 2011; Liddell et al. 2011). They therefore succeed in finding those considered energy poor using the 10% indicator. However, the results of the multiple regression suggest that each energy poverty indicator represents only a relatively narrow subset of socio-spatial vulnerabilities. By centring the analysis upon the 10% indicator, certain socio-spatial vulnerabilities are prioritised. Area-based approaches may benefit from extending their framing beyond existing national indicators to better capture the range of unique socio-spatial vulnerabilities that give rise to energy poverty. Those interested in the design of energy poverty metrics using a vulnerability framing could draw inspiration from indexes that are structured around several domains, for example, the English Index of Multiple Deprivation (IMD).

Spatially-constituted composite indicators

Additionally, Fahmy et al. recognises that existing area-based approaches assume that 'the relationship between energy poverty and its predictors is spatially invariant' (2011, 4376). Area-based targeting approaches tend to use weightings for each predictor variable that are uniform across the country, despite predictors varying in nature and magnitude over space. Having recognised that socio-spatial vulnerabilities have a complex and uneven spatial distribution, these could be reflected in spatially constituted composite indicators of energy poverty. A spatially constituted composite indicator has similar ambitions to area-based measures but recognises that needs and the relative importance of different vulnerabilities vary geographically, depending upon localised challenges. This is an appealing, yet methodologically challenging task. It could be achieved to varying degrees using statistical techniques that account for spatial effects in the data (e.g. Demšar et al. 2013). It could also be achieved by integrating the knowledge of energy poverty practitioners or households about localised challenges within a region, local authority or neighbourhood into the design of the indicator.

Concluding remarks: an explicitly geographic approach

There is increased recognition of the complexity and uneven geographic distribution of the vulnerability dimensions that increase the likelihood of households falling into energy poverty, thus endangering many different aspects of a household's wellbeing. In England, DECC attempts to better represent the phenomenon by shifting from a 10% indicator to a LIHC indicator. However, both indicators are based upon a narrow triad of drivers: income, efficiency and price. The interrogation of the spatial distribution of the indicators within this chapter demonstrates that rather than capturing this complexity the transition to a LIHC indicator has simply shifted the focus towards an alternative subset of socio-spatial vulnerabilities: from pensioners and households without gas central heating towards families with low incomes and high housing costs. Whilst able to represent certain vulnerabilities, the LIHC indicator is designed at the national scale without consideration of many of the diverse socio-spatial vulnerabilities increasingly apparent within wider energy poverty research. These findings are problematic as they imply that national energy poverty measures do not reflect those most in need, a disconnect reflected in wider research (Moore 2012). Thus an explicitly geographic approach to the design of composite indicators, that captures the unique spatial distributions of vulnerability dimensions, is encouraged if policy-makers are to succeed in understanding 'the geography of fuel poverty' (DECC 2015, 7).

Acknowledgements

This research was generously supported by the Engineering and Physical Sciences Research Council (EPSRC) Centre for Doctoral Training in Power Networks at the University of Manchester.

References

Adger, W. N. (2006). Vulnerability. *Global Environmental Change*, 16(3), 268–281.

Ambrose, A. R. (2015). Improving energy efficiency in private rented housing: Why don't landlords act? *Indoor and Built Environment*, 24(7), 913–924.

Anderson, W., White, V. and Finney, A. (2012). Coping with low incomes and cold homes. *Energy Policy*, 49, 40–52.

Baker, W., Starling, G. and Gordon, S. (2003). *Predicting fuel poverty at the local level*. Centre for Sustainable Energy.

Barnes, M., Butt, S. and Tomaszewski, W. (2008). *The dynamics of bad housing: The impact of bad housing on the living standards of children*. National Centre for Social Research. Available at: www.eagacharitabletrust.org/app/uploads/2016/03/natcendynamicsfullreport.pdf.

Barton, C. and Hough, D. (2016). *Briefing paper: Fuel poverty*. Available at: http://research briefings.parliament.uk/ResearchBriefing/Summary/SN05115.

Boardman, B. (1991). *Fuel poverty: From cold homes to affordable warmth*. London: Pinter Publishers Ltd.

Boardman, B. (2010). *Fixing fuel poverty: Challenges and solutions*. London: Earthscan.

Boardman, B. (2012). Fuel poverty synthesis: Lessons learnt, actions needed. *Energy Policy*, 49(0), 143–148.

Bouzarovski, S. (2013). Energy poverty in the European Union: Landscapes of vulnerability. *Wiley Interdisciplinary Reviews: Energy and Environment*, 3(3), 276–289.

Bouzarovski, S. and Cauvain, J. (2016). Spaces of exception: Governing fuel poverty in England's multiple occupancy housing sector. *Space and Polity*, 20(3), 1–19.

Bouzarovski, S. and Petrova, S. (2015). A global perspective on domestic energy deprivation: Overcoming the energy poverty – fuel poverty binary. *Energy Research and Social Science*, 10, 31–40.

Bouzarovski, S. and Tirado Herrero, S. (2015). The energy divide: Integrating energy transitions, regional inequalities and poverty trends in the European Union. *European Urban and Regional Studies*, 24(1), 69–86.

Bouzarovski, S., Tirado Herrero, S., Petrova, S. and Ürge-Vorsatz, D. (2015). Unpacking the spaces and politics of energy poverty: Path-dependencies, deprivation and fuel switching in post-communist Hungary. *Local Environment*, 21(9), 1–20

Bradshaw, J. and Hutton, S. (1983). Social policy options and fuel poverty. *Journal of Economic Psychology*, 3(3), 249–266.

Brunner, K. M., Spitzer, M. and Christanell, A. (2012). Experiencing fuel poverty: Coping strategies of low-income households in Vienna/Austria. *Energy Policy*, 49, 53–59.

Buzar, S. (2007). *Energy poverty in Eastern Europe: Hidden geographies of deprivation*. New York: Ashgate Publishing Ltd.

Day, R. and Hitchings, R. (2011). 'Only old ladies would do that': Age stigma and older people's strategies for dealing with winter cold. *Health and place*, 17(4), 885–894.

Day, R., Walker, G. and Simcock, N. (2016). Conceptualising energy use and energy poverty using a capabilities framework. *Energy Policy*, 93, 255–264.

Demšar, U., Harris, P., Brunsdon, C., Fotheringham, A. S. and McLoone, S. (2013). Principal component analysis on spatial data: An overview. *Annals of the Association of American Geographers*, 103(1), 106–128.

Department for Energy and Climate Change (DECC). (2014). *2012 sub-regional fuel poverty data*. Available at: www.gov.uk/government/collections/fuel-poverty-sub-regional-statistics.

Department for Energy and Climate Change (DECC). (2015). *Cutting the cost of keeping warm: A fuel poverty strategy for England*. Available at: www.gov.uk/government/publications/cutting-the-cost-of-keeping-warm.

Department for Energy and Climate Change (DECC). (2016). *Sub-regional fuel poverty, 2016: Statistical methodology*. Available at: www.gov.uk/government/statistics/fuel-poverty-sub-regional-methodology-and-documentation.

Department for Environment, Food and Rural Affairs (DEFRA). (2013). *Rural urban classification*. Available at: www.gov.uk/government/collections/rural-urban-classification.

Department of Communications, Energy and Natural Resources (DCENR). (2016). *A strategy to combat energy poverty*. Available at: www.dccae.gov.ie/energy/en-ie/Energy-Efficiency/Pages/Combating-Energy-Poverty.aspx.

Druckman, A. and Jackson, T. (2008). Household energy consumption in the UK: A highly geographically and socio-economically disaggregated model. *Energy Policy*, 36(8), 3177–3192.

Dubois, U. (2012). From targeting to implementation: The role of identification of fuel poor households. *Energy Policy*, 49, 107–115.

Eakin, H. and Luers, A. L. (2006). Assessing the vulnerability of social-environmental systems. *Annual Review of Environment and Resources*, 31(1), 365.

Fahmy, E., Gordon, D. and Patsios, D. (2011). Predicting fuel poverty at a small-area level in England. *Energy Policy*, 39(7), 4370–4377.

Gilbertson, J., Stevens, M., Stiell, B. and Thorogood, N. (2006). Home is where the hearth is: Grant recipients' views of England's Home Energy Efficiency Scheme (Warm Front). *Social Science and Medicine*, 63(4), 946–956.

Graham, S. and Marvin, S. (1994). Cherry picking and social dumping: Utilities in the 1990s. *Utilities policy*, 4(2), 113–119.

Hall, S. M., Hards, S. and Bulkeley, H. (2013). New approaches to energy: Equity, justice and vulnerability. Introduction to the special issue. *Local Environment*, 18(4), 413–421.

Harrison, C. and Popke, J. (2011). "Because you got to have heat": The networked assemblage of energy poverty in Eastern North Carolina. *Annals of the Association of American Geographers*, 101(4), 949–961.

Healy, J. D. (2003). Excess winter mortality in Europe: A cross country analysis identifying key risk factors. *Journal of Epidemiology and Community Health*, 57(10), 784–789.

Hills, J. (2012). *Getting the measure of fuel poverty*. London: Centre for Analysis of Social Exclusion.

Hutcheson, G. D. and Sofroniou, N. (1999). *The multivariate social scientist: Introductory statistics using generalized linear models*. London: Sage.

Jansz, A. and Guertler, P. (2012). *The impact on the fuel poor of the reduction in fuel poverty budgets in England*. Available at: www.energybillrevolution.org.

Liddell, C. (2008). *Policy briefing: The impact of fuel poverty on children*. Save the Children. Available at: www.savethechildren.org.uk.

Liddell, C. and Lagdon, S. (2013). *Tackling fuel poverty in Northern Ireland: An area-based approach to finding households most in need*. Belfast: University of Ulster.

Liddell, C. and Morris, C. (2010). Fuel poverty and human health: A review of recent evidence. *Energy Policy*, 38(6), 2987–2997.

Liddell, C., Morris, C., McKenzie, P. and Rae, G. (2011). *Defining fuel poverty in Northern Ireland: A preliminary review*. Belfast: University of Ulster.

Liddell, C., Morris, C., McKenzie, S. J. P. and Rae, G. (2012). Measuring and monitoring fuel poverty in the UK: National and regional perspectives. *Energy Policy*, 49, 27–32.

Lindley, S., O'Neill, J., Kandeh, J., Lawson, N., Christian, R. and O'Neill, M. (2011). *Climate change, justice and vulnerability*. York: Joseph Rowntree Foundation.

Middlemiss, L. (2016). A critical analysis of the new politics of fuel poverty in England. *Critical Social Policy*, 37(3), 425–443.

Middlemiss, L. and Gillard, R. (2015). Fuel poverty from the bottom-up: Characterising household energy vulnerability through the lived experience of the fuel poor. *Energy Research and Social Science*, 6, 146–154.

Moore, R. (2012). Definitions of fuel poverty: Implications for policy. *Energy Policy*, 49, 19–26.

Office for National Statistics (ONS). (2011a). *Neighbourhood statistics: Census 2011*. Available at: www.neighbourhood.statistics.gov.uk/dissemination/.

Office for National Statistics (ONS). (2011b). *Digitised boundary data (England and Wales)*. Available at: http://geoportal.statistics.gov.uk/.

Organisation for Economic Co-operation and Development (OECD). (2008). *Handbook on constructing composite indicators: Methodology and user guide*. Available at: www.oecd.org/std/leading-indicators/42495745.pdf.

Pearce, J. (2013). Commentary: Financial crisis, austerity policies, and geographical inequalities in health. *Environment and Planning A*, 45(9), 2030–2045.

Roberts, D., Vera-Toscano, E. and Phimister, E. (2015). Fuel poverty in the UK: Is there a difference between rural and urban areas? *Energy policy*, 87, 216–223.

Rudge, J. (2012). Coal fires, fresh air and the hardy British: A historical view of domestic energy efficiency and thermal comfort in Britain. *Energy Policy*, 49, 6–11.

Smith, G. R. (1999). *Area-based Initiatives: The rationale and options for area targeting*. London: Centre for Analysis of Social Exclusion.

Snell, C., Bevan, M. and Thomson, H. (2015). Justice, fuel poverty and disabled people in England. *Energy Research and Social Science*, 10, 123–132.

Strakova, D. (2014). Energy poverty in Slovakia. *SSRN*, 2546758. Available at: https://papers.ssrn.com/sol3/papers.cfm?abstract_id=2546758.

Thomson, H. and Snell, C. (2013). Quantifying the prevalence of fuel poverty across the European Union. *Energy Policy*, 52, 563–572.

Thomson, H., Snell, C. and Liddell, C. (2016). Fuel poverty in the European Union: A concept in need of definition? *People, Place and Policy Online*, 10(1), 5–24.

Turner, B. L., Kasperson, R. E., Matson, P. A., McCarthy, J. J., Corell, R. W., Christensen, L. and Schiller, A. (2003). A framework for vulnerability analysis in sustainability science. *Proceedings of the National Academy of Sciences*, 100(14), 8074–8079.

Uswitch. (2016). *Regional energy prices*. Available at: www.uswitch.com/gas-electricity/guides/regional-energy-prices/.

Walker, G. and Day, R. (2012). Fuel poverty as injustice: Integrating distribution, recognition and procedure in the struggle for affordable warmth. *Energy Policy*, 49, 69–75.

Walker, R., Liddell, C., McKenzie, P. and Morris, C. (2013). Evaluating fuel poverty policy in Northern Ireland using a geographic approach. *Energy Policy*, 63, 765–774.

Walker, R., Liddell, C., McKenzie, P., Morris, C. and Lagdon, S. (2014). Fuel poverty in Northern Ireland: Humanizing the plight of vulnerable households. *Energy Research and Social Science*, 4, 89–99.

Walker, R., McKenzie, P., Liddell, C. and Morris, C. (2012). Area-based targeting of fuel poverty in Northern Ireland: An evidenced-based approach. *Applied Geography*, 34, 639–649.

Walker, R., McKenzie, P., Liddell, C. and Morris, C. (2015). Spatial analysis of residential fuel prices: Local variations in the price of heating oil in Northern Ireland. *Applied Geography*, 63, 369–379.

Wallace, M. and Denham, C. (1996). *The ONS classification of local and health authorities of Great Britain*. London: Stationery Office.

Wong, C., Baker, M., Webb, B., Hincks, S. and Schulze-Baing, A. (2015). Mapping policies and programmes: The use of GIS to communicate spatial relationships in England. *Environment and Planning B: Planning and Design*, 42(6), 1020–1039.

Wright, F. (2004). Old and cold: Older people and policies failing to address fuel poverty. *Social Policy and Administration*, 38(5), 488–503.

10 The triple-hit effect of disability and energy poverty

A qualitative case study of painful sickle cell disease and cold homes

Anna Cronin de Chavez

Introduction

There are over 11 million people in the UK with a limiting long-term illness, impairment or disability (Burke et al. 2013). About 6% of children, 16% of working age adults and 45% of adults over state pension age are disabled (Clay et al. 2012). The link between disability and poverty has been well acknowledged (MacInnes et al. 2015). In 2013/14, 27% of people in families where someone is disabled were in poverty, compared with 19% of those in families where no one was disabled. The link between energy poverty and disability however is less defined, yet has the potential to be extremely complex due to the number of variables such as age, health and socio-economic status. People with disabilities may be at risk of energy poverty for different reasons, and the solutions will also vary greatly.

It is therefore useful to explore how energy poverty plays out in everyday life with disabilities. Taking the condition of sickle cell disease (SCD) as a case study, this chapter reports on qualitative research conducted on energy poverty and SCD in children and adults in the Midlands and Northern England in 2015. This research demonstrates how the risk factors for energy poverty of low income, housing conditions and energy efficiency and energy prices affect people with SCD and contributes to a cycle of ill health and further disabilities.

Background

Whilst it may seem plausible that there is a link between energy poverty and disability, this link has only recently been a focus of research. There is some evidence that disabled people experience higher rates of energy poverty (DECC 2016; George et al. 2013). Emerson and Hatton (2005) found families with disabled children were twice as likely to live in a house that could not be kept warm enough. Additionally, disabled people are typically treated as a single group with homogenous needs in energy poverty statistics, despite varying needs and sources of income (Walker and Day 2012). Snell et al. (2015a and 2015b) conducted a statistical analysis of the English Housing Survey and found elevated levels of energy poverty among households with disabilities or long-term illnesses. They also conducted interviews and identified general behaviours observed for people in energy poverty, such as cutting back on food, wearing extra layers instead of having heating on and selling possessions to pay for bills. They identified increased energy needs for some disabled people and argued for greater understanding of how we capture disabled people in energy poverty statistics.

Boardman (2012) and DECC (2012) identified three factors that contribute to the risk of the general population experiencing energy poverty (termed 'fuel poverty' in these documents). These are low incomes, housing conditions (including energy efficiency) and energy prices (Boardman 2012; DECC 2012). There has been some work done to identify how these factors may affect people with disabilities more than the general population. In terms of the first factor, low-income, disabled people are less likely to be employed, less likely to have savings and more likely to have higher general living costs associated with their condition (Morciano et al. 2015). Changes in energy poverty and welfare policy appear to be increasing this vulnerability (Snell et al. (2015a). For the second factor, housing conditions and energy efficiency, one in three disabled households live in non-decent housing conditions and are more likely to live in private rented housing which has been notorious for poorer housing conditions and inadequate energy efficiency (Ambrose 2015). In addition they often need adapted housing with additional space, requiring higher rents and possibly an 'under-occupancy' charge (colloquially known as the 'bedroom tax' in the UK). The need for adapted housing means they are less able to move around and find more competitive rents or find large amounts of money for building works if they are homeowners. Snell et al. (2015b) found there were more energy poor people in households with someone with a disability in the private rented sector. The private rented sector is already notorious for vulnerable tenants finding it difficult to challenge landlords for better living conditions (Cauvain and Bouzarovski 2016). The third factor, energy prices, could disproportionately affect people with disabilities resulting from higher energy needs related to their condition; for example, use of assistive equipment requiring electricity, and the need to maintain a home warm enough to avoid exacerbation of symptoms. The evidence regarding the latter is however still sparse, under-developed and in debate.

The health impacts of cold homes in the general population are vast (Friends of the Earth & Marmot Review Team 2011; NICE 2014). A significant proportion of the general population in the UK now find it hard to maintain a warm home (DECC and ONS 2016). Strained incomes, increase in the cost of living and housing costs and reductions in government and local authority funding to help people in energy poverty are exacerbating the crisis of energy poverty in the UK. This has an impact on the health of the general population in terms of excess winter deaths and morbidity. For example hospital admissions for primary hypothermia in children under the aged 2–5 years old has doubled between 2005 and 2014 (Health and Social Care Information Centre 2014) at the same time as energy prices doubled (Consumer Futures 2014).

A recent Department of Health review concluded that, based on existing evidence, 18°C can be regarded to be a 'healthy room temperature' (Wookey et al.

2014). They did however acknowledge that this is based on existing evidence and that more evidence on different ages and conditions is still needed. The evidence review for the NICE guidance on the prevention of excess winter deaths and morbidity acknowledged that the potential number of conditions affected by cold temperatures was too vast for the remit of their review, so they focused on the conditions of cardiovascular disease, respiratory disease and external causes such as injuries (NICE 2014). Human thermoregulation is complex, and there is good evidence to explain why a one-size-fits-all room temperature cannot support health for all ages and conditions. Thermoregulation is a highly complex interaction of internal physical and psychological systems and external conditions of temperature, humidity and air velocity. Room temperature is only one factor of over at least 40 other factors (British Standards Institute 2007). Cronin de Chavez (2016) proposes a framework, the HeaTmaPPE to identify how a multitude of ages and conditions can be at risk of extra vulnerability to the exacerbations of cold, or cool, room temperatures and why extra heating is essential for some conditions.

Whilst some health conditions may predispose people to being vulnerable to hot environmental conditions, there is good reason to be more worried about disabled people being exposed to cold rather than heat. One is that the room temperature required for a thermo-neutral environment, i.e. that requires an unclothed, healthy adult to have to neither produce nor conserve body heat, is 25–30°C (Parsons 2003). This means for the majority of the year, even with layers of clothing, heating is required to achieve the minimum 18°C. Healthy individuals may not be harmed by intermittent exposure to cooler temperatures. However, people with disabilities and long-term health conditions can experience mild to severe exacerbations in the same conditions. As such, the maintenance of a warm enough home environment is not a question of comfort but, for people with certain conditions, a way of staying out of hospital and surviving.

The invisibility of energy poor disabled people is made worse through current energy poverty definitions not excluding disability-related benefits from income calculations, thus making their income look artificially high and appearing to take them out of energy poverty (Snell et al. 2015b). It could be argued that these disability benefits account for disabled households' extra heating costs, so not excluding disability benefits in energy poverty calculations can be justified. However, firstly there has never been any robust attempt to actually quantify what the extra heating costs of disabled households might be and what the differences are for people with different conditions. Secondly, there are several difficulties with estimating the extra living costs of people with disabilities (Pérez et al. 2016). Thirdly, there has been a reduction in the amount of benefits given for living costs for disabled people and a reduction in the number of people who qualify for such benefits. This makes it very hard to identify disabled people at risk of being energy poor and to include them in current energy poverty statistics. Therefore, it can be seen that a relationship between energy poverty and disability does exist but that it is complex and poorly understood.

One of the most dangerous diseases to have, if exposed to cool temperatures, is sickle cell disease (SCD), also known as sickle cell anaemia. There are

12,000–15,000 people in the UK with SCD (NHS 2015). A sickling crisis occurs when the abnormal sickle-shaped blood cells of people with this hereditary condition get stuck and form blockages in blood vessels in any part of the body. The consequences of this blockage can range from mild pain, hospitalisation due to extreme, unmanageable pain through to organ failure and death. Common consequences of a sickling crisis include stroke, anaemia, osteomyelitis, acute chest syndrome, kidney damage, cardiac failure, multi-organ failure and complications from treatments (NCEPOD 2008) with lifetime hospital costs of a person with SCD at 35 years of age averaging £185,000 (Karnon et al. 2000). Child SCD sufferers can lose weeks of schooling per year (Dyson et al. 2011), and adults may find it difficult to maintain regular employment if they experience regular attacks requiring time off work or lower productivity due to pain levels, complications and anaemia. The main cause of stroke for children is SCD, with a peak age of 2–5 years old (Brousse 2014; Dick 2010). Whilst it is the disease itself that ultimately causes these life-threatening consequences, the triggers for the crisis can be conditions that are quite benign for most people without this condition – these include exposure to cool or cold environments, getting wet, not eating well, being dehydrated or experiencing stress.

There is good evidence that cold stress, i.e. conditions that require the body to make some physiological or behavioural change to keep warm, can trigger a sickle crisis (Jones et al. 2005; Mohan et al. 1998; Molokie et al. 2011; Rogovik et al. 2011; Smith et al. 2009; Brandow et al. 2013). The association between cold and sickle crisis is also regularly observed by people with SCD and their families (Elliot 2007) and doctors regularly advise people with the condition to keep warm (Oni et al. 2013). Although physicians are well aware of the need for people with SCD to keep warm, medical professionals are rarely in a position to have an impact on the housing conditions and income of their patients who are living in cold, damp housing without the funds to pay energy bills. There is therefore a strong medical, economic and social argument for preventing the triggers that set off the damaging, intensely painful crisis in the first place.

The impact of energy poverty among people with SCD is likely to be extreme. Because even temporary exposure to cool environments can result in a dangerous, painful sickle crisis being triggered, people with SCD cannot risk coping measures such as 'self-disconnection' from heating (i.e. turning the heating off when they run out of money) because the danger to their health and survival is so high. To compound the situation further, people from ethnic minorities in the UK are not only more likely to suffer lower incomes (Majeed et al. 2009) and therefore be more at risk of energy poverty, but they are also more likely to inherit SCD, especially for people with African, Caribbean, Middle Eastern and Mediterranean genetic origins (NICE 2012). This is a toxic combination of elevated risk of SCD, energy poverty and danger to life from exposure to cool environments. Some indication that there is a possible link between SCD and energy poverty can be seen through evidence that people with SCD are more likely to be on a low income (Majeed et al. 2009) but also that people with SCD in the deprived group quartile of the Lower Super Output areas in England are twice as likely to die when admitted to hospital than those from more affluent areas (Al Juburi et al. 2013), thus indicating that for some reason their symptoms are more severe. Because of the danger to life, the extreme sensitivity to cold and the higher than average risk of energy poverty, SCD is an important example to focus on in terms of understanding disability and energy poverty. By looking at this group, it may be possible to demonstrate some direct consequences of energy poverty that might be less easy to observe in people with other disabilities and health conditions.

Methods

The aim of the project was to explore the heating and energy requirements and behaviours of people with SCD and to understand what opportunities there are to increase effectiveness and efficiency of delivery and take-up of energy use and services.

A semi-structured questionnaire was used to interview 15 adults with SCD or carers of a child (< 18 years old) with SCD. Data-loggers were used to record temperature and humidity readings over a period of 2 weeks for participants who accepted this. This mixed methods approach of using qualitative interviews with environmental monitoring has been used in other energy poverty research projects (Cronin de Chavez 2017). Recruitment was facilitated through email, telephone or face-to-face contact with people with SCD, with the help of UK SCD charities, SCD researcher colleagues and snowballing techniques. Ethical approval was obtained from Sheffield Hallam University's Health and Wellbeing Faculty Ethics Committee.

Interviews were conducted with a total of 15 adults with SCD or parents of a child with SCD in the Midlands, Manchester and Yorkshire. The spread of locations aided the anonymity of participants who might otherwise have been identifiable by local services because SCD is a rare condition. All of the participants had a more extreme version SCD, apart from one who had sickle cell trait but had experienced a crisis. The process for the research was for a key contact to arrange a convenient time and place for the interview with those who were willing to participate. Interviews lasted between 25–70 minutes. In the interview, the research was explained in more detail, and consent was taken. The interviews were recorded using a digital recorder and transcribed. The qualitative results were analysed using a grounded theory approach (Charmaz 2014) and Gemini TinyTag2 software, and Microsoft Excel was used to analyse the temperature and humidity data.

Six of the participants agreed to having their room temperatures and humidity recorded using Gemini TinyTag2 data loggers recording room temperatures and humidity every hour for a maximum of 2 weeks. All of the interviews were conducted in colder months January to March. It was felt temperatures could be recorded for no longer than 2 weeks because a longer period would make it harder for the participants to recall their heating use during the recording period. For these participants there were two visits, one to drop off the temperature monitors and gain consent and a second approximately 2 weeks later to conduct the interview.

The characteristics of the participants are given in Table 10.1, which shows the participants had a mixture of age, tenure, employment status and energy payment type. Although there were no criteria for selecting by ethnicity in the recruitment process, all participants were Black British, Black Caribbean or Black African. The ethnicity of the participants reflects the higher incidence of SCD in groups of African and Caribbean origin. Unless stated, the information below refers to the participant – i.e. the adult with SCD or the parent of a child with SCD.

There were other participants than those finally included, who were unavailable for interview due to being hospitalised when initially contacted. In terms of research methods for studying energy poverty and disability, illness and

Table 10.1 Participant characteristics

Characteristic	Number in category	
Age of person with SCD (n = 15)	< 18 years	5
	19–35	4
	36–45	3
	41–55	1
	56–65	2
Gender of person with SCD	Male	6
	Female	9
Household tenure (n = 15)	Housing association	3
	Local Authority landlord	3
	Private rented	3
	Home owner	2
	Living with parents	1
	Living with grandparent	1
	Homeless	1
Employment/income status of participant (n = 15)	Working	5
	Claiming benefits	6
	No work or income	3
Highest qualification of participant (equivalent to UK) (n = 12)	University level	6
	A Level	2
	GNVQ	4
Ethnicity of participant (n = 15)	Black British	10
	Black African	2
	Black Caribbean	3
Fuel bill payment type (n = 12)	Meter	4
	Direct debit/bill	7
	Taken out of benefits	1
Heating system (n = 15)	Gas central heating	14
	Storage heating	1
	Electric radiators used as well as heating system (n = 11)	9

hospitalisation must be factored in during recruitment and fieldwork and extra care taken to not put people under pressure to participate.

Results

The results will be presented below in an adapted categorisation to Boardman's (2012) three factors of low income, housing conditions (including energy efficiency) and energy prices and extra cost of heating. The results will be presented in two sections, the first on the additional cost of heating and housing conditions for people with SCD and the second on the difficulty in sustaining and maintaining an income.

Cost of heating and housing conditions

Participants demonstrated several instances when they needed to keep warm at all times. To achieve this, they required heating to be higher than the room temperature recommended for healthy adults and for longer periods. Therefore, participants' heating costs necessary to avoid harm to their health were higher than they otherwise would have been. The consequences of failing to keep adequately warm and prevent a sickle crisis were usually described as an extreme level of pain, plus other complications including kidney failure, bone death and acute chest syndrome. Participants described the severity of the pain caused by a crisis:

> Yeah, because sickle they need someone to talk on their behalf, because the pain is that intense you cannot speak. When you're going through that pain you cannot speak. So you need someone that can tell them their history, and they can tell them how they're feeling, where the sickling is taking place, how it started, and generally allow them to trust the person that's about to touch them when they're in such severe pain.
>
> (P8 talking of her son with SCD)

Parents described how much of an emergency the crisis could be once initiated:

> You can say the ambulance, sometimes it's just delayed before they come, or she will be screaming and screaming, it's really painful.
>
> (P3)

Cold as a trigger for SCD crisis and hospitalisation was identified in 12 scenarios. These included external exposures to cold such as being out in the snow or rain, having an outdoor job or playing outside, swimming, eating an ice cream and indoor exposures such as not setting radiators at the right temperature and going into emergency housing with poor heating. All but one of these 12 examples resulted in a crisis where the person with SCD had to be hospitalised. There was one example of a child of a participant who was washing dishes in cold water whilst living in exile in an African country. The cold water triggered an SCD crisis in her wrists, and because the family did not have access to hospital care, the child died. This made her mother extra cautious about allowing her surviving daughter who also had SCD to be exposed to cold or when there was any sign of a crisis being triggered:

> [E]ven when she says I'm feeling [pain in] my head, I'm not going anywhere. I know, I've experienced it; I saw my daughter die and you can see a big woman like me, I was just.. it's shock, I can't believe. It's so quick! It's so quick!
>
> (P3)

Because of the direct effect of cold on levels of pain, as reported by the participants, there was a high level of vigilance in terms of protection from cold, and participants believed they needed higher room temperatures than people without the condition. The temperature and humidity readings were an opportunity to test out these claims – the temperature readings did not always match the room temperatures participants reported to be ideal.

Poorer households in general are more likely to have compulsory installation of pre-payment meters for energy, due to incurring debts. Energy prices are often higher on pre-payment meters, and they may have standing charges (Vyas 2014). People with SCD try to maintain a warm house at all times and can risk a crisis if exposed to a cold home due to not being able to top up a prepayment meter card:

> With a direct debit as I say I've no idea of how much I pay a month, but yeah, I do definitely prefer, because actually if I've not got that money to top up a meter then I'm just sat in my house freezing which all then equates to be in hospital.
>
> (P13)

Until recently, most energy suppliers would charge for the removal of pre-payment meters when customers wanted access to more competitive rates. As stress is another principle trigger for a sickle crisis, the stress of managing energy payments can also affect the health of those with SCD. Table 10.2 shows the advantages and disadvantages of paying for energy via direct debits versus pre-payment meters, as reported by the participants.

There appears to be a greater source of stress surrounding the pre-payment meter method and more chance that those living with SCD will not be able to keep their home as consistently warm as necessary. Meanwhile, Box 10.1 provides a case study of a participating household that used a pre-payment meter and struggled with their energy costs – as such, they were often unable to achieve the temperatures necessary for the household member with SCD.

Table 10.2 Stresses of different payment methods

Payment method	Advantages	Disadvantages (sources of stress)
Meter	• Avoids the debts and shocks of big bills • You can see what you are using	• Gas or electricity can get cut off when emergency credit runs out • Shop may be shut to top up card • Have to go out in cold to get top up (meters are sometimes located outside the home) • Have to take young children out with you to get top up – they may have SCD and get cold going out, plus it is just harder to get out • If you have gone into debt, even more is needed to get into credit and have some money for heating • Standing charge for meter – even when no gas appliances connected • May not be able to crouch down for meter • Paying up-front in winter
Direct debit/ bills	• Can refuse to have a meter put in on health grounds • Can negotiate monthly payment • You can have heat even when you don't have money • Can't see what you're using • Can spread payments over year	• Frequent drops in income and sanctions can lead to fees for unpaid direct debit/unauthorised overdraft • Risk or a large, unexpected bill or debt

Box 10.1   Case study of the difficulties of pre-payment meters for households with sickle cell disease

Participant 9 was a mother of a 13-year-old girl with SCD. The house was a semi-detached, post-war council house. The mother wanted to drive her daughter home from school so she was not exposed the cold, but the girl had insisted she wanted to walk home with her friends. The mother agreed to allow her to do the 15-minute walk home if she wore very warm clothing. The daughter also got under a duvet for 15 minutes when she got home, and the mother turned the heating on before the daughter arrived home so the house was warm. They could not afford to heat the house all day. They had a pre-payment meter, which meant they were unable to keep the home warm if there was no cash available. One evening they ran out of money, and so the mother drove several miles to borrow £10 from her friend. When she returned, the shop selling the pre-payment top-ups was closed, and so the daughter had to sleep in the parents' bed for body warmth. Data from the temperature monitor in the participant's home showed that the heating was only turned on in the evenings, and the house rarely reached even the minimum temperature of 18°C recommended by the Department of Health for healthy individuals (Wookey 2014). This may explain why the daughter was constantly in pain. However, she was conscious of the money her parents spend on keeping the house warm for her and reluctant to ask for the house to be warmer despite experiencing pain. The mother said:

> But she's always cold. And I can tell that sometimes she can see because we moan about, like me and my husband we're saying oh we have to go and put £10 gas in. We spend already £30 this week. And you can tell, because she's a grown up girl, you can tell that sometimes I'll say oh put the heating on, and she says oh mum I'm fine. But she's got jacket and blanket on you see. And we just put it on, because it's expensive anyway. But she does feel a lot of cold, you can tell that she's cold. And then if I'm late to pick her up, she walks. Like now it's been cold quite often and she's been in crisis all the time. All the time she's in pain, all the time, but I don't know, it's difficult. I don't know how to explain to you because she's been just three months [over the winter] with this like, you feel more sad and upset.

Only 2 of the 15 participants were homeowners, 6 lived in social housing, 3 in rented accommodation, 2 with family members, and 1 who was homeless living with people who took her in. This meant most of the participants had little control over the conditions of their home and improving energy efficiency. One of the participants who lived in a high-rise block of flats was refused energy efficiency improvements. The landlord understood the urgency but needed to find funding to improve the whole tower block. A house that was easy to keep warm was valued, with one participant who consciously chose a mid-terrace new build with the assumption it would be a warmer house because of good energy efficiency. Another participant had been trying to get her private landlord to install double glazing for 10 years and did not want to argue, so intended to move to a warmer house. Moving location in the UK to stay warm was seen in this study and is not unheard of among people with SCD in general.

Difficulty sustaining and obtaining income

As with many people with disabilities, the income of those with SCD can fluctuate over time, and it is difficult to complete education and maximise earning capacity, maintain a job or maintain an income through benefits. SCD can affect children right throughout their school career. Participant 7, for example, found it difficult to trust nursery staff to identify her young son's symptoms before they became serious and to give him the preventative care he needed:

> I can't tell it all [the care needed] but there are so many things that you have to look for. Like for him for instance his spleen, you feel that area and it feels hard you have to rush [to the hospital] with him because it can be fatal. And like him going to nursery and stuff, the sickle cell nurse has to go to the nursery or school and explain the illness.
>
> (P7)

The financial strain on higher and further education students from poorer backgrounds is magnified for students with SCD who may not be able to work to supplement their incomes. Additionally the stresses of learning to live independently and of exams can trigger a crisis:

> [My son] went there for a year just to try and study at university, and he did well, he was doing well. But he was threatened with losing his flat this time, so that caused him stress and then he went into crisis. Then when he entered into crisis down there he was able to go to the South London clinic which he saw like-minded people that understood him immediately, understood what to do, how to do it, spoke to him like he was a man, not like he was a child. And yeah, he liked their care, and he wished he could have stayed in London but obviously he couldn't because he was going to lose his flat.
>
> (P8)

Maintaining employment is also hard for people with SCD.

> Because I have my nephew here as well, he's sickle cell . . . and he's 32. He's a very hard worker but sometimes you can see the agony. But he never claims [benefits]. He always, he got disability allowance but always worked. But his work, but he missed so much job, every time, god knows how many agencies he has been. Because he'll be working, some agency he'll be working for three or four months, and then like he is off for a week, even though

he explained that because I've been ill or because I've got this illness. But people don't understand, they keep sacking him.

(P9)

It is also an issue for their carers, further impacting on the household's income and the carer's ability to maintain their own health and the person with SCD they care for:

With my own situation, if my daughter is sick or I am sick, if I am sick, like I'm not like others, they are paid if they are sick, but for me nothing like that. So sometimes I just try if I see extra hours to just work and make up for the last days. Sometimes even when you're not sick but you just get tired, you want to stay, you know, on your own.

(P3)

Because SCD is a poorly understood, fluctuating condition, people with SCD can find themselves being switched between different types of state welfare when they go through periodic reassessments. If they are on a benefit type that requires attending appointments to sign on and they are ill or in hospital, they may experience being sanctioned for failure to attend, even when they have explained they were in hospital:

And then when he [son with SCD] was 16 he said, we sat down and we spoke about it, he said I feel fit me, I want to go and get a job. So we decided not to re-apply for the carer's allowance, and we would try. Six months after that he had heart failure. He had had a couple of jobs up until then, but couldn't [continue]. It was about a year he got heart failure, then he had to be booked in to have open heart surgery for the second time. And when I went to re-apply for disability living allowance it had all changed and oh no, you said you didn't want it before so you're not having it now, you don't need it now. Did an appeal, that failed.

(P8)

Three of the fifteen participants in the study had no income whatsoever at the time of the interview, other than the voucher given for participating. The case study in Box 10.2 demonstrates the disruption on income caused by being assessed as having a disability in some years but not in others.

Box 10.2   Case study of the relations between sickle cell disease, welfare benefits and insecure income

Participant 10 was a young adult with SCD living alone in a ground floor flat. He had received no state welfare benefits during the measurement period because he was suddenly taken off Employment and Income Support after failing a 'work capacity assessment'. He then had to wait several weeks to receive any new benefits. With £30 debt on his gas pre-payment meter, he said he did not see the point of accepting £30 from a family member to top up his meter card because that would just be taken up by the debt. This meant he could not heat his home while he had no income. He spent most of the day at home and his family dropped round meals for him.

He regularly had periods of no income, so had to walk to the Job Centre for his signing on appointments despite the pain after a hip replacement and being breathless because of his anaemia and heart condition. He did not want to move back with his family because he wanted to live independently as his peers did. He also wanted to socialise with his friends which meant going outdoors in the cold to meet them, sometimes leading to him becoming hospitalised when a sickle crisis was triggered. He had spent years of his childhood in and out of hospital and excluded from friends, so socialising as a young adult was a high priority for him.

Participant 10 had been on a work-based benefit a couple of years previously, having failed to be assessed as disabled. To keep receiving welfare benefits he had to accept a job as a door-to-door salesman for an energy company. Being out in the cold for long periods whilst doing this job resulted in a sickle crisis and his hospitalisation. He had an unstable income for years as a result of his changing eligibility for disability benefits. Becoming ill made him miss appointments at the job centre resulting in sanctions that temporarily stopped his benefit payments. He recognised that the stress of dealing with his insecure income was also a trigger for crisis. Describing the process of going through a 'work-capability assessment', which determined whether and how much welfare benefits he would be entitled to, he recalled:

I mean just obviously [the work capability assessor] they asked me questions, I answered them, and then yeah, when I was on the phone to them, and I said how could I have got no [eligibility] points, and they said it's just what obviously, if you answer a question, that's what they write down, write down my answer. And plus, as I was saying earlier, the woman said I looked fine, so, and that counts towards it as well . . . It's just, yeah, I've got nothing to say about it well, other than it just getting me a bit angry at times, but obviously try not to get angry because then I end up getting ill, so.

(P10)

The temperature data from the data logger showed that his flat was never at even a minimum temperature (18°C) for health in the general population during the recording period, increasing the risk of a sickle crisis. This absence of heating can be directly attributed to the withdrawal of his benefit payments.

The triple-hit effect of disability and energy poverty

From the above evidence, a 'triple-hit' model of the interactions between disability and energy poverty is proposed. This demonstrates how experiencing disability and ill health could potentially send people into a spiral of worsening energy poverty. These factors are shown in Figure 10.1.

In the case of sickle cell disease, for stage 1 of the model – disability reducing income – there was evidence that disability, if experienced in childhood or early adulthood, can reduce educational attainment because of absences and illness. This can then reduce earning capacity as an adult. Furthermore, maintaining employment with good working conditions was difficult if regularly needing to take time off sick, especially if they were employed via a contract without guaranteed hours (often termed 'zero hours' contracts), which some participants were. Those receiving different kinds of state welfare benefits for disability and

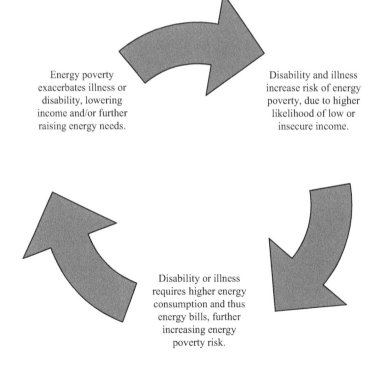

Energy poverty exacerbates illness or disability, lowering income and/or further raising energy needs.

Disability and illness increase risk of energy poverty, due to higher likelihood of low or insecure income.

Disability or illness requires higher energy consumption and thus energy bills, further increasing energy poverty risk.

Figure 10.1 The triple-hit effect of disability and fuel poverty

unemployment found their eligibility constantly being reassessed. This caused fluctuations in income levels and periods of no income whilst benefits changed. The frequent periods of illness also put them at risk of being sanctioned for not attending appointments at employment centres, even if they had given advanced notice. This reduced income results in a higher risk of energy poverty and an inability to maintain adequate temperatures in the home.

Stage 2 of the model relates to higher energy needs. There is evidence that there is a greater need for higher room temperature over sustained periods for those with SCD, thus raising energy costs that some participants struggled to pay on their limited and/or insecure incomes. Furthermore, exposure to even mildly cold environments could trigger a sickle crisis and complications such as severe pain, pneumonia, kidney failure and bone death.

The experience of energy poverty could result in stage 3, as inadequate temperatures exacerbate current illnesses or disability or cause additional ones. This then affects people's ability to find or maintain employment and further increases their energy and heating needs. The cycle then begins again, as these factors lead to an increased risk of more severe energy poverty, leading to cold homes which risks increased severity and incidence of illness. Additional disability can result from complications of SCD such as difficulty walking because of affected bones and dependency on kidney dialysis. One of the most dramatic examples of SCD complications is stroke in children with SCD, which peaks at 2–4 years. Stroke in a young child can result in lifelong disabilities. However, the most dramatic example of all was the case of the daughter of participant 3 who died from a sickling crisis after cold water triggered a crisis where no medical care was available. Whilst this was not in the UK, some complications, such as splenic sequestration, require emergency treatment which might not be immediately available especially in winter where ambulance services are already over-stretched.

There are several ways that limited or insecure income can reduce the ability to pay for energy. There is evidence of disabled people being subject to sanctions (in which they have their welfare payments stopped for weeks at a time) that go against the UK Department for Work and Pensions' (DWP) own guidance. Below is a quote from a DWP guide for assessment decision makers, which makes clear that the impact of sanctions on the health of the individual must be considered:

> 35098 The DM [decision maker] must consider if the health of the person with the medical condition would decline more than a normal healthy adult. The DM should make this comparison based on a normal healthy adult who is in similar circumstances to the person with the medical condition.
>
> 35099 It would be usual for a normal healthy adult to suffer some deterioration in their health if they were without
>
> 1. essential items, such as food, clothing, heating and accommodation or
> 2. sufficient money to buy essential items for a period of two weeks.
>
> (DWP 2015)

With some disability benefits included as an income in energy poverty calculations, it could be argued that this money is intended to cover extra living costs
such as higher heating bills. Even if this was the case, this income should not
be compared to income received by non-disabled people, as in theory the extra
money coming in should then go out on a range of extra expenses. However,
there is evidence that there has been a disproportionate reduction of income for
people with disability, affecting their ability to cover all their living costs. For
example, a United Nations inquiry into the UK government's changes to disability welfare benefits found evidence of a decrease in disabled people's ability to
pay for basic living costs:

> The Committee also received evidence that the cumulative impact in the
> reduction of welfare benefits has led persons with disabilities to struggle to
> maintain minimum level of income, driving many into increased depend-
> ency on relatives and increased levels of indebtedness and resulting in an
> inability to manage the bare essentials and recourse to food banks.
>
> (UN 2016)

Given the potential for harm by cold homes experienced by disabled people and
their increasing risk of experiencing energy poverty, it is urgent that energy poverty research and practices recognises the needs of disabled people to be supported
to stay warm and seeks a greater understanding of how to provide this support.

Conclusion

Despite the tragic energy poverty picture illustrated in the case of people with
SCD, the positive side is that much of this suffering is potentially preventable.
Reducing energy poverty among this group, and of others with disabilities, is potentially a 'simple' matter of increasing access to assistance with energy payments and
improving housing conditions. There is much to learn about how to provide these
in the field of energy poverty research and practice. Furthermore there is still a lot
of work to be done in identifying energy poverty among people with disabilities,
such as: evidence for what room temperatures are needed by people with different
conditions (recognising that the 'disabled population' is not homogenous); health
economics arguments to demonstrate the cost effectiveness of providing a warm
home versus health and social care costs of people with disabilities living in cold
homes; and the most appropriate ways of providing help to those with different
conditions. Alongside more research being needed to deepen the understanding
of the relationship between disability, energy poverty and excess winter deaths
and morbidity, existing health guidelines such as the Department of Health's Cold
Weather Plan (DH 2011) and existing and future NICE guidance provide an
opportunity to raise awareness of the risks disabled people face. As highlighted in
the UN report (UN 2016), there are a significant questions of distributional and
recognition justice (as described in the introductory chapter to this volume) that
need to be urgently addressed in terms of the ability of disabled people to cover
their basic needs and sustain their mental and physical health.

Acknowledgements

With sincere thanks to the Chesshire Lehmann Fund for the funding to make this work possible, to ASYABI (Association of Sickle Cell Sufferers of Yorkshire and Africa and Basic Information), Oscar Birmingham and Oscar Sandwell (Organisation for Sickle Cell Anaemia Relief and Thalassaemia Support) for helping with recruitment. Thank you most of all for the participants in agreeing to participate despite illness, staying up after a night shift, turning down work on a zero hours contract to be interviewed, juggling caring for children and making time in busy lives to speak to me.

References

Al Juburi, G., Laverty, A. A., Green, S. A., Phekoo, K. J., Bell, D. and Majeed, A. (2013). Socio-economic deprivation and risk of emergency readmission and inpatient mortality in people with sickle cell disease in England: Observational study. *Journal of Public Health*, 35(4), 510–517.

Ambrose, A. R. (2015). Improving energy efficiency in private rented housing: Why don't landlords act? *Indoor and Built Environment*, 24(7), 913–924.

Boardman, B. (2012). Fuel poverty synthesis: Lessons learnt, actions needed. *Energy Policy*, 49, 143–148.

Brandow, A. M., Stucky, C. L., Hillery, C. A, Hoffmann, R. G., Panepinto, J. A. (2013). Patients with sickle cell disease have increased sensitivity to cold and heat. *American Journal of Hematology*,88(1), 37–43.

British Standards Institute. (2007). *BS EN ISO 9920:2007 Ergonomics of the thermal environment – Estimation of thermal insulation and water vapour resistance of a clothing ensemble*. BSI.

Brousse, V. (2014). Management of sickle cell disease in the community. *British Medical Journal*, 348, 1765.

Burke, D., Clay, S., Evans, D., Herring, I., Sullivan, J. and Vekaria, R. (2013). *Family resources survey – United Kingdom, 2011/12*. DWP – Department for Work and Pensions & ONS Office for National Statistics. Available at: www.gov.uk/government/uploads/system/uploads/attachment_data/file/206887/frs_2011_12_report.pdf.

Cauvain, J. and Bouzarovski, S. (2016). Energy vulnerability in multiple occupancy housing: A problem that policy forgot. *People Place and Policy*, 10(1), 88.

Charmaz, K. (2014). *Constructing grounded theory* (2nd ed.). Los Angeles, CA, London, New Delhi, Singapore and Washington, DC: Sage.

Clay, S., Evans, D., Herring, I., Sullivan, J. and Vekaria, R. (2012). *Family resources survey – United Kingdom, 2011/12*. DWP Department for Work and Pensions & ONS Office for National Statistics. Available at: www.gov.uk/government/uploads/system/uploads/attachment_data/file/222839/frs_2010_11_report.pdf.

Consumer Futures. (2014). *Retail price information*. Available at: www.consumerfutures.org.uk/our-work/project4/retail-price-information#Bookmark4.

Cronin de Chavez, A. (2017). Using environmental monitoring to complement in-depth qualitative interviews in cold homes research. *Indoor and Built Environment Journal*, in press.

Cronin de Chavez, A. (2016). Challenges for health services in identifying which groups are most vulnerable to health impacts of cold homes. In Heffron, R. and Little, G. (eds.) *Delivering energy policy in the EU and US: A reader*. Edinburgh: Edinburgh University Press.

DECC – Department for Energy and Climate Change and Office for National Statistics ONS. (2016). *Annual report on fuel poverty statistics 2016*. Available at: www.gov.uk/government/uploads/system/uploads/attachment_data/file/557400/Annual_Fuel_Poverty_Statistics_Report_2016_-_revised_30.09.2016.pdf.

DH Department of Health. (2011). *Cold weather plan for England: protecting health and reducing harm from severe cold*. London: Department of Health. Available at: www.dh.gov.uk/health/2011/11/cold-weather-plan/.

Dick, M. (2010). *Sickle cell disease In childhood: Standards and guidelines for clinical care* (2nd ed.). Available at: www.gov.uk/government/uploads/system/uploads/attachment_data/file/408961/1332-sc-clinical-standards-web.pdf.

DWP Department for Work and Pensions. (2015). *Decision makers guide: Hardship*. 6, Ch 35, 29. Available at: www.gov.uk/government/uploads/system/uploads/attachment_data/file/470852/dmgch35.pdf.

Dyson, S., Atkin, K., Culley, L., Dyson, S. and Evans, H. (2011). Sickle cell, habitual dyspositions and fragile dispositions: Young people with sickle cell at school. *Sociology of Health and Illness*, 33(3), 465–483.

Elliot, J. (2007). *Sickle cell: A victim of bigotry?* Available at: http://news.bbc.co.uk/1/hi/health/6936326.stm.

Emerson, E. and Hatton, C. (2005). *The socio-economic circumstances of families supporting a child at risk of disability in Britain in 2002*. Lancaster: Institute for Health Research.

Friends of the Earth and Marmot Review Team. (2011). *The health impacts of cold homes and fuel poverty*. Available at: www.instituteofhealthequity.org/projects/the-health-impacts-of-cold-homes-and-fuel-poverty.

George, M., Graham, C. and Lennard, C. (2013). *The energy penalty: Disabled people and fuel poverty*. Available at: www2.le.ac.uk/departments/law/research/cces/documents/the-energy-penalty-disability-and-fuel-poverty-pdf.

Health and Social Care Information Centre. (2014). *Hypothermia national stats by age 2005–06 to 2013–2014*. Hospital Episode Statistics. Available at: www.hscic.gov.uk/media/15004/Hypothermia-national-stats-by-age-2005-06-to-2013-14/xls/Hypothermia_national_stats_by_age_200506_to_201314.xlsx.

Jones, S., Duncan, E. R., Thomas, N., Walters, J., Dick, M. C., Height, S. E., Stephens, A. D., Thein, S. L. and Rees, D. C. (2005). Windy weather and low humidity are associated with an increased number of hospital admissions for acute pain and sickle cell disease in an urban environment with a maritime temperate climate. *British Journal of Haematology*, 131(4), 530–533.

Karnon, J., Zeuner, D., Ades, A. E., Efimba, W., Brown, J. and Yardumian, A. (2000). The effects of neonatal screening for sickle cell disorders on lifetime treatment costs and early deaths avoided: a modelling approach. *Journal of Public Health Medicine*, 22(4), 500–511.

MacInnes, T., Tinson, A., Hughes, C., Born, T. B. and Aldridge, H. (2015). *Monitoring poverty and social exclusion 2015*. JRF Joseph Rowntree Foundation. Available at: www.jrf.org.uk/mpse-2015.

Majeed, A., Banarsee, R. and Molokhia, M. (2009). Health disparities and community participation in England. *Journal of Ambulatory Care Management*, 32(4), 280–284.

Mohan, J., Marshall, J. M., Reid, H. L., Thomas, P. W., Hambleton, I. and Serjeant, G. R. (1998). Peripheral vascular response to mild indirect cooling in patients with homozygous sickle cell (SS) disease and the frequency of painful crisis. *Clinical Science*, 94(2), 111–120.

Molokie, R. E., Wang, Z. J. and Wilkie, D. J. (2011). Presence of neuropathic pain as an underlying mechanism for pain associated with cold weather in patients with sickle cell disease. *Medical Hypotheses*, 77(4), 491–493.

Morciano, M., Hancock, R. M. and Pudney, S. E. (2015). Birth-cohort trends in older-age functional disability and their relationship with socio-economic status: Evidence from a pooling of repeated cross-sectional population-based studies for the UK. *Social Science & Medicine, 136*, 1–9.

NICE (National Institute for Health and Care Excellence). (2012). *Sickle cell acute painful episode: Management of an acute painful sickle cell episode in hospital.* Available at: www.nice.org.uk/guidance/cg143.

NICE (National Institute for Health and Care Excellence). (2014). *Evidence review & economic analysis of excess winter deaths – review 1' Factors determining vulnerability to winter- and cold-related mortality/morbidity.* Available at: www.nice.org.uk/guidance/gid-phg 70/resources/excess-winter-deaths-and-illnesses-guideline-consultation-supporting-evidence2.

NCEPOD (National Confidential Enquiry into Patient Outcome and Death). (2008). *A sickle crisis? A report of the national confidential enquiry into patient outcome and death.* Available at: www.ncepod.org.uk/2008report1/Downloads/Sickle_report.pdf.

NHS Sickle Cell and Thalassaemia Screening Programme. (2015). *Facts and figures/statistics.* Available at: http://sct.screening.nhs.uk/statistics.

Oni, L., Dick, M., Smalling, B. and Walters, J. (2013). *Care and management of your child with sickle cell disease – A parents' guide.* The NHS Sickle Cell & Thalassaemia Screening Programme. Available at: http://sct.screening.nhs.uk/parentsguide.

Parsons, K. (2003). *Human thermal environments – the effects of hot, moderate and cold environments on human health, comfort and performance.* London and New York: CRC Press.

Pérez, J. I. A., Pino, F. J. B. and de Bustillo Llorente, R. M. (2016). An analysis of the cost of disability across Europe using the standard of living approach. *SERIEs: Journal of the Spanish Economic Association, 7*(3), 281–306.

Rogovik, A. L., Persaud, J., Friedman, J. N., Kirby, M. A. and Goldman, R. D. (2011). Pediatric vasoocclusive crisis and weather conditions. *Journal of Emergency Medicine, 41*(5), 559–565.

Smith, W., Bauserman, R., Ballas, S., McCarthy, W., Steinburg, M., Swerdlow, M., Waclawiw, M. and Barton, B. (2009). Climatic and geographic temporal patterns of pain in the Multicenter Study of Hydroxurea. *Pain, 146*(1–2), 91–98.

Snell, C., Bevan, M. and Thomson, H. (2015a). Welfare reform, disabled people and fuel poverty. *Journal of Poverty and Social Justice, 23*(3), 229–244.

Snell, C., Bevan, M. and Thomson, H. (2015b). Justice, fuel poverty and disabled people in England. *Energy Research & Social Science, 10*, 123–132.

United Nations. (2016). *Inquiry concerning the United Kingdom of Great Britain and Northern Ireland carried out by the Committee under article 6 of the Optional Protocol to the Convention Report of the Committee.* Available at: www.ohchr.org/Documents/HRBodies/CRPD/CRPD.C.15.R.2.Rev.1-ENG.doc.

Vyas, D. (2014). *Topping-up or dropping-out: Self-disconnection among prepayment meter users.* Citizens Advice Bureau/Citizens Advice Scotland. Available at: www.citizensadvice.org.uk/global/migrated_documents/corporate/topping-up-or-dropping-out.pdf.

Walker, G. and Day, R. (2012). Fuel poverty as injustice: Integrating distribution, recognition and procedure in the struggle for affordable warmth. *Energy Policy, 49*, 69–75.

Wookey, R., Bone, A., Carmichael, C. and Crossley, A. (2014). *Minimum home temperature thresholds for health in winter – A systematic Review.* Public Health England. Available at: www.gov.uk/government/uploads/system/uploads/attachment_data/file/365755/Min_temp_threshold_for_homes_in_winter.pdf.

11 The value of experience

Including young people in energy poverty research

Kimberley C. O'Sullivan, Helen Viggers,
and Philippa Howden-Chapman

Introduction

As a matter of course, any 'future' under consideration necessarily involves young people. The need for energy transitions to reduce the impacts of climate change provides opportunities for considering co-benefits as a way of increasing the case for renewable energy and improved energy efficiency to ameliorate energy poverty and improve public health. In recent years, with the development of emancipatory research models such as participatory action research, alongside the growth in popularity and funding for citizen research, and the United Nations Convention on the Rights of the Child (UNCRC) (UNICEF 1989), children and young people have begun to be included more frequently as active participants in social research processes. Yet energy poverty research has continued to prioritise the experiences of adults, particularly older adults, living in cold housing. Relatively few recent studies have given voice to the perspectives of young adults (Butler 2015) and children (Children in Wales 2011), and participation of children and young people in the research process appears a valuable but overlooked approach to understanding energy poverty.

Energy poverty is an important and increasingly researched phenomenon, so the absence of evidence about children's and young people's experiences of energy poverty, and whether these experiences differ from those of adults, needs to be remedied. Three key arguments have been made for focusing on children and young people: children have a legal right to participate under the UNCRC; it is empowering and democratic, providing skills and improving outcomes for the participants as well as other children in the community; it is just and improves equality (Ergler 2017a). In addition, involving children and youth *in* research to explore energy poverty may have additional outcomes, contributing new knowledge and a deeper understanding than if adult researchers conducted the research *on* children and youth.

In this chapter we consider causes of energy vulnerability specific to young people (up to age 18), discuss the effects of living in energy poverty for children and youth, and argue for the inclusion of young people in energy research exploring energy futures. We posit that giving voice to youth perspectives on the effects of energy poverty and cold indoor environments is crucial to implementing successful and cost-effective remedial policies.

Drivers of youth energy poverty

The causes of energy poverty are by now well understood to include building and appliance energy inefficiency, high energy prices, low incomes, and specific needs of households (Thomson et al. 2017). The causes of energy poverty in young people are not markedly different, although adopting a youth perspective highlights some distinct policy challenges at the individual and household levels.

Both young and older people are physiologically more vulnerable to the effects of cold, damp housing than young and middle-aged adult, and yet are the groups most likely to spend more hours inside than these other age groups (Baker et al. 2007). Specific child health risks include asthma, respiratory infections, poor nutrition and weight gain, and injuries (Liddell and Morris 2010; Marmot Review Team 2011; Baker et al. 2012; Maidment et al. 2014). For adolescents, health risks include increased mental health problems, low self-esteem, and anti-social behaviours (Tod et al. 2016).

Policies to ensure homes are warmer tend to be focused on older people in nations such as England (Sovacool 2015) and New Zealand (Viggers, et al. 2013). This is despite strong epidemiological evidence that cold indoor temperatures lead directly and indirectly to higher rates of avoidable hospitalisation amongst young people (Marmot Review Team 2011). Moreover, a recent sociological study demonstrated that parents' inability to pay energy/utility bills is often a key compounding factor in eviction in the USA (Desmond 2016). It is children who suffer the most in these circumstances, but they have the least power to act to avert such a domestic disaster.

While children and young people have similar needs to older adults for maintaining physical health, they tend to use energy differently. There is now an emphasis on the use of energy and technology for important aspects of young people's lives and wellbeing, such as education, entertainment, and social connectedness. Children in households create 'stickier' social practices, which affect home energy use (Shove et al. 2012). This 'family peak' (Nicholls and Strengers 2015) typically coincides with peak demand, making families less able to react to economic incentives available for demand-side management. Households with children have particular routines and requirements that are often impractical to re-order: meals need to be ready in advance of bedtime, bathing is often part of an evening routine, and children's school uniforms or outdoor clothing needs to be ready again for use by morning – English parents in full-time work are more likely to do weekday evening laundry (Anderson 2016). Shifting temporal routines of dishwashing and laundering, two activities often touted as easy targets for load-shifting, were found to be more complicated than is often assumed by policy-makers, particularly for households with children (Friis and Haunstrup Christensen 2016).

While children influence family energy expenditure, little energy research has focused on children and young people's energy needs or use or has included them as active research participants; indeed, it is a moot point to what extent children should be expected to make energy savings (Fell and Chiu 2014; Aguirre-Bielschowsky, Lawson et al. 2015). Some research has shown that younger teens think about their energy use across a broad range of locations, while older teens focused on personal energy use and cited cost as well as environmental reasons as motivators for conserving energy (Toth et al. 2013). Adults in the household are generally considered responsible for conserving energy during cooking and laundry, whereas children's energy use of devices for entertainment and schooling is considered 'necessary' (Schmidt et al. 2014). These intergenerational differences in thinking about 'energy services' (Fell 2017) and 'necessary energy use' (Walker et al. 2016) have broader implications when considering the definition and measurement of energy poor households.

Middlemiss and Gillard (2015) identified six key challenges faced by households in energy poverty – quality of the dwelling fabric, tenancy relations, energy costs and supply, stability of income, social relations, and ill health – and characterised the capacity for action and power that residents may lack to sufficiently address these (Middlemiss and Gillard 2015). The challenge of social relations, particularly within the home, is framed as being difficult to overcome for parents. Similarly, the effects of energy poverty and cold indoor environments on social relations are a challenge for young people (O'Sullivan et al. 2017). Children and young people have even less agency to address other challenges such as the quality of the dwelling fabric and energy costs and supply.

Our own research has found that around 13% of young people contributed to paying for bills, including for electricity, thereby helping to address the energy poverty challenge of low or unstable household income (O'Sullivan et al. 2017). However, despite the efforts of these young people to help their parents, it is both unfair and unrealistic at a policy level to expect young people to be able to alleviate macro-level causes of energy poverty. Indeed, young people may be deterred by parents or guardians from adopting the kinds of coping responses to energy poverty commonly used by adults, such as making hot drinks, wearing additional clothing, or going to bed early. Decisions around how, when, and how long to heat the home are often not made by children.

Nonetheless, there is accumulating evidence that poor energy efficiency is a significant problem in housing, and also in some schools, the other indoor environment where children spend a significant amount of their time (Baker et al. 2007). The school setting is not usually included in energy poverty research, but the particular vulnerability of children to respiratory and other housing-related illnesses are strongly influenced by indoor conditions and often have life-long, cumulative effects on their health and wellbeing. A child living in an energy poor home, who spends the day in a thermally comfortable classroom, may have very different outcomes from a child who goes from a cold home to a cold classroom. Primary hypothermia hospitalisation rates in school-aged children point to protective effects of warm school classrooms in England (Stafford 2015).

However, in New Zealand schools, this protective effect may not be evident, due to poor building quality leading to unhealthy classroom temperatures. The average age of the government's school property estate is 42 years (National Infrastructure Unit 2015), with demonstrable deferred maintenance. An estimated 18% of the Ministry of Education's property portfolio and 41% of buildings require repair (Hampton Jones Property Consultancy 2012), including remediating 'Leaky Building Syndrome' previously identified as a major housing problem with probable health consequences (Howden-Chapman, et al. 2010; Douwes and Howden-Chapman 2011).

The restrictions on children and young people's capability to respond to energy poverty is also present in school and childcare settings. In a discussion of energy retrofits for a resilient childcare centre in Milan, Pagliano and colleagues (2016) note that young children have fewer opportunities than adults to behaviourally or physiologically adapt to improve thermal comfort, and that their teachers are in control of the most important adaptive measures (Pagliano et al. 2016). We believe that their limited capacity to reduce both their household energy poverty and their thermal comfort at school contributes to the strong support that young people in New Zealand express for Government action through policy to improve building quality and access to heating.

Energy use is integral to modern life in developed countries and both parents and young people rely on ready accessibility for social participation, integration, and mobility (Egan-Bitran 2012, Schmidt et al. 2014; O'Sullivan et al. 2017). Any attempts to encourage energy conservation must be balanced with maintaining energy access to avoid increasing inequities between age groups.

Including children and young people in the research process

The 'participation' Article 12 of the United Nations Convention on Rights of the Child has contributed to the increasing use of child participation in research (Horgan 2016). Different models of child participation exist, from Hart's (Hart 1997) 'ladder of participation' through to Ergler's (2017b) co-constructive model.

We have recently begun to include youth participation in the research process, as part of the ongoing mixed methods research undertaken by *He Kainga Oranga/* Housing and Health Research Programme (O'Sullivan and Howden-Chapman 2017). As a further prompt for this, there is also evidence that participation in collaborative public health research can be beneficial to youth health in itself, through increasing community engagement which, when successful, may have beneficial effects on health (Ballard and Syme 2016).

Our approach to participation has been to engage with youth and explain the proposed research and process, and to invite their collaboration as far as they would like to be involved. Using mixed methods participatory research undertaken in collaboration with young people, we have found that youth report more problems with residential building quality and thermal comfort than adults across New Zealand (O'Sullivan et al. 2017). Our research has shown that youth are articulate and can offer sensible, policy-relevant ideas about current constraints on their energy use and future energy needs. For the remainder of this chapter, we draw on two case studies of our research experiences working with young people from Waiopehu College, Levin. We reflect on the insights gained and provide suggestions for meaningful inclusion of children and young people in future energy research.

Case study 1: cool? Exploring youth experiences of living in or at risk of energy poverty

The *Cool?* study used mixed methods, participatory action research to systematically explore youth experiences of cold housing and energy poverty risk factors (O'Sullivan et al. 2017). From the outset, we had an explicit goal of including youth in the research process, with as much equality with adult researchers as possible. After successfully recruiting a school into this part of the study, it was suggested we work with a specific social science teacher and Year 10 class (usually aged 14–15 years), as this would allow sufficient time and space for the students to be involved. After the students decided that they wanted the highest level of involvement possible, the teacher was able to incorporate the study into the curriculum to replace a previously planned module. This gave 6 weeks of class time, which we split into three sets of workshops held in March, June–July, and October–November 2015, a total of 24 hours during class.

At the completion of the second set of workshops, we collected anonymous feedback from the youth researchers for a process evaluation of the early stages of this work. Based on their suggestions for how they would like to contribute their feedback, youth researchers were asked to reflect on five questions, writing their responses to be collected together anonymously. As the purpose of this evaluation was simply to describe youth views on the research and process being used, content analysis was performed to collate the data using a qualitative descriptive approach (Neergaard et al. 2009, Sandelowski 2010).

The majority of the youth researchers agreed that cold housing is a problem, although their responses at this stage were likely to have been influenced by prior discussions of why energy poverty and cold housing might be problematic for young people. They were most concerned about potential health problems and school performance. Some also commented on psychosocial effects of cold housing, for example not being happy at home or difficulties with having friends over. A couple of respondents did not think it was an issue for youth as it was not a problem for them personally; conversely, a couple said it was an issue for them in their own homes and therefore was an issue for youth generally. This latter view was better supported by a subsequent nationwide study, which found that young people acknowledged that, although they themselves may not struggle with energy poverty, they were aware of friends or other people that did (O'Sullivan et al. 2017). This also may have been influenced by the increased likelihood that the youth included as researchers were from households with relative socioeconomic privilege, as the class put forward to work with us on the research was the highest achieving academic class of the year group in this school. There were also a few young researchers who noted that it might affect young people without their knowledge or, if it was 'normal' to them, that it might be more problematic than current research suggests.

When asked whether it was important to involve youth in the research process the young people unanimously agreed. In particular, they felt that youth perspectives are required to contribute their distinct voices and opinions, to give insights adults might not be able to access through either personal experience or what they know about their peers and because the youth perspective is valid. A couple also noted that, if youth are involved as researchers, youth participants might then be more inclined to share their experiences than they would if speaking to an adult. Including youth researchers in the development of the survey did result in several wording changes to make the questions more 'youth-friendly'. Despite our best efforts, we were politely informed that the youth researchers did not believe that their peers would be comfortable with some of the language that we had proposed. They also strongly favoured the inclusion of response categories, reasoned by lack of privacy and time for students to type lengthy answers as surveys would be completed during class time. Included in the survey were several open-ended text boxes; however, many of the respondents did not use these at all, or gave very sparse responses.

In terms of the practicalities of undertaking such collaborative research, the youth researchers highlighted that providing food during workshop sessions encouraged them to participate more fully in the break-out group discussions used to develop survey questions, work on initial analysis, develop interview questions, and develop a presentation of the research. Having the opportunity to participate and gain real-world experience, working as a team, and the chance to participate as co-authors to benefit their own careers were also mentioned as incentives for youth to participate as researchers.

We believe that this process has been successful in achieving 'deeper' participation, supported by the continuing relationship with the school and some of the students who were in the class group for the second study described below. Similar results on youth experiences of energy poverty may have been achieved without using participatory methods. Indeed most studies of energy poverty among other at-risk groups have not included participatory methods. However, incorporation of youth researchers onto the research team, rather than including youth on an advisory group, which would likely have taken less time and flexibility on our part, has served as a constant reminder to view energy poverty from a youth perspective and encouraged us to develop more youth-centric policy recommendations and future research. Furthermore, the deep participation model used for this study has provided additional gravitas to the research, with highly positive responses from policy-makers and researchers towards results and recommendations.

Case study 2: cool at school? Pilot study: classroom temperatures and thermal comfort in the Horowhenua

As stated earlier, limited available research suggests that New Zealand classroom temperatures may be a problem. After completion of the above study, our young colleagues identified a new research priority, stating that while they felt it important that we had discovered during our research that many young people experience thermal discomfort at home, their classroom temperatures were also often not providing thermal comfort. Increasing the energy efficiency of school buildings is a plausible pathway to improving thermal comfort and the indoor environment of classrooms. As such, we developed a new research question: do classroom indoor environments in the Horowhenua, an area north of Wellington, New Zealand, provide thermal comfort?

To test the feasibility of measuring indoor temperatures using small data-loggers in classrooms installed by our young collaborators, the teacher installed these in ten high-school classrooms February/March 2016. The classrooms were selected to provide a range of building quality and anecdotal thermal comfort. The data-loggers were returned to us by courier for analysis. Following this, for the main part of this study, a class of Year 11 students was visited by the first author. At this visit, students were invited to participate, after explanation of the research problem and the proposed process. After discussion, the young researchers decided that they wanted to perform the study without further input from us as adult researchers, but we could help with recruiting four primary schools, supplying equipment, and answering questions. Therefore, this study became almost entirely youth-driven, and we (as adult researchers) had no further control over the data collection.

The results from the initial measures of indoor temperatures conducted by teachers showed that temperature regulation was a problem not only in winter, but was also during the height of summer. The World Health Organization has recommended indoor temperatures of at least 18°C, with recommendations of higher temperatures for vulnerable populations (such as young children) (World Health Organization 1987, Ormandy and Ezratty 2016). The Ministry of Education's (MoE) Designing Quality Learning Spaces guidelines for New Zealand schools recommend that classrooms are kept between 18°C and 20°C during the school day (BRANZ Ltd 2007).

Figure 11.1 shows the range of temperatures experienced in each monitored high-school classroom during the school day in the summer. The flat grey colour indicates a measurement inside the MoE guidelines. All the classrooms spent most of the school day above the 20°C recommended maximum. For at least half of the high-school hours (weekdays 8:50am to 3:10pm), all ten classrooms were above 22°C; five were above 22°C for more than 90% of the school day. Two classrooms were cooler than 18°C but only for around 3% of the school day. Overall, all the monitored rooms experienced an average of just under 15 minutes per day inside the 18°C–20°C range, and half of the rooms experienced no time inside the temperature guidelines during the school day. Importantly, classrooms were routinely too hot even when the external temperature was about 15°C (the lowest during the sampling period), although the more extreme overheating tended to occur at higher external temperatures.

Based on these summer results, children and teachers successfully lobbied school management to install heat pumps to improve thermal comfort in the two worst classrooms before winter temperature monitoring was carried out.

In winter, the youth participants then conducted their own classroom temperature measurements in primary schools as part of the research process. Results from these confirmed anecdotal reports of cold temperatures in some classrooms,

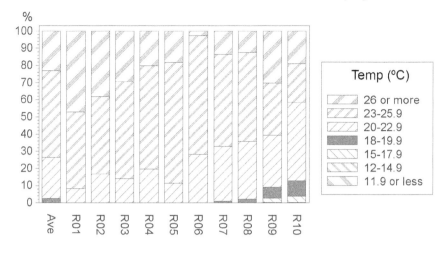

Figure 11.1 Summer temperatures by classroom

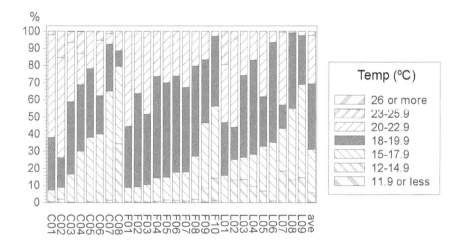

Figure 11.2 Winter temperatures by classroom/school

although others overheated. Not all the classrooms monitored could be analysed, as not all necessary information was recorded by the youth researchers, but 27 classrooms across 3 of the 4 schools yielded data for analysis.

Figure 11.2 shows the range of winter temperatures experienced in the classrooms during the primary school day (weekdays 9am – 3pm). Different schools are indicated by different letters. There was considerable variation both within and between schools. However, all but two schools had classrooms less than 15°C at least some of the day, all were colder than 18°C (the MoE guideline minimum) at least for part of the day, and half were colder than 18°C for a quarter of the day. One classroom was below 15°C for a third of the school-time. Overall, in winter the classrooms were colder than guidelines for approximately the same amount of time they were too hot, although this differed strongly by classroom – the coldest was too cold for 80% of the school day, and the hottest too hot for 74% of the school day. The extent of these very cold temperatures varied strongly by school – one school had five out of nine measured rooms colder than 15°C for approximately 1 hour per day of school. Overall, all the monitored rooms experienced an average of at least an hour a day outside the 18°C–20°C guidelines from the Ministry of Education, while a typical room experienced about 3.25 hours outside the guidelines, and the worst 4.75 hours. Some overheating was experienced when external temperatures were as low as 5°C; likewise some under-heating occurred even when the external temperature was 15°C.

Alongside this temperature data, at each school, the youth researchers facilitated a classroom workshop with primary school children, aiming to obtain qualitative data about how children felt their classroom environments affected their learning and health. These were designed and undertaken entirely by the young researchers, and videos and reports that some prepared were shared with us.

At the workshops, the young researchers discussed the research problem with the primary students and ran three exercises. The data have some caveats: for example, the exercises were repeated in three different schools, but data were not always available for every exercise at each school. However, in the absence of any other New Zealand data, these data give indicative insights into children's perceptions of classroom comfort.

Two exercises were aimed at focusing the younger children on the topic: a quiz, including some pop-culture and general knowledge questions alongside questions about thermal comfort at school and home, and a 'game-show' exercise, where three of the students from the primary classes answered questions. The game-show aimed to demonstrate how being 'too hot' or 'too cold' might be distracting for learning. One of the students volunteered to become 'too hot' with extra clothing, blankets, and hot water bottles, and a second student volunteered to become 'too cold' with their feet in a bucket of cold water and ice packs applied under their arms and hands, while the third remained the same or 'just right'. The young researchers stated that usually the 'just right' participant answered the most questions correctly, although they noted that they could not be sure whether this was due to temperature.

A third exercise with various conditions, for example 'a hot classroom', 'a noisy classroom', or 'a cold classroom', was used to capture discussion by the children about whether these conditions were healthy or unhealthy for their learning environment. This exercise illustrated that children are able to articulate their preferences for certain classroom environmental conditions and have some knowledge of environmental risk factors for health. For example, children described having a very hot classroom as being unhealthy, commenting that 'it can give you a headache sometimes' and 'you can get dehydrated' and that a cold classroom is unhealthy 'because you might get a cold virus'. Children indicated broader wellbeing was affected by being in a cold classroom, for example 'I feel like I'm getting a cold, but I'm at school, not with my Mum and Dad'. One child said that, in a cold classroom, 'you can't concentrate properly because you're only concentrating on – you want to be warm – or something', while another simply stated that 'it makes it too hard to learn, because it's too cold'. They also gave examples of individual responses to thermal discomfort such as 'I have to keep stopping my work and getting a drink', and commented that their teachers may adjust the classroom temperature. We later invited the teaching staff to describe the effects on teaching and learning, and they broadly agreed with what the children had reported.

The results from this small research project demonstrate that, even with very little collaboration with adult researchers, young people are able to design energy research studies and adequately collect data, although their failure to record installation dates led to the temperature data from one primary school being excluded from the analysis. As part of their school assessments, the young researchers also wrote detailed reports about their involvement in and results of the research. The young researchers were not involved in the analysis presented here, but have subsequently been involved giving a research presentation about the study. This project therefore better fits a flexible model of child participation in research as put forward by Ergler (2017b), whereby participation and collaboration are fluidly negotiated to fulfil both child and adult expectations and motivations for undertaking research so that both parties may benefit, than Hart's linear ladder of participation (Hart 1997). The study finds that children and youth consider both home and school energy services (particularly in this case, heating and cooling) as necessary for their health and wellbeing. Working with youth researchers has encouraged us to consider whether school buildings can be included in future as *part of* energy poverty research, at least sometimes, as well as a distinct topic of study given the importance of classroom environments to children's experiences of energy poverty.

Planning a youth-friendly energy future

As we have demonstrated here, it is possible, and indeed necessary, to include meaningful participation by youth in research to explore energy poverty. Our young colleagues have been unanimous in their assertion that youth can and should be involved in research investigating youth issues. By its nature, future energy use and planning for an energy-poverty-free future is a youth problem, as the consequences of current decisions on how best to achieve the transition to clean energy will be experienced most keenly by today's young people. For example, in planning for future energy use and discussing what is 'necessary energy use' (Walker et al. 2016), or when designing demand-side management strategies for increasing energy conservation, including smart-homes or through the more traditional route of load-shifting, including young people in the discussion may provide additional information different to that opined by adults.

Initial findings from our youth-driven research show that, as well as in housing, gains can be made in schools to improve thermal comfort and reduce the risk of exposure to both cold, and overly hot, indoor temperatures among young people. They highlight the central contribution of school environments to child health, and situate the school as an important site for energy (poverty) research. Our results are consistent with other research, showing that, while achieving adequate heating of energy-inefficient school buildings is problematic and costly in the winter, even in milder climates use of cooling or air conditioning may be required in the summer to achieve adequately cool classroom temperatures and improve student performance (Wargocki and Wyon 2007). Under high-carbon future climate scenarios, summer temperatures are expected to increase, with expected high heat days (over 25°C) for many parts of New Zealand reaching at least 80 days per year, increased from 20–40 days per year currently (Renwick et al. 2016). Risk of diminished school performance due to heat in summer is emerging as a public health threat for children (Sheffield and Landrigan 2011; Bidassey-Manilal et al. 2016). Results from this research have been used to develop a research proposal to undertake a new nationwide study investigating classroom thermal comfort and child health in New Zealand.

Energy efficiency and building improvement are increasingly important pathways of delivering co-benefits by mitigating the effects of climate change, while also improving public health (Watts et al. 2015). Benefits of improving energy efficiency in public buildings include: reduced costs to municipalities and governments, reduced greenhouse gas emissions, and the promotion of a 'culture of energy efficiency among the population' (Dall'O' and Sarto 2013), as well as the macro-economic benefits of stimulating employment opportunities (International Energy Agency 2014). Studies show increasing energy performance in existing school buildings and behaviour change could provide school energy savings ranging from 13–40% (Dall'O' and Sarto 2013; Brás et al. 2015; Craig and Allen 2015).

Future research exploring the problem and solutions for energy poverty among households with children and young people will be richer and more successful for having participatory research with young people included, at least as a component of research investigations in this area.

Acknowledgements

We wish to thank our young research collaborators at Waiopehu College in 2015 and 2016, for their contributions to the research we use as examples here. Special thanks to Mr Daniel Hutchinson, Head of Department – Junior Social Studies, and Mr Mark Robinson, Principal, Waiopehu College, Levin for facilitating our ongoing collaboration. The first author was funded by a Lotteries Health Research Postdoctoral Fellowship while undertaking this research. The research was funded by *He Kainga Oranga*/Housing and Health Research Programme, funded by the New Zealand Health Research Council. The second case study was funded by the University of Otago's Otago Energy Research Centre.

References

Aguirre-Bielschowsky, I., Lawson, R., Stephenson, J. and Todd, S. (2015). Energy literacy and agency of New Zealand children. *Environmental Education Research*.

Anderson, B. (2016). Laundry, energy and time: Insights from 20 years of time-use diary data in the United Kingdom. *Energy Research & Social Science*, 22, 125–136.

Baker, M., Keall, M., Ee Lyn, A. and Howden-Chapman, P. (2007). Home is where the heart is – most of the time. *The New Zealand Medical Journal*, 120(1264), 67–71.

Baker, M., Telfar Barnard, L., Kvalsvig, A., Verrall, A., Zhang, J., Keall, M., Wilson, N., Wall, T. and Howden-Chapman, P. (2012). Increasing incidence and inequalities in infectious diseases in a developed country. *The Lancet*, 379(9821), 1112–1119.

Ballard, P. J. and Syme, S. L. (2016). Engaging youth in communities: A framework for promoting adolescent and community health. *Journal of Epidemiology and Community Health*, 70(2), 202–206.

Bidassey-Manilal, S., Wright, C. Y., Engelbrecht, J. C., Albers, P. N., Garland, R. M. and Matooane, M. (2016). Students' perceived heat-health symptoms increased with warmer classroom temperatures. *International Journal of Environmental Research and Public Health*, 13(6).

BRANZ Ltd. (2007). *Designing quality learning spaces: Heating & insulation*. Wellington: Ministry of Education.

Brás, A., Rocha, A. and Faustino, P. (2015). Integrated approach for school buildings rehabilitation in a Portuguese city and analysis of suitable third party financing solutions in EU. *Journal of Building Engineering*, 3, 79–93.

Butler, D. E. (2015). *An interpretative phenomenological analysis of the perceptions, attitudes and experiences of energy vulnerability among urban young adults*. Master of Science by Research. Salford, UK: University of Salford.

Children in Wales. (2011). *Keeping warm this winter: Hearing the voices of children and young people in tackling fuel poverty in Wales*. S. O'Neill. Cardiff: Children in Wales, Consumer Focus Wales.

Craig, C. A. and Allen, M. W. (2015). The impact of curriculum-based learning on environmental literacy and energy consumption with implications for policy. *Utilities Policy*, 35, 41–49.

Dall'O', G. and Sarto, L. (2013). Potential and limits to improve energy efficiency in space heating in existing school buildings in northern Italy. *Energy and Buildings*, 67, 298–308.

Desmond, M. (2016). *Evicted: poverty and profit in the American city*. London: Allen Lane/ Penguin Books.

Douwes, J. and Howden-Chapman, P. (2011). An overview of possible health effects from exposure to "leaky buildings". In *The leaky building crisis: Understanding the issues*. Wellington: Thomson Reuters.

Egan-Bitran, M. (2012). *Our views matter: Children and young people talk about solutions to child poverty – a consultation carried out for the Children's Commissioner's Expert Advisory Group on Solutions to Child Poverty*. Wellington: Office of the Children's Commissioner.

Ergler, C. (2017a). Participation. In *Encyclopedia of educational philosophy and theory*. M. Peters. Singapore: Springer.

Ergler, C. (2017b). Beyond passive participation: From research on to research by children. *Methodological Approaches*. R. Evans and L. Holt. Singapore, Springer Singapore, 97–115.

Fell, M. J. (2017). Energy services: A conceptual review. *Energy Research & Social Science*, 27, 129–140.

Fell, M. J. and Chiu, L. F. (2014). Children, parents and home energy use: Exploring motivations and limits to energy demand reduction. *Energy Policy*, 65, 351–358.

Friis, F. and Haunstrup Christensen, T. (2016). The challenge of time shifting energy demand practices: Insights from Denmark. *Energy Research & Social Science*, 19, 124–133.

Hampton Jones Property Consultancy. (2012). *Ministry of Education – National Schools Weathertightness Survey – final report*. Wellington, New Zealand: Ministry of Education.

Hart, R. (1997). *Children's participation: The theory and practice of involving young citizens in community development and environmental care*. London: Earthscan.

Horgan, D. (2016). Child participatory research methods: Attempts to go 'deeper'. *Childhood*.

Howden-Chapman, P., Bennett, J. and Siebers, R. (eds.) (2010). *Do damp and mould matter? Health impacts of leaky homes*. Wellington: Steele Roberts.

International Energy Agency. (2014). *Capturing the multiple benefits of energy efficiency*. Paris: International Energy Agency.

Liddell, C. and Morris, C. (2010). Fuel poverty and human health: A review of recent evidence. *Energy Policy*, 38(6), 2987–2997.

Maidment, C. D., Jones, C. R., Webb, T. L., Hathway, E. A. and Gilbertson, J. M. (2014). The impact of household energy efficiency measures on health: A meta-analysis. *Energy Policy*, 65, 583–593.

Marmot Review Team. (2011). *The health impacts of cold homes and fuel poverty*. London: Friends of the Earth and the Marmot Review Team.

Middlemiss, L. and Gillard, R. (2015). Fuel poverty from the bottom-up: Characterising household energy vulnerability through the lived experience of the fuel poor. *Energy Research & Social Science*, 6, 146–154.

National Infrastructure Unit. (2015). *The thirty year New Zealand infrastructure plan*. Treasury. Wellington: New Zealand Government.

Neergaard, M. A., Olesen, F., Andersen, R. S. and Sondegaard, J. (2009). Qualitative description – the poor cousin of health research? BMC *Medical Research Methodology*, 9, doi:10.1186/1471-2288-9-52

Nicholls, L. and Strengers, Y. (2015). Peak demand and the 'family peak' period in Australia: Understanding practice (in)flexibility in households with children. *Energy Research & Social Science*, 9, 116–124.

O'Sullivan, K. C. and Howden-Chapman, P. (2017). Mixing methods, maximising results: use of mixed methods research to investigate policy solutions for fuel poverty and energy insecurity. *Indoor and Built Environment*.

O'Sullivan, K., Howden-Chapman, P., Sim, D., Stanley, J., Rowan, R., Harris-Clark, I., Morris, L. and the Waiopehu College 2015 Research Team. (2017). Cool? young people investigate living in cold housing and fuel poverty: A mixed methods action research study. *Social Science & Medicine Population Health*, 3, 66–74.

Ormandy, D. and Ezratty, V. (2016). Thermal discomfort and health: Protecting the susceptible from excess cold and excess heat in housing. *Advances in Building Energy Research*, 10(1), 84–98.

Pagliano, L., Carlucci, S., Causone, F., Moazami, A. and Cattarin, G. (2016). Energy retrofit for a climate resilient child care centre. *Energy and Buildings*, 127, 1117–1132.

Renwick, J., Anderson, B., Greenaway, A., King, D. N., Mikaloff-Fletcher, S., Reisinger, A. and Rouse, H. (2016). *Climate change implications for New Zealand*. Wellington: The Royal Society of New Zealand.

Sandelowski, M. (2010). What's in a name? Qualitative description revisited. *Research in Nursing & Health*, 33(1), 77–84.

Schmidt, L., Horta, A., Correia, A. and Fonseca, S. (2014). Generational gaps and paradoxes regarding electricity consumption and saving. *Nature + Culture*, 9(2), 183–203.

Sheffield, P. E. and Landrigan, P. J. (2011). Global climate change and children's health: threats and strategies for prevention. *Environ Health Perspect*, 119(3), 291–298.

Shove, E., Pantzar, M. and Watson, M. (2012). *The dynamics of social practice: Everyday life and how it changes*. London: Sage.

Sovacool, B. K. (2015). Fuel poverty, affordability, and energy justice in England: Policy insights from the Warm Front Program. *Energy*, 93 (Part 1), 361–371.

Stafford, B. (2015). *Fuel poverty, families, and children*. Presentation at seminar, Belfast, University of Ulster, 13 October.

Thomson, H., Bouzarovski, S. and Snell, C. (2017). Rethinking the measurement of energy poverty in Europe: A critical analysis of indicators and data. *Indoor and Built Environment*.

Tod, A. M., Nelson, P., Cronin de Chavez, A., Homer, C., Powell-Hoyland, V. and Stocks, A. (2016). Understanding influences and decisions of households with children with asthma regarding temperature and humidity in the home in winter: A qualitative study. *BMJ Open*, 6(1).

Toth, N., Little, L., Read, J. C., Fitton, D. and Horton, M. (2013). Understanding teen attitudes towards energy consumption. *Journal of Environmental Psychology*, 34, 36–44.

UNICEF. (1989). *United Nations convention on the rights of the child*. London: United Nations.

Viggers, H., Howden-Chapman, P., Ingham, T., Chapman, R., Pene, G., Davies, C., Currie, A., Pierse, N., Wilson, H., Zhang, J., Baker, M. and Crane, J. (2013). Warm homes for older people: Aims and methods of a randomised community-based trial for people with COPD. *BMC Public Health*, 13(176).

Walker, G., Simcock, N. and Day, R. (2016). Necessary energy uses and a minimum standard of living in the United Kingdom: Energy justice or escalating expectations? *Energy Research & Social Science*, 18, 129–138.

Wargocki, P. and Wyon, D. P. (2007). The effects of moderately raised classroom temperatures and classroom ventilation rate on the performance of schoolwork by children (RP-1257). *HVAC&R Research*, 13(2), 193–220.

Watts, N., Adger, W. N., Agnolucci, P., Blackstock, J., Byass, P., Cai, W., Chaytor, S., Colbourn, T., Collins, M., Cooper, A., Cox, P. M., Depledge, J., Drummond, P., Ekins, P., Galaz, V., Grace, D., Graham, H., Grubb, M., Haines, A., Hamilton, I., Hunter, A., Jiang, X., Li, M., Kelman, I., Liang, L., Lott, M., Lowe, R., Luo, Y., Mace, G., Maslin, M., Nilsson, M., Oreszczyn, T., Pye, S., Quinn, T., Svensdotter, M., Venevsky, S., Warner, K., Xu, B., Yang, J., Yin, Y., Yu, C., Zhang, Q., Gong, P., Montgomery, H. and Costello, A. (2015). Health and climate change: Policy responses to protect public health. *The Lancet*, 386(10006), 1861–1914.

World Health Organization. (1987). *Health impact of low indoor temperatures: Report on a WHO meeting*. Copenhagen: WHO.

12 Energy poverty in the Western Balkans

Adjusting policy responses to socio-economic drivers

Slavica Robić, Ivana Rogulj, and Branko Ančić

Introduction

The Western Balkans (WB) region – which for the purpose of this research is understood to consist of the post-socialist countries Albania, Bosnia and Herzegovina (BiH), Croatia, Kosovo, Macedonia, Montenegro and Serbia –[1] faces many difficulties regarding energy poverty. These problems are driven by a range of regional and historical contingencies, which play a significant role in the prevalence and characteristics of energy poverty in the region (Robic et al. 2016). The ability to afford adequate amounts of energy and adequate quality of energy services is an important governance issue and a key social policy concern (Walker, Liddell et al. 2014).

Energy price rises pose a significant social and political issue in the whole of Europe. A liberalisation process started in 1990s in the EU, with the aim of privatising previously monopolised national electricity and gas markets and of allowing market prices based on competition. In the WB, the liberalisation process began with the 2005 Energy Community Treaty, and to date, only Croatia has fully liberalised its electricity and gas markets. While the argument is that liberalisation will lead to lower energy prices, in the WB region, energy prices have historically been regulated and heavily subsidised by national governments and are still lower than the EU28 average. The gradual shift to a competitive market has seen a corresponding increase in prices that has been burdensome for many domestic consumers, particularly as social safety nets for vulnerable groups are inadequate (Buzar 2007; Boardman 2010; Tirado Herrero and Ürge-Vorsatz 2012; Petrova et al. 2013).

Moreover, appliances and the housing stock in this region are notoriously inefficient (Buzar 2007; Matković et al. 2007; Tirado Herrero and Ürge-Vorsatz 2012), and there is a high-rate of electrical heating systems in homes that consume high-amounts of energy compared to gas or other heating systems (KOSID 2013). As such, households in the WB are often burdened with unnecessarily high electricity consumption. For example, Kosovo, the poorest WB country with record rates of unemployment, electricity consumption per household amounts to 8,600kWh/annum compared to the 3,633kWh average of average EU28 households.[2] In larger cities, apartment buildings are often connected to out-dated and inefficient oil-powered district heating systems, usually without individual metering or regulation. As a result, the energy provided is very expensive, and households have no ability to control their own heating bills by reducing their consumption.

Energy poverty in the WB is thus widespread. Affected families are forced to choose between food and basic energy services. Those living in individual homes often resort to living in inadequate conditions, attempting to reduce their heating consumption by living only in a few rooms during winter (in our study described below, more than 50% of visited families did this). Meanwhile, in urban, residential multifamily buildings many families, who lack the ability to control their heating, actually experiencing *excessive* heat and commonly open windows to cool down. The harmful consequences of living in energy poverty are well known (Thomson et al. 2013; Lacroix and Chaton 2015; Camprubí et al. 2016; Teller-Elsberg et al. 2016), but there has been little focus on analysing the magnitude of health consequences of energy poverty in the Western Balkans.

The aim of this chapter is to highlight the adverse effects of living in energy poverty in the WB and to investigate which paths these countries should take to protect vulnerable citizens and ultimately eradicate energy poverty. It assesses current definitions of energy vulnerability and the policies currently in place protect vulnerable groups, while also providing insights into the lived reality of those stricken by severe energy poverty. By combining analysis of existing legislation with data gathered through field visits to energy poor homes in the region, the chapter provides policy-relevant insights on costs and benefits of different energy efficiency strategies to reduce energy poverty, whilst demonstrating the necessity for immediate action and change of current policy practices.

The data that comprises aspects of this chapter were collected from 824 field visits to vulnerable households were undertaken (Albania N = 10, BiH N = 103, Croatia N = 397, Kosovo N = 10, Macedonia N = 206, Montenegro N = 97, Serbia N = 10) between April 2015 and October 2016, during which we collected qualitative data on experiences of energy poverty. The respondents targeted were either those who receive compensation and/or receive social welfare support which is in line with current energy vulnerability criteria in the region. Subject to available funding, in Croatia, Bosnia and Herzegovina, Macedonia and Montenegro, a questionnaire was also used to gather standardised quantitative data on energy consumption habits[3] and the self-assessed physical and mental health of the participants (Blaxter 1990; Pierret 1995).[4] All respondents gave their informed consent to participate in the research, and their identities have been anonymised.

Manifestations and experiences of energy poverty in the Western Balkans: results of field visits to energy poor households

The average visited household has three to five household members (50.5%) and lives in a family house (85%) which was built more than 35 years ago (49.5%).

More than 67% of visited families live in dwellings which have no insulation (N = 612).

As Figure 12.3 shows, mould and draughts were part of the reality of life for many of those we visited, due to inadequate heating, poor insulation and old, single-glazed windows creating permanent exposure to a cold and damp environment (Kolokotsa and Santamouris 2015; Robić 2016). 45% had visible mould in their homes (Figure 12.1), some of which was very severe (Figure 12.2), and 74.68% report some form of draught (Figure 12.3).

In terms of health conditions, 612 (48%) of respondents to the survey were suffering from long-term illness, chronic illness or have certain disabilities, with

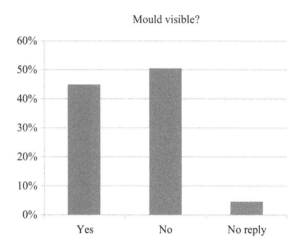

Figure 12.1 Occurrence of visible mould amongst respondents

Figure 12.2 Photo of severe mould taken during field visits in Croatia

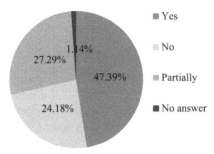

Figure 12.3 Occurrence of draught through windows and/or doors amongst respondents

more than 17% assessing their overall health as 'weak'. 50% stated that, in the last 4 weeks (at the time of survey), they had had difficulty in carrying out work or household activities due to health problems, whilst around 54% had bodily aches or pain and around 49% felt unhappy and depressed. Kruskal-Wallis and Mann-Whitney tests showed that self-reported mental and physical health was significantly worse ($p < 0.05$) among those respondents living in households with occurrences of mould or draughts. Additional in-depth analysis conducted in Croatia also showed households who were exposed to a continuous flow of cold air around the window to a significant extent report worse physical health (Ančić et al. 2015). The inability to heat homes and the permanent exposure to high levels of damp and mould appear to harm mental and physical health damage. This is in line with previous research; for example, long exposure to high levels of indoor damp and mould has been shown to increase the risk of asthma exacerbation (Sharpe et al. 2015) among respondents living in households with occurrence of mould and/or draught.

What is also worrisome is that many households in our sample with a pre-existing illness or disability were living in cold and damp homes – potentially exacerbating their problems (Snell et al. 2015). With the severe conditions that we observed (see Figure 12.2), and with the region being, as mentioned, particularly vulnerable to energy poverty as result of inefficient housing and appliances, it is furthermore likely that the consequences for health are far beyond those commonly reported for Western Europe.

A final important point is that many respondents (over 50%) felt completely, very or fairly happy with their lives in general (based on indicator of personal well-being), despite living in conditions that could be considered 'objectively' poor and inadequate – permanent exposure to moisture, mould and draught and inadequate internal temperatures. This echoes previous research by Chard and Walker (2016), who found that energy poor and vulnerable households 'normalised' and accepted cold room temperatures and the need to adopt 'coping strategies' to keep warm. More theoretically, the finding relates to the concept of 'adaptive preferences', which posits that those living in hardship often develop lower expectations compared to those living in relative comfort (Nussbaum

2011). This is potentially problematic for energy poverty alleviation measures that attempt to target and identify vulnerable households via self-reporting.

Energy poverty policies in the Western Balkans

The idea of energy poverty came into the EU legal framework for the first time via the so-called 'Third Energy Package' when the protection of 'vulnerable' energy consumers was first defined with the goal of reducing energy poverty. On the basis of the EU Internal Market in Electricity (2009/72/EC) and Natural Gas (2009/73/EC) Directives, member states must define energy poverty and protect vulnerable energy consumers. The Internal Market in Electricity Directive (2009/72/EC) states that energy regulators should be empowered to contribute to ensuring a high standard for universal and public services in compliance with the open market, protection of vulnerable consumer, and fully efficient measures of consumer protection. The Energy Efficiency Directive (2012/27/EU) states that member states should be enabled to include, within their own national systems of energy efficiency obligations for communal energy enterprises, demands in relation to the realisation of social goals – specifically in order to ensure access to greater energy efficiency to vulnerable consumers. It is now up to each government to find their own way to deal with this complex issue.

In this context, policy attempts have been applied throughout the Western Balkans, aiming to help vulnerable energy consumers. Social policies in the Western Balkans are considered as typical for post-socialist transformation. The legacy is worsened by after-socialist conflicts and devastated institutional capacities. Social policies in general are functioning merely as politically-motivated care of state for the people (voters) and without covering targeted vulnerable groups (Babović and Vuković 2015). As with social legislation, energy legislation suffers from lack of strategic planning and consistent policies. The main 'driving force' of energy policy development is the implementation of the *acquis communautaire*, compliance with (Second and Third) Energy Package.

The most common (and basically only) approach to dealing with energy poverty in the WB region has so far been through financial support targeted at socially vulnerable groups based on low income and disability status. While it is good that at least some action has been taken – showing governments' attempts to address the issue – direct financial support and guaranteed provision of electricity/gas/district heating are the only measures in place (Table 12.1). Direct financial support does, to some extent, alleviate burdens related to high energy costs. However it only deals with the consequences of energy poverty, not with the causes. Families receiving this kind of support still live in the same damp, deteriorated, draughty and dark dwellings, without any options that would enable them to change any of those symptoms.

It is also important that none of the countries have definition of energy poverty. Defining energy poverty is important for enabling statistical monitoring of its prevalence (Simcock et al. 2016) and thus to assess of impacts of alleviation policies. Definitions are also vital for putting energy poverty high on the political

Table 12.1 National legislation for the protection of vulnerable consumers in Western Balkan countries

	Protection mechanisms	Vulnerable energy consumers definition
Albania	*Electricity:* Vulnerable consumers can have subsidies on their electricity bills, those who use up to 300 kWh though a monthly deduction of 648 ALL (4.7 EUR) and are ensured universal access to electricity supply. *Gas:* N/A *Other:* N/A	*Electricity:* The Albanian Law on the Power Sector (OG 43/2015) defines a vulnerable customer as a household consumer who, due to social reasons (low income, single-phase grid of maximum 16A, maximum level of energy consumption per person), is entitled to certain special rights regarding the supply of electricity. *Gas:* The Law on the Natural Gas Sector defines a vulnerable customer as the one who (low income) cannot afford the price of gas. *Other:* N/A
Bosnia and Herzegovina	The Commission for the Development of a Programme for the Protection of Vulnerable Household Electricity Buyers was formed (OG 51/15). Programme for the protection of Socially Vulnerable Categories of Electricity Consumers in RS defines subsidies for 150 kWh of electricity per month (2008–2010). *Gas and other:* N/A	*Electricity:* The Brčko District legal framework enforces protection of customers under general public service. The existing legislation of the Federation defines protected customers, but allows discrimination between customers through price regulation. The Electricity Act (OG 66/13) states that energy policy needs to provide a programme for the protection of vulnerable energy consumers which needs to protect them from disconnections and provide protection in remote areas. In 2007, the RS Government adopted a Programme for the protection of Socially Vulnerable Categories of Electricity Consumers. *Gas and other:* N/A
Croatia	Financial support is secured trough a solidarity fee, 0.4EUR cents/kWh (paid by all final customers). Through money collected by solidarity vulnerable customer are entitled to 200 HRK/month (26EUR) deduction of electricity bill. To date (March 2017) an agreement with suppliers is in effect in which they forswear profit as a way to satisfy funding, and as result, social compensation for the end consumer is currently set to zero. It is unclear for how long will this agreement be valid.	*Electricity:* Vulnerable consumer is defined as a consumer from the household category who, due to their social welfare status and/or due to health status has the right to receive energy under specific conditions (Energy Act OG 120/12, 14/14, 95/15, 102/15). The Regulation on criteria for achieving the status of vulnerable consumer was adopted in September 2015 (OG 95/15). *Gas and other:* N/A

(Continued)

Table 12.1 (Continued)

	Protection mechanisms	Vulnerable energy consumers definition
Kosovo	*Gas and other:* Social Welfare Act (OG 157/13, 152/14) states that all vulnerable consumers have the right to financial aid for housing expenses and related bills and heating and for households which use wood heating enables either 3 m³ of stacked fuel-wood for heating or money equivalent.	*Electricity:* Customers who are recipients of social aid as defined by the Law on the Social Assistance Scheme (OG 2003/15) and the Law on the Status and Rights of Families of Martyrs, Disabled People, Veterans and Members of the Kosovo Liberation Army and Families of Civil War Victims (OG 04/L–054) are considered vulnerable. *Gas and other:* N/A
Macedonia	*Electricity:* Vulnerable consumers have right to a cheaper tariff for electricity for personal use. The Law on the Energy Regulator (OG 03/L – 185, Article 45) grants possibility of providing subsidies. About 10% of households meet the criteria for subsidies related to electricity consumption. *Gas and other:* N/A *Electricity, fuelwood, coal, light heating oil for households/ oil for households and district heating:* In 2015 the amount subsidised was 700 denars for bills from 1 January to 30 June 2015 and 800 denars (13 EUR) to cover bills from 1 July to 31 December 2015.	*Electricity, fuelwood, coal, light heating oil for households/ oil for households and district heating:* Vulnerability criteria are targeting households entitled to social welfare and to permanent financial support.
Montenegro	*Electricity:* Subsidies, with monthly limit of electricity and gas consumption by which the subsidy can be applied and ensured supply from October until end of April, regardless of arrears or non-payment. *Gas and other:* N/A	*Electricity:* The requirement for protection of vulnerable consumers is stated in the Act on the Energy Sector (OG 05/2016) – vulnerability criteria are defined based on health status and social status. *Gas and other:* N/A
Serbia	*Electricity and gas:* An energy vulnerable customer is entitled to electricity or natural gas supply with a reduction of the monthly payment. The monthly income thresholds for eligibility are defined by the Regulation on harmonised amounts of household's monthly income as eligibility criteria for acquiring status of vulnerable energy buyer (40/2015).	*Electricity, gas and district heating:* The Act on the Energy Sector (145/14) defines a vulnerable energy buyer based on social and health status if household 1) falls in lowest earnings per household member category; 2) it does not own or use another residential unit.

agenda and to ensure it gets proper recognition as a key policy issue (Thomson et al. 2016). A total lack of definitions in the WB region indicates that energy poverty is yet to become a recognised problem, amongst the general public and decision-makers, requiring immediate action.

A further issue is that current practice defines specific groups which are 'vulnerable' – i.e. those who have a higher risk of being energy poor than the general population – and focuses policies towards them. Good targeting of policies per specific vulnerable group is important and can help ensure energy poverty measures improve the lives of those most in need (Boardman 2010). However, depending on accuracy, targeting can also increase energy inequality (Dubois and Meier 2016).

Throughout more than 30 years of research in the field of energy poverty, attempts have been made to provide a comprehensive definition of vulnerable groups; however, no consensus exists on this. Furthermore, there is no comprehensive guidance on how specific countries or regions should approach this issue. A European Commission Working Group for Vulnerable Consumers was established in 2013. The Working Group was formed with the goal of performing a qualitative and quantitative review of different aspects of vulnerability and to give recommendations for defining vulnerable consumers in the energy sector (European Commission 2013). It concluded that it is not possible to have a unified definition of vulnerable consumers which would apply to the entire EU. However, there are some indications of groups that tend to be most vulnerable in the academic literature. Older people are commonly affected by energy poverty as they may require more home heating than others for physiological reasons and they spend most of the time at home, unlike the employed population (Healy and Clinch 2004; Walker and Day 2012; Legendre and Ricci 2015; Snell et al. 2015). Disabled, ill and single parent families are more likely to be energy poor than general population (Snell et al. 2015). It has been determined that recipients of social welfare are three times more likely to be energy poor than the average (Healy and Clinch 2004).

In Western Balkan countries, the definition of energy vulnerability is still solely related to general welfare criteria (details provided in Table 12.1). The energy vulnerability criteria is automatically awarded to those who are in various existing support schemes based on their income (and other welfare indicators in some countries), and no attempts have been made to widen energy vulnerability criteria to groups other than disabled and recipients of permanent social welfare. Such an approach is extremely limited as, although it provides some protection to groups that are likely to be severely affected by energy poverty, it discriminates many others who are falling just outside of general welfare criteria and who are likely to be suffering from adverse impacts of energy poverty.

Adjusting policy responses: insights from Croatia

In this section, we focus on Croatia, which is the only EU member state from the analysed region and which has most advanced energy policies in the region.

Furthermore, data for Croatia was easier to access and analyse than other countries.

In Croatia, as was described in Table 12.1 there is a system in place which is designed to provide direct financial support to socially vulnerable enabling them a 200 HRK (27 EUR) monthly deduction from their electricity bills. The money needed for this is collected through the social levy paid by all electricity consumers. However, there are clear limitations to this approach. First, Croatian policy related to energy poverty and energy vulnerability so far focuses solely on electricity, which is a severely limited and exclusive approach as no other forms of energy are taken into consideration. While electricity use is important segment of households' total energy needs, creating policies that only take into consideration one type of energy are likely to have limited impacts. This type of policy is limited, not only because if offers no help in covering costs of other forms of energy (i.e. district heating, gas etc.) to vulnerable households, but because it also only penalises electricity utilities, and other energy providers are out of the scheme. But perhaps more importantly, the Croatian policy focuses only on the symptoms of energy poverty, not its real underlying causes.

Prior to devising any national policies to alleviate energy poverty, it is important to understand how energy prices are formed, as well as the main components that determine the final cost for consumers. The main components of electricity price are the costs of distribution and transmission system network use, the costs of energy and supply (wholesale and retail) and, last but not least, taxes and levies. Between 2008 and 2014, for the EU 28+Norway, average electricity price levies (various policy support costs, PSC) increased on average by 170% for households. In 2014, the weight of the levies was almost equal to the energy and supply component for the average residential consumer (EURELECTRIC 2016). Such levies have been widely critiqued in the academic literature as unfair and regressive, because low-income households who may be vulnerable to energy poverty pay a larger proportion of their income on the levies (Boardman 2010; Oppenheim 2016). Indeed, the European Commission states that it is of crucial importance to understand energy pricing mechanisms and structures when defining possible financial and legislative frameworks for tackling energy poverty to prevent passing on costs to consumers (European Commission 2014).

It is therefore significant that Croatia's energy poverty policy is funded, as mentioned, through a social levy on energy bills. Although an agreement between the electricity distributor and the Croatian government means that the levy is currently effectively set to zero for consumers[5] and financed by distributor giving up a share of their profit, it is only a matter of time before the distributor refuses to give up their profits and electricity bills will once again be on the rise – even for the poor.

The first and foremost step in tackling energy poverty should involve dealing with main causes of energy poverty, instead of easing its consequences through mechanisms whose adverse effects we can only estimate and which have proven to increase overall energy costs. The principal solution to most energy poverty – related hardships is energy efficiency. Energy efficiency helps improve quality of life through decreased air humidity, leaking roofs and mould; it eliminates cold draught, resulting in improved health conditions. Improving the energy efficiency of dwellings and of household appliances, while improving the heating and ventilation systems is the most effective and sustainable approach to alleviating energy poverty (Maidment et al. 2013; Thomson et al. 2013; Walker, Liddell, et al. 2014; Walker, McKenzie, et al. 2014; Sharpe et al. 2015; Robic et al., 2016). What is even more interesting is that poorer households seem to experience greater benefits of such improvements (Maidment et al. 2013), and while most of the studies have reported small but significant health improvements, it is likely that even greater health improvements occur but are not recorded as they appear through longer time periods than those analysed (Thomson and Thomas 2015).

In our own study, when we visited respondents as well as conducted interviews and questionnaires, we also provided all respondents with a range of simple energy efficiency measures. These included LED light bulbs, reflective foils for radiators, timers for electrical boilers, draught proofing for doors and windows and water-saving tap adaptors. The goal was to improve respondents' comfort, quality of life and reduce energy consumption. All visited household members were also advised on the efficient use of energy by the field-workers and through brochures and leaflets. Though inexpensive, the actions taken resulted in estimated calculated annual energy savings in the 2–8% range, with water savings estimated at approximately 10%. Given the low income levels in relation to high energy costs, those savings offer relief while somewhat improving living conditions. Six months after the field visits in Croatia, a phone survey was undertaken to assess the impact of measures implemented and advice provided. For almost 75% of the households their general comfort had improved, although for some a few problems with cold, humidity or draught remain. (42% stated their general comfort improved a lot, 19% state their comfort has improved a lot but they still feel cold in their home, 9% have improved comfort a lot but still feel draught and 17% still have issues with damp.)

To illustrate differences and possible benefits an assessment of costs was made for four different energy efficiency measures scenarios (Table 12.2). The house to which measures are applied is assumed to be 70m^2 size, E energy class, wood-heated dwelling with an assumed heating system efficiency of 70%, located in continental Croatia. The household is assumed to consume an average amount of energy per year. Energy savings related to building measures are calculated using the methodology for energy audits in buildings, with CO^2 emission factors based on calculations provided by Croatian Ministry of Economy (2014). Water and electricity related measures are calculated using technical parameters of the devices installed. The measures planned included:

- Thermal insulation of walls, with 12cm – EPS ETICS system to a final heat transfer coefficient of 0.25 W/m^{2}K, total wall surface 100m^2
- Thermal insulation of roof with 14 cm of mineral wool (with vapour barrier) towards unheated ceiling, installation of doors and windows, specifically 11.5 m^2 of 5-chamber system windows, with heat transfer coefficient of maximum 1,2 W/m^{2}K, total roof surface 70m^2

Table 12.2 Costs and benefits of different energy efficiency measures and combinations

	Measures combinations				Cost per measure
	Low-cost	Low-cost and appliances	Refurbishment	Refurbishment and appliances	EUR
Wall insulation			+	+	3,333
Roof insulation			+	+	933
Doors and windows			+	+	1,687
New biomass heating system			+	+	1,720
Standby costs elimination	+	+	+	+	4
Old-new refrigerator		+		+	293
Old-new washing machine		+		+	333
Classical bulb to LED 7pcs	+	+		+	20
Hot water saving in kitchen and toilet 2 pcs	+	+	+	+	13
Shower water saving 1pc	+	+	+	+	8
Draught proofing sealing 18m	+	+			7
Energy advisors and campaign (calculated on the bases of 5000 households)	+	+	+	+	234,267
Cost for 1 households [EUR]	132	759	7,782	8,408	
Cost for 5.000 HH	662,250	3,795,600	38,908,950	42,042,250	
Savings					
Electricity savings [kWh/y]	3,532,500	13,572,500	3,532,500	13,572,500	
Heat savings [kWh/y]	3,235,000	3,235,000	68,930,000	68,930,000	
Water savings [m³/y]	39,500	156,500	39,500	156,500	
Savings in energy bills[EUR/y]	617,105	2,055,629	1,904,605	3,403,947	
Simple payback period [y]	1	2	20	12	
Spent on solidarity tariff during the SPP time/5000HH [EUR]	1,653,600	2,886,000	31,870,800	19,266,000	

- Installation of 12–15 kW biomass boiler and heating system including radiators and thermostat valves
- Elimination of standby costs using multi-socket extension cable with switch; it was assumed all devices having standby consumption are plugged into one multi-socket extension cable and switched off for 8 hours daily; assumed standby savings 15W, with total 43.4kWh/year total saving
- Replacement of seven classical bulbs (a combination of 100W, 60W and 40W) with LED bulbs of equivalent illuminance; assumed use 3 hours daily per bulb (1.062 h/year per bulb)
- Installation of two hot water aerators (in kitchen and toilet)
- One efficient shower head
- Replacement of 1970s manufactured refrigerator with new, combined A+ 150l refrigerator with 50l freezer
- Replacement of pre-1970 washing machine with new, A+++ appliance

Costs accounted for in the scenarios: salaries for national coordinator (gross salary of one person for national coordination, half time, 12 months), local coordinator (gross salary for local coordinator, one person, one third work time, 12 months), mentors (20% gross salary for 12 months), advisors (4 advisors, fulltime) and PR expert (10% worktime, 12 months), expenses related to education, teachers' honoraria, travel and accommodation, dissemination and promotion expenses.

The results indicate that some measures, the 'low-cost' combination, have a simple payback period as short as 1 year (Table 12.2), while even the most costly combinations of measures, i.e. the full refurbishment of the building envelope including replacement of household appliances, show that, although the payback period is lengthy (in some cases over 20 years), it is still an investment. If at the same time policy which is currently in place in Croatia would continue, up to 31,870,800 euros would be spent without living conditions being improved or adverse impacts on health and environment removed. In comparison, the most costly scenario (energy efficiency retrofitting of the building and replacement of household appliances with more efficient ones) requires 42,042,250 euros, and unlike the solidarity tariff, it is a long-term infrastructural investment. When energy service deprivation is widespread, the cost of policies is high in any case (Dubois and Meier 2016), which also indicates the necessity for designing such policies that can be seen as an investment rather than a cost with no return.

Conclusions

Energy poverty is a serious problem and an ever-present threat in the Western Balkans. Manifestations of energy poverty are severe and clearly indicate adverse impacts on physical and mental health. Health issues result not only in impacts on the well-being of those affected but also on increased health costs which thus impact the national economy.

In the scenario where households are heavily dependent on inefficient electricity use, when increases in prices occur, especially when coupled with electrical heating, vulnerable groups are left with limited means to decrease their energy costs. They are forced to make decisions which often leave them in dark, cold and damp homes, often leaving them in hunger. A distinct problem of energy poverty is directly related to distributional injustice where poorer and more vulnerable households live in more deteriorated dwellings and have almost no chance to invest in energy efficiency improvements (Walker and Day 2012). This can be seen across the WB. Marginalised groups, the disabled, elderly and ill are more likely to be affected by the consequences of energy poverty (Snell et al., 2015).

While there have been some efforts to design policies for protecting vulnerable energy consumers in the WB, those policies primarily focus on short-term energy price relief. However, ultimately such measures are, in our view, not long-term solutions and, because they are funded through levies on energy bills, can actually increase energy prices in the longer term. There is a need for change in policy thinking towards more sustainable solutions. Such solution as a first step is energy efficiency. As it was shown through field research in WB countries, energy poverty is a social issue requiring primarily technical energy solutions followed by financial support mechanisms. Energy efficiency should be the first step in tackling energy poverty in the WB, and both social and energy policies should widen the definition of vulnerability as current policies focus only on those affected by low income and ill health. Further research should be undertaken as to understand the magnitude of the energy poverty prevalence and to enable better design of protection mechanisms. Energy poverty is not solely an issue of expenditure as it is often interpreted; it is a development issue. Current situation where groups which are by current policies defined as vulnerable (affected low income, disability, ill health, as shown in Table 12.1) are living in inadequate living calls for immediate action, both on the national and on the EU level, to provide help and support to those in need and to alleviate adverse impacts of energy poverty while eradicating its causes.

While some countries of the WB region have recently started providing different support schemes for residential housing energy efficiency improvement, energy poor households typically fail to use available mechanisms because the application documentation is too demanding and they do not have any funding available to close the financing gap. Energy efficiency support schemes typically offer only a percentage of the needed investment, leaving the poor out of their scope. The lack of private and state capacity to invest in energy poverty abatement measures is a common problem in the region. EU funding, i.e. through the Cohesion Funds and the Instrument for Pre-Accession, should offer schemes targeted specifically for tackling energy poverty. On the national level, attention should be given to making grants accessible to vulnerable households.

Programmes for increasing 'energy literacy' and energy advising should interlink with other energy efficiency programmes. Vulnerable groups should be provided with the information needed to understand their energy habits and read energy bills. Information on costs and benefits of different energy efficiency and energy savings should be available and presented in a simple manner.

Although the results of undertaken visits to energy poor households in the WB region which are presented in this research are indicative and clearly stress the importance of immediate action, it is highly recommended that further detailed research is conducted using representative samples in each country. Such research would provide valuable insights and ensure solid basis for adequate policy responses in each country.

Acknowledgements

The data used here have been obtained through the projects 'Reduce Energy Use and Change Habits' (REACH),[6] REACH CEI, 'With Knowledge to Warm Home'[7] and the South East Europe Sustainable Energy Policy. In order to analyse energy poverty in the seven countries, a review of national legislation was undertaken for each country by local partners thus enabling access to legislation available only in local languages, in addition to a review of existing research. Special thanks to all of the volunteers and partners from Albania, Bosnia and Herzegovina, Bulgaria, Croatia, Kosovo, Macedonia, Montenegro, Serbia and Slovenia who have made this research possible.

Notes

1 Except Albania, all of the countries of the WB were parts of the former Socialist Federal Republic of Yugoslavia.
2 Calculated using Eurostat data (Eurostat 2016) and data on number of households from most recent census for every country.
3 The second part of the questionnaire relating to the energy aspects of households includes basic information about the household electricity consumption, water consumption, the consumption of thermal energy and the general conditions of relevance in the context of energy poverty, such as temperature, damp and mould in the household. It is important to note that certain estimates have been made for the calculations. Data on electricity consumption was collected through energy bills; however, in cases when respondents did not have bills available, a calculation was made based on the price of the monthly bill they reported. For heating, as most of the households use fuelwood, they reported the consumption in space metres. Heat consumption was calculated based on the assumption that 1srm = 1.575 kWh.
4 Indicators of self-assessment of psychological and physical health (ISPPH) – respondents were asked to estimate during the past 4 weeks how often did they experience difficulties in business or household activities because of health problems, had health problems that limited their usual social activities with family or friends, had a physical pain, felt unhappy or depressed, lost confidence in themselves, had a feeling that they cannot overcome their problems. For all six questions the same scale with five answers was used (1 – never, 2 – rarely, 3 – sometimes, 4 – frequently, 5 – very often). Indicator of illness (II) – respondents were asked to indicate if they are suffering from some long-term disease, chronic illness or disability, whereby it was possible to respond with 1-yes or 2-no. Indicator of personal well-being (IPW) – as a measure of personal well-being respondents were asked, 'If you were to consider your life in general these days, how happy or unhappy would you say you are, on the whole?'. Answers were on a 7-point scale where is 1 – completely happy, 2 – very happy, 3 – fairly happy, 4 – neither happy nor unhappy, 5 – fairly unhappy, 6 – very unhappy and 7 – completely unhappy. Indicator of general self-assessment of health (IGSH) – respondents were asked to rate their health in general from 1 – excellent to 5 – poor. Index of the self-rated mental health (ISMH) and Index of the self-rated physical health (ISPH) were calculated based on the indicators of self-assessment of psychological and physical health. The

questionnaire was consisted with basic socio-demographic indicators that are relevant to research related to health outcomes – age, gender and education.
5 The solidarity tariff is 0.03HRK/kWh (approx. 0.4 euroCent/kWh) with 100% discount provided at the moment.
6 www.reach-energy.eu, co-funded by the Intelligent Energy Europe Programme of the European Union.
7 Funded by the European Union through European Social Fund and Government of the Republic of Croatia Office for Cooperation with NGOs.

References

Ančić, B., Domazet, M. and Grbavac, K. (2015). *Istraživački izvještaj o energetskom siromaštvu*. Zagreb, Croatia: Društvo za oblikovanje održivog razvoja.
Babović, M. and Vuković, D. (2015). Shaping social policies in the Western Balkans: Legal and institutional changes in the context of globalisation and post-socialist transformation. In Thomas, M. and Bojicic-Dzelilovic, V. (eds.) *Public policy making in the Western Balkans*. Dordrecht: Springer Netherlands, pp. 17–43.
Blaxter, M. (1990). *Health and lifestyles*. London: Routledge.
Boardman, B. (2010). *Fixing fuel poverty: Challenges and solutions*. London: Earthscan.
Buzar, S. (2007). The "hidden" geographies of energy poverty in post-socialism: Between institutions and households. *Geoforum*, 38(2), 224–240.
Camprubí, L., Malmusi, D., Mehdipanah, R., Palència, L., Molnar, A., Muntaner, C. and Borrell, C. (2016). Façade insulation retrofitting policy implementation process and its effects on health equity determinants: A realist review. *Energy Policy*, 91, 304–314.
Chard, R. and Walker, G. (2016). Living with fuel poverty in older age: Coping strategies and their problematic implications. *Energy Research & Social Science*, 18, 62–70.
Dubois, U. and Meier, H. (2016). Energy affordability and energy inequality in Europe: Implications for policymaking. *Energy Research & Social Science*, 18, 21–35.
Eurelectric. (2016). *Drivers of electricity bills: Supporting graphs, methodology and country notes*. Belgium: Brussels.
European Commission. (2013). *Vulnerable consumer working group guidance document on vulnerable consumers*. Available at: http://ec.europa.eu/energy/sites/ener/files/documents/20140106_vulnerable_consumer_report_0.pdf.
European Commission. (2014). *Energy prices and costs in Europe*. Brussels: European Commission.
Eurostat. (2016). *Electricity consumption by households*. Available at: http://ec.europa.eu/eurostat/tgm/table.do?tab=table&init=1&language=en&pcode=tsdpc310&plugin=1.
Healy, J. D. and Clinch, J. P. (2004). Quantifying the severity of fuel poverty, its relationship with poor housing and reasons for non-investment in energy-saving measures in Ireland. *Energy Policy*, 32(2), 207–220.
Kolokotsa, D. and Santamouris, M. (2015). Review of the indoor environmental quality and energy consumption studies for low income households in Europe. *The Science of the Total Environment*, 536, 316–330.
Kosovo Civil Society Consortium for Sustainable Development (KOSID). (2013). *Electricity score*. Prishtine: GAP, INDEP and FIQ.
Lacroix, E. and Chaton, C. (2015). Fuel poverty as a major determinant of perceived health: The case of France. *Public Health*, 129(5), 517–524.
Legendre, B. and Ricci, O. (2015). Measuring fuel poverty in France: Which households are the most fuel vulnerable? *Energy Economics*, 49, 620–628.

Maidment, C. D., Jones, C. R., Webb, T. L., Hathway, E. A. and Gilbertson, J. M. (2013). The impact of household energy efficiency measures on health: A meta-analysis. *Energy Policy*, 65, 583–593.

Matković, T., Sucur, Z. and Zrinscak, S. (2007). Inequality, poverty, and material deprivation in new and old members of the European Union. *Croatian medical journal*. Medicinska Naklada, 48(5), 636–652.

Nussbaum, M. C. (2011). *Creating capabilities: The human development approach*. Cambridge, MA: Harvard University Press.

Oppenheim, J. (2016). The United States regulatory compact and energy poverty. *Energy Research and Social Science*, 18, 96–108.

Petrova, S., Gentile, M., Mäkinen, I. H. and Bouzarovski, S. (2013). Perceptions of thermal comfort and housing quality: Exploring the microgeographies of energy poverty in Stakhanov, Ukraine. *Environment and Planning A*, 45(5), 1240–1257.

Pierret, J. (1995). Constructing discourses about health and their social determinants. In Radley, A. (ed.) *Worlds of illness biographical and cultural perspectives on health and disease*. London: Routledge, pp. 9–26.

Robić, S. (2016). *ENERGETSKO SIROMAŠTVO U HRVATSKOJ -rezultati terenskog istraživanja provedenog u Sisačko-moslavačkoj županiji*. Zagreb, Croatia: Društvo za oblikovanje održivog razvoja.

Robic, S., Zivcic, L. and Tkalec, T. (2016). *Energy poverty in South-East Europe: Challenges and possible solutions*. Available at: http://reach-energy.eu/wordpress/wp-content/uploads/2015/01/Policy-reccomendations-SEE-and-EU.pdf.

Sharpe, R. A., Thornton, C. R., Nikolaou, V. and Osborne, N. J. (2015). Fuel poverty increases risk of mould contamination, regardless of adult risk perception & ventilation in social housing properties. *Environment International*, 79, 115–129.

Simcock, N., Walker, G. and Day, R. (2016). Fuel poverty in the UK: beyond heating? *People, Place and Policy*, 10(11), 25–41.

Snell, C., Bevan, M. and Thomson, H. (2015). Justice, fuel poverty and disabled people in England. *Energy Research & Social Science*, 10, 123–132.

Teller-Elsberg, J., Sovacool, B., Smith, T. and Laine, E. (2016). Fuel poverty, excess winter deaths, and energy costs in Vermont: Burdensome for whom? *Energy Policy*, 90, 81–91.

Thomson, H. and Thomas, S. (2015). Developing empirically supported theories of change for housing investment and health. *Social Science & Medicine*, 124, 205–214.

Thomson, H., Snell, C. and Liddell, C. (2016). Fuel poverty in the European Union: A concept in need of definition? *People, Place and Policy*, 10(1), 5–24.

Thomson, H., Thomas, S., Sellstrom, E. and Petticrew, M. (2013). Housing improvements for health and associated socio-economic outcomes. *The Cochrane Database of Systematic Reviews*, 2, CD008657.

Tirado Herrero, S. and Ürge-Vorsatz, D. (2012). Trapped in the heat: A post-communist type of fuel poverty. *Energy Policy*, 49, 60–68.

Walker, G. and Day, R. (2012). Fuel poverty as injustice: Integrating distribution, recognition and procedure in the struggle for affordable warmth. *Energy Policy*, 49, 69–75.

Walker, R., Liddell, C., McKenzie, P., Morris, C. and Lagdon, S. (2014). Fuel poverty in Northern Ireland: Humanizing the plight of vulnerable households. *Energy Research & Social Science*, 4, 89–99.

Walker, R., McKenzie, P., Liddell, C. and Morris, C. (2014). Estimating fuel poverty at household level: An integrated approach. *Energy and Buildings*, 80, 469–479.

13 Lighting up rural Kenya

Lessons learnt from rural electrification programmes

Dorice Agol

Introduction

This chapter gives insights into rural electrification programmes (REPs) designed and implemented to accelerate access to electricity in Kenya, East Africa. The advent of Kenya's REP in the 1970s was driven by the realization that the level of access to electricity in rural areas was very low (just 4% of the rural population) and that this was a critical barrier to development. According to the Ministry of Petroleum and Mining (MoEP) of Kenya, the REP is a strategic approach which is aligned with the Government's development goal of Vision 2030 and aims to improve electricity supplies to accelerate economic growth in rural areas (MoEP 2015). Currently, access to electricity in rural areas in Kenya is less than 50%, despite various efforts across the country to enhance the availability of this resource (MoEP 2015).

The chapter provides a critical analysis of the REP through the lens of energy poverty. The correlation between access to electricity and socio-economic growth is at the core of the energy poverty discourse worldwide (Barnes et al. 2011; Giannini et al. 2011; Sovacool 2012; Reddy 2015; Bouzarovski and Tirado Herrero 2017). Lack of access to electricity is a form of energy poverty (e.g. Day et al. 2016). This is because electricity can enhance human well-being through better health, education, housing and improved income (Bouzarovski et al. 2012; Sesan 2012; González-Eguino 2015; Reddy 2015). Subsequently, rural electrification programmes and policies continue to gain much attention due to their potential to alleviate energy poverty (Cecelski 2000; Tanguy 2010; Ahlborg and Hammar 2014; Slough et al. 2015; Lee et al. 2016; Xu et al. 2016). In Bangladesh, India and Kenya, studies have shown that improved access to electricity through REPs can minimize energy deprivation (Barnes et al. 2011; Sesan 2012; Smith and Urpelainen 2016).

As part of socio-economic policies, many governments worldwide have introduced REPs to supply clean and reliable energy in order to reduce poverty and promote equitable development (Giannini et al. 2011). Historically, REP policy prescriptions have been shaped by affordability presumptions, based on the belief that rural populations cannot afford electricity – in response, REP interventions tend to subsidize electricity in order to attract customers and create demand.

Despite such efforts, experience has shown that access to electricity is still relatively low in rural areas compared to their urban counterparts (e.g. Lee et al. 2016). This calls for a critical analysis of REPs to identify reasons for limited success in electricity access in rural areas.

The extent to which electricity helps in alleviating energy poverty is context-dependent as some households may be much more vulnerable than others, based on factors such as their physical location and type of housing (see Slough et al. 2015). This statement contributes to the debate on the geographies of energy injustice where recent studies have shown the ways in which vulnerabilities are driven by demographics and housing factors (Bouzarovski and Tirado Herrero 2017).

The chapter ignites the debate on REPs' contribution to rural welfare through improved access to electricity. To date there is hardly thorough interrogation of REPs with regard to its role in energy poverty alleviation. For example, there are no enquiries on how REPs themselves might be sources of energy poverty. This study fills this gap by using key concepts such as energy vulnerabilities and injustices to unpack ways in which REP interventions facilitate and/or hinder energy poverty alleviation efforts in rural areas of Kenya. Exploring this multi-dimensional nature of REPs helps to deepen the understanding of the institutional, social, economic, cultural and environmental influences of energy poverty. It is anticipated that findings from this study will inform policy prescriptions for REP interventions in similar contexts.

The study focuses on electricity use in homes and small and medium businesses in three sites in rural areas of Kenya – Makueni, Naivasha and Kisumu counties. Information was gathered through key informant interviews (mainly with electricity service providers), focus group discussions with household members and business owners (half of which were connected to electricity and half of which were not connected), observations and literature reviews.

The first section gives a brief snapshot of the situation of electricity industry in Kenya, mainly relating to its sources, actors involved and regulatory and policy environment. This is followed by an introduction of the REP, its opportunities and challenges and local perceptions on the value of electricity. The next section presents the Last Mile Programme (LMP), a strategy for accelerating electricity access through subsidies and prepayment metering system. Then discussion on key findings is presented, and key lessons learnt from implementing rural electrification programmes are highlighted. The last section concludes the chapter.

Electricity industry in Kenya

Kenya's electricity comes from diverse sources including hydro-power, geothermal, oil, gas, coal, solar, wind and biogas. According to Kenya Power and Lighting Company (KPLC), the electricity sector has grown with an increase of power generation from 1765 Megawatts (MW) in March 2013 to 2341MW in mid-2016 (KPLC 2016a). The MoEP approximates that 70% of electricity is generated from renewables, mainly hydro-power[1] and geothermal[2] (MoEP 2015). Despite this growth, electricity contributes to only 9% of the total energy consumption in Kenya (MoEP 2015).

The government encourages private sector participation to generate electricity from renewable sources (Ken Gen 2014). Renewable sources of electricity such as solar photovoltaic (PV) systems have become common in remote areas where grid extension is still scarce. Solar PV is already serving many remote areas in Marsabit, Wajir and Turkana counties. Improved solar technologies have created new demands leading to increased use of solar panels in rural areas. These are mounted on rooftops, and energy is channelled to a battery to store power. Homes and other establishments which have installed solar panels use the generated electricity mostly for lighting and charging phones. There are also portable solar panels which can be put out in the sun during the day to tap the sun's energy, and these can cost as little at Kes 3000 (~ 30 USD) a piece.

Since the mid-1990s, the electricity industry in Kenya has been reformed. As a result, the industry is managed by multiple stakeholders with various roles and responsibilities ranging from policy guidance, electricity generation to transmission (Table 13.1). Key policies and regulations that guide the electricity industry include: the Energy and Petroleum Policy (2015), the Energy Bill (2015) and the Petroleum Bill (2015). These frameworks promote adequate reliable and sustainable energy supplies to meet the needs of the various sectors across the country (MoEP 2015).

Rural electrification programme (REP): barriers to electricity access in rural areas

This section introduces the REP, presents the challenges of being connected and gives local insights into the value of electricity. Kenya's REP was initiated in 1973 to accelerate electricity supplies[3] in order to modernize the countryside and reduce socio-economic gaps between rural and urban populations. The REP was previously implemented by the KPLC until 2007 when the REA was established and took over. The REA's overarching goal is to extend electricity to all Kenyans by the year 2030, via national grid supplies and off-grid extension, isolated diesel stations, solar photovoltaic (PV), wind and biogas systems (MoEP 2015). When REP projects are complete, they are handed over to the KPLC to distribute electricity, although they remain REA's property (KPLC 2016b). REA's strategy is to connect all public institutions and spaces such as schools, health facilities, markets and trading centres so that households along the transmission lines[4] would easily be connected.

According to the REA, access to electricity in rural areas of Kenya has grown from 4% in the 1970s to just under 50% (observation notes from REA meeting, May 2016). Much still needs to be done to reach the target, which is access to electricity by all in 2030.

The next sub-section gives a detailed account of the barriers and challenges of being connected to electricity, drawing on findings from the empirical data collection of this research.

Table 13.1 Key institutions in the electricity industry in Kenya

Institution	Responsibility
Ministry of Energy and Petroleum (MoEP)	Provides an enabling policy environment in the energy and petroleum sector. National energy and petroleum planning, training of manpower and mobilisation of financial resources.
Energy Regulatory Commission (ERC)	Energy sector regulator: responsible for economic and technical regulation of electric power, renewable energy and downstream petroleum sub-sectors. Tariff setting, review, licensing, enforcement, dispute settlement and approval of power purchase and network service contracts.
Energy Tribunal	To hear appeals against the decisions of ERC. It also has jurisdiction to hear and determine all matters referred to it relating to the energy sector.
Kenya Power and Lighting Company Limited (KPLC)	State Corporation with the government shareholding of 50.1% and private shareholding of 49.9% as of June 2014. Purchases electrical energy in bulk from KenGen and other power producers and carries out transmission, distribution, supply and retail of electric power.
Kenya Electricity Generating Company Limited (KenGen)	State corporation with the government shareholding of 70% as of June 2014. Currently producing the bulk of electricity consumed in the country.
Rural Electrification Authority (REA)	Corporate body responsible for extending electricity supply to rural areas, managing the rural electrification fund, mobilizing resources for rural electrification and promoting the development and use of renewable energy.
Geothermal Development Company Limited (GDC)	100% state-owned company established by the Government of Kenya as a special-purpose vehicle for the development of geothermal resources.
Kenya Electricity Transmission Company Limited (KETRACO)	State company responsible for the development, maintenance and operation of the national transmission grid network. It is also responsible for facilitating regional power trade.
Independent Power Producers (IPPs)	Private companies which generate power and sell electricity in bulk to KPLC. As at November 2014, there were nine IPPs in operation, accounting for about 24% of the country's installed capacity.
Kenya Nuclear Electricity Board (KNEB)	Charged with spearheading development of nuclear electricity generation.
Centre for Energy Efficiency and Conservation (CEEC)	The Centre was established jointly by the government and the Kenya Association of Manufacturers to champion energy efficiency and conservation efforts in Kenya.
Kenya Revenue Authority (KRA)	KRA is responsible for collection of taxes from energy and petroleum related transactions in line with relevant laws and regulations.
National Environmental Management Authority (NEMA)	Enforcement of environmental laws and regulations including those associated with electricity generation and transmission.
Kenya Bureau of Standards	Responsible for setting and regulating standards including those of electricity supplies.

Source: Ministry of Energy and Petroleum (2015)

The logistics of being connected to electricity in rural areas

Access to electricity in rural areas is inhibited by some critical barriers. The application process involving electricity connection is long. The first step is making a payment of Kenya shillings (Kes) 35,000 (~ 350 USD) to the KPLC and the response period can take between weeks to several months. Once the application is approved, the KPLC's technical personnel conduct a site survey to assess the viability of installing electrical infrastructure. From discussions, it appeared that having money does not guarantee access to electricity. Three household members said that they had applied for electricity and paid the full fee but had not heard back from the KPLC for months. In one case, a respondent narrated that multiple households pooled resources together and raised the full amount of connection fee. Collectively they applied for electricity and were still waiting for over 18 months. They have visited the KPLC's offices several times to make inquiries but were unsuccessful. These households lack collective bargaining power to demand better services. KPLC asserted that each case is special and that among the reasons for such delays were limited access to private land and difficult terrain.

But even after successful applications, customers face additional hurdles. For example, all the 30 households in this study who had electricity had paid an additional fee to speed up the process of being connected. In addition, key respondents revealed that a lack of access to private land is a common barrier to installing electrical infrastructure in rural areas. Often, tree felling is necessary to clear land, and it is not uncommon for private landowners to resist installation of electrical poles on their property. The KPLC and REA confirmed that, while some landowners have cooperated, others have declined leading to suspension of projects. According to government policies, private landowners should be compensated, but this too can take a long time to materialize.

Another challenge related to infrastructure development is the difficulty of connecting remote villages in sparsely populated areas. According to the KPLC and REA, it is costly to reach remote scattered villages in arid and semi-arid areas such as Northern and North Eastern parts of the country. For example, it costs the REA approximately Kes 1.5 million (USD 15000) to transmit electricity over a distance of 1 kilometre. The profits accrued from remote areas tend to be low. Consequently, companies try to avoid carrying out grid extension in scattered villages because they are expensive investments with relatively little returns. This is a huge disadvantage to those living in remote rural areas.

The logistical challenges of connecting rural houses constructed with basic materials was also noted. Observations showed that many rural houses have weak reinforcement since they are made of mud walls and thatched roofs, which make them unsuitable for electrical wiring installation. Such homes remain underprivileged because they do not qualify for electrical connection in accordance with health and safety rules of the KPLC and REA. Nevertheless, even houses built with more substantial construction materials in rural areas face connection challenges. Many houses or establishments are built without pre-electrical installation and where applications have been successful, customers have to make arrangements to have their homes wired incurring additional costs and expenses.

KPLC's policy stipulates that electrical wiring should be done by a fully qualified electrician in accordance with their health and safety regulations. The fee for a certified electrician range from Kes 5000 (~ 50 USD) to thousands of shillings.

During focus group discussions, 12 out of 30 households who were connected said that they were not sure whether their houses were wired by a certified electrician. Many respondents said that they could not afford a certified electrician but instead hired the services of any individuals they considered had the skills to carry out the task of wiring. However, they could not verify that such individuals were fully qualified and certified, and according to the KPLC, it is possible that some homes have been wired poorly. The KPLC is aware of 'rogue' electricians and the potential to cause accidents through their poor wiring activities. Yet, ironically, it is the company's responsibility to ensure that all electrical wires are installed in accordance to their rules and regulations. During discussions, the issue of poor wiring was found to be a sensitive topic, because it is linked with corruption. As one respondent indicated, 'Does it matter whether you find a qualified person? So long as you give him something [*meaning money*], nobody will bother to verify anything'.

Being disconnected when payments are delayed and frequent power cuts were identified as important barriers to access to electricity. Households with post-paid meters are billed monthly, and the payments vary depending on the intensity of use. On average, customers who use electricity for basic purposes such as lighting and charging electronic appliances pay about Kes 800 (~ 8 USD) per month while those who use it for business purposes pay anything from Kes 1000 (~ 10 USD). After being disconnected, respondents narrated how they went through 'a nightmare' when seeking re-connection services from the KPLC. Paying for re-reconnection fee does not guarantee efficient services because, on average, it takes about 4 working days to get reconnected and nearly always extra costs are incurred to speed up the process. According to the KPLC, reconnection delays are due to difficulties of reaching out to customers who are geographically far away from their offices.

The problem of frequent power outages was indicated as the biggest livelihood disruption especially for those running business in rural areas. Findings revealed that on average, customers experienced power cuts five days a week and said that they were 'fed up' with unreliable electricity supplies. The KPLC and REA suggested the root causes of power outages as vandalism, poor weather conditions and electricity rationing during short supplies. These multiple challenges reflect common barriers to access to electricity in rural areas and influence the ways in which rural people value electricity in rural areas.

The next section explores local perceptions on the value of electricity in attempts to understand demand and the intensity of energy poverty within rural households.

Local perception on the value of electricity

Rural electrification interventions are anticipated to give households a choice of switching from unsustainable traditional energy to clean reliable sources (Tanguy

2010; Sesan 2012) so that they can climb the 'fuel ladder' (Andadari et al. 2014). Thus promoters of REP interventions such as the MoEP, the KPLC, the REA and the ERC proclaim that this can be achieved by electricity connection. However, energy poverty alleviation is a complex undertaking and is not simply a matter of connecting to households. During discussions with those connected 'fuel stacking', whereby households use multiple different types of fuels for energy, was found to be a common practice. Electricity is not a household priority in rural areas, and if a household is connected, it is used for lighting and charging electronics such as mobile phone. No evidence was found to suggest a high demand for electricity in rural households for basic needs such as cooking and heating. Biomass was found to be the most common source of energy among households. Biomass tends to be the predominant energy source and accounts for over 80% consumption in rural areas (MoEP 2015). Of the 65 household investigated across different areas, the majority used wood and charcoal for cooking and heating, and many used alternative sources of energy for lighting – mainly kerosene and solar lamps. This was partly due to unreliable electricity supplies.

The fact that traditional sources of energy are still preferred undermines chances of climbing the fuel ladder as the majority indicated using a minimum of three different energy sources. For example, biomass, gas and kerosene were used for cooking. Kerosene, solar and electricity were used for lighting. Thus rather than moving up the ladder, fuel stacking is a common cultural practice in rural areas and is a key coping mechanism for reducing uncertainties associated with electricity and gas supplies.

Further enquiries on the value assigned to electricity showed that, out of the 30 respondents who were connected, 23 said that being connected was prestigious and inspirational and that it earned them some kind of social status. For example:

> When your house and home is well lit at night, it is a prestigious thing as people see you as different.

> People respect you when you have electricity; . . . it feels like you are living in town.

Seventeen respondents indicated that electricity earned them income while nine indicated that it enhanced learning at home through prolonged hours of studying. The rest identified benefits such as improved communication, networking and awareness when used for charging mobile phones and radio. The value assigned to electricity was linked to its actual utility where the most common use is lighting followed by charging electronics and running businesses.[5] Other uses include heating, ironing, preserving food and cooking.

However, during discussions, there were nonetheless varying perceptions about the advantages and disadvantages of being connected to electricity. While the majority considered electricity as a useful resource that can improve social and economic welfare of those connected, others perceived it as a dangerous resource that could cost lives of people and their resources (e.g. poultry and livestock). Interestingly, while some respondents considered being connected as a security measure – a well-lit home or establishment can deter intruders – others feared that electricity could actually attract criminal acts. For example:

> When your home is well lit, they think that you have much money and wealth and they are easily led to your house; . . . this is risky.

One respondent said that, despite having installed security lights, they deliberately switched them off every night to deter intruders who perceived them as rich. Respondents also revealed that some homes have been burnt and lives have been lost due to electrical accidents such as exposure to 'live' wires. Key informants from service providers indicated that such accidents may have been caused by lack of technical skills and infrastructural installation. Culturally, it was interesting to find that accidents caused by electricity were perceived to be associated with 'evil spirits' and bad luck in some communities.

Thus while electricity is perceived to be valuable by some households, others associate it with risks. These findings challenge the notion that household electricity access is always an unquestionable 'good thing' – instead, it is necessary to understand how such access relates to further complexities such as the affordability of such electricity, and to broader cultural practices and social inequalities.

The next section discusses the Last Mile Programme, a current strategic approach which has been adopted by the government of Kenya to accelerate electricity supplies and improve access especially for low-income households.

Accelerating electricity access through the Last Mile Programme (LMP)

The government launched the Last Mile Programme (LMP) in 2015 to increase the rate of electricity connection across the country, by subsidizing the connection fee from Kes 35,000 (~ USD 350), to Kes 15,000 (~USD 150), although some customers indicated that they paid as little as Kes 2,500 (~ USD 25) to get connected. The LMP targets households and/or entities located within 600 metres of an existing electrical transformer. Currently there are approximately 40,000 transformers spread across the country, typically in densely populated areas that provide the lowest connection cost per household. Closely spaced villages have a higher chance of being connected than those which are sparsely populated. The main sources of funding for the LMP are the government through a government Constituency Development Fund (CDF) and loans from external development partners such as the African Development Bank (AfDB), the European Union and the European Investment Bank (KPLC 2017). An advantage of the LMP is that customers do not have to pay the connection fee upfront, and no formal application is required as long as they are located within 600 metres from a transformer. Furthermore, once connected, customers have control over their electricity use through a prepayment metering system. The LMP targets both rural and urban areas and KPLC's statistics show that customer base throughout the country increased from 2.3 to 4.9 million[6] between 2013 to 2016 (*Ibid*). The question posed in this study was whether these LMP strategies – the subsidies and prepayment metering system – are ameliorating risks and vulnerabilities associated with energy poverty in rural areas.

Subsidizing electricity through the LMP

According to the Ministry of Energy and Petroleum (MoEP), electricity subsidies are important market incentives that attract investments in the REP. During discussions, it was a widely held belief among service providers that subsidizing the connection fee through the LMP was making electricity much more affordable and accessible to low-income households. Findings revealed that this statement holds true for certain groups, particularly small to medium-sized businesses situated near and along power transformers and power lines, such as flour mills, shops, cafes and fuel stations.

The extent to which the subsidies were increasing household electricity access and subsequent energy poverty alleviation was found to be uncertain at best. There is no doubt that subsidizing the connection fee has attracted certain households to get connected. However, respondents from unelectrified homes living within 600 metres from the main transformer indicated that, despite subsidies, electricity costs – including upfront payments and internal wiring – were a significant barrier towards being connected. More interestingly, those without electricity supply said that they would only try to get connected if they were sure that the resource would enhance their livelihoods. Among the household engagements that were identified that would improve their livelihoods include irrigated farming and water vending, both of which require pumping water by use of electricity.

Despite subsidies, access to electricity remains a challenge in rural areas for multiple reasons. With subsidized electricity, the KPLC and REA have had to serve a growing number of customer base, mostly small to medium-sized businesses. Key respondents were concerned that there was a high chance that the capacities of electrical transformers were being exceeded in some areas. Consequently, power cuts are common during most days in villages and it can take days before transmission is re-established. More interestingly, respondents asserted that power cuts were due to unstable infrastructure (i.e. regular tripping) exposing homes and businesses to high risks. For example, respondents narrated how power destroyed their stereo systems and mobile phones in one incident when electricity was reconnected after power cut. The KPLC and REA are aware that power transformers are failing to establish reliable transmissions due to 'overload', but they declined to confirm whether this is due to increased number of connections.

During discussions, there were various views on electricity subsidies based on experiences. Some respondents asserted that subsidies encouraged corruption whereby customers have been asked to pay money but were never connected. Others asserted that subsidies were a government's campaign strategy used to secure electoral votes from citizens. Some key informants were concerned that due to the fact that the LMP is also externally funded means that it is unlikely to be sustainable when such assistance exits.

The prepayment metering system: issues of affordability for households

After successful piloting and rolling out of prepayment metering in urban areas, the KPLC introduced the system to the countryside. The REA and KPLC listed various advantages of prepayment metering system including enhanced efficiencies in electricity transmission and distribution, minimized corruption and improved customer services. In comparison to the traditional post-payment method, the service providers asserted that the prepayment system was incentivising customers to use electricity efficiently in their homes since they only consumed the amount which they could afford to pay for. Both KPLC and the REA agreed that the prepaid meters prevented unnecessary disconnection and high reconnection fees and the consequent inconvenience often associated with post-payment schemes.

Out of 30 customers with electricity, 15 were on prepayment billing arrangement, and the other half were on post-payment scheme. The most commonly identified advantages of prepayment system were: taking control over electricity consumption and budgeting, avoidance of worrying about accumulated bills and not having to queue up to pay for electricity.

When asked about the limits of prepayment system, the main challenge was the need to have money at one's disposal before they could access electricity. Respondents perceived this as a major hindrance towards access. Further discussions revealed that most service users were extremely cautious about their consumption, and some confessed to disconnecting the meters deliberately just to ensure that they were completely cut off. However, being too careful put limits to power consumption and restricted access.

Further analysis revealed that payment for electricity was not a priority for household expenditure. Respondents ranked key areas of household expenditure including food, fuel (mainly kerosene), mobile telephone top up, education, health and so on. Based on an average weekly income of Kes 3000 (~ USD 30), it was not surprising to find that the majority of households spent 40% of their money on food and that only less than 10% went to payment of electricity. Priority was granted to what were considered essential needs mainly food, water and education, before prepaying for electricity. For example:

> I only pay for electricity when I have extra money because you see I have to buy food, pay for the water vendor and pay for my daughter's schools fees.

> When my son sends me money, I can afford to pay for electricity . . . but he also has family burden and he cannot send money all the time. So I manage with other fuel types such as kerosene.

These testimonials suggest that prepayment metering system does not really guarantee access to electricity unless one can afford to make regular upfront payments. Furthermore, findings showed that even for those households connected via the LMP, expenditure on electricity was relatively lower compared to other uses.

During discussions, opponents of prepayment systems asserted that it can create new forms of poverty in households, when incomes are put under strain. An additional concern with the prepayment metering system was that many customers said that they had little understanding on its price variabilities. For example, a voucher worth Kes 200 (~ USD 2) can give variable amounts of electricity units on each occasion when a top-up is made. KPLC explained that this variability is dependent on elasticity of fuel prices, meaning less electricity per unit cost during high fuel prices, and vice versa. This sort of information is not readily available for service users, and this has led to misunderstandings as some customers suspected that the KPLC overcharged them.

How significantly has the REP helped to alleviate energy poverty in rural areas of Kenya? Are there specific lessons learnt so far from implementing the REP, and what are key policy implications? While REP interventions aim to accelerate access to electricity, their proponents tend to pay little attention to the socio-economic factors and household cultural needs, practices and priorities and how these influence household demands for energy. These issues are discussed below.

Lessons learnt and policy implications

There is a whole body of literature on rural electrification programmes and their potential to reduce energy poverty through improved access to electricity (Cecelski 2000; Tanguy 2010; Ahlborg and Hammar 2014; Slough et al. 2015; Lee et al. 2016; Xu et al. 2016). The potential of REPs to ameliorate energy poverty in rural areas is determined by the quality and level of service provision and the geography of an area as well as the physical location of a household. Through a critical analysis of the REP in Kenya, this section argues that alleviating energy poverty is a complex situation which is entwined with wider socio-economic, cultural and environmental challenges as well as institutional and technological barriers and that the quality and level of service provision influences an REP's capacity to tackle energy poverty. It identifies potential sources of risks and vulnerabilities and discusses the energy injustices within the context of rural electrification programmes.

As this study has demonstrated, the logistical challenges of being connected to electricity in rural areas influence the quality and level of service provision negatively. This is due to institutional, technical and environmental barriers, a finding which is supported by studies elsewhere (Reddy 2015; Alkon et al. 2016; Panos et al. 2016; Wolf et al. 2016; Herington et al. 2017; Stojanovski et al. 2017; Tait 2017). Notable barriers such as the long application processes, conflicts over land, unsuitable household structures, inaccessible terrain and climate change all limit access to electricity in rural areas. This finding demonstrates how the causes of energy poverty are spatially contingent and extend beyond the affordability which is a common discourse in developed countries (Day et al. 2016; Reddy 2015; Scarpellini et al. 2015; Tait 2017).

A lack of affordability remains the basis on which REP policy and interventions are implemented, especially in developing countries, where it is argued that high costs is a barrier to electricity access (e.g. Tait 2017). However, there is no evidence from this study to show that the electricity subsidies introduced through the REP enhanced household affordability and subsequently ameliorated energy poverty in rural areas. A recent study conducted in Kenya on the REP by Lee and colleagues showed that, despite subsidies and significant infrastructural investments in grid extension, levels of electrification rates remained low among households and businesses in rural areas (Lee et al. 2016). In Ethiopia for example, both electricity and kerosene subsidies did not significantly increase the purchasing power of low-income household (Kebede 2006). REP proponents also need to consider the environmental impacts of subsidies which can lead to over-exploitation of natural resources (Smith and Urpelainen 2016) and climate change (Lin and Jiang 2011).

Certainly, many rural economies are fast growing and demand modern forms of energy (Lee et al. 2016). The Last Mile Programme aims to meet a growing demand for energy in rural areas but without a deeper understanding of the demographics, i.e. which areas most require electricity and for what purposes. The decision to connect only households which are 600 metres through the LMP appears to be arbitrary and reflects inequality in electricity distribution. What about households which are outside the 600 metre mark and are in need of electricity? In reflecting the demographics of electricity distribution under the LMP framework, the study argues that favouring areas which are within 600 metres denotes distributional energy injustice which is characterized by inequalities in electricity access (see Simcock and Mullen 2016). By being pragmatic (cost efficiency), the LMP reflects the limits of spatial targeting (e.g. Roberts et al. 2015; Reames 2016) by serving only those situated near electrical infrastructure but while excluding those living in remote areas and subjecting the latter to risks and vulnerabilities. Policy prescriptions should adopt a more strategic targeting approach for REPs, and this requires systematic monitoring of dynamics of electricity demand and use. A deeper knowledge on the value of electricity to potential service users can better inform rural electrification policies particularly with regard to targeting the right populations (Hirmer and Guthrie 2016).

The ultimate goal of most rural electrification interventions is to lift households out of energy poverty by helping them climb the fuel ladder from traditional sources such as kerosene to electricity (Slough et al. 2015; Smith and Urpelainen 2016; Xu et al. 2016; Stojanovski et al. 2017). But traditional energy sources like biomass are largely preferred in rural areas (e.g. Malla 2013), and the culture of fuel stacking is a common phenomenon (Andadari et al. 2014; Cheng and Urpelainen 2014). While improved sources can reduce energy vulnerabilities such as risks to health, the study argues that a complete switch to electricity is risky for households which experience frequent power cuts. It is not certain therefore if electricity supplies in rural areas can reduce vulnerabilities and ultimately reduce energy poverty amongst low-income households. Studies have shown that climbing the energy ladder may alleviate extreme energy poverty, particularly among medium- to higher-income households who are likely to switch to an improved source (Andadari et al. 2014). Thus rather than focusing too much on electricity, REPs should put greater efforts on improving traditional forms such as energy-saving stoves (Barnes et al. 2011).

The prepayment metering system (Depuru et al. 2011) may not resolve the problem of energy poverty (e.g. Oseni 2015) and can be a source of risks and vulnerabilities especially when households fail to make upfront payments. Evidence from New Zealand showed that prepayment metering for electricity was more expensive than other methods (O'Sullivan et al. 2011). Thus, there is need to strengthen service users' capacities on prepayment metering system and create awareness on its pros and cons in order to improve service provision (Vyas 2014).

The universal acceptance that rural households are deprived of electricity needs further interrogation taking into account issues of demand and value addition (e.g. Hirmer and Guthrie 2016). For example, are households getting less than they demand and need? A study in rural Kenya revealed that the level of acceptance of a proposed energy use technology was determined by user needs and priorities rather than those expressed by the implementers (Sesan 2012). As this study revealed, the demand for energy in rural areas resonates with its perceived benefits and personal values. Being connected to electricity has multiple connotations which range from earning social status (prestige), risks, personal security and safety and income generation. This is a reminder of the importance of understanding perceptions on the value of electricity as it determines the level of demand and intake of the service. Hence, policy prescriptions on REPs need to be informed by facts on user perceived value of electricity and how this resonates with the actual customer demands.

Conclusions

Rural electrification is widely endorsed as a strategy for accelerating growth and human well-being because it can improve access to electricity in low-income households. While REP interventions can improve access to electricity, they can simultaneously act as sources of energy deprivation. For example, by targeting only specific demographics, the basic orientation of the REP can be problematic, leading to energy injustices through inequitable access. Yet ironically, the basis of designing rural electrification programmes is to minimize energy inequalities in the countryside. In essence, REPs might be promoting energy justices only amongst certain groups such as the middle- and higher-income households who are situated within their areas of operations.

The study has successfully identified the key factors that contribute to the success and/or failure of REP interventions and the ways in which they are embedded in socio-cultural, political, economic and environmental dynamics of rural areas. Findings from this chapter show that, while REPs are designed to provide opportunities to ameliorate energy poverty in rural areas, they often face multiple challenges that shape their outcomes and impacts. These include technological (e.g. poor infrastructure, energy inefficiency); institutional barriers (poor service provision, corruption), socio-cultural practices; and environmental impacts such

Figure 13.1 Sources of vulnerability in rural electrification programmes

as climate change. These different factors can be considered different sources of energy vulnerability (Figure 13.1), as they shape the risk of a household living in energy poverty.

Policy prescriptions in REPs consider access to electricity by the poor as optimal, but without fully recognizing that the success of these interventions is surrounded with and shaped by multiple forms of vulnerabilities. This study provides a strong example of how the causes of energy poverty are geographically variable and contingent, embedded in particular places and contexts. A key lesson learnt from the REP is that much emphasis is put on outputs, with an intention to serve as many rural households as possible without an understanding of how institutional, social, economic, cultural and environmental factors influence service delivery. This chapter questions the design and implementation of these programmes and argues that the REP's role in rural economies tend to be overrated and should be interrogated in order to maximize their benefits in alleviating energy poverty.

Notes

1 Much potential of hydro-power is located within five water drainage systems in Lake Victoria, the Rift Valley, the Tana River, the Athi River and the Ewaso Ng'iro River.
2 Mainly in the Rift Valley, Lake and Coastal regions.
3 The REP's key funding source was a 5% levy charged to all electricity users across the country.
4 Particularly those located approximately 1.2 kilometres from the main network.
5 Electricity used for pumping water for sale to household for domestic use.
6 Unfortunately, attempts to obtain disaggregate data on customers being served in rural areas for this study was unfruitful.

References

Ahlborg, H. and Hammar, L. (2014). Drivers and barriers to rural electrification in Tanzania and Mozambique – Grid-extension, off-grid, and renewable energy technologies. *Renewable Energy*, 61, 117–124.

Alkon, M., Harish, S. P. and Urpelainen, J. (2016). Household energy access and expenditure in developing countries: Evidence from India, 1987–2010. *Energy for Sustainable Development*, 35, 25–34.

Andadari, R. K., Mulder, P. and Rietveld, P. (2014). Energy poverty reduction by fuel switching: Impact evaluation of the LPG conversion program in Indonesia. *Energy Policy*, 66, 436–449.

Barnes, D. F., Khandker, S. R and Samad, H. A. (2011). Energy poverty in rural Bangladesh. *Energy Policy*, 39(2), 894–904.

Bouzarovski, S. and Tirado Herrero, S. (2017). Geographies of injustice: The socio-spatial determinants of energy poverty in Poland, the Czech Republic and Hungary. *Post-Communist Economies*, 29(1), 27–50.

Bouzarovski, S., Petrova, S. and Sarlamanov, R. (2012). Energy poverty policies in the EU: A critical perspective. *Energy Policy*, 49, 76–82.

Cecelski., E. (2000). *Enabling equitable access to rural electrification: Current thinking and major activities in energy, power and gender*. Asia Alternative Energy Policy and Project Development Support: Emphasis on Poverty Alleviation and Women. Washington, DC: World Bank.

Cheng, C. and Urpelainen, J. (2014). Fuel stacking in India: Changes in the cooking and lighting mix, 1987–2010. *Energy*, 76, 306–317.

Day, R., Walker, G. and Simcock, N. (2016). Conceptualising energy use and energy poverty using a capabilities framework. *Energy Policy*, 93, 255–264.

Depuru, S. S. S. R., Wang, L. and Devabhaktuni, V. (2011). Smart meters for power grid: Challenges, issues, advantages and status. *Renewable and Sustainable Energy Reviews*, 15(6), 2736–2742.

Giannini, P. M., Vasconcelos Freitas, M. A and da Silva, N. F. (2011). The challenge of energy poverty: Brazilian case study. *Energy Policy*, 39(1), 167–175.

González-Eguino, M. (2015). Energy poverty: An overview. *Renewable and Sustainable Energy Reviews*, 47, 377–385.

Herington, M. J., van de Fliert, E., Smart, S., Greig, C. and Lant, P. A. (2017). Rural energy planning remains out-of-step with contemporary paradigms of energy access and development. *Renewable and Sustainable Energy Reviews*, 67, 1412–1419.

Hirmer, S. and Guthrie, P. (2016). Identifying the needs of communities in rural Uganda: A method for determining the 'User-Perceived Value' of rural electrification initiatives. *Renewable and Sustainable Energy Reviews*, 66, 476–486.

Kebede, B. (2006). Energy subsidies and costs in urban Ethiopia: The cases of kerosene and electricity. *Renewable Energy*, 31(13), 2140–2151.

Ken Gen. (2014). *Annual report & financial statements for year ended 30 June 2014: KenGen*. Nairobi: Kenya Electricity Generating Company Limited.

KPLC. (2016a). *State of electricity Kenya*. Available at: www.kplc.co.ke/.

KPLC. (2016b). *Five year corporate strategic plan 2016/17–2020/21*. Nairobi: The Kenya Power and Lighting Company Limited.

KPLC. (2017). *The last mile programme*. Available at: www.kplc.co.ke/.

Lee, K., Brewer, E., Christiano, C., Meyo, F., Miguel, E., Podolsky, M., Rosa, J. and Wolfram, C. (2016). Electrification for "Under Grid" households in Rural Kenya. *Development Engineering*, 1, 26–35.

Lin, B. and Jiang, Z. (2011). Estimates of energy subsidies in China and impact of energy subsidy reform. *Energy Economics*, 33(2), 273–283.

Malla, S. (2013). Household energy consumption patterns and its environmental implications: Assessment of energy access and poverty in Nepal. *Energy Policy*, 61, 990–1002.

MoEP. (2015). *Draft national energy and petroleum policy*. Nairobi: M. o. E. a. Petroleum, Nairobi Government Publisher.

O'Sullivan, K. C., Howden-Chapman, P. L. and Fougere, G. (2011). Making the connection: The relationship between fuel poverty, electricity disconnection, and prepayment metering. *Energy Policy*, 39(2), 733–741.

Oseni, M. O. (2015). Assessing the consumers' willingness to adopt a prepayment metering system in Nigeria. *Energy Policy*, 86, 154–165.

Panos, E., Densing, M. and Volkart, K. (2016). Access to electricity in the World Energy Council's global energy scenarios: An outlook for developing regions until 2030. *Energy Strategy Reviews*, 9, 28–49.

REA. (2016). *Rural electrification biannual news*. Nairobi: Ministry of Energy and Petroleum.

Reames, T. G. (2016). Targeting energy justice: Exploring spatial, racial/ethnic and socioeconomic disparities in urban residential heating energy efficiency. *Energy Policy*, 97, 549–558.

Reddy, B. S. (2015). Access to modern energy services: An economic and policy framework. *Renewable and Sustainable Energy Reviews*, 47, 198–212.

Roberts, D., Vera-Toscano, E. and Phimister, E. (2015). Fuel poverty in the UK: Is there a difference between rural and urban areas? *Energy Policy*, 87, 216–223.

Scarpellini, S., Rivera-Torres, P., Suárez-Perales, I. and Aranda-Usón, A. (2015). Analysis of energy poverty intensity from the perspective of the regional administration: Empirical evidence from households in southern Europe. *Energy Policy*, 86, 729–738.

Sesan, T. (2012). Navigating the limitations of energy poverty: Lessons from the promotion of improved cooking technologies in Kenya. *Energy Policy*, 47, 202–210.

Simcock, N. and Mullen, C. (2016). Energy demand for everyday mobility and domestic life: Exploring the justice implications. *Energy Research & Social Science*, 18, 1–6.

Slough, T., Urpelainen, J. and Yang, J. (2015). Light for all? Evaluating Brazil's rural electrification progress, 2000–2010. *Energy Policy*, 86, 315–327.

Smith, M. G. and Urpelainen, J. (2016). Rural electrification and groundwater pumps in India: Evidence from the 1982–1999 period. *Resource and Energy Economics*, 45, 31–45.

Sovacool, B. (2012). The political economy of energy poverty: A review of key challenges. *Energy for Sustainable Development*, 16(3), 272–282.

Stojanovski, O., Thurber, M. and Wolak, F. (2017). Rural energy access through solar home systems: Use patterns and opportunities for improvement. *Energy for Sustainable Development*, 37, 33–50.

Tait, L. (2017). Towards a multidimensional framework for measuring household energy access: Application to South Africa. *Energy for Sustainable Development*, 38, 1–9.

Tanguy, B. (2010). Impact analysis of rural electrification projects in sub-saharan Africa. *World Bank Research Observer*, 27(1), 33–51.

Vyas, D. (2014). *Topping-up or dropping-out: Self-disconnection among prepayment meter users*. London, Citizen Advice.

Wolf, F., Surroop, D., Singh, A. and Leal, W. (2016). Energy access and security strategies in Small Island Developing States. *Energy Policy*, 98, 663–673.

Xu, Z., Nthontho, M. and Chowdhury, S. (2016). Rural electrification implementation strategies through microgrid approach in South African context. *International Journal of Electrical Power & Energy Systems*, 82, 452–465.

14 Urban energy poverty

South Africa's policy response to the challenge

Peta Wolpe and Yachika Reddy

Introduction

> When we hear a scream we know something has happened; a rape or burglary.
> When we hear a mother cry we know another child has been electrocuted.
>
> (SEA, 2016a)

These are the poignant realities of the women of Thembelihle, an informal unelectrified settlement located on the margins of one of South Africa's major cities – Johannesburg. It is established on fairly barren land with no streetlights, where the majority of households reside in shack dwellings with makeshift outdoor ablution facilities. Despite the City of Johannesburg introducing several 'pro-poor' policies, over half the households in Thembelihle remain below the poverty threshold (deemed to be an income less than R3200 or 240 US dollars per month, (Stats SA 2011)). Those with access to electricity often obtain it through 'illegal connections', and those without electricity use unsafe fuels such as paraffin and wood to meet their basic household energy needs (SEA 2016b). This situation is typical of the urban poor settlements in South Africa and points to the policy challenges associated with the complex issues of energy poverty – an inability to attain the energy services necessary to sustain economic and human development (UNDP 2000) – in present-day South Africa (SEA 2014; Wolpe et al 2012; Visagie 2008; SANERI 2008).

In 1994, the provision of modern energy services was high on the agenda of the newly elected government, as part of addressing the historic inequalities and severe poverty of the past Apartheid era. National government introduced many laudable pro-poor policies in its quest to achieve universal access to energy for households, notably the White Paper on Energy (1998), Free Basic Electricity (FBE), Free Basic Alternative Energy (FBAE), and an impressive national electrification and housing programme. However, despite these enormous efforts, South Africa's response to energy poverty alleviation has not been completely successful; 47% of South Africa's households are deemed to be energy poor based on the affordability measure (DoE 2013).

This chapter aims to analyse the key factors that have hindered the effectiveness of energy poverty alleviation policies, with a particular focus on the 'micro-' or local-level factors, and to provide recommendations for future policy design. We illustrate that, despite the good intentions, these issues create a disjuncture between national imperatives and the ability of local government to deliver on its energy service delivery mandate, resulting in the reduction of energy poverty not occurring at the desired or intended pace.

This chapter begins with an overview of energy poverty policy in South Africa, before describing the current situation in the country. We move on to analyse the key factors that have hindered the effective implementation of these policies and then provide some policy recommendations in our conclusions.

Energy poverty policy in South Africa: a history and overview

South Africa is recognised as an 'emerging' economy; whilst there has been growth in the economy, it has not been at a rate expected and has not produced the desired degree of change and social development. Prior to 1994, the country was distinguished by an Apartheid system, a system of governance which called for the separation of people on the basis of race, codified into law. This translated into black people and people of colour living in dire poverty with little access to development and economic opportunities. It resulted in the majority of the population being discriminated against by the minority white population. In 1994, the Apartheid system was dismantled through the election of a new democratic government.

Since 1994, policy development has aimed to redress the systemic injustices of the Apartheid era. This commenced with the crafting of the democratic Constitution of South Africa, established in 1996, which is developmental in nature and adheres to the concepts of interrelatedness, cooperation, and interdependence between the three spheres of government.

This was followed by the Reconstruction and Development Programme (RDP), an overarching socio-economic policy framework for the country. It aimed to transform the country from a segregated to a democratic state, with a focus on the development of infrastructure in poor communities. This led to an impressive national electrification programme, the building of close to 3 million homes to address the massive housing backlog, job creation and land redistribution, amongst other measures (DoE 2014; Presidency 2014).

An important aspect of South Africa's developmental goals has been the introduction of policies that aim to dramatically reduce energy poverty, which was deep and widespread. In 1994 only 36% of the population had access to electricity, which was denied to the majority of South Africans during the Apartheid era. The White Paper on Energy (1998) is the overarching policy approach for the energy sector in South Africa. It was significant in that it shifted energy policy away from a predominantly supply-side focus to including the demand-side perspective of the energy sector, bringing to the fore energy poverty. A key objective of the White Paper is to widen access to affordable, adequate, and secure energy services for small businesses and disadvantaged households in urban and rural areas. Promoting universal access to electricity in order to reduce the harmful health impacts caused by poor-quality domestic fuels was deemed particularly important. In order to widen access, the South African government undertook the Integrated National Electrification Programme (INEP). Initially, this aimed to achieve universal (100%) access to electricity by 2012, but this was later revised to a new target of 97% by 2025 (Presidency 2014; DoE 2013; Barnard 2011). Nonetheless, by 2016, 87% of the population was electrified (Madzhie 2016), a substantial increase of 51% in two decades.

Over time, it became evident that access to electricity alone was not sufficient. Poor households that were electrified were also constrained by the affordability of electricity, and so were unable to derive the full socio-economic benefits anticipated from the enormous electrification investment (Tait 2015; DoE 2013; Winkler 2006; Borchers et al 2001). As a result of this realisation, the Free Basic Electricity (FBE) and Free Basic Alternative Energy (FBAE) policies were introduced, to enable the affordability of energy use by the poor (DME 2007; 2005). The FBE policy (2005) was developed to help poor electrified households by providing 50kWh of free electricity per month (DME 2005). This was the amount deemed sufficient for meeting 'basic energy needs', although it has been questioned whether this is sufficient for contemporary energy requirements (Jaglin 2009). In line with this, some municipalities are subsidising larger amounts of free electricity. Meanwhile, the FBAE policy (2007) emerged from recognition that not all households were electrified, particularly in the rural areas. It provides support for impoverished households via a monthly allowance to purchase alternative fuels such as paraffin.

The next section discusses the extent to which these policies have been successful in addressing the challenges of energy poverty.

Energy poverty: the situation today

Currently, South Africa is 63% urbanised (Stats SA 2011) and urban populations are forecasted to reach 70% by 2030 (NPC 2011). Those previously forced to live under impoverished circumstances in rural areas during the Apartheid era, far away from economic and resource opportunities, have moved to the cities in search of employment and better opportunities (COGTA 2014). Much of the urban growth has been in the poor and informal housing sectors, impacting on the scale of energy poverty in the urban nodes of the country.

There are currently about 2,700 informal settlements spread across South Africa, comprising 13.6% of the national population (HDA 2012; Stat SA 2011). These settlements are typically situated on land unauthorised for residential development, with residents living in overcrowded and poor conditions (see Knox et al., this volume). Informality in South Africa includes those households living in temporary structures, often termed 'shacks', which tend to be constructed adjacent to a low-income formal house (serviced plot), accommodating families who cannot afford to live independently (Turok 2015; HDA 2012).

South African cities have historically developed along sprawling, low-density suburban lines. As outlined in detail by Knox et al. (this volume), this urban form was rooted in Apartheid's inequitable and segregated spatial-land distribution policies but is also a consequence of how post-democracy government housing programmes have been delivered (Turok 2015; COGTA 2014; Ewing and Mammon 2010). The success of such programmes were measured purely by output (quantity), and they were driven by private companies whose central rationale was profit and so located settlements on the urban margins where land is cheaply available. These houses were poorly built, lacking thermal insulation such as ceilings, resulting in high energy costs to the household (DHS 2014; Turok and Borel-Saladin 2013; Ewing and Mammon 2010). As a consequence, South African cities are socially exclusive with the poor living on the distant margins experiencing persistently inadequate levels of service delivery (Turok 2015; COGTA 2014; Sustainability Institute 2009; Jaglin 2009). They are unable to access the social amenities and employment opportunities that cities have to offer, and are often without access to basic services such as modern forms of energy or are unable to afford the constant supply of safe and reliable energy.

Whilst South Africa has experienced an overall decline in income poverty levels, due largely to the introduction of state grants, the magnitude of absolute poverty and inequality currently prevailing in the country remains high. Thus 27% of the population are unemployed, and 63% of households live below the poverty line, largely concentrated in urban areas (Stats SA 2011, 2017; SEA 2014; Leibbrandt et al. 2010).

In this context, a survey conducted by the National Department of Energy in 2013 on energy-related behaviour and perceptions in the residential sector (DoE 2013), demonstrated – using an expenditure-based measure where a household is in energy poverty if they expends more than 10% of their income on energy – that 47% of the country is considered energy poor. Thus many households are burdened with relatively high energy costs compared to wealthier households, who typically spend 2–3% of their income on energy (SEA 2015, 2006) and must make difficult choices about everyday expenditure taken for granted by wealthier households. Lack of affordability means households often cut back on electricity consumption and use polluting and unsafe fuels instead, and therefore energy poverty is also manifest in the enduring and persistent multiple fuel use patterns amongst households despite high levels of electrification (Mzini and Lukamba-Muhiya 2014; SEA 2015; GNESD 2013; DoE 2013). Limited resources and unpredictable incomes lock low-income households into making frequent purchases of small quantities of fuel such as paraffin, which tends to be more expensive than buying such fuels in larger quantities. Approximately 7 million households continue to rely on a range of unsafe, unhealthy traditional fuels including paraffin, candles, coal, and biomass (GNESD 2013), resulting in poor indoor air quality that creates health problems such as acute low respiratory infections (ALRIs) and chronic obstructive pulmonary disease (GDARD 2015; DEA 2013; Mduli et al. 2005; UNDP 2000). ALRIs are among the leading causes of death among South African children under the age of 5 (DEA 2013; Poggiolini 2007; Mduli et al. 2005).

As outlined in more detail by Knox et al. in an earlier chapter of this book, those living in informal settlements face a number of disadvantages that make them particularly vulnerable to energy poverty. Electricity tends to be significantly more expensive for such households – it is often obtained and purchased from neighbours through makeshift and informal connections extending from a 'main house' and often charged at a higher rate than formal municipal billing tariffs (CCT 2014; Franks and Prasad 2014; Gaunt et al. 2012; GNESD 2013; Misselhorn 2010; SANERI 2008; SEA 2014, 2016b; Tait 2015; Visagie 2008). Informal dwellings, as well as government-delivered housing, are not adequately insulated (majority without ceilings) – meaning they are not thermally efficient. Thus, they are too cold in the winter and too hot in the summer and require proportionally more resources in order to maintain comfortable temperatures (DHS 2014, 2013).

In summary, energy poverty remains a significant problem in South Africa. This is despite the consistent economic growth and a number of national policies and frameworks aiming to alleviate energy poverty, and various local level initiatives – notably, the City of Cape Town laying of foundations for electrifying informal settlements, the City of Johannesburg's widespread delivery of solar water heaters to low-income houses, and the City of Polokwane's introduction of a package of alternative energy technologies for non-electrified settlements (SEA 2015; Gaunt et al. 2012). Whilst interventions are happening, the scale of implementation is not occurring at a level intended by the national policies and frameworks, or at a rate that can match increasing urban populations and energy consumption. In the next section, we analyse the reasons why this is the case.

Key factors hampering energy poverty policies

This section discusses some of the key factors hampering the implementation of energy poverty policies, shedding light on why they have not entirely succeeded in alleviating energy deprivation. We begin by briefly discussing broad national level factors, before moving on to discuss four specific issues that have contributed to hampering effective policy implementation: a lack of coordination and alignment, an inadequate financial framework, a lack of technical and human resource capacity, and poor and inconsistent targeting.

Macro-scale political and economic factors

In analysing the Reconstruction and Development Programme, Wolpe (1995) argues that, whilst it gave effect to enormous social change including that of other government programmes, it was not undertaken at a systemic level. The institutions and bureaucracies that were in place to support and uphold the Apartheid regime were not fundamentally transformed and remained in place to support a new post-Apartheid society. To this end, solely implementing progressive policies would not yield an inclusive and developmental transformation that was envisaged for the nation. As Wolpe (1995, 1) writes, 'The transition from Apartheid thus [requires] not merely changes in specific policies, but also extensive cultural and ideological, as well as institutional and social structural transformations'. Supporting this notion, Turok and Borel-Saladin (2013) assert that it is critical for urbanisation to be addressed systemically (at an institutional and structural level) by government for greater economic growth to be 'secured' to sustain the fast-growing urban populace who are, and will in the foreseeable future be, largely poor. South African cities are neither equitable nor efficient, and the solution does not rest solely with increasing infrastructure and basic service delivery. The authors emphasise that the 'whole apparatus of government needs to be better prepared' for the provision of 'decent' services to the burgeoning urban populace and to 'facilitate accelerated economic development' (Turok and Borel-Saladin 2013, 35).

Additionally, the macro-economic policies which have emerged since the RDP are not aligned with the national developmental agenda and to this end perpetuate an unequal system. Indeed, it can be argued that such policies have actually adversely impacted development goals by promoting competitive growth, beginning with the GEAR policy of 1996 (which promoted Growth, Employment and Redistribution). Such policies presupposed that economic growth within a market-driven environment would create employment opportunities and the kind of transformation needed to overcome the legacy of Apartheid. In many respects these policies have not fundamentally shifted the status quo; the systemic social and economic exclusion, established under Apartheid continues to prevail, as manifest in the rise of income inequality since 1994 (Habib 2013). Habib (2013) states that, although the National Development Plan (2011), the first country plan since the RDP which addresses energy poverty directly, is a robust document, it uses the same indictors to address poverty and inequality as pre-1994 – again indicating the lack of a systemic transformation, and the inability of a key plan to be responsive to the current context.

For the past hundred years, South Africa's economy has been built on the export of minerals (such as gold, platinum, and associated smelting production) that continues to overshadow all other areas of economic activity (Fine and Rustomjee 1997). The power sector is reliant on mining of coal (generating 93% of the country's electricity) and has, in turn, been built to support further mining and mineral processing notably gold and platinum and associated smelting production (Eberhard 2011). As a result, South Africa has developed an energy-intensive industrial sector, which must compete for electricity with households at a time of on-going rural to urban migration and increasing household electricity demand, leading to capacity constraints. Indeed, the national government acknowledged that such constraints were among the prime reasons that the goal of 100% electricity access by 2012 would not be achieved.

In short, the very core of the country's political and economic base is not completely conducive to (and indeed are often in conflict with) reducing energy poverty and South Africa's development agenda more broadly. Changing such macro-economic conditions is a long-term process. Many cities have implemented new approaches in their path to sustainable energy transitions. It is clear that a bottom-up approach, and implementing pilot projects at the local or micro-level, can leverage the change required to alter the urban energy poverty picture, and this is the focus of the following discussion.

Lack of coordination and alignment in governance

The Constitution of South Africa informed the creation of the three spheres of government – national, provincial and local – each with distinctive functional and independent responsibilities but operating as a single system of cooperative government. National government develops strategies, frameworks, and policies provide guidance for the country, while provincial and municipal governments are constitutionally mandated to put these into practice.

A challenge to energy poverty policy implementation at the local level is a lack of coordinated and integrated planning between the national and local spheres of government and between the departments within local government. A gap or disjuncture exists between national and local levels of government. National-level actors experience local government as uncooperative and blocking the changes that need to take place, and local government actors perceive that they operate in a vacuum with insufficient financial, resource, and capacity support in the face of the dilemmas they are confronted with – keeping pace with the increasing demand for services of their fast-growing, predominantly poor, populations and at the same time with promoting economic development (SEA 2015; Wolpe et al. 2012).

The different spheres of government are not always aligned and operating in a cooperative manner as intended. In part, this is due to the 'silo' nature in which government departments operate – weak alignment of policies, and lack of coordinated planning, between departments and across spheres of government hamper the process of implementation (De Visser 2009; SEA 2015). This is particularly critical for energy, which is an issue that cuts across many departmental functions. For example government housing programmes proceed without adequate coordination with the electricity departments, and as a result, houses often sit empty awaiting electricity connections to take place. Municipal officials have identified that there is not strong political will and leadership at the local level, which results in energy poverty projects not being sufficiently mainstreamed and integrated into all municipal planning structures (SEA 2015).

Inadequate financial framework

The municipal service delivery model developed for municipalities is progressive and based on the notion of redistribution in favour of the poor (De Visser 2009). However, the financial model for service delivery has been influenced by neo-liberal principles, emphasising a cost recovery and technocratic approach to delivery which is often conservative and does not adequately address the needs of poor households (Jaglin 2009; Parnell and Pieterse 2002). Ultimately, such financial models do not match the constitutional developmental brief, including the servicing of informal households. Thus, there sits a tension within municipalities between the need to be financially sound on the one hand and to deliver on the developmental agenda on the other. The role of municipalities is to deliver services and promote local economic development without compromising their financial security, which often leads to municipalities having to focus on cost recovery over the provision of services (Habib 2013). This in turn has led to a disjuncture between national policy directives and the ability of municipalities to deliver on their developmental mandate.

National Government allocates a number of grants to municipalities to assist in their service delivery mandate. One key funding source relevant to energy service delivery is the Local Government Equitable Share Grant (LGES), a grant disbursed to municipalities to fund free basic amounts of water, electricity, sanitation services, and refuse removal for low-income households. The size of the equitable share allocation is largely determined by the number of low-income households (indigents) and the capabilities of the municipalities to raise their own revenue. However, these allocations are based on data that can be as much as 10 years old (Moore 2014), and figures point to an under-utilization of this subsidy (SEA 2014; Tait 2015; SANERI 2008). Moreover, once the LGES is disbursed to municipalities, it may not necessarily be used to deliver services that benefit those living in energy poverty. This is because the grant is unconditional in nature – therefore, FBE allocations are sometimes spent on other urgent competing demands faced by a municipality, thus compromising its intended use of assisting households with the cost of energy.

At the same time as receiving direct grants, municipalities are structured such that they are obliged to raise their own funds through, for example the sale of electricity. Revenue from this source is substantial, particularly for municipalities with a large high-income household base and a large commercial and industrial sector, allowing for the cross subsidisation of services to the poor (SEA 2015; Winkler 2006). However, in recent years. this strategy has been compromised – high increases in the cost of electricity have resulted in large electricity consumers reducing their consumption, resulting in less revenue for municipalities.

Municipalities are constrained by their financial accounting and the regulations they are accountable to. The decisions that they take are driven by these regulations and the need to generate income in order to deliver on their constitutional mandates. This in turn impacts on the delivery of their developmental agenda. They are constantly balancing between service delivery and good financial accounting with limited resources.

Lack of technical and human resource capacity

South Africa's municipalities are varied in their capabilities and circumstances with respect to human resources, infrastructure, and finances, and this impacts the scale and reach of energy poverty interventions. The metropolitan cities tend to be better resourced than smaller municipalities; this is in part a legacy of Apartheid, but also because this is where economic and employment opportunities lie and where more people are concentrated (Turok and Borel-Saladin 2013).

As cities grow, the demands on municipal officers to deliver on basic services and deal with competing demands results in different sets of priorities emerging. Whilst there are highly skilled people in senior positions, there remains a lack of organisational capacity generally to undertake the extent of the work required to implement, not only energy poverty policies, but all policies at the local level. In particular, poorer municipalities experience limited technical and human resource capacity to implement both FBE and FBAE. For example, some lack the skills required to identify appropriate energy sources that would meet informal household needs (SANERI 2008). There is the added problem that some alternative fuels are not regulated in price, meaning that neither municipalities nor households can depend on the same quantity or quality of fuel being delivered each month should the costs or standards vary. In addition, cooking appliances are often of poor quality. The aforementioned silo nature of local governments constrains the building of capacity, information exchange, and communication on energy poverty.

Poor and inconsistent targeting

Whilst the intention of FBE is to ease the energy burden of the poor, its reach is limited partly due to the approach adopted by municipalities in identifying poor households. Some municipalities work on the basis of indigent register whilst others administer FBE on the basis of low levels of electricity consumption. This variety of implementation approaches across municipalities has resulted in not all poor households being classified as impoverished nor in all cases receiving the benefit. This has also given rise to some wealthy households receiving FBE due to low electricity consumption levels. Furthermore, where multiple households (such as backyard dwellers, who are often among the most deprived) are connected to one meter, their combined consumption exceeds the FBE benefit threshold. Those households receiving electricity via illegal means or who are disconnected due to non-payment will not be eligible for FBE, and so their ability to meet basic energy needs and indeed develop their human potential is impeded. The number of people accessing FBE is not officially known. The figures for the adoption of FBE range from 30% to 70% depending on varying government department estimates (SEA 2014).

In terms of the FBAE, there has been little successful implementation, largely because it is difficult to administer and monitor (Tait 2015; SEA 2014; SANERI 2008). Municipal officials have noted that there is a strong reluctance by households to accept alternative fuels and technologies other than electricity, even if these alternatives are safe (SEA 2015; SANERI 2008). Households perceive these fuels as inferior to electricity and are of the notion that if they accept them they lose their opportunity to be electrified (DME 2007; DPLG 2005). Current thinking within the National Department of Energy is to diversify reliable and safe forms of energy (DoE Roundtable Meeting with Sustainable Energy Africa 2014, pers. comm., 6 August), but within low-income households, this concept is not well understood or explained. Low-income households do diversify their energy use for meeting their energy needs, but this is driven by cost and not safety. It is clear that awareness and education on energy issues is required, alongside the inclusive participation of energy poor households in energy poverty policy-making.

Community engagement in municipal affairs and decision making is a key objective of local government as defined by the Constitution and put into effect through a progressive legal framework for participatory governance. As such local government is tasked to involve communities in engaging in decisions relating to service delivery. In-depth engagement with civil society and community leaders is needed to improve the understanding of the barriers and constraints communities face and to help to identify joint solutions and interventions towards overcoming barriers of household energy access for the urban poor in South Africa.

Conclusions and policy implications: overcoming the challenges of alleviating energy poverty amongst the urban poor

To conclude, South Africa faces substantial energy poverty challenges. Whilst there is strong articulation in almost all national government policies of the need to enhance development, increase employment, grow the economy, and reduce all forms of poverty, the country continues to experience challenges and policy implementation has not been as effective as many had hoped. The issues are complex but the ingredients for change are in place. Key factors identified as hindering the success of energy poverty policies are a disjuncture between macro-economic goals and socially equitable development, a lack of integration and coordination between the spheres of government, inadequate financial frameworks for local government, a lack of technical and human resource capacity, and poor and inconsistent identification of vulnerable and energy poor households.

In order to hold the energy poverty agenda in a cohesive manner and to enable political buy in at a high level, the country needs to develop an integrated energy poverty framework that addresses the following elements:

- Aligning and integrating energy (poverty) policies across and within all three spheres of government is needed for overcoming the 'silo'-based nature of policy-making at national and local levels. This is particularly important given that energy cuts across so many governmental departments. The National Development Plan (2011) is intended to be the overarching plan from which all government policies are guided, yet to date this has not been implemented.
- The municipal financial frameworks and regulatory environment need to be reviewed by the relevant national departments in collaboration with local government. Related to this, national government needs to review how municipalities are funded to deliver basic services including energy.
- Improved collaboration, integration, and coordination between all government departments, by clarifying the roles and functions of the various energy

institutions and building partnerships, would facilitate implementation. For example, a low-income housing development in Joe Slovo in Cape Town has been successful because of a partnership building approach amongst key stakeholders. Formally, an informal shack settlement, this area now has formal houses and services, including a suite of sustainable energy interventions including solar water heaters, efficient lighting, and roof overhangs. It is the result of a National Housing flagship project that aims for a new approach to government-delivered homes. Key to the success of this project (with donor support) was cooperation between local, provincial, and national government, alongside building partnerships with businesses, civil society, and local communities (DHS 2014). In addition, capacity building at the local government level, through peer-to-peer learning and information exchange platforms, is crucial for enhancing and strengthening implementation efforts.

• Raising awareness and educating households on the benefits of clean and affordable energy alternatives and technology choices will strengthen implementation of energy poverty measures. This can be undertaken by community meetings, stakeholder engagements, and inclusive projects that provide the chance for the voices of the energy poor to be heard. The potential impact of such an approach is illustrated by a small demonstration project in the City of Johannesburg, which is rolling out 'hot bags' to households. Hot bags are made from insulation material; for example once a pot of rice or stew is brought to the boil, it is placed in the bag where it continues to cook for hours at no cost. This technology can bring down costs of using other fuels in cooking and making the bags is a potential employment generator. Through this pilot experiment, community awareness and engagement have been greatly increased (SEA 2016a).

In order to reach effective solutions to alleviate energy poverty in urban areas, the institutional and governance challenges outlined earlier, in conjunction with the participatory role of civil society and communities in energy decision making, need to be addressed so as to bring about systemic change. If all of these components work together cohesively, a space for substantial change to take place is possible. Of crucial importance is the need to engage in integrated and holistic planning, given that energy poverty is an issue that cuts across many sectors of government. To this end, it is essential to develop an integrated energy poverty policy/framework for the country – one that considers the institutional coordination of different spheres of government and alignment across stakeholders and departments, and involves consultative engagements with communities and awareness campaigns.

References

Barnard, W. (2011). Keynote address at the Association of Municipal Electricity Undertakings (AMEU) Technical Convention. AMEU Proceedings 2011. South Africa.

Borchers, M., Qase, N., Gaunt, T., Mavhungu, J., Winkler, H., Afrane-Okese, Y. and Thom, C. (2001). *National electrification programme evaluation: Summary report. Evaluation commissioned by the Department of Minerals and Energy and the Development Bank of Southern Africa*. Cape Town: Energy Research Centre, University of Cape Town.

CCT [City of Cape Town]. (2014). *Low Income Energy Services Strategy (LIESS)*. Cape Town, South Africa: City of Cape Town.

COGTA [Department of Cooperative Government and Traditional Affairs]. (2014). *Integrated urban development framework*. Pretoria: COGTA.

De Visser, J. (2009). Developmental local governance in South Africa: Institutional fault lines. *Commonwealth Journal for Local Governance*, 2 (January).

DEA [Department of Environmental Affairs]. (2013). *Strategy to address air pollution in dense low income settlements*. Draft version: November 2013. Pretoria, South Africa.

DHS [Department of Human Settlements]. (2014). *Energy efficiency and sustainable settlements for the N2 Gateway Joe Slovo 3 Precinct – Lessons Learnt Report*. Report prepared by Sustainable Energy Africa for Department of Human Settlements. Pretoria, South Africa.

DME [Department of Minerals and Energy]. (2005). *Free basic electricity policy*. Department of Minerals and Energy. Pretoria: Republic of South Africa.

DME [Department of Minerals and Energy]. (2007). *Free Basic Alternative Energy Policy (Households Energy Support Programme)*. Department of Minerals and Energy. Pretoria, Republic of South Africa.

DoE [Department of Energy]. (2013). *A survey of energy-related behaviour and perceptions in South Africa – the residential sector*. Pretoria, South Africa.

DoE [Department of Energy]. (2014). *Presentation on the integrated national electrification programme made to the parliamentary Portfolio committee on energy on 26 August 2014*. South Africa: Department of Energy.

DPLG [Department of Provincial and Local Government]. (2005). *Free basic services – guidelines for the implementation of municipal indigent policies*. Available at: www.western cape.gov.za/text/2012/11/national_framework_for_municipal_indigent_policies.pdf.

Eberhard, A. (2011). The future of South African coal: market, investment and policy challenges. *Working Paper #100*. Program of Energy and Sustainable Development. Freeman Spogli Institute for International Studies, Stanford University, USA.

Ewing, K. and Mammon, N. (2010). Cape Town Den[city]: Towards sustainable urban form. In Swilling, M (ed.) *Sustaining Cape Town, imagining a liveable city*. Stellenbosch, Cape Town: SUN MeDIA Stellenbosch and the Sustainability Institute.

Fine, B. and Rustomjee, Z. (1997). *South Africa's political economy: From minerals-energy complex to industrialisation*. Johannesburg, South Africa: Wits University Press.

Franks, L. and Prasad, G. (2014). *Informal electricity re-selling: Entrepreneurship or exploitation*. South Africa: Energy Research Centre, University of Cape Town.

Gaunt, T., Salida, M., Macfarlane, R., Maboda, S., Reddy, Y. and Borchers, M. (2012). *Informal electrification in South Africa: Experience, opportunities and challenges*. South Africa: Sustainable Energy Africa.

GDARD [Gauteng Department of Agriculture and Rural Development]. (2015). *Feasibility study and implementation plan of alternative energy technology options for unelectrified informal settlements in Gauteng Province*. Report prepared by Sustainable Energy Africa for GDARD. South Africa.

GNESD [Global Network on Energy for Sustainable Development]. (2013). *Energy poverty in developing countries' urban poor communities: Assessments and recommendations*.

Country Report 2013. Case Study – South Africa. Report prepared for GNESD by the Energy Research Centre, University of Cape Town. Riso Centre, Denmark.

Habib, A. (2013). *South Africa's revolution, hopes and prospects.* Johannesburg, South Africa: Wits University Press.

HDA [Housing Development Agency]. (2012). *South Africa: Informal settlement status.* Johannesburg, South Africa: Housing Development Agency.

Jaglin, S. (2009). *Between electricity crisis and "green hub" marketing: Changes in urban energy policies and governance in Cape Town.* Paper presented at the International Roundtable Conference: 'Cities and energy transitions: past, present, future' Autun, France, 1–4 June 2009.

Leibbrandt, M., Woolard, I., Finn, A. and Argent, J. (2010). Trends in South African income distribution and poverty since the fall of Apartheid OECD Social, *Employment and Migration Working Papers, No. 101,* OECD Publishing. Available at: http://npc.gov.za/MediaLib/Downloads/Home/Tabs/Diagnostic/HumanConditions2/Trends%20in%20South%20African%20income%20distribution%20and%20poverty%20since%20the%20fall%20of%20apartheid.pdf.

Madzhie, L. (2016). Telephone interview with Mr Lufuno Madzhie, Department of Energy, by Peta Wolpe, Sustainable Energy Africa, 14 November.

Mduli, T., Piketh, S. and Igbafe, A. (2005). Assessment of indoor air respirable particulate matter (PM7) in township houses with coal – fired stoves at Kwaguqa (Witbank). *National Electricity Regulator Quarterly Journal 12.*

Misselhorn, M. (2010). A new response to informal settlements. *Transformer*, December/January.

Moore, M. (2014). Personal communication with Marissa Moore, Department of National Treasury in South Africa, 12 September.

Mzini, L. and Lukamba-Muhiya, T. (2014). An assessment of electricity supply and demand at Emfuleni Local Municipality. *Journal of Energy in South Africa*, 25(3).

NPC [National Planning Commission – The Presidency Republic of South Africa]. (2011). *Diagnostic overview.* Pretoria: Presidency of South Africa.

Parnell, S and Pieterse, E. (2002). Developmental local government. In Parnell, S., Pieterse, E., Swilling, M. and Wooldridge, D. (eds.) *Democratising local government: The South African experiment.* Cape Town: UCT Press, pp. 79–92.

Poggiolini, D. (2007). Pacifying the air pollution killer. *African Energy Journal*, 9(3), 26–27.

Presidency. (2014). *Twenty year review, South Africa, 1994–2014.* Pretoria: Department of Performance Monitoring and Evaluation.

SANERI [South African National Energy Research Institute]. (2008). *Improving energy welfare in unelectrified urban informal households.* Report prepared by Sustainable Energy Africa for SANERI: Project Number EU 06/07–103. Pretoria, South Africa.

SEA [Sustainable Energy Africa]. (2006). *State of energy in South Africa's cities – setting a baseline.* Cape Town, South Africa: SEA.

SEA [Sustainable Energy Africa]. (2014). *Tackling urban energy poverty in South Africa.* Cape Town, South Africa: SEA.

SEA [Sustainable Energy Africa]. (2015). *State of energy in South Africa's cities.* Cape Town, South Africa: SEA.

SEA [Sustainable Energy Africa]. (2016a). *Lessons learnt from the implementation of a sustainable energy intervention to improve the energy welfare of low-income households in Johannesburg: The Hot Bag pilot project in the Riverpark Community.* A report compiled by

Sustainable Energy Africa as part of the Heinrich Boell Stiftung funded Africa's Energy Future Project. Cape Town, South Africa.

SEA [Sustainable Energy Africa]. (2016b). *Sustainable gender sensitive energy solutions for low income households in the City of Joburg.* Report prepared for the City of Johannesburg as part of the Heinrich Boell Stiftung funded Africa's Energy Future Project. Cape Town, South Africa.

Stats SA [Statistics South Africa]. (2011). *South African census 2011.* Pretoria: Statistics South Africa.

Stats SA [Statistics South Africa]. (2017). *Quarterly Labour Force Survey (QLFS 04:2016).* Pretoria: Statistics South Africa.

Sustainability Institute. (2009). *Sustainable Neighbourhood Design Manual: A non-technical guide.* Funded by the National Department of Housing and Cordaid, The Sustainability Institute.

Tait, L. (2015). *Evaluating the electrification programme in urban settlements in South Africa.* Research Report Series, Energy Research Centre, University of Cape Town, South Africa.

Turok, I. (2015). *South Africa's new urban agenda: Transformation or Compensation?* South Africa: Human Science Research Council.

Turok, I. and Borel-Saladin, J. (2013). *The spatial economy Background Research Report for the Integrated Urban Development Framework Draft.* South Africa: Human Sciences Research Council.

UNDP [United Nations Development Program]. (2000). Overview. In Goldemberg, J. (ed.) *World energy assessment: Energy and the challenge of sustainability.* New York: United Nations Development Programme.

Visagie, E. (2008). The supply of clean energy services to the urban and peri-urban poor in South Africa. *Energy for Sustainable Development,* XII(4), 14–21

Winkler, H. (ed.) (2006). *Energy policies for sustainable development in South Africa – options for the future.* Cape Town: Energy Research Centre, University of Cape Town.

Wolpe, H. (1995). The uneven transition from Apartheid in South Africa. *Transformation,* 27, 88–101.

Wolpe, P., Reddy, Y. and Euston-Brown, M. (2012). *Energising urban South Africa: Poverty, sustainability and future cities.* Paper presented at the conference on 'Strategies to Overcome Poverty and Inequality, Towards Carnegie3'. University of Cape Town, South Africa.

15 Conclusions

Neil Simcock, Harriet Thomson,
Saska Petrova, and Stefan Bouzarovski

We began this book with the aim of providing the first global and comparative perspective on energy vulnerability, in order to advance debates on the systemic processes and conditions that (re)produce domestic energy deprivation. By bringing together 13 chapters that cover 14 countries in total, the volume provides the first instance where such divergent contexts are brought together to discuss energy vulnerability in one common space. In this concluding discussion, we look across the range of contributions and draw out some overarching lessons, policy implications and future research directions.

Commonalities and differences across the chapters

One of the key advantages of considering studies from such diverse settings though a single lens is the ability to identify commonalities and differences in the underpinning drivers of energy poverty across the globe. In terms of similarities, it is notable that many of the factors identified in the existing literature as direct causes of energy deprivation were present in some form in all of the national settings analysed. The 'triad' of low incomes, high energy prices and the material condition of the home is highlighted as important contingencies shaping energy vulnerability in every chapter.[1] Beyond this, the expanded list of factors identified in more recent conceptualisations of energy poverty (Bouzarovski 2014; Middlemiss and Gillard 2015; Snell et al. 2015) are also evident across the chapters. All document the important role of households' particular *needs* and *everyday practices* in determining how energy poverty emerges and is experienced. These are shown to shape how (much) energy and what forms of energy services are required and used in the home (see, for example, Chapters 6 and 11), or whether and how households engage with energy poverty amelioration policies and support networks (see Chapters 3 and 4). Several of the chapters also report a lack of *access* to adequate and appropriate energy carriers as an issue, further disturbing the representation of this as solely an issue for households living in the 'Global South'. Overall, that these various factors were present across such a diverse range of settings validates their positioning as central causes of domestic energy deprivation in many contemporary theorisations of energy poverty.

However, alongside such commonalities, the chapters also provide detailed accounts of a range of differences in some of the processes that (re)produce domestic energy deprivation in particular spaces and contexts. Firstly, comparing nation states, the chapters evidence how in each national context the aforementioned 'direct' causes of energy poverty are underpinned and driven by wider-scale processes and contingencies that are specific to the historical, cultural, material, economic and political context of each country, and which shape the particular emergence, form, prevalence and patterning of household energy vulnerability (Bouzarovski et al. 2017). To name only a few examples, Knox, De Groot and Mohlakoana (Chapter 5) and Wolpe and Reddy (Chapter 14) provide rich accounts of how a particular set of spatial planning regimes and housing policies in South Africa, deeply linked to the past Apartheid system of governance, have contributed to a geographically dispersed and segregated urban landscape, resulting in an increased risk of energy poverty for those living on the urban peripheries and in informal or low-income housing. Meanwhile, in China, a very different history and set of underpinning processes are at play, and consequently, a unique geography of vulnerability is evident (see Chapter 6). The Huai River policy developed in the 1950s has led to vast differences in thermal comfort infrastructures in the north and south of the country and subsequently differences in vulnerabilities of residents in these two regions – whilst those in the south often suffer from inadequate thermal comfort in the winter, people in the north have their thermal comfort needs met at the expense of air quality. In the UK context, both Connon (Chapter 4) and Cronin de Chavez (Chapter 10) document how the emergence and subsequent mainstream dominance of neoliberalism since the 1980s has had several repercussions for energy vulnerability. These include a hardening of stigmatising attitudes toward those living in material deprivation – with the consequence that households suffering from energy poverty feel ashamed of their situation – and recent welfare reforms that have made accessing financial support more difficult for vulnerable households. These are just a few examples – we could also have highlighted the role of economic crisis and austerity policies in Greece (Chapter 7), communist legacies of out-dated district heating systems in the Western Balkan region (Chapter 12) or building standards in New Zealand (Chapter 3 and 11), among others.

Secondly, at finer scales of analysis, many of the chapters also point to spatial and social differences *within* nation states, in both the extent of energy poverty and the specific causes that are most fundamental. In line with current literature (Baker et al. 2008; Kaygusuz 2011; Roberts et al. 2015), several chapters discern important distinctions between rural and urban areas. For example, Lis, Miazga and Sałach (Chapter 8) find that larger dwelling size and lower incomes are key drivers of energy poverty in rural Poland, whilst poor energy efficiency and dated heating systems are the prime cause in urban settings. In China, alongside the North-South divide, there is uneven infrastructural development related to heating between urban and rural areas. Spatial variation and unevenness are also reported within the grain of cities themselves; as noted, those living on the peripheries of South African cities often face particular energy vulnerability-related difficulties (Chapter 5). In Chapter 7, Chatzikonstantinou and Vatavali report vast spatial differences in the quality of housing infrastructure and price of heating fuels across Athens, Greece, whilst those who live in apartment buildings with shared heating systems face a unique set of challenges and constraints that shape their energy vulnerability. Finally, multiple chapters also demonstrate differences in the specific drivers of vulnerability between households (e.g. Chapters 2, 3, 6). Households vary in terms of their energy needs, practices or the material configurations of their home, with some groups, based on factors such as age, gender, ethnicity or health status, facing particular disadvantages due to increased energy requirements or systemic relations of prejudice and misrecognition – pointing to the importance of wider systems of inequality and discrimination in underpinning household energy deprivation (see Chapter 2).

Table 15.1 summarises the multiple commonalities and differences discussed thus far. The key point is that these differences lead not only to spatially unequal vulnerabilities – i.e. those living in certain countries, regions, cities or neighbourhoods are at a heightened risk of experiencing domestic energy deprivation (see Chapters 8 and 9) – but also that the very processes and contingencies that (re)produce energy poverty vary across space. Not all of the 'direct' causes of energy poverty, although broadly shared across national contexts, will always be present or equally significant for particular places or households.

How do such broad conclusions bring us into conversation with established academic concepts and debates? The spatial and social variation in the causes and extent of energy poverty supports an explicitly *geographical* reading of energy vulnerability and the operation of energy systems more broadly (Bridge et al. 2013). In particular, two concepts can usefully explain the differentiated geographies described in this volume. The notion of 'landscape' draws attention to how the dynamic economic, material and cultural features of particular geographical settings interact to (re)produce particular outcomes, in this case energy vulnerability, that vary over space and time. 'Spatial embeddedness', meanwhile, explains how distinct landscape features may become 'locked-in' to particular spaces and thus produce path-dependencies (ibid.), as is evident in the chapters here that demonstrate how historical policies and decisions continue to have agency in shaping forms and patterns of energy vulnerability in the present.

The elucidations in many chapters of how underpinning processes and contingencies, operating at wider temporal and geographical scales than the household, work to produce and maintain domestic energy deprivation also draws us into synergy with recent literature on energy justice. Of particular relevance here is work that highlights how energy poverty and vulnerability can be seen as an outcome of structural inequities that are engrained in various stages of the energy system (Jenkins et al. 2016) and, more fundamentally, of wider dynamics of discrimination and injustice in the political, economic and cultural relations of societies (Bouzarovski and Simcock 2017; Walker and Day 2012). Energy poverty is, we would argue, a geographically *constituted* phenomenon, rather than an issue that simply *affects* places.

Table 15.1 Commonalities and differences between the chapters in the driving forces of energy poverty

	Driving forces of energy poverty
Common factors	• Inadequate energy efficiency or poor material conditions of the home • Low or insecure household incomes • High or rising energy prices • Household needs and/or practices increasing energy requirements and consumption • Lack of access to adequate or appropriate energy carriers (most countries)
Country-specific contingencies	• China: Huai River policy and the 'Heating Line' lead to uneven heating infrastructure and affordability • Germany: Energiewende increasing energy bills for some households • Greece: economic crisis and subsequent austerity policies straining incomes of many households • Kenya: cultural preferences for biomass fuel and suspicion toward electric lighting; poor-quality transmission infrastructure • New Zealand: lack of insulation in homes and schools due to inadequate building standards • South Africa: dispersed and segregated planning patterns of Apartheid system; prevalence of poor-quality informal homes • UK: neoliberal ideology and policy reforms leading to hardening stigmatisation of the poor; reductions in availability of state welfare; increasing insecurity in labour market • Western Balkans: rapid energy price increases since liberalisation of energy market; socialist legacy of inefficient housing and heating systems; lack of political recognition
Intra-country spatial and social differences	• Rural vs. urban differences reported in the Western Balkans, Poland, UK, China, Kenya • In China, North-South divide in terms of heating affordability and infrastructure, alongside differing household expectations of thermal comfort • Spatial variation within urban areas – in Athens, Greece, reduced energy efficiency and access to natural gas network in central areas; heightened vulnerability on urban periphery in South Africa • Differences between individual households depending on needs and practices; particular disadvantages based on age, gender, ethnicity, health or other aspects of social status

Policy recommendations

From these overarching findings, some broad policy recommendations can be made. First, it is clear that, in many settings, improving domestic energy efficiency remains a crucial part of tackling energy poverty and enhancing living conditions and quality of life (see Chapter 12). However, whilst measures to improve domestic energy efficiency are undoubtedly vital, it is also important to recognise that the causes of energy poverty are often multiple and complex, and infrastructural investment in energy efficiency will not necessarily be the only (or best) solution to energy vulnerability problems. The appropriateness of housing stock upgrades will depend on the specifics of the place in which they are set, the features of the housing and individual household needs. This is a point made by the authors of several chapters, including McKague et al. (Chapter 3), Lis et al. (Chapter 8) and Robić et al. (Chapter 12).

Policy-makers should attempt to develop comprehensive and holistic strategies that account for and are sensitive to a wider range of issues than only energy efficiency – such as household needs, practices, incomes and also other factors relating to the materiality of the home (for example, its ability to absorb passive heat). Beyond the household level, policies are likely to be more effective at addressing energy poverty in the long-term when they address the larger-scale processes and histories, such as uneven development, the operation of energy markets and stigmatising cultural discourses, that contribute to households being unable to meet their basic energy needs (Bouzarovski and Simcock 2017). These often extend beyond the typical domain of 'energy policy', and thus, there is a need for 'joined-up' policy-making and collaboration and communication across conventional departmental divides (see Chapter 14). A focus on only one or two causes of energy poverty – such as *solely* energy efficiency (Middlemiss 2016) or household income (see Chapter 12) – can obscure this range of complexities, nuances and broader structural factors, offering simple but ultimately limited policy prescriptions.

Second, and relatedly, the fact that the causes of energy poverty are spatially embedded and contingent suggests that policies to alleviate the condition would do well to be attuned and tailored to the particular context in which they are being implemented. This cautions against one-size-fits-all measures that can simply be 'plugged-in' to new localities or settings and instead calls for a greater openness to diversity – both in terms of the exact measures that are implemented and the particular manner in which they are implemented.

The findings of this book come at a time when improving access to affordable, modern energy services has moved into the mainstream of international policy-making (Brunner et al. in press), with increased policy recognition for the role of energy in human and economic development (Sustainable Energy for All 2016). The UN declared 2012 the 'International Year of Sustainable Energy for All' and in 2015 adopted the 'Sustainable Development Goals for 2030' (SDGs). Goal 7 of the SDGs recognises that whilst access to electricity is increasing globally, a significant proportion of the world's population still lacks access, thus there is a need to "ensure access to affordable, reliable, sustainable and modern energy for all" (UNDP 2015). In 2016, the historic Paris Agreement reached the threshold for entry into force, having been ratified by 145 parties. This global agreement seeks to reduce vulnerability to climate change, with a core goal of "holding the increase in the global average temperature to well below 2°C above pre-industrial levels and pursuing efforts to limit the temperature increase to 1.5°C above pre-industrial levels" (United Nations Framework Convention on Climate

Change 2015, 3) via investment in mitigation and adaptation strategies. Crucially, the Paris Agreement recognises the specific needs and circumstances of 'least developed' countries, as reflected by common but differentiated responsibilities and requirements for developed countries to fund adaption work in least developed countries. At the same time, we have seen a fundamental shift change in the European Commission's approach to tackling energy poverty, in which it has moved from a position of historically opposing efforts to measure and define energy poverty (Thomson et al. 2016), to investing over a million euros since 2014 in new studies and the European Energy Poverty Observatory. These global processes of institutional thickening around the issue of energy poverty represent significant opportunities for enacting path-breaking changes to the policy agendas followed to date and create an even greater need for robust scientific knowledge on the contexts in which energy vulnerabilities are (re)produced.

Future research directions

This volume also suggests a number of directions for future research. Similar to much scholarship on energy poverty that utilises primary data, the chapters in this book are largely single-country studies. Although clearly valuable, research projects that studies of energy poverty and vulnerability in multiple countries, through a consistent research design, could be particularly useful in terms of enabling systematic and detailed comparison of the prevalence, causes and consequences of the condition – and the role of economic, social, political and cultural contexts in shaping these. Such a method has been successfully adopted to unpack the lived experiences of income poverty (Walker et al. 2013), and a similar approach could also be utilised in the energy poverty domain.

Several studies in this volume also demonstrate the value of qualitative methods for enabling detailed and contextualised insights into the complex causes of energy poverty and the practices, perceptions and experiences of those living with domestic energy deprivation. However, such approaches remain relatively rare in the field, which tends to be dominated by more quantitative methodologies. There would therefore be value in future research adopting a qualitative methodology in order to understand the drivers and experiences of energy deprivation in different settings – or, perhaps even better, in adopting a mixed-methods design that combines both the strengths of both qualitative and quantitative approaches.

Although much of the energy poverty literature has historically focused on deprivation of adequate space heating, there has recently been recognition of the need for energy poverty research to also engage with other energy services to provide a fuller account of the causes and consequences of the condition. Several chapters in this volume highlight how deprivation of non-heating energy services, such as lighting and even mobility (see Chapter 5) can also be implicated in how energy vulnerabilities manifest and are experienced by households – not to mention the relation of energy services with water provision and usage, as explored by Browne et al. (Chapter 6). Future research can continue to explore such avenues. Two particularly pertinent areas may be, first, the capacity for households to attain adequate space *cooling* (particularly during summer months) in a context of rising global temperatures and, second, the ability for people to access and use information and communication technologies (ICT) as they proliferate and become an increasingly important part of participating in many contemporary societies.

While this book has not adopted a justice framing, the need for a more explicit dialogue between energy vulnerability and justice approaches is a consistent thread throughout many of the contributions presented here. Therefore, a key avenue of future research could centre on the manner in which justice frameworks can be used to understand the distributional or procedural drivers of energy vulnerability – including both 'whole-systems' thinking and energy end-use issues. Of particular importance in this context are notions of recognition – as it is clear that energy poor households often fall through the gap in terms of being identified and supported by public policies and discourses (Bouzarovski and Cauvain 2016). The suggestion that energy vulnerability is both constitutive and constituted by the socio-spatial context in which it arises also opens a number of questions around the spatial embeddedness of the phenomenon and its relationship with wider spatial and economic inequalities. This is where scholarship on energy poverty connects with feminist work on intersectionality, as well as critical theories of precarity and precarisation. We hope, therefore, that the chapters presented here signal the start of a new generation of efforts to study and address energy poverty and vulnerability, both building on existing scholarship while pushing knowledge and policy boundaries.

Note

1 In rural Kenya (see Chapter 13), because the major concern for many households is (a lack of) access to electricity, the crucial material contingency of the home is not its thermal efficiency but the ability for the structure to safely incorporate electrical wiring.

References

Baker, W., White, V. and Preston, I. (2008). *Quantifying rural fuel poverty: Final Report.* Bristol: Centre for Sustainable Energy.

Bouzarovski, S. (2014). Energy poverty in the European Union: Landscapes of vulnerability. *Wiley Interdisciplinary Reviews: Energy and Environment*, 3(3) (May 1), 276–289.

Bouzarovski, S. and Cauvain, J. (2016). Spaces of exception: Governing fuel poverty in England's multiple occupancy housing sector. *Space and Polity*, 20(3) (September 1), 310–329.

Bouzarovski, S. and Simcock, N. (2017). Spatializing energy justice. *Energy Policy.* Available at: www.sciencedirect.com/science/article/pii/S0301421517302185.

Bouzarovski, S., Herrero, S. T., Petrova, S., Frankowski, J., Matoušek, R. and Maltby, T. (2017). Multiple transformations: Theorizing energy vulnerability as a socio-spatial phenomenon. *Geografiska Annaler: Series B, Human Geography*, 99(1) (January 2), 20–41.

Bridge, G., Bouzarovski, S., Bradshaw, M. and Eyre, N. (2013). Geographies of energy transition: Space, place and the low-carbon economy. *Energy Policy*, 53 (February), 331–340.

Brunner, K-M., Mandl, S. and Thomson, H. (in press). Energy poverty. In Davidson, D. J. and Gross, M. (ed.) *Energy and Society Handbook*. Oxford: Oxford University Press.

Jenkins, K., McCauley, D., Heffron, R., Stephan, H. and Rehner, R. (2016). Energy justice: A conceptual review. *Energy Research & Social Science*, 11 (January), 174–182.

Kaygusuz, K. (2011). Energy services and energy poverty for sustainable rural development. *Renewable & Sustainable Energy Reviews*, 15(2), 936–947.

Middlemiss, L. (2016). A critical analysis of the new politics of fuel poverty in England. *Critical Social Policy* (October 18), 261018316674851.

Middlemiss, L. and Gillard, R. (2015). Fuel poverty from the bottom-up: Characterising household energy vulnerability through the lived experience of the fuel poor. *Energy Research & Social Science*, 6 (March), 146–154.

Roberts, D., Vera-Toscano, E. and Phimister, E. (2015). Fuel poverty in the UK: Is there a difference between rural and urban areas? *Energy Policy*, 87 (December), 216–223.

Snell, C., Bevan, M. and Thomson, H. (2015). Justice, fuel poverty and disabled people in England. *Energy Research & Social Science*, 10(November), 123–132.

Sustainable Energy for All. (2016). *Strategic framework for results 2016–2021*. Vienna: Sustainable Energy for All.

Thomson, H., Snell, C. and Liddell, C. (2016). Fuel poverty in the European Union: A concept in need of definition? *People, Place & Policy*, 10(1), 5–24.

UNDP. (2015). *Sustainable development goals*. New York: United Nations Development Programme.

United Nations Framework Convention on Climate Change. (2015). *Paris agreement*. Geneva, Switzerland: United Nations.

Walker, G. and Day, R. (2012). Fuel poverty as injustice: Integrating distribution, recognition and procedure in the struggle for affordable warmth. *Energy Policy*, 49. Special Section: Fuel Poverty Comes of Age: Commemorating 21 Years of Research and Policy (October), 69–75.

Walker, R., Kyomuhendo, G. B., Chase, E., Choudhry, S., Gubrium, E. K., Nicola, J. Y., Lødemel, I. et al. (2013). Poverty in global perspective: Is shame a common denominator? *Journal of Social Policy*, 42(2) (April), 215–233.

Index

188, 203; income poverty *vs.* 48, 49; indicators *see* energy poverty indicator; intersectionality *see* intersectionality; Italy 120; justice-based approach 2; Kenya REPs 8, 218–19, 224, 226, 228–31; New Zealand 191, 192, 198; perceptions of shame 49; Poland (voivodeships) 7, 119, 120–36, 139–40, 250; qualitative research *see* case studies and interviews; quantitative research *see* quantitative methods; social inequality and 4–5, 15, 27, 255; social isolation 49, 53, 142; socio-cultural norms and i, 46, 47, 49, 52, 54, 55, 57–8; South Africa 6, 8, 61–2, 64, 69–73, 75, 76, 235–45, 250; Switzerland 120; triad 2, 5, 12–15, 21, 25, 34, 35, 46, 48, 58, 141–3, 162, 164, 169, 170, 175, 189, 249; UK 1, 7, 35, 46–9, 52–8, 119, 120, 141–2, 145–61, 163, 164, 169–70, 172–4, 250; vulnerability dimensions 144; vulnerability variables *see* vulnerability variables; Western Balkans 8, 63, 202–15

energy poverty indicator: 10% *see* 10% indicator; area-based composite 162, 163–4; fuel poverty (FPI) 163; LIHC *see* low-income high-cost (LIHC); national composite 162–3; risk index 163–4; spatially-constituted composite 164; *see also* DECC indicators

energy practices 6, 36–8, 40–2, 143, 144, 184, 251–4

energy precariousness 142

energy price 2, 3, 12, 13, 38, 119, 120, 142, 170, 190, 202, 252; China 81; Germany 12, 14, 15, 20, 21, 24–9; Greece 96, 103, 110, 251; Kenya 228; New Zealand 40; Poland 7, 121, 123, 133–6; South Africa 62, 67, 69, 71, 75, 76, 238, 242, 243; UK 56, 58, 144–6, 149, 151, 163, 176, 183; Western Balkans 202, 206, 207, 210–15, 252; *see also* metering

energy provider: Germany 14, 15, 17, 20, 22–5, 27–9; Greece 104, 105, 107, 109, 111, 112; Kenya 219, 221–7; Poland 135; South Africa 73; UK 6, 56, 119, 144, 181; Western Balkans 210; *see also* infrastructure

energy (re)source: alternative 34, 61, 83, 224, 237, 243, 245; biogas 219, 220; biomass 33, 63, 71, 85, 86, 224, 229,

238, 252; brushwood 122; candle 4, 69, 238; charcoal 224; coal 4, 71, 82–5, 87, 126, 134, 135, 208, 219, 238, 240; commercial 85; corncob 86; dung 4; gas 7, 12, 15, 21, 23, 38, 52, 99, 103, 110, 112, 119, 129, 134, 141, 144, 151, 174, 177, 178, 181, 198, 202, 206–8, 210, 219, 224, 252; geothermal 219, 221; green energy *see* green energy; hydropower *see* hydropower; kerosene 4, 71, 224, 227, 229; liquefied petroleum gas (LPG) 69, 85, 86; mineral 85, 211, 240; natural gas 99, 101, 110, 112, 114, 119, 126, 134, 135; non-commercial 83, 85; non-fossil 83; oil 15, 83, 96, 99, 102, 103, 107–12, 115, 163, 203, 208, 219; paraffin 69, 71, 235, 237, 238; renewable *see* renewable energy; solar 219–20, 224, 239; solid 4, 52, 126, 129; water *see* water-energy (WE) nexus; wind 219, 220; wood 4, 41, 61, 63, 69, 86, 115, 126, 208, 211, 215, 224, 235

energy-stacking 63, 224, 229

energy supply 3, 4, 15, 16, 52, 54, 62, 90, 173, 190, 210, 218, 231, 236, 238, 240–4; coal 84; electricity 72, 99, 111, 207, 208, 221, 226; gas 21, 208; solar 239; water 81, 84, 85; WE 80–7, 90

energy transition 14, 85, 188, 240

energy vulnerability i, 2, 3, 13, 34–5, 48, 62–4, 113, 141–5, 249–50, 251–5; children and young people 7, 188; China WE 6, 80–90, 250; Croatia 210; dimensions 144; Germany 19, 22, 24, 27, 28; Greece 6, 97, 102, 103, 113, 251; Hungary 63; Kenya REPs 219, 226, 228–31; Poland 121; South Africa 6, 61–4, 68–76, 239, 244, 251, 252; Switzerland 120; UK 7, 54, 141, 144, 250; variables *see* vulnerability variables; Western Balkans (legislation and definition) 203, 206–9, 214; *see also* socio-spatial vulnerability

English Housing Condition Survey 163

English Housing Survey 147, 161, 169

English Index of Multiple Deprivation (IMD) 164

environmental sustainability 67, 80, 83, 86

European Commission Working Group for Vulnerable Consumers 209

European Energy Poverty Observatory 1, 254